Manchester Unite

Despite a myriad of popular and journalistic expositions, up to this point there have been virtually no academic discussions of the Manchester United phenomenon. This anthology represents the first concerted academic examination of Manchester United F.C. in its contemporary guise as a both widely followed, and highly emblematic, sporting institution.

Bringing together respected academics from an array of disciplinary backgrounds including Cultural Studies, Sociology, English, History, Media Studies, Sports Management, Gender Studies and Economics, the essays gathered within this anthology each interrogate various interrelated dimensions of the Manchester United universe.

The primary aim of this collection is to illustrate how the structure and experience of Manchester United is implicated in broader social shifts, within which the boundary between cultural and commercial concerns have become increasingly indivisible. The chapters are presented within five thematic sections – 1. *Becoming United*, 2. *Economy United*, 3. *Embodied United*, 4. *Local United*, 5. *Global United* – each focused on specific elements of the Manchester United condition. It is hoped that readers will engage in chapters as individual entities, as part of a thematic section, and as a contribution to the project as a whole.

David L. Andrews is Associate Professor and member of the Physical Cultural Studies Research Group in the Sport, Commerce and Culture Program, Dept. of Kinesiology, and an Affiliate Faculty in the Department of American Studies, University of Maryland, USA. His research is concerned with crafting a sociology of late capitalist sport. He has been guest editor of the *Sociology of Sport Journal*, and is on the editorial board of the *Journal of Sport and Social Issues* and the *Sociology of Sport Journal*.

Manchester United
A thematic study

Edited by David L. Andrews

Routledge
Taylor & Francis Group

LONDON AND NEW YORK

First published 2004
by Routledge
2 Park Square, Milton Park, Abingdon, Oxfordshire OX14 4RN

Simultaneously published in the USA and Canada
by Routledge
29 West 35th Street, New York, NY 10001

Routledge is an imprint of the Taylor & Francis Group

© 2004 David L. Andrews

Typeset in Goudy by
HWA Text and Data Management, Tunbridge Wells
Printed and bound in Great Britain by
MPG Books Ltd, Bodmin

Every effort has been made to ensure that the advice and
information in this book is true and accurate at the time of going
to press. However, neither the publisher nor the authors can
accept any legal responsibility or liability for any errors or
omissions that may be made. In the case of drug administration,
any medical procedure or the use of technical equipment
mentioned within this book, you are strongly advised to consult
the manufacturer's guidelines.

British Library Cataloguing in Publication Data
A catalogue record for this book is available from the British
Library

Library of Congress Cataloging in Publication Data
A catalog record for this book has been requested

ISBN 0-415-33333-4 (hbk)
ISBN 0-415-33334-2 (pbk)

Contents

Illustrations

Figure

Tables

Contributors

John Amis is an Associate Professor at the University of Memphis where he holds joint appointments in the Department of Health and Sport Sciences and the Department of Management. Amis' research interests have predominantly centered on organizational change and the identification, utilization and management of intangible resources. His work has appeared in journals such as *Academy of Management Journal, Journal of Applied Behavioral Science, Journal of Sport Management, European Marketing Journal, European Sport Management Quarterly,* and *Leisure Studies.* He serves on the editorial boards of four international journals.

David L. Andrews is an associate professor and member of the Physical Cultural Studies Research Group located in the Sport Commerce and Culture Program, Department of Kinesiology, and an Affiliate Faculty in the Department of American Studies, at the University of Maryland, USA. His research is concerned with crafting a sociology of late capitalist sport, to which end he is presently working on two books, *Sport Culture* (Blackwell), and *Sport and Cultural Capitalism* (Peter Lang). He has been guest editor of the *Sociology of Sport Journal,* and is currently on the editorial board of the *Journal of Sport and Social Issues* and the *Sociology of Sport Journal.*

Alan Bairner is a graduate of the universities of Edinburgh and Hull. He worked in Northern Ireland for 25 years before moving in 2003 to take up his present position as Reader in the Sociology of Sport at Loughborough University. He has written extensively on sport, politics and society and is the author of *Sport, Nationalism, and Globalization: European and North American Perspectives* (SUNY, 2001), co-author (with John Sugden) of *Sport, Sectarianism and Society in a Divided Ireland* (Leicester University Press, 1993) and joint editor (with John Sugden) of *Sport in Divided Societies* (Meyer and Meyer, 1999).

Carlton Brick lectures in Social Sciences at the University of Paisley. A founding member of the football supporters' civil rights campaign, *Libero,* he has written widely on such issues as consumption, commodification and regulation in soccer culture. He is currently working on a book on *jouissance,* enjoyment and Manchester United. He lives on the west coast of Scotland with his wife, Linda, and two children, Megan and Daniel.

Adam Brown is Research Fellow at the Manchester Institute for Popular Culture, Manchester Metropolitan University. His research areas include the football industry and its fans and fan culture; sport and community; and sport and regeneration. Adam is currently working on a major football research project, 'Football and its Communities', and has recently completed research for the UK Sports Council on the Commonwealth Games. He has published on sport and football and is editor of one football book, *Fanatics!* (Routledge, 1998) and co-author of another, *Not For Sale* (Mainstream, 1999). Adam is a Manchester United season ticket holder and supports the team home and away.

Emma Chumley graduated with a first-class Bachelor of Arts Honours degree from De Montfort University in 2001. She gained her Masters degree in Sport & Leisure Studies from the Department of Human Movement Sciences at The University of Memphis in 2003. She is currently an instructor at Epping Forest College in the UK. Her research interests focus around the intersections between gender, sexuality and local/national identities.

Jim Denison is a lecturer in Coach Education and Sports Development at the University of Bath, UK. He is the co-editor of *Moving Writing: Crafting Movement in Sport Research* (Peter Lang, 2003), and the author of *Bannister and Beyond: The Mystique of the Four-Minute Mile* (Breakaway Books, 2003). He is currently researching and writing the official biography of legendary Ethiopian distance runner, Haile Gebrselassie.

Grant Farred is an Associate Professor in the Literature Program at Duke University. He is author of *What's My Name? Black Vernacular Intellectuals* (University of Minnesota Press, 2003) and *Midfielder's Moment: Coloured Literature and Culture in Contemporary South Africa* (Westfiew Press, 2003), and editor of *Rethinking CLR James* (Basil Blackwell, 1996). He is a lifelong fan of Liverpool Football Club.

Bill Gerrard is Professor of Sport Management and Finance at Leeds University Business School in the UK. He has published academic papers on various aspects of the economics and finance of professional team sports, including football transfer fees, measuring player and team quality, coaching efficiency, media owner-ship of teams, and sport sponsorship. Proud of his Celtic and Tartan Army allegiances, Bill is a Leeds United fan, season ticket holder and shareholder. As a founding member of the Leeds United Independent Fans Association (LUIFA), he has campaigned against the recent financial mismanagement of the club.

David Hand works at the Manchester Metropolitan University. His research focuses on the analysis of discourses of national identity with particular reference to football writing. He is also interested in issues in football culture such as identity, gender and fandom. He has published on the relationship between French football and society and on the symbolism of the 1998 World Cup mascot. His work on the representation of national identities in European journalism includes the ground-breaking *Football, Europe and the Press* (Frank Cass, 2002), co-authored with Liz Crolley. A Mancunian, he naturally supports Manchester City as well as following the triumphs and tribulations of the French national team.

Eileen Kennedy is a Senior Lecturer within the Centre for Cultural Research in Sport, at University of Surrey Roehampton, where she teaches courses in sport, media and visual culture and convenes the MA in Sport and Culture. Her research interests centre on the exploration of the relationship between sport and leisure cultures and identity construction. She is particularly concerned with the interconnections between sport, gender and national identity, and the analysis of representations of sport in a range of audio-visual media.

Pirkko Markula is currently a Senior Lecturer in Sport Sociology and a member of the Qualitative Research Unit in the School of Sport and Health Sciences at the University of Exeter. She is an ethnographer with special interest in poststructuralist feminist analysis of dance, fitness, and health. She is the co-editor of *Moving Writing: Crafting Movement in Sport Research* (Peter Lang, 2003).

Gavin Mellor has taught at the University of Central Lancashire and Liverpool Hope University College in the Sociology and History of Sport. He is currently working as a research associate at the Manchester Institute for Popular Culture (MIPC) at Manchester Metropolitan University. His research interests are mainly concerned with the study of sport, community and social identity. He has published in a number of sport- and non-sport-related academic journals and is currently Senior Reviews Editor for the international journal *Soccer and Society*.

Toby Miller is Professor of Cultural Studies and Cultural Policy in the Center for Latin American and Caribbean Studies, the Program in American Studies, and the Department of Cinema Studies at New York University. He is the author and editor of more than twenty books, including: *The Well-Tempered Self: Citizenship, Culture, and the Postmodern Subject* (The Johns Hopkins University Press, 1993); *Technologies of Truth: Cultural Citizenship and the Popular Media* (University of Minnesota Press, 1998); *Popular Culture and Everyday Life* (Sage Publications, 1998) with Alec McHoul; *SportCult* (University of Minnesota Press, 1999) edited with Randy Martin; *Globalization and Sport: Playing the World* (Sage Publications, 2001) with Geoffrey Lawrence, Jim McKay, and David Row; and, *Sportsex* (Temple University Press, 2001). He is the editor of *Television & New Media*, co-editor of the Sport and Culture book series for University of Minnesota Press, editor of the Popular Culture and Everyday Life series for Peter Lang, and co-editor on the Web of *Blackwell/Polity Cultural Theory Resource Centre*.

Bo Reimer is Professor of Media and Communication Studies at the School of Arts and Communication, Malmö University, Sweden. He is the author of *The Most Common of Practices. On Mass Media Use in Late Modernity* (Almqvist & Wiksell International, 1994) and *The Politics of Postmodernity* (Sage 1999) with John R. Gibbins. He has also written a book on the history of sports on Swedish television (in Swedish).

Kirstin Rosaaen received her Master's degree from the University of Memphis in December 2002. Rosaaen's graduate research focused on the FedEx St. Jude Golf Tournament and the relationships between sponsor and client, as well as the cultural impact of the Manchester United football club. On graduation, she worked for a sport marketing agency running Nokia's sponsorship of the Nokia Sugar Bowl National

Championship football game, and currently works as an Account Manager in Client Development managing sponsors for a grassroots soccer and basketball tournament.

Andrew Ross is Professor of American Studies at New York University. He is the author of several books, including, most recently, *Low Pay, High Profile: The Global Push for Fair Labor* (New Press, 2004), *No-Collar: The Humane Workplace and its Hidden Costs* (Basic Books, 2003), and *The Celebration Chronicles: Life, Liberty and the Pursuit of Property Value in Disney's New Town* (Ballantine, 2000). He has also edited several books, including *No Sweat: Fashion, Free Trade, and the Rights of Garment Workers* (Verso, 1997), and, most recently, *Anti-Americanism* (NYU Press, 2004).

Michael Silk is an Assistant Professor and a member of the Physical Cultural Studies Research Group located in the Sport Commerce and Culture Program, Department of Kinesiology, at the University of Maryland. His work is committed to the critical, multidisciplinary and multi-method interrogation of sporting practices, experiences, and structures. He has published a number of book chapters and journal articles in *Media, Culture, Society, Journal of Sport and Social Issues, Sociology of Sport Journal, International Review for the Sociology of Sport, Sport, Culture and Society, Journal of Sport Management* and *Media Culture: A Review*.

John Sugden is Professor in the Sociology of Sport at the University of Brighton. He studied in the UK at the universities of Essex and Liverpool and completed his postgraduate education in the USA at the University of Connecticut where he earned his doctorate in 1982. He is well known for his ethnographic work on boxing, his studies of sport and politics in divided societies and, with Alan Tomlinson, is considered to be a leading expert on the politics of the governing body of world football(soccer), FIFA. Professor Sugden's contribution to this book is based on his investigative work into professional football's underground economy in the UK.

Alan Tomlinson is Professor of Leisure Studies at the University of Brighton, where he is the area leader of Sport and Leisure Cultures in the Chelsea School, Head of the Chelsea School Research Centre and Deputy Chair of the university's Research Degrees Committee. He teaches and writes on the social history and sociology of consumption, leisure and sport. His latest research concern is the changing nature of popular spectacle.

Stephen Wagg teaches the politics and history of sport at Roehampton University, London in the United Kingdom. He wrote *The Football World: A Contemporary Social History* (Harvester Press, 1984). He co-edited *British Football and Social Change* (with John Williams) (1991) and edited *Giving the Game Away: Football, Politics and Culture on Five Continents* (1995) (both Leicester University Press). Most recently he edited *British Football and Social Exclusion* (Routledge, 2004). He also writes on the political aspects of childhood, comedy and cricket.

Introduction

Situating Manchester United plc

David L. Andrews

The choice of Manchester United as the empirical locus of this project was based
on a number of factors, not least of which was the prominent place occupied by
the club within the everyday lives of the English populace. Whether one loves,
hates, or is indifferent toward the club, some semblance of its material, symbolic
and/or commercial presence is difficult to avoid when traversing England's high
streets, out-of-town shopping centres, school playgrounds, myriad newspapers or
television channels. Within the context of contemporary consumer society,
perhaps the most tangible criteria through which it is possible to evaluate
Manchester United's cultural significance are economic in nature. As testament
to its broad-based appeal, and unlike most other football clubs within what is a
recession-hit culture industry, in recent years Manchester United has generated
increased rates of profit, with earnings per share doubling between 2001 and
2003. Moreover, in 2003 profits reached £50 million, from turnover of £173
million, resulting in a market valuation approaching £610 million. Also, unlike
many clubs whose reliance upon television broadcast rights fees necessarily places
them in a perilous financial position, a breakdown of United's 2003 turnover
reveals a much healthier, balanced fiscal landscape derived from match day (41
per cent of turnover), media (32 per cent) and commercial (27 per cent) revenue
sectors.

Not that Manchester United should be considered a fundamentally parochial
phenomenon, as evidenced by its growing presence and aspirations within overseas
markets. As the club's 2003 annual report effused:

> Manchester United is one of the leading clubs in world football, with a global
> brand and following that embodies the passion and excitement of the world's
> most popular sport. Our goal is, through innovation, commitment and
> evolution, to protect and develop the brand by sustaining the playing success
> on the field and growing the business to enhance the financial strength of
> the Group.
>
> (Anon., 2003: 2)

Manchester United's rising status within the global cultural economy of sport
can be attributed to its position at the vanguard of the commercialising processes

that commandeered English football over the past two decades. This financial-isation (Martin, 2002) of the game was wrought from the introduction of new sources, and previously unimagineable scales, of capital investment from, amongst other media, marketing and commercial innovations: 'satellite and pay-per-view television networks, Internet and telecommunications corporations, transnational sports equipment manufacturers, public relations companies, and the major stock markets through the sale of club equity' (Giulianotti, 2002: 29). The latest phase in this process merely speaks to the growth strategies demanded by any successful corporate entity confronted with a saturation of their home market. For this reason, the Manchester United administration readily acknowledges the need to 'leverage the global brand' with the aim of 'converting more' global 'fans into customers' (Anon, 2003: 9).

The emergence of the emblematic Manchester United plc illustrates broader societal shifts within which the boundaries between cultural and commercial spheres have become increasingly indivisible. As such, the complex web of institutional forces and relations through which Manchester United is presently constituted speaks to Jameson's (1991; 1998) suggestive characterization of the late capitalist condition as being marked by the *collapsing* of the cultural and the economic 'back into one another' (Jameson, 1991: xxi), otherwise referred to as a 'dedifferentiation of fields, such that economics has come to overlap with culture: that everything, including commodity production and high and speculative finance, has become cultural; and culture has equally become economic or commodity oriented' (Jameson, 1998: 73). Certainly, contemporary sport culture can be considered an outgrowth of late capitalism's propensity for sectoral and institutional convergence (Andrews, 2001; Giulianotti, 1999; Goldman and Papson, 1998; Miller *et al.*, 2001; Rinehart, 1998; Roche, 2000; Whitson, 1998). In this regard, Manchester United represents a popular cultural institution that occupies the space between – and therefore shapes its very being in relation to – contemporaneous social forces and conditions. This, of course, has always been the case. For instance, the origination of the club in 1878 with the founding of Newton Heath (a name which endured until 1902), by the male workers of the Lancashire and Yorkshire Railway, spoke to the manner in which accelerating urbanising and industrialising processes contributed to the corporeal, spatial and temporal regulation of working-class leisure at that juncture. The relatively recent, yet rapid, transformation of Manchester United into an 'American-style, brand-led media business' (Maidment, 2002), exhibits the extent to which sport, in the late twentieth and early twenty-first centuries, has become inextricably entangled with the values and directives of an increasingly dominant global corporate capitalist order (Maguire, Jarvie, Mansfield and Bradley, 2002). In McKay and Miller's (1991: 87) terms, Manchester United plc thus represents a prototypical 'corporate sport' institution.

Manchester United presently occupies a relational and dynamic space, positioned in relation to external social fields (Kay and Laberge, 2002) many of which are dominated and defined by commercial dictates. Thus, the club's major shareholders, the organizational and representative bodies of the game (FA

Premier League, UEFA, Professional Football Players Association, G-14 European Football Clubs Association), primary corporate sponsors (Nike, Vodafone), and broadcast media interests (Sky Sports, ITV), all contribute toward shaping the club's corporatist demeanour, in ways which may, or indeed may not, accommodate the wishes and ambitions of its supporters (not infrequently a football club's most overlooked constituency). Within the relational space created by these inter-secting commercial forces and relations, the late capitalist Manchester United has become actualised as much by the workings of the previously distinct advertising, marketing, promotion, public relations and mass media sectors, as by its own internal mechanisms. As such, Manchester United plc exemplifies the type of horizontally integrated and flexible organizational network, indicative of the post-Fordist structures that have come to dominate and define the late capitalist cultural economy (c.f. Castells, 1996; Harvey, 1989; Murray, 1990). Indeed, in Jameson's (1991; 1998) terms, Manchester United's structure, goals and objectives can no longer be easily differentiated from those of the core institutional elements and relations through which it has come to exist in its present form. Moreover, such is the degree to which they have been seamlessly sutured into the very essence of the Manchester United experience – and such is the hegemonic influence of the club – that its various commercially based institutional interdependencies have come to be viewed by many as 'naturalized and indispensable' (Rowe, 1995) elements of the contemporary football club.

At the behest of the commercialising, mass-mediating, and globalising forces that simultaneously compel and propel many of its core constituents, Manchester United plc has effectively become a highly diversified (both in its structure and focus) platform for the delivery of mass entertainment. Hence the club, its history, stadium, players and playing exploits are mobilised as the centrepiece of an array of branded experiences and commodities designed to stimulate public interest (match attendance, television viewership, books and magazines, video games, video documentaries and season reviews, replica team shirts and other licensed merchandise, stadium tours, theme restaurants *et al.*) with the aim of generating – as the normative expectations of the stock market dictate to any public corporation – ever-increasing rates of investment return. While Manchester United may have taken the lead in English football's newly found preoccupation with markets and consumers (King, 1997), the football public's engagement with the club does not necessarily foreground commercially inspired relations; they are, however, almost unavoidably present in some capacity. Put another way, hypercommercial football clubs such as Manchester United still command the same type of obsessive and, at times, irrational loyalty identified as being characteristic of the traditional football supporter (Giulianotti, 2002). The difference within the present football context is that the cleverly crafted normative expectations of behaviour, which can compel (however unwillingly) the aforementioned traditional *supporter* to invest in what are not inconsiderable commercial exchanges (such as those demanded by season ticket, satellite television and pay-per-view subscription and replica team shirt purchases), in order to both publicly and privately announce a Manchester United subjectivity beyond reproach. That having been said, the hypercommercialism of the new football economy has stimulated the emergence of new categories of spectators. For, as the 'commodity-centered mediation of football qua entertainment intensifies', so the presence of spectators with more celebrity-driven (fans) and ephemeral (flaneurs) relations to specific clubs becomes more evident (Giulianotti, 2002: 38). The changing experience of football spectatorship is also linked to the expanded spatial reach of mega-clubs. No longer reliant solely upon the locally grounded, near mythical, working-class communities with which football club support has been traditionally associated, major clubs represent a point of coalescence for a transnational, televisually based neo-tribalism (Maffesoli, 1995), substantiated through the establishment of truly global, satellite distribution networks (for further explication of the changing relations between football and its communities, see Brown et al., N.D.). Thus, Manchester United operates, at one and the same time, in a manner that accommodates its local and national spectator bases, while it looks to colonise the rest of the acknowledged football world and beyond (i.e. the United States).

From a number of vantage points, Manchester United clearly represents a prescient and illuminating problematic. Somewhat surprisingly, therefore, up to this juncture there have been remarkably few considered academic analyses of even the more discrete aspects of the Manchester United question, let alone a fully comprehensive study. The most notable contributions in this regard are Brown and Walsh's (1999) thoughtful and rigorous analysis of the political machinations surrounding Rupert Murdoch's unsuccessful bid to purchase the club, and Cashmore's (2002) lively deconstruction of one-time United icon, David Beckham. Indeed, while it cannot be considered in the same vein as a considered scholarly work, Bose's (2000) mildly sensationalist exposé of the commercial reinvention of the club is arguably the most comprehensive analysis of Manchester United to date. Dropping down (or is it up?) the publishing food chain, there is of course a flourishing Manchester United sub-industry consisting of descriptive popular histories, player (auto)biographies, fan narratives, annual reflections and even national curriculum related workbooks (c.f. Broadbent, 2000; Connor, 2004; Gregg, 2002; Hughes, 2003; Kelly, 2003; Shindler, 1999). However, in order to address the relative disregard shown by the academic community toward Manchester United as the focus for serious study, this anthology seeks to situate and excavate the Manchester United phenomenon in a manner which renders intelligible its social, cultural, economic, and political significance.

Broadly speaking, this project can be viewed as an attempt to contextualise Manchester United through a multi-themed, interdisciplinary, interpretive approach, premised on the understanding that 'An event or practice does not exist apart from the forces of the context that constitute it as what it is' (Grossberg, 1997a: 255). In a previous discussion (Andrews, 2002), I sought to outline a contextually grounded approach toward developing a comprehensive under-standing of sport culture, in all its myriad manifestations. According to this dialectic materialist schema, sport is a fluid, relational and processual entity, whose culturally and historically contingent iterations can only be understood in relation to the complex matrix of forces with which it is constitutively bound. Differently put, sport 'identities, practices, and effects generally, constitute the very context within which they are practices, identities, or effects' (Slack, 1996: 125), and hence they need to be addressed as such. In light of this, the aim of any contextually driven research is to map the sport entity under scrutiny – in this case Manchester United – within, and through, the precise set of social, cultural, economic and/or political conditions and relations operating at the moment of analysis.

Though generally acknowledged as a legitimate mode of critical intellectual inquiry, there continues to exist a relative scarcity of sport-oriented studies advancing Grossberg's directive to the effect that 'context is everything and everything is context for cultural studies' (1997b: 7–8), for which the notable exceptions merely underscore the greater absence of this approach (c.f. Carrington, 2001; Cole, 1996; Giardina, 2003; Gruneau and Whitson, 1993; Howell and Ingham, 2001; McDonald, 2000; Miller, 1998). Of course this relative dearth of contextual cultural studies of sport is wholly understandable. Put simply, the associated craft of mapping the 'rich aggregate of many determinations and relations' (Marx, 1977: 351) that dialectically link, or articulate, a discrete sporting entity to the broader social context, is indeed a bewildering task for any individual researcher. For this reason, it is by no means surprising that *Policing the Crisis: Mugging, the State, and Law and Order* (Hall et al., 1979) – generally considered to be a benchmark cultural studies project in terms of empirical depth, political commitment, theoretical sophistication and contextual reconstruction – was a collaborative endeavour in the truest sense of the term. While by no means intended to be, or indeed realised as, as close a research collaboration as that which spawned *Policing the Crisis*, in combination the substantive and disciplinary diversity of the Manchester United analyses incorporated within this anthology seeks to make a similar contribution. Through a collective linking of Manchester United to the 'determinate effects' and 'concrete relations' characteristic of the social context in which it exists and operates (Hall, 1996: 45), the aim of the book is to explicate the complexities of the Manchester United phenomenon, while simultaneously providing some important insights into the forces shaping contemporary society as a whole.

The process of contextualising Manchester United is realised within five thematic sections, each focused on somewhat discrete, yet necessarily interrelated, aspects of inquiry. As befits the study of what is a necessarily complex and multifaceted problematic, the chapter authors speak from a variety of disciplinary vantage points, including Cultural Studies, Sociology, English, History, Media Studies, Sport and Leisure Management, Gender Studies, Economics and the Sociology of Sport. The aim is to encourage readers to engage in their own form of disciplinary boundary crossing (Klein, 1996), and hopefully generate a more holistic and contextual understanding, as they encounter the various elements of the Manchester United phenomenon. Part I, 'Becoming United', provides a historical backdrop to Manchester United's present incarnation, through discussions which, to differing degrees and in differing ways, address the Munich air crash in February 1958 as a pivotal moment in the club's recent evolution.

Focusing on the symbolic influence of the iconic Matt Busby, Stephen Wagg outlines the manner in which the mythology that enveloped the team that perished in Munich was, and continues to be, responsible for anchoring the club firmly in the collective consciousness of the global football public. Acknowledging the importance of the Munich disaster to the self-reflexive understanding of the Manchester United supporter's experience, Gavin Mellor uses archival and oral histories in identifying how this tragic event evolved into an important moment for the supporters of rival teams looking for points of attribution, in justifying their increasing disdain for an ascendant Manchester United. Lastly in Part I, from a strategic management perspective, Kirsten Rosaaen and John Amis examine the intangible resources, particularly in terms of the public interest and empathy, deriving from involvement in the Munich disaster. Albeit emergent from the midst of tragedy, Rosaaen and Amis argue that the club's elevated popular profile and reputation was subsequently capitalised upon through the adoption of corroborative management and branding strategies.

In Part II, 'Economy United', the discussion turns to contrasting readings of Manchester United's commercial being. Utilising a method of quantitative bench-marking, Bill Gerrard highlights the sources of Manchester United's competitive advantage, which he identifies as deriving from the mobilising of key strategic resources in a superior fashion to its leading Premier League rivals. Andrew Ross provides a more critical interpretation of football's new business model, of which Manchester United is the leading exemplar, through an examination of com-mercial relations, and political contestations, responsible for the instantiation of the United megabrand. Furthermore, his explication of the exploitative labour relations engaged through the club's commercial relationship with Nike – the producer of team apparel – represents an ironic updating of the unequal economic interdependencies that have, for centuries, linked Manchester with South East Asia. Focusing on the politics of replica shirt consumption, Carlton Brick high-lights how Manchester United fan cultures have scorned the consumption of licensed merchandise as being a soulless, commodified expression of club loyalty. In doing so, Brick, following Žižek, identifies a core paradox within late capitalism, namely, that devotional anti-consumptuary resistance, or non-consumption, actually mirrors the commodified excesses of that which it purportedly abhors. Lastly within Part II, John Sugden provides a rich ethno-graphic reading of an illegimate commercial subculture centred on the provision of counterfeit clothing, merchandise and independent ticket and travel *et al.* to Manchester United supporters. Ironically, this urban underground economy effectively uses the club's popularity as a mechanism for enabling its workers to immerse themselves within the ideology and excess of Britain's mainstream enterprise culture.

Part III, 'Embodied United', turns the attention to the players, the embodied representatives of Manchester United. Alan Bairner uses George Best as a suggestive vehicle through which to examine the complex relationship between Manchester United and the Northern Ireland population. Specifically, he identifies how Best's iconic status as player and personality, in combination with his understated Protestantism, allowed support for Manchester United to – however superficially and ephemerally – transcend the religious and cultural divides within Northern Ireland. Through a variety of theoretical lenses, Eileen Kennedy discusses how different representational modes influence the manner in which footballers' bodies become visible. In doing so, she illuminates the shifting gender and class politics of late capitalist sport. Pirkko Markula continues the focus on the gendered nature of the Manchester United spectacle. Through a Deleuzian informed feminist interrogation, Markula challenges the popular disdain for Victoria Beckham (wife of former Manchester United icon, David Beckham) and offers an alternative reading of her as a progressive female subject.

Turning to issues of football, community and identity, Part IV, 'Local United', illustrates the various local rivalries with which Manchester United, and most pertinently its Mancunian supporters, are implicated. Adam Brown discusses Manchester's contested footballscape within the context of a period of significant urban investment and regeneration. This leads to a focus on the relations between rival clubs, Manchester United and Manchester City, their fans and the city itself. Evidencing Manchester's football-based divisions, David Hand outlines the common perceptions held by Manchester City supporters concerning their domineering local rivals. He graphically illustrates how these antagonistic United imaginings play an important role in the discursive constitution of antithetical City identities. Alan Tomlinson broadens the issue of rivalry with Manchester United to include its Lancastrian neighbours, specifically Burnley. Through a detailed socio-historical analysis, Tomlinson outlines the contrasting evolutions of Manchester United and Burnley, as expressed through changing relations between administrators, players and supporters. Finally in Part IV, Grant Farred provides an illuminating window into Liverpool fans' haughty disregard for Manchester United's position of ascendancy within English football, due to its failure to emulate Liverpool's onetime dominance of the European sphere. As Farred acknowledges, this disdain is as much a mechanism for coping with Liverpool's relative decline, as it is a critique of Manchester United's corporatised sensibility.

Lastly, Part V, 'Global United', focuses on Manchester United's aspirations and presence within the broader football universe. Toby Miller provides an insightful overview of the contextual forces and conditions operating in contradistinction to Manchester United's market expansionist ambitions, as it seeks to penetrate the United States' sporting landscape. From a more discrete US perspective – that of Memphis, Tennessee – Silk and Chumley offer an ethnographically based understanding of the hierarchies and complexities operating within the consumption communities, which have coalesced around the televisual globalisation of the Manchester United spectacle. Focusing specifically on particular Manchester United supporter groups, Bo Reimer underscores the fact that Scandinavian interest in British football has to be understood as part of broader social and historical relations between these contrasting parts of Northern Europe. Reimer identifies how the complexities and contradictions within contemporary English football culture, wrought by the mass-mediated hyper-commercialisation of the game, has similarly affected the constitution and experience of Scandinavian Manchester United supporter groups. Finally in Part V, Jim Denison inverts the focus of the previous discussions by focusing on an immigrant's seemingly unavoidable compulsion to become a Manchester United fan. In pinpointing the centrality of Manchester United within English culture, and its increasing international presence, Denison suggests how the newly landed immigrant can derive a sense – however superficial – of belonging, through exposure to the globally familiar.

References

Andrews, D.L. (2001) 'Sport', in R. Maxwell (ed.) *Culture Works: The Political Economy of Culture*, Minneapolis: University of Minnesota Press.

Andrews, D.L. (2002) 'Coming to terms with cultural studies', *Journal of Sport and Social Issues*, 26(1), 110–17.

Anon. (2003) *Annual Report*, Manchester: Manchester United plc.

Bose, M. (2000) *Manchester Unlimited: The Money, Egos and Infighting Behind the World's Richest Football Club*, London: Texere.

Broadbent, P. (2000) *The Official Manchester United Maths Workbook 5*, London: Letts Educational.

Brown, A., Mellor, G., Crabbe, T., Blackshaw, T. and Stone, C. (N.D.) *Football and its Communities*, Manchester: The Football Foundation.

Brown, A. and Walsh, A. (1999) *Not for Sale: Manchester United, Murdoch and the Defeat of BSkyB*, Edinburgh: Mainstream.

Carrington, B. (2001) 'Postmodern blackness and the celebrity sports star: Ian Wright, "race" and English identity', in D.L. Andrews and S.J. Jackson (eds) *Sport Stars: The Cultural Politics of Sporting Celebrity*, London: Routledge.

Cashmore, E. (2002) *Beckham*. Cambridge: Polity Press.

Castells, M. (1996) *The Rise of the Network Society*, Cambridge, MA: Blackwell Publishers.

Cole, C.L. (1996) 'P.L.A.Y., Nike, and Michael Jordan: national fantasy and the racialization of crime and punishment', *Working Papers in Sport and Leisure Commerce* (Bureau of Sport and Leisure Commerce: The University of Memphis), website.

Connor, J. (2004) *The Lost Babes: The Untold Stories of Manchester United and Munich*, Edinburgh: Canongate Books.

Giardina, M.D. (2003) '"Bending it like Beckham" in the global popular: styling hybridity, performativity, and the politics of representation', *Journal of Sport and Social Issues*, 27(1): 65–82.

Giulianotti, R. (1999) *Football: A Sociology of the Global Game*. Cambridge: Polity Press.

Giulianotti, R. (2002) 'Supporters, followers, fans, and *flaneurs*: a taxonomy of spectator identities in football'. *Journal of Sport and Social Issues*, 26(1): 25–46.

Goldman, R. and Papson, S. (1998) *Nike Culture*, London: Sage.

Gregg, H. (2002) *Harry's Game: An Autobiography*. Edinburgh: Mainstream Publishing.

Grossberg, L. (1997a) 'Bringing it all back home: pedagogy and cultural studies', in *Bringing it all Back Home: Essays on Cultural Studies*, Durham: Duke University Press.

Grossberg, L. (1997b) 'Cultural studies, modern logics, and theories of globalisation', in A. McRobbie (ed.) *Back to Reality? Social Experience and Cultural Studies*, Manchester: Manchester University Press.

Gruneau, R. and Whitson, D. (1993) *Hockey Night in Canada: Sport, Identities, and Cultural Politics*, Toronto: Garamond Press.

Hall, S. (1996) 'The problem of ideology: Marxism without guarantees', in D. Morley and K.H. Chen (eds) *Stuart Hall: Critical Dialogues in Cultural Studies*, London: Routledge.

Hall, S., Critcher, C., Jefferson, T., Clarke, J. and Roberts, B. (1979) *Policing the Crisis: Mugging, the State, and Law and Order*, London: Macmillan.

Harvey, D. (1989) *The Condition of Postmodernity: An Enquiry into the Origins of Cultural Change*, Oxford: Blackwell.

Howell, J. and Ingham, A. (2001) 'From social problem to personal issue: the language of lifestyles', *Cultural Studies*, 15(2): 326–51.

Hughes, B. (2003) *The King: Denis Law, Hero of the Stretford End*, Manchester: Empire Publications.

Jameson, F. (1991) *Postmodernism, or, the Cultural Logic of Late Capitalism*, Durham: Duke University Press.

Jameson, F. (1998) *The Cultural Turn: Selected Writings on the Postmodern 1983–1998*, London and New York: Verso.

Kay, J. and Laberge, S. (2002) 'Mapping the field of "AR": adventure racing and Boudieu's concept of field', *Sociology of Sport Journal*, 19(1): 25–46.

Kelly, N. (2003) *Manchester United: The Untold Story*: London: Michael O'Mara Books.

King, A. (1997) 'New directors, customers, and fans: the transformation of English football in the 1990s', *Sociology of Sport Journal*, 14(3): 224–40.

Klein, J.T. (1996) *Crossing Boundaries: Knowledge, Disciplinarities, and Interdisciplinarities*, Charlottesville, VA: University of Virginia Press.

Maffesoli, M. (1995) *The Time of the Tribes*, London: Sage.

Maguire, J., Jarvie, G., Mansfield, L. and Bradley, J. (2002) *Sport Worlds: A Sociological Perspective*, Champaign, IL: Human Kinetics.

Maidment, P. (2002) 'Manchester United expands its global reach', *Forbes*, 30 September.

Martin, R. (2002) *Financialization of Daily Life*, Philadelphia: Temple University Press.

Marx, K. (1977) 'Grundrisse', in D. McLellan (ed.) *Karl Marx: Selected Writings*, Oxford: Oxford University Press.

McDonald, M.G. (2000) 'The marketing of the Women's National Basketball Association and the making of postfeminism', *International Review for the Sociology of Sport*, 35(1): 35–48.

McKay, J. and Miller, T. (1991) 'From old boys to men and women of the corporation: the Americanization and commodification of Australian sport', *Sociology of Sport Journal*, 8(1): 86–94.

Miller, T. (1998) 'Commodifying the male body, problematising "Hegemonic Masculinity"?' *Journal of Sport and Social Issues*, 22(4): 431–46.

Miller, T., Lawrence, G., McKay, J. and Rowe, D. (2001) *Globalization and Sport: Playing the World*, London: Sage.

Murray, R. (1990) 'Fordism and post-Fordism', in S. Hall and M. Jacques (eds) *New Times: The Changing Face of Politics in the 1990s*, London: Verso.

Rinehart, R.E. (1998) *Players All: Performances in Contemporary Sport*, Bloomington: Indiana University Press.

Roche, M. (2000) *Mega-Events and Modernity: Olympics, Expos and the Growth Of Global Culture*, London: Routledge.

Rowe, D. (1995) *Popular Cultures: Rock Music, Sport and the Politics of Pleasure*, London: Sage.

Shindler, C. (1999) *Manchester United Ruined my Life*, London: Headline.

Slack, J.D. (1996) 'The theory and method of articulation in cultural studies', in D. Morley and K.H. Chen (eds) *Stuart Hall: Critical Dialogues in Cultural Studies*, London: Routledge.

Whitson, D. (1998) 'Circuits of promotion: media, marketing and the globalization of sport', in L.A. Wenner (ed.) *Mediasport*, London: Routledge.

Part I
Becoming United

1 The team that wouldn't die

On the mystique of Matt Busby and Manchester United

Stephen Wagg

Ransom Stoddard: 'You're not going to use the story, Mr Scott?'
Maxwell Scott: 'This is the West, sir. When the legend becomes fact, print the legend.'
From: The Man Who Shot Liberty Valance (Directed by John Ford, 1962)[1]

Many English football people of a certain age – born, that is, before or just after the Second World War – have long since wearied of the growing global pre-occupation with Manchester United and its personnel. If the much-feted David Beckham were to be holding a photo shoot in their back garden, or the graceless, gum-chewing Sir Alex Ferguson were to be conducting a press conference there, they would probably prefer to draw the curtains. But the United teams of 1948 or the mid-1950s might be a different matter; these sides would now very likely inspire the same feelings of warmth and identification beyond the immediate Manchester conurbation as they did then.

I confess I'm one of those people (b. 1947) and this essay is about the legend of Manchester United which formed in those years and which provided the basis for, but is importantly in some ways distinct from, the current international fascination for the club. In trying to suggest the appeal of Manchester United outside its own locality during this period the essay is necessarily speculative. It treats United, inevitably, as a text, but it also considers key recent texts on the mythology of Manchester United and of their most celebrated manager Matt Busby. Three are especially important – *A Strange Kind of Glory: Sir Matt Busby and Manchester United* by the Irish writer Eamon Dunphy (Dunphy, 1991); a three-part *Arena* documentary made by the leading sports journalist Hugh McIlvanney about three football managers born on the same Scottish coalfield: *Busby, Stein, Shankly: The Football Men*, broadcast on BBC in 1997 (McIlvanney, 1997); and *Matt Busby: The Boss*, another TV documentary, this time for BBC2's *Reputations* series, put out in May of 1999. There are others.

My main purpose is to outline the legend and to suggest its seductiveness at certain times and in certain social places. The legend is clearly what counts and I'm not concerned to 'debunk' popular myths about the club or their famous manager, although I will, where I feel it's appropriate, seek to unpack important notions about post-war Manchester United. I'm using the word 'myth', therefore, not so much in its everyday usage which refers to a popular but mistaken view, as in the meaning given to it by Roland Barthes of 'depoliticized speech' (Barthes, 1973: 142)

My argument, in summary, is this: Manchester United became one of the most loved and admired football teams in the world because they represented, variously, a tantalising balance between vitally opposed ideas – between tradition and modernity, between the local and the global (or, at least, the continental), between Anglo Saxon sobriety and Celtic romance, between freedom and constraint, between the individual and the collective. The Manchester United team which appeared most successfully to embody the tensions between these ideas came together in the mid-1950s, under the charismatic manager Matt Busby, and was broken up in what has arguably become world sport's most remembered catastrophe: the Munich air crash of February 1958. This disaster froze an important and attractive young team in the act of becoming. Although a number of its members survived, this team – the so-called 'Busby Babes' – remains, in perpetuity, what it might have been, and public interest in the tragedy has not, apparently, abated.

A meeting of myths: Matt Busby and Manchester United

Manchester United, as is well known, began life as Newton Heath, a football club formed by workers on the Lancashire–Yorkshire railway in the late 1870s. In 1978 Geoffrey Green, the languid football correspondent of the London *Times*, published the official history of Manchester United at the club's first centenary. It begins, however, in 1945. This strategy for the book's organisation is explained by the author by the fact that before the 1940s United had been 'just another provincial club with a minimal national following', which had accomplished little of note since the early 1900s. 'Only those living in Lancashire and the environs of Manchester knew or cared much about United ...', wrote Green. Indeed they weren't even the best team in these environs, Manchester City being by common consent the more prestigious side in the 1920s and 1930s (Green, 1979: 25–6). All this changed, according to virtually every popular account, with the arrival of Matt Busby as team manager in 1945. Busby, it's said, was the principal instrument in the transformation of Manchester United, the second best football club in Manchester, into the Manchester United of popular myth. There are several important elements to the Busby mythology, which I'd like to discuss.

Busby as manager

In the mythology of Matt Busby as a football manager, there is a strong hint of the modern. He typifies a process I have previously described whereby managers at English football clubs during the 1940s and 1950s became progressively more identified with their team's performance. This was not an entirely new phenomenon – Herbert Chapman, for example, at Huddersfield Town (1921–

5) and then at Arsenal (1925–34) and Boer War veteran Major Frank Buckley (Wolverhampton Wanderers 1927–44) had both been regarded as strategists who planned their players' performances and who wished to be in sole charge of team matters. But this notion of managerial responsibility was amplified after the Second World War, so that, as I observed in 1984, by the late 1960s 'most people knew who, say, Matt Busby was, or Bill Shankly or Don Revie or Jimmy Hill ... But practically none of them, outside of the respective communities, would have known who had managed Manchester United before Busby, Liverpool before Shankly ...' (Wagg, 1984: 162).

Busby happily embraced this notion of manager as sole arbiter of team affairs. He is said, when asked to become Manchester United manager in 1945, to have informed the club that he would only accept the job on these terms (Dunphy, 1991: 100). Later, in an autobiography published in the early 1970s, he told of how he resisted repeated attempts by the United chairman Jimmy Gibson to dictate team policy to him (Busby, 1973: 13 and 17).

Two things are important about this notion of Busby-as-His-Own-Man: first, the stark contrast he provided to a previous kind of discredited football management and, second, the ambiguity surrounding the kind of new management he actually represented. In English football discourse after the 1970s, there was a favoured way of recalling football management in the 1940s and 1950s. This held that during the post-war period a generation of desk-bound, time-serving men in waistcoats and watch chains were elbowed aside in favour of a new kind of 'boss' – a 'hands-on' coach in muddy boots, anxious to work with his players to 'organise victory' (Chapman's preferred phrase) the following Saturday (Wagg, 1984: 73–100). Thus, histories of United refer routinely to the fact that Scott Duncan, Busby's predecessor at Old Trafford, invariably wore spats and a flower in his buttonhole, while Matt, having taken the United job, was soon out on the training ground, kicking a ball about with the lads (see, for example, Glanvill, 1994: 51; Meek and Tyrell, 2001: 13). This is the classic marker of political cultural change. Effete traditionalism had to step aside and watch egalitarian modernity take over.

More importantly, in this new popular discourse about football, the manager now becomes the paradigm for the popular understanding of football. However, Busby was a text more open than most: traditionalists might regard him as the keeper of the true faith, while modernisers could perceive him to be a new broom. For example, Charlie Mitten and Johnny Morris, both of whom played for United under Busby in the 1940s, recently challenged the idea of Busby as the great team maker. 'I never saw him coaching anybody at all,' said Mitten. 'He never said once to me anything about improving my play at outside left.' Morris spoke, importantly, as a man who'd played before the invention of the Great Football Manager: 'All managers get a bit stronger if you're top t'League. Win something. And that's what you've got to do to keep your job. So, we kept his job for him' (*Reputations* 'Matt Busby: The Boss', BBC2, 17 May 1999). Later, when the discourse of English football became more technocratic, this became the yardstick against which Busby was judged. In this context, he was either efficient, or he wasn't. Noel Cantwell, for instance, who went to Old Trafford in 1960 and captained United's FA (Football Association) Cup winning side in 1963, recalled asking Busby 'How do we play?' and receiving the reply: 'We play football'. This story appears in different places, with subtly different inflections. In *Reputations* it's seen as evidence of Busby's sloppiness, while in the club's official biography of Busby it affirms his charisma (Glanvill, 1994: 144–5). Others were equally adamant that Busby *was* a tactician and that he had a plan. His biographer Rick Glanvill suggests that 'the 1955–8 team gives the lie to the idea that Matt was no tactician. Throughout this period, United employed a 4-2-4 formation ... before world champions Brazil made it fashionable.' His close friend Paddy McGrath, who ran the Cromford, Manchester's first nightclub, confirms this: 'He used to say "There's only one way to play football ... and that's four at the back, two in midfield and four up front"' (Glanvill, 1994: 102, 110).

But most devotees and exponents of the Busby myth preferred to believe that Busby intervened only to set his players free to do what they did best. In this he was said to reconcile the art and the science of the game – combining nature and nurture, spontaneity and artifice, tradition with modernity. He took what he inherited – his first United team was a collection of established players returning to the club after the war – and creatively nurtured them, soon arranging for two established attacking players, Johnny Carey and John Aston, to move into defensive positions. From then on, the implication within the discourse was that Busby's team now embraced new, exciting, audacious ideas, with the intention to 'play football from the back' (Dunphy 1991: 109). As Dunphy points out, it was this team which crowds flocked to see in the late 1940s. In the season 1946–7 well over a million people came to watch them play at Maine Road, Manchester (their temporary home while bomb damage at Old Trafford was repaired), and the following year they won the FA Cup in what many observers 30 years later still considered to be the best post-war final (Dunphy, 1991: 109, 131–8; Green, 1979: 38–40). It's at this point that Manchester United first became a phenomenon of interest to football-minded people outside the club's own backyard.

In the late 1940s, Matt Busby became a popular manifestation of the football-manager-as-arbiter-of-team-performance and he was invited to manage the Great Britain football team at the London Olympics of 1948. He was often asked how he produced the exciting performances of his teams and he liked to respond with a story likely only to enhance his mystique. A sculptor he knew had, similarly, been asked how he sculpted an elephant, and had replied that he'd take a block of stone and knock off all the bits that didn't look like an elephant (Green, 1979: 53; Glanvill, 1994: 83). This allowed the romantics to claim him as their own, and the technocrats equally to suppose that he had a closely guarded stock of expertise. The former liked to cite his frequent pre-match advice – 'Give it to a red shirt' (Dunphy, 1991: 133) – and the latter to argue that there was, necessarily, much more to it than that. 'People say about Matt that all he used to tell us was to "just go out and play", remembers Wilf McGuinness, a United player in the late 1950s and Busby's successor as the club's manager. 'He did tell you that, but we used to have a team talk on the Friday. He'd go through the opposition individually and we were always amazed how much he knew about them' (Glanvill, 1994: 90).

Busby as Celt

Busby's Manchester United was extraordinary in inspiring loyalty across a range of British ethnicities, whether based on religion, national identity and/or relationship to England and the English. Busby was born on the Lanarkshire coalfield to a Catholic family. His grandfather had been an Irish immigrant. He was, according to Paddy McGrath, 'a bloody good Christian' (Glanvill, 1994: 62) – a devout Catholic who received a papal knighthood in 1967. But he was equally devout in his anti-sectarianism and the corresponding (and modern) belief that religion was a private matter (Dunphy, 1991: 14). He similarly discouraged any thought that United might be a Catholic club (McIlvanney, 1997: Programme 2) and, although his assistant Jimmy Murphy was also a practising Catholic, other members of his training staff were not: trainer Tom Curry was an Anglican, and coach Bert Whalley a Methodist lay preacher (Roberts, 1988: 59; Dunphy, 1991: 127). Moreover, there was no perceptible religious pattern to United's recruitment policy under Busby. Indeed, the only teams in the British Isles thought to practise religious discrimination in their selection were Glasgow Rangers and the Scottish national side: Busby had only played once for the latter and this, according to United player Paddy Crerand, was widely thought to be because he was a Catholic (Glanvill, 1994: 28–9).

Busby's Scottishness was important in the globalising of Manchester United's popularity. For one thing, as Stuart Cosgrove has observed, '[m]ore than any other nation, including Brazil, the Scots elevate football to its proper status' (1986: 99). Scottish football, traditionally, was widely perceived to be 'a confused blend of Calvinist and Celtic elements', the former represented as doggedness and hard work, the latter as daring and virtuosity, placing style above safety (Holt, 1994: 66). North of the border Busby was seen as introducing a brand of football that expressed the poetry of the Celtic soul. He was doing it, moreover, not only in the northwest of England where English professional football had been forged, but mostly with English players, in a city that was historically the fortress of Liberalism, Protestant nonconformism and free trade.

Manchester also had a long history of Irish Catholic migration, and Irish descended families were a strong feature of the city's working class (Herbert, 2001: 9–18; Messinger, 1985: 177–9). A part of Manchester was known as 'Little Ireland' and there had been periodic ill feeling between Protestants and Catholics in the nineteenth century (Herbert, 2001: 33–41). Sectarianism, however, was never on the scale of other British cities such as Liverpool and Glasgow. Irishmen had played for Manchester United since its formation as Newton Heath (Scally, 1998: 45). But, although the board of the latter had voted to rename the club 'Manchester United' instead of 'Manchester Celtic' by only three votes to two (Green, 1979: 280), there was no discernable link from then on between the club and the Manchester Irish. Busby, however, noted the Celtic connection. The captain of United's popular team of the late 1940s was Johnny Carey, another Irish Catholic who had played both Gaelic and association football for the Republic before coming to United. He was selected to captain the Rest of Europe in 1947 against Great Britain and Dunphy suggests that a similar legend began to form around Carey as the one that formed around Busby (1991: 137–8). Busby established a scout in the south of Ireland around this time, but made sure to have one in the north too.

A decade later enthusiasm for Manchester United among the southern Irish seemed as strong as ever. In 1957, Manchester United were drawn to begin their European Cup campaign against Shamrock Rovers at Dalymount Park in Dublin. When the draw was made in Zurich, Matt Busby turned to the Rovers chairman and said: 'You've just got a licence to print money'. United attracted a sell-out crowd of 40,000 people (Scally, 1998: 60–1, 71). Busby was conscious of the importance of foreign markets, and of United's advantageous relationship to them. From early in his managership he took the team abroad where they could be seen – notably to the United States in 1950 and again in 1952. The USA, of course, was an important place of settlement for Irish migrants and, as in the Republic of Ireland itself, its association football culture had been partially submerged by nationalist elements (Wagg, 1995; Sugden and Bairner, 1993). They played to big crowds.

So Busby's early United sides were enormously engaging both to communities identifying themselves in some way as Celtic – which, given the global reach of the Irish diaspora (Coogan, 2000), might be a huge constituency – and to football people in different countries likely to be discomfited if United had carried any specific ethnic or sectarian affiliation. As Dunphy observes, Busby's vision of football travelled across national and cultural boundaries and had a special appeal to the wretched of the earth: 'Football's properties – imagination, courage, grace and wit – were God's gifts, belonging to the humblest person, be he in Orbiston [Busby's birthplace], Manchester, urban ghetto, mining village, the slums of Naples or the *barrios* of South America' (Dunphy, 1991: 292).

Moreover, United's attractiveness and Busby's status as bold, Celtic outsider were enhanced by the club's entry into European competition. As is well known, Manchester United, at Busby's instigation, defied the English Football League authorities to take part in the European Cup in 1956. The League's obstructive stance might be read as imperialist disdain or Little Englandism, producing Busby's defiance as representative of the Other, subject peoples. The crowds that subsequently flocked to various European airports and hotels to see the United players and seek their autographs no doubt did so partly in homage to a Britishness more humble and open to the outside world than English football authorities had hitherto expressed. If they went to see United play it's likely that they experienced United as not typically English, since their game was not based on the traditionally English virtues of hard tackling and the long ball. Significantly, the other leading English team prepared to take on European opposition, Wolverhampton Wanderers, had done so in the apparent belief that other countries could be shown the superiority of the English style. However, following England's landmark defeat by Hungary at Wembley in 1953, this style was already being questioned (Wagg, 1984:85–9), causing Busby to be seen by many as a prophet. Dunphy hints that United's team of the mid-1950s may have restored national pride on this score: 'They were exhilarating, carefree, unconventional. And British, not Hungarian ...' (1991: 207)

Busby as paterfamilias

Matt Busby was often called 'The Father of Football' and this soubriquet cropped up in his obituaries when he died in 1994 (see, for example, Keating, 1994). The football writer Frank Taylor called him a 'Father Confessor' (2003: 92). He was styled as a father for at least two reasons. His physical appearance – pipe, Crombie overcoat, trilby hat – was almost cinematic in its suggestion of an authoritative, middle-aged, middle-class Western male of the mid-twentieth century. And, secondly, his managerial regime at Old Trafford was consciously based on the notion of family. In this he had something of the same public impact as Dr Benjamin Spock in the United States following the publication of his *The Common Sense Book of Baby and Child Care* in 1946. 'Trust yourself,' Spock had famously told parents. 'You know more than you think you do' (Spock, 1946: 1; see also Bloom, 1972: 121–49). Busby similarly asked players to be confident enough to 'go out and express yourselves'. And his team policy during the 1950s, the pre-war old guard having moved on, was virtually child-centred. In 1953, he famously picked seven teenagers to play for the United first team at Huddersfield. In the English football world, according to ex-United player Bobby Charlton, Busby's policy provoked resentment: 'They're playing babies ... They can't possibly win anything' (Brown, 1998). Busby, like Spock, caught the 'do it for the kids' mood of the post-war West and, again like Spock, he exuded the same 'reassuring, apolitical quality' as US President Eisenhower (see Maier, 1998: 201–3).

Busby's sponsoring of a family atmosphere and an egalitarian, one-for-all camaraderie at Manchester United seems genuine enough. Irene Ramsden, for example, who did the laundry at Old Trafford in the 1950s, remembers being told by Busby that 'If anybody ever upsets you, you must come to me. Because this club is just a wheel, and everybody is a cog turning that wheel ... No one's bigger than the club' (Glanvill, 1994: 65). Likewise, the reasons given for the fashioning of this football family seem valid, as far as they go. They are part of a story frequently told about Busby, his social class origins and pre-war experiences as a player. But, to paraphrase Marx, Busby could not make history simply as he pleased; he made it in circumstances not chosen by himself. And, in relation to these circumstances, Busby, as Dunphy points out, was not a rebel (1991: 63).

Hugh McIlvanney has powerfully argued that the Old Trafford family originated in the pit tunnels and miners' welfare clubs of the Lanarkshire coalfield where Busby was born. Sectarianism, the argument runs, though it thrived in the smallest villages, could not be sustained down the mines. Ever-present dangers would make men recognise their dependence on each other and, thus, cancel all particularism.

Similarly, above ground, union culture did not allow for dissent from collective action. Busby, then a miner, took part in the General Strike of 1926 and is rumoured, according to his half brother Jimmy Mathie, to have dealt with blacklegs during that time (McIlvanney, 1997, Programme 1). According to at least one account (Glanvill, 1994: 230) he remained a lifelong socialist. Subsequently, as a professional footballer, he was miserable at Manchester City, where players' welfare was not considered, but much happier at Liverpool, where it was. Busby himself said he 'hoped to treat players the way I'd expect to be treated myself and this I set out to do at the start' (McIlvanney, 1997: Programme 1). But Busby's moral and managerial regime at United had a political and economic framework and was dictated to some extent by this framework.

After the Second World War, across a range of British institutions, there was a growing recognition that the authoritarian relationships of the pre-war era might no longer be viable. Critical thinking among the rank and file of British troops, and the subsequent, unanticipated landslide victory of the Labour Party in the General Election of 1945, strongly implied that the Conservatives represented to most voters an outmoded social order, based on deference, on which their verdict was 'never again' (Hennessy, 1993; Calder, 1971: 605–77). Homecoming professional footballers were unlikely now to be satisfied with managers in hats and overcoats who met them only in the dressing room half an hour before kick-off to offer a brief word of advice. Besides which, renewed tensions were inevitable in English football's skewed labour market. A campaign on the maximum wage restriction was likely and could expect political support (Wagg, 1984: 101–20). The demand from players for perks and under-the-counter payments was meanwhile likely to increase and, with full employment in Britain in the post-war years, there were always other jobs for disgruntled footballers to go to. Busby's United is reliably said to have refused to make concealed payments on top of the stipulated maximum wage. Busby, as manager, resolved instead to ensure that his men received as many goodwill, non-monetary benefits as he could procure for them. So United players of the late 1940s, aside from their £14 per week, received membership of a local golf club, nights in the best hotel in the northern resort of Blackpool, free passes for a local cinema, and more (Dunphy, 1991: 128, 131). Busby accompanied the players when they played golf or took the sea air, in the process bonding them to their manager and, thus, to their employing club.

United's refusal to sanction illegal payments no doubt had a moral basis, emanating partly from the devoutly Catholic Busby. But the club had not been well off financially. With the death of their president J.H. Davis, a wealthy local brewer, in 1927 the club had lost an important benefactor. During the 1930s, as I observed earlier, Manchester City, not United, had been the bigger spenders and in the 1940s money had been needed to restore Old Trafford following German bombing. Busby's zeal to engage in European competition is believed partly to have derived from his wish to raise money for some new floodlights. Busby's most sympathetic biographer makes clear that both he and the club profited from the maximum wage: in 1948 he signed a contract for a salary of £3,250 a year (four times his starting salary in 1945) and the club, over the period of his management thus far, had cleared its overdraft and was around £100,000 in the black (Glanvill, 1994: 65).

There was also a political economy to the world famous youth scheme, which gave rise to the ubiquitous media label 'Busby Babes'. It had actually been started as the Manchester United Junior Athletic Club by then manager Walter Crickmer in 1938. Crickmer had done this with the encouragement of the chairman James Gibson, who believed that, since the club could not pay high transfer fees, they had better develop their own players. Busby had simply renewed this policy after the war, directing his staff to scour the country for the best schoolboys. 'The main factor', Matt said later, 'was that they were brought up in the club from ... basically young boys, schoolboys. We liked school-leaving age. And they become part of the club itself, dedication to the club and trying to get into the team ...' (*Reputations*, BBC2, 17 May 1999). In this context, though, the Busby-United family regime was not as benign as it seemed. Within Old Trafford Busby and his assistant manager Jimmy Murphy resembled the Eisenhower–Nixon partnership in the US presidency in the 1950s. Busby dispensed the love and paternalism, while Murphy put the fear of God into the youngsters on the training field or at half time in a youth team game. 'He didn't encourage you at all. He told you. You could hear him shouting in the other dressing room, "get bloody stuck in" that was his favourite expression,' one United veteran told Dunphy (1991: 167). Busby was well aware, of course, of the commercial dimension to this youth development and proudly told the annual general meeting of Manchester United in 1953 that '£200,000 worth' of young football talent now resided in the club's reserve and youth teams (Dunphy, 1991: 178).

When the Football League's maximum wage ceiling was abolished in 1961 the Busby family ethos could be seen in a slightly different political light, its bonds beginning to weaken. John Giles, who left Manchester United for Leeds United in 1963, remembers: 'Matt used to say ... "You should all be on £100 a week", but after abolition Manchester United's first offer was £25 per week plus £5 appearance money' (McIlvanney, 1997: Programme 3). Here the notion that the 'club was bigger than anybody' could be seen more clearly as an instrument of negotiation between capital and labour.

By then, English football and Manchester United had entered an era, and a new set of political and commercial circumstances, increasingly incompatible with Busby's benevolent paternalism. By now, though, the mystique of his Manchester United was well established across the world in communities where football was discussed. The principal factor in this was the plane crash at Munich airport in 1958, in which eight players were killed. The next section discusses the importance of this event.

Who knows how good they might have been? The Munich air crash and popular culture

'Before Munich it was Manchester's club', said Bobby Charlton, one of the survivors. 'Afterwards, everyone felt they owned a little bit of it' (quoted in

Dunphy, 1991: 249). A similar tragedy, when players of the Italian club Torino died in an air crash in 1949, is largely forgotten (Green: 1979: 98–9). By contrast, the Munich air crash remains strong in football's collective folk memory, a fact reflected and supported by substantial media material. A website is dedicated to the incident (http://www.munich58.co.uk/index.asp), two books recount the disaster in great detail – who sat where, who sustained what injuries – (Roberts, 1988; Taylor, 2003), biographies were recently published of Roger Byrne and Tommy Taylor, two of the United players to die (Hughes, 2001; McCartney, 2000) and there was a commemorative TV documentary to mark the 40th anniversary of the crash (Brown, 1998).

Some of this no doubt supports a growing mini-heritage industry within Manchester United's huge global fan base. Partly too it keeps alive the memory of a singular football team, cut down in early maturity. 'I'm probably not alone in rating this second team, the "Busby Babes", as the greatest of his three' wrote football correspondent Donald Saunders on the day of Busby's death. 'No one can know how good the "Busby Babes" might have become' (*Daily Telegraph*, 21 January 1994: 3). Many, including survivors of the crash itself, have claimed that this team was, or would have been, the best British club side ever – perhaps the best club team of all time. Football reporter Frank Taylor, for example, who was injured in the accident, went on to write that the 'Babes' were the 'most talented group of young footballers ever seen at any one club' (Taylor, 2003: 15). Many superlatives have been lavished on Duncan Edwards, one of the eight players killed. Edwards, who was 21 when he died, had been playing for England since he was 18 and was variously canvassed as the best English player of his time and as one of the greats in the history of the world game. Tributes to him abound in British football literature. Murphy called him 'the Kohinoor diamond amongst our crown jewels' (Green, 1979: 81). Duncan's mother, still alive 40 years on, told television viewers in 1998 that Duncan 'was kicking a ball before he could walk' (Brown, 1998). He, it seemed, had been the greatest talent in the greatest team to emerge from Busby and Murphy's secular seminary. (There is also a website devoted to Edwards' memory: http://www.duncan-edwards.co.uk/index.asp.) The team had been adventurous to the last, drawing 3–3 in Belgrade, having the previous Saturday scored five goals away at Arsenal, conceding four.

But the loss of talented and exciting young footballers cannot, on its own, explain the mystique that strengthened, and remained, around Manchester United after the Munich tragedy.

In the Munich literature and discourse, the deceased footballers emerge as heroes, as opposed to celebrities. Some of their heroism could have been drawn, undiluted, from the dialogue of a British war film of the immediate post-war era. The last words of Liam Whelan, United's Irish inside forward, uttered as the plane took off for the last time, are said to have been: 'If the worst happens, I am ready for death. I hope we all are' (Roberts, 1988: 132). In hospital, Duncan Edwards, though fatally injured, reputedly asked of Murphy: 'What time is the kick-off against Wolves on Saturday, Jim? I mustn't miss that match' (Taylor, 2003: 59). Gerda Thiel, a nurse at the hospital, likewise testified that the stricken players had been true to Busby's family ethic: 'Their first thoughts were for their colleagues ... Their spirit of community was amazing' (Brown, 1998).

This latter remark, however, coupled with the extensive written, oral and photographic evidence of the team dismembered at Munich, hints at the most powerful meaning of the crash – across the generations, but most likely for those now aged 50 and over. This meaning is rooted in notions of class, community and sensuality.

Social theorists have always deliberated upon the need in human relationships for security and freedom, and on the difficulty of reconciling the two. Marx, Durkheim, Freud – and, most recently, Zygmunt Bauman (Bauman, 2003) – have all been centrally concerned with these themes, which were, in turn, vital debates about the English working class in the post-war period. Here security, in the form of family and community, had somehow to be squared with the equally desirable goals of social mobility, self-expression and sexual enlightenment.

One of the most eloquent, and pessimistic, voices in these debates was that of the liberal academic Richard Hoggart, whose semi-autobiographical *The Uses of Literacy* warned of the harmful effects on working-class life of the new, commercial Americanised popular culture. The young of the working class should beware a 'candy-floss world' typified by milk bars, full of nasty 'modernistic knick-knacks' and young men with 'an American slouch' (Hoggart, 1958: 203). His arguments found some favour with the left, who were concerned that the working-class appetite for political action and self-improvement would now be sapped. They resonated also with the right who feared that brash, American-bred violence and a degeneration of English national culture.

Busby, within certain limits, encouraged the pursuit of pleasure. The players should take out their wives and girlfriends, drink, dance and bet in moderation, and feel free to call into the Cromford Club, whose proprietor Paddy McGrath went on to establish a Playboy Club in Manchester. Busby's young players willingly sampled his qualified hedonism. They went to the local Plaza ballroom, whose assistant manager Jimmy Savile at weekends hoisted a (for then) shameless poster announcing 'Saturday Night is Crumpet Night' (Roberts, 1988: 45; Savile, 1976: 43). Young left winger David Pegg bought a Vauxhall Victor, the British car closest to the American aesthetic (Roberts, 1988: 85) and became aware of his glamorous good looks when Manchester barbers began offering 'David Pegg Cuts' (Brown, 1998). Wing half Eddie Colman liked the drainpipe trousers and winklepicker shoes of the Teddy Boy style. 'They were,' recalled Savile, 'the first non-musical megastars.' This might be overstating it, but these footballers had certainly begun to sense a little of their own celebrity and to enjoy freedom in the form of the urban, commercial popular culture of the time.

But, equally conspicuously, they inhabited a world of apparent security. Most of them lived in digs and were seen on newsreels being served their evening meal by their landlady, Mrs Watson. They loved animals and walked out with steady girlfriends. They had modest aspirations – captain Roger Byrne, for instance, was studying to be a physiotherapist. Above all they had strong roots in the northern industrial working class, whose best virtues Busby, it's often been claimed

(McIlvanney, 1997; Dunphy, 1991) was trying to preserve. Four of the eight to die – Mark Jones, Tommy Taylor, David Pegg and Geoffrey Bent – were the sons of miners. Eddie Colman was from Salford. According to the town's historian, there were 'few more extreme examples' of the 'poverty, misery and ill health of the common people of industrial Britain' than Salford (Greenall, 2000: 9). The Colmans lived on Archie Street, the model for ITV's *Coronation Street* (launched in 1960), and Eddie's father had scored three goals in the Salford Unemployed Cup Final of 1933. Being paid only the League's maximum wage, and at Busby's behest, most of the eight had either a trade (e.g. Mark Jones was a bricklayer) and/or had recently put in time learning one on some Manchester shop floor.

The camera captures them happy and uncynical, lads-becoming-men. They died at a point when they had moved out of the world of outside toilets and dole queues, were enjoying a few quid in their pockets, eyeing the 'crumpet' at the Plaza, thinking of proposing to their girlfriends and wondering what they might do when they'd finished playing. They died on the cusp between security and freedom, community and celebrity. They have a powerful aura, therefore. To some they will represent the last working-class football heroes, killed when they were still of, and among, the people. To others they will be Savile's first non-musical megastars, who perished at base camp on a peak later scaled by the Beatles. To others still, in the transient world that Busby helped to create, the young men of Munich had it all: the proximity of strong communities, family and worker solidarity balanced by the roar of the crowd and the uptown fun of the ballroom jive. Perhaps they, and Busby, met Hoggart halfway: a little bit of candy floss did you good.

Conclusion: love the team, hate the club?

As Dunphy observes, Matt Busby did not want to change the world, although he did seek to alter his own immediate part of it (Dunphy, 1991: 141). In the period between 1945 and 1960 he created a kind of qualified dressing-room socialism at Manchester United. Young players balanced individual self-expression and a sense of adventure with team work and mutual regard. Busby presided, with benevolent firmness. The context for this arrangement was the prevailing labour market conditions imposed by the Football League. These conditions were archaic and restrictive – although, arguably, more democratic than today's. The conditions were progessively removed after 1961 and during that time the link between football club and place has been loosened. Football has long since become a television show.

The heirs to Duncan Edwards and David Pegg included George Best and David Beckham. Best came to United in 1961 from a Protestant housing estate in Belfast. He became a celebrity in March of 1966 when, before a big international TV audience, he put in an exciting performance against Benfica in Lisbon. The following day the British press gave him the title 'El Beatle'. Best undoubtedly swelled the global appeal of Manchester United, but the fascination of Best could hardly be in starker contrast to that of the 'Babes' of the 1950s. They were a cheery collective of playful but, ultimately, domestic creatures. Best, in global popular culture, signifies individuality and hedonism. Endlessly replayed TV film shows him in acts of solitary virtuosity, opponents falling to the turf as he tricks them, teammates arriving to embrace him once the ball is safely in the net. His private life, organised for many years around sex and drink, is equally well documented (see, for example, Parkinson, 1975). A uniquely gifted footballer, as a man he was Hoggart's, and Busby's, worst fears made flesh.

Beckham is the consummation of the small compliments once paid to David Pegg by the hairdressers of Manchester. At the time of writing, hundreds of magazines across the world are carrying pictures of his new, closely woven hairstyle, along with the exhortation, punning on the title of the recent feature film that bears his name, to 'braid it like Beckham'. Born in East London, to a gas fitter and a hairdresser, Beckham, like Best, carries little in the way of class signifiers. In any event the identity-conferring, working-class communities which spawned Colman, Pegg, Taylor and the others have disappeared. As the writer Peter Conrad recently remarked, he is a 'floating signifier' (2003: 4) – a leading example in the global marketplace of Brohm's 'human sandwich board' (Brohm, 1989). Unlike Best, Beckham does not stand apart from Manchester United as a player, but he rivals them as a brand and contract talks with the club have been protracted while Beckham's people discuss his 'image rights'.

In contemporary Britain there is much talk of the over-commercialisation of football, and a good deal of this talk indicts Manchester United. Indeed, sections of the club's vast constituency of supporters argue that the club's global marketing operation and the personal enrichment of individual directors has betrayed Busby's legacy. They therefore shun the club and get behind the team. Club director Martin Edwards responded to this in the late 1990s: 'Never mind betraying a legend. We're actually capitalising on all the hard work that they did in the early years' (*Reputations*, BBC2, 17 May 1999).

The road past Old Trafford has been re-named 'Sir Matt Busby Way'. A statue of Busby stands outside the stadium – one of several recently put up outside English football grounds to commemorate managers and players of the 1950s and 1960s. (There's a similar statue of their former manager Sir Alf Ramsey outside Ipswich Town's ground, for example, and one of the 1960s captain, Billy Bremner, at Leeds United.) A clock on the wall rests permanently at the time at which the club's plane foundered at Munich airport. This event anchors Manchester United in the consciousness of the world's football public, and beyond. The contrast between Duncan Edwards and George Best or David Beckham as signifiers is as sharp as the contrast between socialist realism and pop art. In a sense this makes Munich more vital. Every corporate enterprise wants to display its humble origins. For Manchester United, the global brand of the Munich team is the metaphorical sepia photograph. It is the brilliant prototype, fashioned in a shed by quiet, determined men-with-a-dream, which perished on the runway, that sleeker subsequent models might prosper.

Football is like art in another respect. People talk of it as being 'commercialised' and, in doing so, invoke a mythical time when it was not. But football, like art, is produced in identifiable material circumstances. Manchester United, in Busby's era no less than the contemporary one, have operated according to market, profit-and-loss criteria. The Munich families, whose menfolk were so central to the club's mystique, have seen this. After the disaster, the 'bereaved families were given little and injured players were told to leave their club houses' (*Reputations*, BBC2, 17 May 1999) and 40 years later, in 1998, the club refused to underwrite a benefit for Munich survivors at old Trafford, meaning that the game's expenses would have to be paid from proceeds (see http://www.munich58.co.uk/features/wood1.asp). Ironically, it's the ever-present memories of Munich that persuade so many who follow Manchester United that they should embrace the team but reject the club (Brown and Walsh, 1999). So Busby's famous 'Babes' – a term he hated – still carry a powerful mystique. For football's political left, for its activists, for its traditionalists and sentimentalists, Munich represents the world we have lost. For the postmodern entrepreneurs of twenty-first century Manchester United, it is the motif on which they must continue to trade.

Acknowledgements

For help in the preparation of this chapter I'd like to thank Anne Philpott, Steven Fielding, Ron Greenall, Helen Pussard, Carlton Brick, Ian Bent, Garry Whannel, Rogan Taylor, Marsha Jones, Kathryn Dodd, and Kathleen Dickson and Ian O'Sullivan in the library of the British Film Institute.

Note

1 John Ford's The Man Who Shot Liberty Valance had three credited scriptwriters – James Warner, Bellah Goldbeck and Willis Goldbeck. Any one of these could have been responsible for the famous piece of dialogue I have used to preface this essay.

References

Barthes, R. (1973) *Mythologies*, St Albans: Paladin.
Bauman, Z. (2003) *Liquid Love*, Cambridge: Polity.
Bloom, L.Z. (1972) *Doctor Spock: Biography of a Conservative Radical*, Indianapolis, IN: Bobbs-Merrill.
Brohm, J.-M. (1989) *Sport: A Prison of Measured Time*, London: Pluto.
Brown, A. (Director) (1998) *The Busby Babes: End of a Dream*, ITV, 1 February.
Brown, A. and Walsh, A. (1999) *Not For Sale: Manchester United, Murdoch and the Defeat of BSkyB*, Edinburgh: Mainstream.
Busby, M. (1973) *Soccer at the Top: My Life In Football*, London: Sphere Books.
Calder, A. (1971) *The People's War*, London: Panther Books.
Conrad, P. (2003) 'Blend it like Beckham', *Observer*, Review Section, 25 May: 1, 4.
Coogan, T.P. (2000) *Wherever the Green is Worn: The Story of the Irish Diaspora*, London: Hutchinson.
Cosgrove, S. (1986) 'And the Bonnie Scotland will be there: football in Scottish culture', in A. Tomlinson and G. Whannel (eds) *Off the Ball*, London: Pluto Press.

Dunphy, E. (1991) *A Strange Kind of Glory: Sir Matt Busby and Manchester United*, London: Heinemann.

Glanvill, R. (1994) *Sir Matt Busby: A Tribute*, Manchester/London: Manchester United Football Club/Virgin Publishing.

Green, G. (1979) *There's Only One United: The Official Centenary History of Manchester United*, London: Coronet (first published 1978, London: Hodder and Stoughton).

Greenall, R.L. (2000) *The Making of Victorian Salford*, Lancaster: Carnegie Publishing.

Hennessy, P. (1993) *Never Again: Britain 1945–1951*, London: Vintage.

Herbert, M. (2001) *The Wearing of the Green: A Political History of the Irish in Manchester*, London: Irish in Britain Representation Group.

Hoggart, R. (1958) *The Uses of Literacy*, Harmondsworth: Pelican, in association with Chatto and Windus.

Holt, R. (1994) 'King across the border: Denis Law and Scottish football', in G. Jarvie and G. Walker (eds) *Scottish Sport in the Making of the Nation*, Leicester: Leicester University Press.

Hughes, B. (2001) *The Tommy Taylor Story*, Manchester: Empire Publications.

Keating, F. (1994) 'Busby, the father of football, dies aged 84', *The Guardian*, 21 January: 1.

Maier, T. (1998) *Dr Spock: An American Life*, Orlando, FL: Harcourt Brace.

McCartney, I. (2000) *Roger Byrne: Captain of the Busby Babes*, Manchester: Empire Publications.

McIlvanney, H. (1997) *Busby, Stein, Shankly: The Football Men*, BBC2:
  Programme 1 'Underground', 28 March
  Programme 2 'Football is the faith', 29 March
  Programme 3 'The price of glory', 30 March.

Meek, D. and Tyrrell, T. (2002) *Manchester United in Europe: The Complete Journey 1956–2002*, London: Hodder and Stoughton.

Messinger, G.S. (1985) *Manchester in the Victorian Age: The Half-Known City*, Manchester: Manchester University Press.

Parkinson, M. (1975) *Best: An Intimate Biography*, London: Arrow Books.

Roberts, J. (1988) *The Team That Wouldn't Die*, London: Methuen.

Savile, J. (1976) *Love is an Uphill Thing*, London: Coronet.

Scally, J. (1998) *Simply Red and Green: Manchester United and Ireland*, Edinburgh: Mainstream.

Spock, B. MD (1946) *The Common Sense Book of Baby and Child Care*, New York: Pocket Books (Simon and Schuster).

Sugden, J. and Bairner, A. (1993) *Sport, Sectarianism and Society in a Divided Ireland*, Leicester: Leicester University Press.

Taylor, F. (2003) *The Day a Team Died*, London: Souvenir Press (first published 1983).

Wagg, S. (1984) *The Football World: A Contemporary Social History*, Brighton: Harvester.

Wagg, S. (1995) *Giving the Game Away: Football, Politics and Culture on Five Continents*, London: Leicester University Press.

2 'We hate the Manchester Club like poison'

The Munich disaster and the socio-historical development of Manchester United as a loathed football club

Gavin Mellor

On 6 February 1958, an airliner carrying Manchester United players and officials home from a European Cup match with Red Star Belgrade crashed after refuelling in the German city of Munich. The incident resulted in the deaths of 23 passengers, including eight of the famous 'Busby Babes' Manchester United team.[1] The Munich Disaster, as the air crash came to be known, is today remembered as one of the most significant tragedies in the history of English football: an event that cost Manchester United and the England national team a generation of young, promising players.[2]

The importance of the Munich Disaster to Manchester United and their supporters is today represented by a permanent memorial at the club's Old Trafford stadium and by tributes to the crash victims that are usually organised by the club on significant anniversaries of the tragedy. In 2003 – the 45th anniversary of the Disaster – Manchester United's plans to remember the victims of Munich coincided with the club's 'derby' match against local rivals Manchester City. In the run up to the game, the *Times* newspaper reported that City supporters had been specifically asked by Manchester United to respect the tribute to the victims of the air crash.[3] The paper noted, however, that a traditional minute's silence had not been organised for the match because of fears that City fans would not properly observe such a mark of respect. The *Times* pointed out that many City fans routinely refer to their United counterparts as 'Munichs' and that difficult relations between City and United supporters tend to be exacerbated by any mention of the Munich Disaster. The paper did not speculate about what exactly Manchester City fans find so difficult or objectionable about the Munich Disaster, but had it spoken to Leeds United fans, Liverpool fans or any other groups of fans who regard themselves as direct rivals of United, it would have found that they too occasionally refer to United fans as Munichs, and regularly sing songs that celebrate the deaths of the United players in 1958.[4] Clearly, the Munich Disaster and its place in the history of Manchester United Football Club is central to how rival fans perceive United. The question is, why do United's rivals view the Munich Disaster in this way, and when did the events of 45 years ago become such a strong signifier of everything that non-United football supporters find so objectionable about the club?

The solution to these questions comes from the common interpretation of the legacy of the Munich Disaster for Manchester United, rather than the event itself. In the history of Manchester United, the Munich Disaster is frequently identified as a fundamental turning point in the emergence of the club as a 'super' football club, capable of drawing supporters from all over the world. From the initial sympathetic reporting that the disaster received, to the 'mythical' status that developed around the players killed in the tragedy, it is argued that the Munich Disaster ensured that United entered the late 1960s with a reputation quite unlike any other club. This idea is summed up by Colin Shindler, Manchester City supporter and author of *Manchester United Ruined My Life*, when he states that 'Munich is where it all started' in the development of Manchester United. Shindler claims: 'Manchester United used to be supported by people who lived in Manchester. But after Munich, United were supported by people who couldn't find Manchester on a map'.[5] Stephen F. Kelly also expresses similar sentiments to this in his history of Manchester United when he writes:

> If any good did come out of Munich it was reflected in a changing view of the club, turning the name of Manchester United into an international institution. Before, they were simply another football club. After Munich, they were, rightly or wrongly, the nation's club.[6]

The key to Shindler's and other non-United supporters' interpretation of the importance of the Munich Disaster stems from a belief that Manchester United somehow exploited the events of February 1958 to create a 'super-club' status for themselves. When supporters of United's rival clubs comment on this issue, there are frequent statements that United have wallowed in the misery of Munich, and have utilised the Munich Disaster as part of the overall 'branding' of the club. In a recent exchange of views on the Munich Disaster on a Manchester City supporters' website, one supporter summed up this point of view by asking a United supporter, 'When are your club going to stop squeezing every last dollar out of that air crash?', whilst another City fan commented, 'I don't like the way they [Manchester United] ruthlessly prolonged and marketed the wave of sympathy that followed the Munich thing. You have to ask yourself honestly – did Man U benefit or suffer as a result of that air disaster?'[7] It is views such as these that make some Manchester City, Liverpool, Leeds and other supporters feel justified in celebrating the Munich Disaster through songs and other practices.

The aim of this chapter is to analyse the early history of the Munich Disaster and to investigate the point at which criticisms about United's response to the tragedy became visible in the media and audible amongst supporters. Evidence is taken from oral history interviews with Manchester United, Manchester City and other supporters, and from the press in the northwest of England. As will be shown, the meaning of the Munich Disaster for Manchester United and other supporters has been contested from almost the day it happened. To explain this, a brief and tentative account will be given of the growth of 'one-club parochialism' amongst English football supporters in the 1950s and 1960s, and how this may have helped to fuel a hatred of Manchester United and a lack of sympathy that many football clubs and football supporters had for the club in the months and years after Munich.

A disaster for Manchester?

To begin an investigation into public responses to the Munich Disaster in 1958, it is simplest to analyse how people reacted to the tragedy in the city that it affected most. As one would expect, the popular memory of the direct aftermath of the Munich Disaster in Manchester is of people, regardless of interest in football or team affiliation, being deeply shocked by the tragedy and supportive of the Old Trafford club. In interviews with Manchester City supporters from the late 1950s, very precise memories of where they were when they heard about the plane crash and clear accounts of their distress at hearing the news frequently emerged. The following account from a Manchester City supporter is typical:

> I remember quite a lot about it [the Munich Disaster] because that particular night I'd been out playing table tennis in a table tennis competition on the other side of Manchester. And I'd come into Manchester to get the bus home and they were selling newspapers in the city centre. And I knew that something most unusual had happened. And of course the word was spreading around by then. And of course I remember the feeling of horror that this had happened. I couldn't get home quick enough to put the television on, because of course I had a television then. The sadness to me was for everyone but particularly for Frank Swift who was a newspaper reporter for the *News of the World*. And he'd been one of my idols as a boy because he was the old goalkeeper [for Manchester City].[8]

Another Manchester City supporter recalled similar feelings:

> I was at work on a Thursday afternoon and ... about half past three something came in through the newspaper. And it said 20 dead or something like that. And I went down into Manchester then. And everybody was out with radios and it was dreadful, I just couldn't believe it.[9]

These Manchester City supporters and others like them stated, implicitly or explicitly, that their feelings of shock in the aftermath of Munich were informed by a football culture in Manchester that was based on mutual respect and relatively fluid boundaries between the two main Manchester clubs. Indeed, it has been noted elsewhere that Manchester United and Manchester City supporters frequently attended each other's matches in the period after 1945, especially when the two clubs were sharing the Maine Road stadium as a result of the wartime bombing of Old Trafford.[10] This, coupled with the feelings of close social proximity that many supporters claimed existed between supporters and players in Manchester in the 1950s, led many Manchester City fans to claim a stake in the tragedy and a feeling that it had happened to 'them', too. One City fan remembered:

> I knew quite a few of them [the victims of the crash] even though they were United. Roger Byrne, who was the captain of this particular team, lived quite locally and we all knew him. I used to watch City with his father. His father was a keen City fan, and he [Roger Byrne] used to go to the local high school ... As far as we were concerned, they were Manchester people, and the sadness was citywide.[11]

The apparent sadness of Manchester City supporters in the wake of the Munich Disaster expressed itself in a number of ways. More than one supporter recalled standing on Princess Parkway in Manchester watching the dead being taken from Manchester Airport to Old Trafford on their return from Germany.[12] Others felt compelled to attend United's matches in the weeks after the tragedy in an effort to pay their respects. One City supporter recalled:

> So within about two or three weeks, I think it was within 19 days or three weeks, I can't remember now, United should have been playing Sheffield Wednesday at Old Trafford. I think it's the most emotional game I can ever remember. And in all honesty Sheffield Wednesday didn't stand a chance. The total wave of emotion went totally against them. There was no way that Sheffield Wednesday were going to win that game. They [United] won 3–0.[13]

The supportive actions of these City fans did not go unnoticed by United supporters. Many of them recalled the support that City fans had shown for United in the wake of the air crash, and could not remember any City fans showing disrespect for the memory of the dead.[14] Others recalled specifically how busy matches at Old Trafford were in the aftermath of the disaster and that many of the increased numbers were City fans:

> In about 40 years I only missed about three games at Old Trafford and one of them was when they [United] played West Brom in a replay in the Cup [in 1958]. We'd been to West Brom on the Saturday. I was working in Broughton at the time and I was meeting somebody in Manchester, and we said we'll get the train from Central [railway station]. Well, we couldn't even get near Central Station. And we still hadn't got on to the station, we were milling around the Free Trade Hall trying to get in, when the police came round with a loudspeaker saying the gates to the game had been closed. Now that was because a lot of City fans had gone up for the game.[15]

These memories of Manchester United and Manchester City supporters sharing in the sadness of the Munich Disaster in February 1958 are certainly held strongly by a large number of Mancunian football supporters from that period. However, there are others who remember the days and weeks after Munich differently. A small number of Manchester City fans remembered a sometimes hidden and occasionally explicit pleasure being expressed amongst fellow City fans that their greatest rivals had lost a number of their best players in the crash. One City fan stated:

> I was very depressed [by the Munich Disaster] ... but some were, like, 'good'. Not good that they'd died, but good that they'd, you know. And then they allowed them [United] to play players who'd played in the Cup matches for other teams, and some were like, 'that's wrong, typical' and all that.[16]

Another City supporter recalled his feelings at the time of the crash with some regret. When asked what the Munich Disaster had been like for City fans, the respondent stated:

> I'm sorry you asked me that. What do you want me to say? Honest? ... I know a lot who went out and got drunk. I did. I'm not proud of the fact. I am *not* proud of the fact. But, I don't know. It had been thrust down our throats for so long and, erm, isn't it terrible? As soon as you asked me that I thought, 'Oh dear.' All that shows is the strength of the rivalry. I know United supporters who said, 'I bet you went out and got drunk,' and I said 'Yeah and I had an extra one on you,' you know. But I know they felt the same way [about Manchester City]. I know many United supporters, including one leading light down there ... who said he wouldn't be happy until they built council flats on Maine Road. So it's tit for tat. But I'm not proud what I did. It was a night out I was going on and we all had an extra one and said 'Cheers, bad luck, and who do we play next week?' ... The football was great, looking back now. They [United] played some great football, and they had some brilliant youngsters come through. And it was a tragedy that any youngster had to die like that. But just taking it as a City fan I thought anything that can harm United was good. But I'm not proud of it ... I was only 23 or 24 at the time and I was still impressionable.[17]

Both of these recollections contain suggestions that the Manchester United team of the late 1950s, the so-called 'Busby Babes', were feted to such a degree by the football world that pleasure amongst City supporters in United's misfortune in Munich was understandable. The claim that it was 'typical' that United were allowed to break Football Association (FA) rules and play 'Cup-tied' players in the aftermath of Munich,[18] and the assertion that Manchester City fans had had the successes of the pre-Munich United team 'thrust down [their] throats', underlines the hostility that existed between City and United supporters before the Munich Disaster occurred. Clearly, the mutual respect and shared interest that existed between City and United supporters in the immediate post-war years was undermined to some degree during this period.

Hostility toward Manchester United in the wake of the Munich Disaster also began to appear in the Manchester local press in the weeks after the tragedy.

Arguments about the correct level of respect that should be accorded to the Munich team abound. The first of these, reported in the *Manchester Evening Chronicle*, centred on commercial and retail organisations in Manchester that had refused to fly flags at half-mast in recognition of the Munich Disaster and had, therefore, shown 'a disregard for public feeling'.[19] This claim was rebuked in a number of letters to the *Evening Chronicle* from business people in Manchester, including one that stated:

> Business people whom [your newspaper] accuses of showing a lack of respect by not lowering their flags to half-mast are not all imbued with the same mass hysteria that causes 'the sheep', for the want of something better to do, to flock to Old Trafford terraces on Saturdays. Everybody deeply regrets the sad deaths of the United players and the sports writers. But every day there are many Manchester citizens who also meet tragic ends by other means.[20]

Football supporters in letters to the Manchester press also expressed concerns about local 'overindulgence' in the disaster. One Rochdale fan wrote to the *Evening Chronicle* with the following thoughts:

> I and thousands of other people who read your paper are fed up with all the bunkum that is written about Manchester United. We will grant that they have been a good team, but why not face facts ... We know you have to rely on Manchester readers for the bulk of your circulation, but people of other towns are fed up with biased reports and comments.[21]

This led the *Chronicle*'s sports editor, Arthur Walmsely, to state that:

> Manchester, especially its soccer public and its press, is under fire from without and WITHIN. We are accused of prolonging the Manchester United agony beyond the bounds of genuine sorrow and sympathy. We are accused of an unhealthy, mass hysterical support of a football club which violates the borders of sport and trespasses on the forbidden ground of maudlin spirit. Bluntly, we are accused of making a meal of that Munich Disaster by carrying it on through the present United side.[22]

He defended these criticisms by stating that they were, 'inspired by sour grapes and even an inverted form of envy of the tremendous loyalty displayed by the Manchester public to the United club'.

The debate about what constituted an appropriate response to the Munich Disaster continued in the Manchester press for much of the remainder of the 1958 football season. Arthur Robertson, a vicar from County Durham, was quoted in the *Evening Chronicle* in an article entitled 'Was mourning for United overdone?' as asking, 'Have we exalted the world of sport above its station in human experience?'[23] A letter to the same newspaper rejected this and other criticisms of United supporters' handling of the disaster under the headline 'Sour grapes flavour criticism of United'. With specific reference to newspaper reporting that had followed Manchester United's victory over West Bromich Albion in the FA Cup, the letter stated:

'Bubbling cauldron', 'seething crucible' – these are among the highly coloured descriptions of Old Trafford I have seen since the defeat of West Bromwich Albion in the sixth round replay [of the FA Cup]. And the Manchester United supporter – brother, is he popular? 'Loutish legions on the terraces', 'mass hysteria', 'the most partisan crowd anywhere', 'shrieking women midst milling hordes of angry shut-out fanatics', 'howling and inhibited savages'. Well, well, well!!! Apparently you have all missed your cue in Manchester. Properly fluffed your lines you have. It seems the way the drama SHOULD have unfolded after Munich was one single great demonstration of loyalty, one brave fight by the remoulded team and then a series of shattering defeats. If this had happened, the same critics who see physical peril in even venturing near Old Trafford would have been engulfing us in a treacle of their boundless sympathy.[24]

Clearly, some United fans felt that the continued success of their club in the aftermath of Munich was the real reason why sections of the media and others were questioning the appropriateness of United supporters' feelings of mourning.

The reaction to the Munich Disaster outside Manchester

The first argument about the Munich Disaster that emerged outside Manchester came within two weeks of the tragedy occurring. On 19 February 1958, the *Manchester Evening Chronicle* reported that Burnley Chairman Bob Lord had criticised other Football League clubs for loaning players to Manchester United after the air crash. He reportedly claimed that United had 'gone into the European Cup with their eyes open' and had gained in cash, glamour and the attraction of youngsters to the club as a result.[25] This argument continued into March when Burnley and Manchester United met in a League match that was dubbed by the press 'The Battle of Burnley' after it had descended into a 22-man brawl.[26] On this occasion, Bob Lord proclaimed that United had played like 'Teddy Boys', and stated his intention to report United to the Football League following an incident in which a Manchester United official allegedly stormed into the Burnley dressing room and had to be restrained.[27] These incidents and the reported comments of Lord led to a deluge of letters to the Manchester press, most of which proclaimed that Lord was simply jealous of United's recent success.

The argument between Manchester United and Burnley football clubs in the aftermath of the Munich Disaster showed a marked lack of solidarity between two relatively close geographical rivals. By the end of the 1957–8 football season, this row had been superseded by comments that were appearing in the Manchester and Bolton press about Bolton Wanderers' forthcoming FA Cup Final appearance against a patched-up post-Munich Manchester United team. In the national press, Manchester United were frequently commended for their achievement in reaching the Final with a team of young and inexperienced players, and it was often commented that the Final would be an overwhelmingly emotional occasion as the victims of the air crash were remembered. The impression given, in fact, was that the entire country, and certainly the majority of Lancashire, would be supporting United in the Final in a celebration of their distinctive 'phoenix from the ashes' story.

In Bolton, however, it appears that a set of rather different sentiments were in evidence in the weeks leading up to the Final. For a period of around three weeks, the *Bolton Evening News* never tired of printing letters that were critical of the national press coverage of the Manchester United team, and others that doubted just how 'sensational' United's feat of reaching the Final had been. One letter mocked the national press for using terms such as 'magnificent, scintillating and fantastic' to describe United's Cup run,[28] while another stated that Bolton had as many problems as United in getting to the Cup Final because of the gulf in resources between the two clubs:

> Manchester United have worked wonders in reaching the Cup Final ... but I would like to remind [readers] that they never lost the bulk of their supporters. Bolton Wanderers have reached Wembley after about 15,000 regular supporters turned their back on them – an even more remarkable feat. The Wanderers will be the cheapest team ever to play at Wembley in the Final, and I think they will prove themselves one of the best.[29]

Another letter showed the level of contempt shown for Manchester United by some Bolton fans when it stated:

> On Cup Final day I hope that Bolton will beat Manchester United to a frazzle ... [I] shall be hoping for a blow that will shatter the prayers of the distinctly unhealthy and morbid sensation mongers whose sentimental partisanship is no more than a wallowing in momentary misery. I am afraid they will enjoy themselves anyway. If Manchester United win, these people will be drenched in tears of joy, relief and pride. If Bolton Wanderers win, they will break into brokenhearted sobbing.[30]

Another letter, written by 'a supporter of Bolton Wanderers and Manchester United', exemplified the lack of empathy for United in Bolton further by stating:

> I am really disgusted with the day-by-day sentiments expressed about Manchester United by the national press. If Bolton do win the papers will say they beat a poor team, but if they lose, the Munich to Wembley team will be toasted everywhere. All I can say is: 'Carry on Bolton and get 'em beat. Take the Cup back to Bolton.'[31]

In the days immediately preceding the Final, sentiments of this kind even took on a political dimension as Ald. J. Vickers, Leader of the Labour Party on Bolton Council, stepped into the controversy. The *Bolton Evening News* reported that Vickers had warned that the Cup Final was 'in danger of becoming an emotional spectacle as a result of the disproportionate amount of publicity given by the press to Manchester United'. To clarify his comments, Vickers stated that:

> I thought the public were getting tired of all the tremendous amount of publicity concerning Manchester United ... and I hoped on Saturday to see not an emotional spectacle but rather 22 fit players giving a good game of football – with the best team winning.[32]

At no time in the run-up to the Final did the *Bolton Evening News* itself make comments which supported this line. However, it was clear that any compassion that was felt for Manchester United in Bolton in 1958 was complicated by the sporting rivalry that existed between the two clubs.

The criticism and concerns that were expressed in Bolton prior to the 1958 FA Cup Final did register to some degree in Manchester. In the Manchester press, concerns about the build-up to the Final being entirely focused on the Munich Disaster were expressed regularly, culminating in a debate about the possible appearance of Manchester United manager Matt Busby at the event. Busby had been seriously injured during the Munich Disaster and had not appeared at any Manchester United match since the crash. However, in the weeks before the FA Cup Final, rumours abounded that the manager could be well enough to lead his team out for the Wembley Final. The Manchester press's attitude towards this news was surprisingly hostile. In the context of months of concern that the media and Manchester United had exploited the Munich Disaster, sections of the local press stated that Busby's appearance at the Final could be interpreted badly in Bolton and elsewhere. As Arthur Walmsley, Sports Editor for the *Manchester Evening Chronicle*, wrote: 'Matt's appearance on the field at Wembley could intensify that wave of sympathy beyond reasonable bounds and make the Cup Final a cruel farce for Bolton – both in victory and defeat.'[33]

After weeks of concern and argument in Bolton and Manchester over the 1958 FA Cup Final, Bolton Wanderers eventually won the game 2–0. However, the day itself was not without controversy, as Nat Lofthouse, Bolton's centre forward, was alleged to have barged United keeper Harry Gregg when scoring Bolton's second goal. This incident and the acrimonious build-up to the Final were not quickly forgiven or forgotten in Manchester. One oral history interviewee recalled that 'trouble' had occurred in Manchester as a result of United's loss in 1958, which resulted in anger being turned on the Bolton players themselves: 'I remember that the Bolton coach was stoned as it came from Piccadilly Manchester through the Kearsley area, you know, through Salford and that, by United fans for beating them and all that had happened.'[34]

Furthermore, in recent articles written on the legacy of the Munich Disaster for Manchester United supporters, United fans of the 1950s have recalled the lack of sympathy that Bolton supporters showed for their near neighbours in the run-up to the FA Cup Final. One supporter, writing for a Manchester United fans' website, recently explained why the events of 1958 meant that Bolton Wanderers, and not Manchester City, should be considered the natural enemies of Manchester United:

> Then came Munich, when I was 10 years old. The whole of Manchester and Salford mourned and yes, even the Scousers. My Dad had some friends in Liverpool and I can remember going to their house not long after Duncan Edwards died and seeing Dad's friend (a regular at Anfield) with tears running down his cheeks as he talked of the loss of Big Dunc – it's one of the most vivid memories of my childhood ... Of course, going to school in Salford I didn't come across many young City fans, but I did come across a few Bolton fans, and to my amazement and shock they actually made jokes about Munich. The only time I met anything but sadness and sympathy in the days immediately following Munich was from a couple of young Bolton fans in my own school playground. A feeling I had never felt before began to foster and to simmer. Then, on a wave of emotion we made it to the Cup Final – to win what should have been 'our' Cup, dedicated to the lads who died. But we didn't win it, not because we weren't good enough, but because Nat Lofthouse, of Bolton Wanderers, cheated. From that day to this, I have hated Bolton (and Nat Lofthouse in particular) with a passion unreserved for any other team, to the point where, when Lofthouse walked out on the pitch on Feb 6th [the anniversary of the Munich Disaster] a couple of seasons ago, I was almost physically sick.[35]

From evidence presented earlier in this chapter, it is clear that Bolton Wanderers supporters were not the only football fans who were critical of Manchester United in the aftermath of Munich, but the passage above underlines the special tension that emerged between Manchester United and Bolton Wanderers as a result of the events of 1958.

The legacy of Munich: the 1960s

From the previous two sections, it is clear that many non-Manchester United supporters from the late 1950s regard the Munich Disaster as an event that was accorded too much attention at that time. Whether this resulted from the actions of the Club or the appetite of the media for a particularly emotional story, the results were the same for many fans. Of course, the real area of contention that emerged between United and non-United supporters since the Munich Disaster has been the question of whether Manchester United exploited the events of 1958, and used the air crash as a basis for launching the club's national and international image and appeal. Clearly, not all fans of even United's closest rivals believe this to be the case, but many do see a link between the Munich

Disaster and United's 'super-club' status.[36] One Manchester City supporter summarised his feelings on the matter in the following way:

> After Munich, and I'm trying to be careful here. I'm not saying that United capitalised because I don't think that the intention was there to do so. But there was a mystique at Old Trafford that no other club had. We certainly didn't in England. They may have had one in Italy 'cause Torino lost a lot of their players in the late 1940s. But United had this mystique that no other club could match, and United essentially built on this. Don't get me wrong, I don't think there was any sinister intention, I think it just happened. But subsequently, United never really looked back in terms of finance. They were able to have the money to bring Denis Law back from Italy, which City probably couldn't have done during that time, and probably very few other clubs could have done ... I think subsequent to that, there was always this thing about United. They'd had this Munich Disaster and people tried to be identified, however tenuously, with the fact that they were United orientated, even if they weren't United fans. And I think it was built on that ... I think their gates always maintained a very high level after that, because I think people tried to associate themselves, even in a tenuous way, with United. And of course it helped that within five years they had a great side.[37]

Evidence of the link between the Munich Disaster and United's emergence as a super-club is in fact more complicated than is traditionally acknowledged. Whilst United's attendances did increase in the direct aftermath of the air crash (from a home average League crowd of 45,583 in 1957–8 to an average of 53,258 in 1958–9), the club's average attendances declined for much of the early 1960s in line with overall League trends. In fact, United's average attendance did not break 50,000 again until 1966–7 – the season after they had reached the semi-final of the European Cup for the first time since 1957. Tellingly, it is at this point that regular comments began to appear in the press about Manchester United's growing national and international support, and how this differentiated the club from all others. It is also at this point that sharply critical statements about United began to appear in the press. In 1966, Manchester United drew Derby County in the third round of the FA Cup. In anticipation of the match, the *Manchester Evening News* reported the Derby County chairman as stating that the people of Derbyshire 'hate the Manchester club like poison'.[38] As United and Derby County had no particular history of extreme rivalry, the *Evening News* expressed surprise at the chairman's comments and retorted, 'Could it be that they hate Manchester United because the club has been successful in the post-war years?'[39]

In the late 1960s and early 1970s, references to the Munich Disaster in critical press articles about Manchester United became commonplace, particularly after United won the European Cup in 1968, thereby completing the club's and manager Matt Busby's journey through adversity. United supporters were referred to as 'ignorant big mouths ... [who] never watched a match until the hysteria of Munich' in the *Manchester Evening News* in 1971, and from that time onwards Manchester United and their fans have been regularly chided in the press and elsewhere for exploiting the memory of Munich to create a marketable mystique on which the club's current status is based. It appears that Manchester United gained at least as many enemies as friends as a result of the Munich Disaster, and that opinions about the club will continue to crystallise around the events of 1958 for years to come.

Conclusion: 'one-club parochialism' and the hatred of Manchester United

Having outlined the different reactions to the Munich Disaster that emerged in the days, months and years after 1958, it is important to place the incident in some form of historical context that enables us to understand why events unfolded as they did. Whilst this chapter is not the place to present a full socio-economic analysis of changes in football supporter behaviour in England in the late 1950s and 1960s,[40] it is worth mentioning how football fans were relating to one another at this time, and how this may have influenced people's understanding of the Munich Disaster.

As mentioned earlier, in the late 1940s and early 1950s it was common in Manchester for supporters of the two main clubs to attend each other's matches. Indeed, this practice of people attending the matches of more than one club was not unique to Manchester and extended to a culture of support for English football that was based to some degree on respect and keen partisanship, rather than fanatical parochialism.[41] In geographical areas with high concentrations of professional football clubs, such as the northwest of England, this culture resulted for some fans in loose local and regional affiliations with small numbers of football clubs, rather than hardened support for one club. Because of this, it was more exceptional during this period to find hatred, parochialism and intense rivalry amongst football supporters than it is today.

During the 1950s, and particularly the 1960s, this mutual respect and cross-club support declined rapidly in English football and was replaced by a culture of passionate one-club loyalty and more intense rivalries between supporters of competing teams. This culture was particularly evident amongst younger supporters who distanced themselves from older football traditions by not attending the matches of more than one club, and by developing a keen hatred of perceived rivals. In areas such as the northwest of England, the loose regional affiliations that had existed between football supporters began to dissipate, and were replaced by something much more akin to English football supporter culture in the late twentieth and early twenty-first centuries.

The reasons for a generational shift in English football supporter culture during the 1950s and 1960s are currently underresearched and undertheorised. In an identifiable geographical area like Lancashire in the northwest of England, it is possible that the cross-club, regional football culture was undermined by the decline of the region as a strongly identifiable landscape. Many of the economic, cultural and political signifiers of Lancashire were gradually removed from the lived experience of young people in the post-war period, as the county's dialect, diet, core industries and historical borders were all undergoing gradual change.[42] On a national scale, reasons for the hardening of football supporter rivalries are more difficult to identify. To begin the process of investigating this phenomenon, it may be useful to analyse changes within British working-class culture during the period and question whether socio-economic shifts in working-class life in the late 1950s including increasing affluence, the continuing decline of organised religion, and new educational philosophies based on free expression rather than disciplined instruction caused a decline in 'respectable working-class values' such as collectivism, good manners, and mutual respect, and resulted in a certain degree of cynicism, individualism and the deriding of other people's interests.[43] These are starting points for discussion and certainly not answers in themselves. If proved useful, however, they may help explain the apparent generational divide in attitudes towards cross-club football support in the 1950s and 1960s, and why certain teams became hated and resented by football supporters rather than respected.

Whatever the reasons for the emergence of sharper rivalries between football supporters in England in the 1950s and 1960s, it is inarguable that this process did occur, and that it coincided with the Munich Disaster and the emergence of Manchester United as a 'super-club'. At exactly the moment when Manchester United were emerging as a distinctive and highly successful football club with 'mythical' properties brought about by the deaths of eight of their young star players, rivalries between English football supporters were hardening as fans increasingly defined themselves by who they hated as much as who they liked. In this context, the constant national visibility of Manchester United in the media, coupled with the sense that the club had exploited the Munich Disaster to accrue an unfair advantage over other clubs, ensured that Manchester United became many non-United football supporters' hate team. In the new supporter culture of loving one's club and hating all others, Manchester United emerged as *the national* football adversary. They were different and 'bigger' than all others, but not, according to many fans, because they deserved to be: it was all because of Munich.

Notes

1 The Manchester United players killed in the Munich air crash were Roger Byrne (aged 28), Eddie Coleman (21), Duncan Edwards (21), Mark Jones (24), David Pegg (22), Tommy Taylor (26), Liam Whelan (22) and Geoffrey Bent (25).

2 Manchester United fans today tend to refer to the Munich Disaster as the 'Munich Air Crash' or simply 'Munich'.

3 *The Times*, 7 February 2003.

4 It is worth noting that Manchester City supporters did sing songs celebrating the Munich Disaster at the derby match in February 2003.

5 *Manchester United Ruined My Life*, BBC2 documentary, 1998.

6 Kelly, S.F. (2000) *Red Voices*, London: Headline Book Publishing: 96–7.

7 'Blue View' Manchester City supporters' website (accessed on 27 May 2003): available online at http://boards.rivals.net/default.asp?sid=914&p=16&style=2&forumId=4501&action=1&replytoid=2133796061.

8 Interview with Keith, 18 November 1997. Oral history interviews quoted in this chapter were conducted in 1997 as part of my PhD research into the history of football supporters in the northwest of England. For a full discussion of these interviews, see Mellor, G. (2002) 'Professional football and its supporters in Lancashire, circa 1946–1985', PhD thesis, University of Central Lancashire.

9 Interview with Anthony, 13 November 1997.

10 See Mellor, G. (1999) 'The social and geographical make up of football crowds in the northwest of England, 1946–62', *The Sports Historian*, 19, 2, pp. 25–42.

11 Interview with Keith, 18 November 1997.

12 For instance, interview with George G., 4 November 1997.

13 Interview with Anthony, 13 November 1997.

14 For instance, interview with Eric, 18 November 1997.

15 Interview with George D., 14 November 1997.

16 Interview with George G., 4 November 1997.

17 Interview with John, 14 November 1997.

18 For teams playing in the English FA Cup, it is ruled that a team cannot use players for FA Cup matches who have played for other teams in earlier rounds of the competition in the same year. Any player who moves clubs during the FA Cup is therefore identified as being 'Cup-tied'. This rule was suspended by the FA for Manchester United in 1958, as they had lost so many players in the Munich Disaster.

19 *Manchester Evening Chronicle* (hereafter MEC), 11 February 1958.

20 MEC, 26 February 1958.

21 MEC, 5 March 1958.

22 Ibid.

23 Ibid.

24 MEC, 15 March 1958.

25 MEC, 19 February 1958.

26 MEC, 17 March 1958.

27 MEC, 19 March 1958.

28 *Bolton Evening News* (hereafter BEN), 5 April 1958.

29 BEN, 8 April 1958. The loss of support for Bolton Wanderers referred to in this quote was part of a national trend of declining English football attendances in the mid-to-late 1950s.

30 BEN, 18 April 1958.

31 BEN, 25 April 1958.

32 BEN, 30 April 1958.

33 MEC, 15 April 1958.

34 Interview with George G., 4 November 1997.

35 'Who do you hate the most?', 24 February 2001: available online at http://www.red11.org/mufc/devilsadvocate/articles/whodoyouhatemost.htm.

36 For a full discussion of Manchester United's development into a super-club, see Mellor, G. (2000) 'The genesis of Manchester United as a national and international super-club, 1958–68', *Soccer and Society*, 1, 2, pp. 151–66.

37 Interview with Anthony, 13 November 1997.

38 *Manchester Evening News*, 6 January 1966.

39 Ibid.

40 Few historical studies have been conducted into the 'everyday' practices and habits of English football supporters. The following provide useful starting points: Fishwick, N. (1989) *English Football and Society 1910–50*, Manchester: Manchester University Press; Hill, J. (1996) 'Rite of spring: cup finals and community in the north of England',

in Williams, J. and Hill, J. (eds) *Sport and Identity in the North of England*, Keele: Keele University Press; Holt, R. (1989) *Sport and the British: A Modern History*, Oxford: Blackwell Publishing; Mason, T. (1980) *Association Football and English Society 1863–1915*, Brighton: Harvester Press; Russell, D. (1997) *Football and the English: A Social History of Association Football in England, 1863–1995*, Preston: Carnegie Publishing; Taylor, R. (1992) *Football and its Fans: Supporters and their Relations with the Game*, Leicester: Leicester University Press; Walvin, J. (1994) *The People's Game* (2nd edition), Edinburgh: Mainstream.

41 Mellor, G., 'The social and geographical make up of football crowds in the northwest of England', pp. 34–9.

42 Mellor, G., *Professional Football and its Supporters in Lancashire*, pp. 268–72.

43 A large number of studies of changes in post-war British working-class life have been conducted. For a useful summary see Devine, F. (1992) *Affluent Workers Revisited: Privatism and the Working Class*, Edinburgh: Edinburgh University Press.

3 From the Busby Babes to the Theatre of Dreams

Image, reputation and the rise of Manchester United

Kirsten Rosaaen and John Amis

With an annual turnover in excess of £147 million, a stadium that has more than doubled in capacity over the last 10 years to 67,700, and a stock market listing that topped £1 billion in the year 2000, Manchester United (MU) has confirmed its reputation as the richest football club, and arguably most valuable sporting franchise, in the world (see Maidment, 2002; CNN, 2001; www.manutd.com, accessed 17 March 2003). The club's revenue is generated from four main areas: ticket receipts, media rights, commercial revenue including sponsorship, and branded merchandise. For the 2002 fiscal year MU reported a gross profit of £33.9 million with ticket receipts accounting for £56.3 million of the club's turnover, media rights £51.9 million, commercial revenue £26.5 million, and income from branded merchandise £11.4 million (see Maidment, 2002; www.manutd.com, accessed 17 March 2003).

Of course, much of MU's income is directly attributable to on-field performances. Since its Football Association (FA) Cup win in 1990, the first trophy won under manager Alex Ferguson, MU has won seven Premier League trophies, three FA Cups, one European Cup Winners Cup, and the European Champions League in 1999. However, it is not possible to place the financial success of MU solely on footballing performances. Liverpool Football Club, for example, enjoyed even greater levels of footballing success during the 1970s and 1980s, and yet MU even then retained their mantle as the best-supported club in the country (Szymanski, 1998). Consequently, it is necessary to look to other avenues to try to explain why MU has become such a dominant brand, both in Britain and abroad. It is our contention that the commercial success of MU has been based upon two key intangible resources – image and reputation – that the club has established and managed over a number of years.

Image has been defined as the 'internal collective state of mind that underlies [an organisation's] corporate communications efforts to present itself to others' (Bromley, 2001: 317). Thus, image denotes the ways in which an organisation (re)presents itself to various stakeholders and the meanings influential organisation members attempt to affix to that representation. According to Harvey (2001), a favorable image can make an organisation more attractive than the individual good or service the company provides. Reputation refers to courses of action that an organisation has already engaged in and how these actions have been perceived. Michalisin *et al.* (2000: 94) defined reputation as the 'perception of customers, competitors, potential recruits, and other stakeholders about a firm's quality of management; quality of products and services; innovativeness; long-term investment value; financial soundness; ability to attract, develop, and keep talented people; community and environmental responsibility; and use of corporate assets.' As a consequence of the positive emotional response that can be generated, interested individuals are more likely to develop 'strong, favorable and unique associations' towards an organisation (Keller, 2000: 115).

While there has been some empirical evidence as to the utility of such resources (e.g. Deephouse, 2000; Fombrun, 1996; McMillan and Joshi, 1997), the ways in which they contribute to a firm's position of sustainable competitive advantage is not well understood. Consequently, the purpose of this chapter is twofold. First, we draw upon an influential stream of the strategic management literature, known as the resource-based view, to better understand how MU has attained and retained such a dominant industry position. Second, we use the investigation to extend our theoretical and empirical understanding of the ways in which such resources are actively managed to impact firm performance.

Intangible resources and competitive advantage

During the 1980s, a dominant theme in the strategy literature was that a firm's advantage was largely down to its ability to adopt and defend a privileged product-market position. Proponents of this industry structure perspective argued that performance depended upon how well a firm was able to influence various environmental contingencies (e.g., Buzzell and Gale, 1987; Porter, 1985). However, it has been widely recognised that in fact industry structure accounts for a relatively small component of the differences in firm performances (Black and Boal, 1994). Consequently, it has been suggested that a much likelier explanation of a firm's advantage stems from the idiosyncratic resources and capabilities that it controls (Barney, 1991, 2001a, 2001b; Grant, 1991; Peteraf, 1993; Wernerfelt, 1984).

Barney (2001a: 54) defined resources as 'the tangible and intangible assets that a firm uses to implement its strategies'. Clearly not all resources held by a firm are of equivalent value. Barney (1991) suggested that resources with the capability of assisting a firm to a position of sustainable competitive advantage must satisfy four criteria. First, the resource must be valuable; that is, it must allow the firm to exploit some opportunity or neutralise a particular threat. Second, the resource must be rare. Generally, the number of firms that control a resource must be less than the number needed for perfect competition, otherwise any advantage generated would be immediately negated by the actions of competitors. Third, the resource must be imperfectly imitable, usually a consequence of the social complexity of the resource or the ambiguity of the link between the resources controlled and the advantage accrued. Finally, there must be no equivalently valuable substitutes for the resource.

Tangible resources such as physical plant, equipment or distribution systems tend to diffuse rapidly through an industry, resulting in any advantage generated being relatively short-lived. Thus, the more tacit a resource, the longer its likely duration as a source of advantage (Wright, 1994). Resources that are intangible are more difficult to observe and understand, making them hard to imitate or duplicate. Consequently, they are more likely to form a more durable source of competitive advantage. Indeed, it has been suggested that only resources that are intangible possess the characteristics necessary to generate a position of sustainable competitive advantage (Grant, 1991; Itami and Roehl, 1987; Michalisin *et al.*, 2000; Sanchez *et al.*, 2000).

Over recent years, it has become increasingly recognised that intangible resources such as image and reputation constitute the most valuable resources that a firm may own because they are durable, difficult for rivals to identify, imperfectly transferable, and not easily replicated (e.g., Grant, 1991; Hall, 1992, 1993). Further, while it may be difficult to place a precise value on them, it has been argued that intangible resources such as image and reputation constitute the bulk of the worth of many firms (Doyle, 2001; Fombrun, 1996; Hall, 1992). Thus, according to Amis, Pant and Slack (1997: 83), 'if managers can enhance and actively promote their firm's image and reputation, they have a potential resource that is capable of conferring a sustainable competitive advantage.'

Much of the discussion on corporate or product image has centred on the ways in which brands are developed and managed. Brand image consists of 'the perceptions about a brand as reflected by the brand associations held in consumer memory' (Keller, 1993: 3). Thus, a key component of delivering customer value depends upon the ways in which a particular brand communicates certain values (Doyle, 2001). These values may draw on shared experiences and emotions such as Nike's 'Just do it!' or Guinness' 'Believe' campaigns, or they may be the more aspirational values espoused by firms such as Ferrari. In the latter example, the brand image that has been built up over many years, in large part as a result of its long association with Formula 1 motor racing and its persona of exclusivity, has been subsequently leveraged into merchandise such as casual clothing, luggage, children's toys, coffee mugs and computer accessories (see, for example, www.scuderiaferrari.com, accessed 23rd August 2002). The financial value of brand image can be immense. Doyle (2001) suggested that while tangible assets account for less than 20 per cent of the value of the world's top 20 companies; brand image forms a significant part of the balance. Similarly, *Forbes'* valuation of the Washington Redskins ($800 million) and the New York Yankees ($730 million) (Heller, 2002), are far in excess of the tangible assets that each firm owns.

Corporate reputation is similarly seen as a potentially valuable resource (Deephouse, 2000; Fombrun, 1996; Fombrun and Rindova, 2000; Hall, 1993). Because reputation provides easily accessible and general information about a firm, favourable reputations can provide an advantage to an organisation over its competitors (Fombrun and Shanley, 1990). Olins (2000) suggested three main reasons for this. First, he held that in highly competitive marketplaces with very similar products, it is virtually impossible for consumers to make rational choices; second, brands offer the promise of a consistent experience; finally, association with a particular brand projects something about who we are, or who we would like to be. Thus, being able to rely on a positive corporate reputation to aid decision-making can be a considerable asset. The financial value of a strong reputation can be immense. The reputational capital of Coca-Cola, for example, has been estimated to be $42.1 billion (Fombrun, 1996). Hall (1993) suggested that the value of reputation lies in the time that it would take to replace or rebuild. As he suggested, a strong reputation depends upon fame and esteem: 'fame can be bought with advertising spending in the short term, but esteem has to be earned, usually over a long period of time' (Hall, 1993: 138). However, reputation is also extremely fragile. Nike, Enron, Arthur Anderson and World Com are all firms that have, to greater or lesser degrees, been severely affected in recent years because of damage to their corporate reputations. Consequently, reputation is a resource that must be carefully developed and protected (Petrick et al., 1999).

Thus, image and reputation are two separate but related intangible resources. Both are rare and difficult to imitate due to the long time it takes to develop them. Therefore, both have great potential to lead to a sustainable competitive advantage. With a positive image and reputation, an organisation will be well positioned to achieve greater marketing communication effectiveness, attract better applicants, generate greater margins by charging higher prices, have lower marketing costs, retain employees, enjoy enhanced access to capital markets, attract investors and generate increased consumer loyalty (Fombrun, 1996; Fombrun and Shanley, 1990; Keller, 1993).

Ferrari and the Dallas Cowboys are examples of sporting organisations that have gained significant advantages from their positive image and reputation. Both organisations have been recognised for their strong brand names. For example, one international study ranked the Dallas Cowboys as the top global brand despite the team not winning a Super Bowl since 1996 and finishing the 2000–1 season last in their division, with 11 losses and only five wins. Similarly, Ferrari, the fourth-ranked sporting brand in Europe, did not win a Formula 1 driver's championship between 1979 and 2000 (CNN, 2001). Both the Dallas Cowboys and Ferrari have seen the benefits of this strong fan loyalty through high revenue and increased profit streams, even during times when neither enjoyed sustained periods of success. In other words, the image and reputation of both brands remained relatively intact despite poor competitive performances. We now examine MU to try to better understand why the football club has been so successful and how it has managed its image and reputation to achieve its position of financial dominance.

Tragedy to triumph: the foundations of success at Manchester United

The rise of MU into the transnational brand that we now see can be traced back to the post-war period and the legendary Busby Babes. Matt Busby was hired as manager on 19 February 1945, and according to Bose (2000: 123), 'before he arrived at Old Trafford the club was nothing; after him it was set on the path to glory which others, who have come in his wake, have struggled to emulate'. Busby focused on acquiring the best players for United, and was the man behind entering English football clubs into European and international competitions (Bose, 2000). Busby had a style markedly different to those of his contemporaries. Rather than the administrator role favoured by his peers, Busby actively coached his players on the training pitch. According to a club website, 'he established the club's footballing ideology, its playing style and philosophy, while in the process building two of English football's most famous ever teams' (Manchester United Zone, 2002).

Busby favoured an exciting, attacking brand of play that would become a hallmark of MU teams. In the 1950s, when Busby thought his team had lost its edge, he decided to dramatically alter his starting lineup by introducing several young players (Manchester United Zone, 2002). These young men famously became the Busby Babes. Players such as Bobby Charlton, Duncan Edwards, Eddie Colman, Dennis Viollet, Tommy Taylor, Bill Foulkes and Jackie Blanchflower provided Manchester with a fresh, optimistic feel for post-war England, quickly winning two league titles.

On 6 February 1958, the team left Belgrade on a chartered aircraft after overcoming Red Star Belgrade in the semi-finals of the European Cup. The team was finally on the verge of winning the coveted European Cup, signifier of the best football club in Europe. However, on the third take-off attempt after a stopover in Munich, the plane crashed into a house at the end of the runway, killing 23 players and journalists. While horrific for the club, the disaster precipitated an outpouring of sympathy from individuals all over the world. According to Bose (2000: 129):

> Manchester United were a well-known, well-respected club before Munich, but the air crash elevated them to another level. The glory had been touched with tragedy and one in which young lives which seemed destined for greatness had been destroyed and the whole nation was drawn to Old Trafford.

Manchester United gained many new fans after this disaster, as sympathy for the club was translated into widespread support. Mellor (2000) suggested:

> It is almost certainly the case that the Munich disaster was something of a catalyst for Manchester United's popularity in the late twentieth century, particularly after the crash and its victims had achieved mythical status in the public's imagination in the 1960s and 1970s.

The Munich disaster set United apart as a unique team with which people from all over the world wanted to be associated. This support was exacerbated by the English and Irish diasporas through which MU was often a nostalgic link to 'home'. Displaced MU fans not only remained loyal followers, they also converted local people to support the club. This became especially true with the rise of terrestrial and then satellite television as increased numbers of ever more diffusely located people gained opportunities to watch the team play.

Fortunately, Matt Busby survived the plane crash and returned to build another successful MU team. The team excelled on the field, and 'as a result of their success in the late 1960s, Manchester United not only built an extremely large following, but also drew national and international support for the first time' (Mellor, 2000). In 1968, Manchester United became the first English club to win the European Cup, the 'Holy Grail of Old Trafford' (Bose, 2000).

Despite the club's success on the field in the late 1960s, the team struggled over the next two decades. However, the fan base did not decline; it continued to grow. The club's reputation of youth and excitement was compelling even in times of little success. In the 1970s and 1980s, the club 'possessed a reputation for style and glamour which was to alter the image of the club forever and ensure United's place in British popular culture's most famous and influential period' (Mellor, 2000). In a period when British culture dominated world style with the likes of the Beatles and James Bond, Manchester United was also developing its own international following. The players and style of play closely resonated with the culture of the time. This provided Manchester United with two main benefits. First, it gained supporters from England and other parts of the world. Second, 'and more importantly in terms of the club's long-term status as a super-club, it also ensured that United retained the image of a glamorous and exciting club long after the team had ceased to be successful in the 1970s' (Mellor, 2000).

Recruiting young, entertaining players ensured that the club would keep this reputation. For example, George Best, perhaps the most written-about player of all time, had a weakness for alcohol and tended to think of himself as an entertainer rather than necessarily a footballer. Good enough to be voted as European Player of the Year in 1968, he was 'the first footballer to take advantage of the mass media age and demonstrate conclusively to the watching world that football could be an art as well as a sport' (Kurt, 1998: 74). Dubbed the 'Fifth Beatle', Best is one of the players who helped MU achieve the popular culture reputation of excitement and style. The ultimate consequence of the mass appeal of Best and the club was that MU became the best-supported club in England, despite the lack of on-field success (Szymanski, 1998). This is a mantle they have retained ever since.

Although the club retained its popular iconic status, the void left by Best, Charlton, and Dennis Law was unfilled on the pitch throughout the late 1970s and 1980s. Outstanding players such as Bryan Robson and Norman Whiteside, along with high-profile managers Tommy Docherty and Ron Atkinson, helped keep the club in the spotlight, but it was to take another manager, Alex Ferguson, and a new crop of young players to revive fortunes on the pitch in the 1990s.

Alex Ferguson was appointed as manager in November 1986. The immediate results were largely indifferent. Ferguson did not win many games, and spent a lot of money bringing in new players. However, the MU board supported Ferguson's long-term strategy of replicating what Busby had done: 'taking the club apart from top to bottom' (White, 1999: 36). Looking for long-term success instead of short-term, ephemeral rewards, Ferguson established a reputation for excellence. His ultimate impact led Bose (2000: xxii) to suggest:

Just as in the standard United myth, before Busby came to Old Trafford in 1945, there was darkness and then he said let there be light and Old Trafford was bathed in glory, so all the success United has had since 1990 has been put down to just one man: Sir Alex Ferguson.

The volatile but highly talented Eric Cantona was the initial catalyst to MU's success. Cantona arrived at the club in 1992, was famously banned for eight months for kicking a Crystal Palace fan in 1995, but was talented enough to be voted Player's Player of the Year in 1993 and play an integral role in the club winning its first Premier League title in 1993. Ryan Giggs also achieved much prominence through the 1990s, often as much for his off-field, high-profile girlfriends as his on-field performances. However, it was David Beckham who really took the Best mantle of a celebrity as much embedded in mainstream popular culture as he is in English football. Outstanding on the field, he was voted runner-up in the World Player of the Year Award in 1999 and 2001, and was also runner-up as 1999 European Player of the Year. In 2001, his public popularity in Britain was demonstrated when he was voted as BBC Sports Personality of the Year, an astonishing turnaround for a player who had been vilified following his sending off in the 1998 World Cup Finals match against Argentina. His film star looks, celebrity marriage to Spice Girl Victoria Adams and numerous endorsements have accorded him an iconic status that has, temporarily at least, placed him at the centre of media attention. This was cemented by his appointment as captain of the England national team in 2001. Until his departure to Real Madrid in the summer of 2003, Beckham, and his colleagues in the MU team, continued to purvey a high-profile image of youth, vibrancy, glamour and excitement that proved highly attractive and provided a strong basis for the ongoing economic success of the football club.

The (brand) management

Manchester United's reputation for on-field excellence, particularly with the talents of individuals such as Best and Beckham, has clearly played a large part in the development of the club's financial success. However, the off-field management has played an equally important role in leveraging the club's popularity into commercial income. In this respect, perhaps the most important figure in the development of the club into a modern transnational brand is Martin Edwards. Edwards became chairman of Manchester United in 1980 when his father, Louis, died (Perry, 2001). Edwards helped define the values of the business, particularly the shift to an explicitly corporate orientation with a primacy placed on the creation of shareholder wealth. After unsuccessfully attempting to sell his majority shareholding for £10 million in 1989 to Michael Knighton, Edwards turned his attention to strategic issues, specifically the need to raise funds for ground improvements at Old Trafford and to pay off his own debts (Bose, 2000; Szymanski, 1998). In 1991, he decided to float the club, with the football club becoming a wholly owned subsidiary of the newly created Manchester United Public Limited

Company. The club was listed on the London Stock Exchange at a price of 32p per share, giving it a market capitalisation of £40 million. Additional share issues followed in 1994 and 1997 that led Edwards to accumulate £71 million as he reduced his stake to 6.5 per cent (Perry, 2001).

While Edwards' off-field leadership certainly contributed to the development of the club into a global brand, arguably as important was the creation of the FA Premier League and the subsequent gentrification of what had traditionally been a working-class sport. Following a decade in which English football had been blighted by hooliganism and the tragedies at Bradford in 1985, Heysel in 1987 and Hillsborough in 1989, the need to redefine English football and the stadiums in which it was played was apparent to those governing football and the country (Scraton, 2000). The move to all-seated stadiums following Lord Justice Taylor's report into the Hillsborough disaster and the use of the Premier League as a platform for attracting new subscribers to News Corporation's BSkyB satellite television service were integral parts in the reimaging of English football. Supporters who had been herded into pens like cattle and provided with the most rudimentary toilet and catering services were increasingly treated as discerning customers with a multitude of options as to how they might spend their entertainment pound. Hooliganism was virtually eradicated from football grounds. Television coverage that had stagnated under the limited though increasing airing on the BBC and ITV underwent a paradigmatic shift as the number of cameras, technological augmentation and vastly increased number of 'live' games combined to represent football as a sophisticated form of entertainment that appealed to the middle classes with the disposable income required to pay for subscription television and the products pushed by both the Premier League's and Sky's corporate sponsors and advertisers. Thus, while the cost of consuming football either at the ground or at home significantly increased, the vastly improved product – including an increasing number of foreign stars – and channels of consumption provided a springboard for English football to rise in popularity, not just in England but worldwide.

Manchester United was at the forefront of this growth, and was thus positioned to take maximum commercial advantage. This was partly serendipitous. The period of MU's on-field dominance coincided with an unprecedented commercial and global demand for English football that allowed MU to massively expand its popular appeal, both with new fans in different parts of the world and with transnational sponsor companies such as Sharp, Nike, Pepsi, Anheuser-Busch and Vodafone. The Premier League is now seen in 152 countries, with a cumulative audience in excess of 1.3 billion; the extensive airing of its games has helped MU to reap the benefit of truly global coverage.

In May 1997, Edwards brought in Peter Kenyon, previously Chief Executive at Umbro, to advance the club's image (Bose, 2000). Kenyon's job, as Deputy Chief Executive, was to broaden United's supporter base, the rationale being that 'the greater the support, the greater the potential to sell club merchandise' (Perry, 2001). In September 1999, Kenyon brought in Peter Draper, also from Umbro, to assist with the club's marketing. As MU's Marketing Director, Draper was responsible for the merchandising and sponsorship of MU, playing a major role in the 'commercial direction of the club as it builds its global position as the richest, and best supported, team in the world ... he will act as a brand guardian, ensuring that licensing and sponsorship deals do not tarnish the strength of the brand' (Darby, 1999a: 14). Draper has made great use of direct marketing to increase loyalty among existing fans and to target new fans (Darby, 1999b).

One marketing initiative of Kenyon and Darby has been the 'Theatre of Dreams' project, an attempt to replicate the Old Trafford experience for United's fans in other countries. The 'Theatre of Dreams' was the first main project to come from Manchester United International, a subsidiary established in 1998 to develop the MU brand across the world (Bawden, 1999). This project strives to exploit the large fan base in the Far East, which has developed through the extensive use of the Internet and satellite TV broadcasting. The club estimates that it has 30 million fans in Asia (Maidment, 2002). The 'Theatre of Dreams' project provides consumers in the Far East, and elsewhere, with Internet access to club merchandise, a virtual museum, and interactive games.

> The strategy is for Manchester United to develop its brand across a global stage, building the concept of a Theatre of Dreams with the retail format varying from shop to shop. So in Dublin, Singapore, Dubai, Shanghai, Hong Kong, United have developed partnerships with regional and local businesses where the locals provide the site ... and the staff, while United supply the goods; United make no capital investment and are assured of a profit on the sales of goods they provide.
>
> (Bose, 2000: 232)

In February 2000, Manchester United struck an innovative partnership with Vodafone AirTouch, the British mobile phone network. Under the agreement, Vodafone paid Manchester United £30million over four years to put its name and logo on the players' shirts (Wood, 2000). While the opportunity to directly market products and services to the MU fan base was attractive, particularly appealing was the association with a global brand that has such a notable presence in the Asian market that Vodafone was anxious to enter.

Manchester United has also stepped up its marketing efforts in the United States, where it estimates that it has five million fans (Maidment, 2002). In 2001, MU joined with the New York Yankees to enhance the brand's global reach. The two organisations, both marketing powerhouses, joined together to advance their own team in the other's country. Manchester United, with their already worldwide following, will help the Yankees extend their merchandise sales around the world. In exchange, the Yankees 'will help United pry open a US market that has stubbornly refused to embrace the world's number one sport' (Piore and Chan, 2001: 60). Manchester United hopes to do this by relying on the strong fan base and profile of the Yankees to attract more fans to the football club. Further, MU games are being shown on the New York Yankees' subscription 'YES' network. Peter Draper is confident in the union, stressing that the US will not be able to resist supporting his team: 'Manchester United is pop meets sport. We're as sexy and glamorous as we can be' (Piore and Chan, 2001: 60). Participation in the summer 2003 'Champions Tour' of the US was also intended to increase exposure of the team to this emergent market.

Manchester United has also focused on community involvement and charitable foundations to improve its corporate image. Initiatives such as a three-year partnership to raise £1 million for the United Nations Children's Funds (UNICEF) (Perry, 2001), the support of various environmental policies, community programmes, local, national and global charities, and various educational initiatives (Manchester United, 2002), as well as allowing local schoolchildren and disabled groups to use some of the clubs facilities, have all been explicitly aimed at improving the way stakeholders view MU.

More commercially, MU has tried to increase brand value by attempting to become a life-services brand. According to Simms (2002), such brands offer simplicity and convenience for consumers overwhelmed by information and product choices. In this way, firms seek to reach beyond their typical goods and services and offer customers a full range of products. As England's best supported football club, Manchester United intends to extend its brand into the life-services arena, exploiting both its reputation for quality and the loyalty of its fans. For example, in 2002, Manchester United announced that it would offer branded gas and electricity. The club also offers mobile phone services through its sponsor Vodafone, and has teamed up with Zurich, Bank of Scotland, and Britannia Building Society to offer personal loans, investments, mortgages and general insurance products (Simms, 2002). Also in 2002, MU joined with Terra Lycos, the largest global Internet network, to allow the club to 'exploit its content and brand strength ... around the world for the benefit of its many non-English speaking fans' (Terra Lycos, 2002). This agreement will significantly extend MU's reach into China, Latin America, Europe, Asia and the US.

Image, reputation and the rise of Manchester United

At a time when English football faces one of the 'biggest crises to ever hit football' with more than 90 per cent of English football clubs facing serious financial problems (BBC, 2002), MU's 'twin-track business strategy' of dominating the football business both on and off the field has led to rapid commercial growth through a sustained period of global expansion (Manchester United Annual Report, 2001). To understand this phenomenon, we have split our analyses into three distinct areas. First we discuss the ways in which the image of the club has developed into one that has a mass public appeal and resonance. Second, we note the ways in which the club's reputation has impacted on the longevity and extension of the brand. Finally we comment on the ways in which image and reputation have been translated into mass appeal through particular events, some strategically orchestrated, others more emergent and unplanned. While these are discussed separately, the closeness and complexity of their interaction should not be underestimated. Indeed, the close relationship between such resources is important because of the ways in which they complement and magnify the effects of one another (Amit and Schoemaker, 1993; Black and Boal, 1994; Keller, 2000).

Image: four pillars of brand development

Brand image comprises the perceptions about a brand that are retained by actual and potential consumers. In this respect, as we noted earlier, an important component of delivering customer value depends upon the ways in which a brand image can communicate certain values (Doyle, 2001). As we now show, there are four key pillars that have constituted MU's brand image. The first of these centres on the desire to produce an on-field product that epitomises passion and excitement. Sir Matt Busby is attributed with being responsible for this philosophy, one that not only brought success to the club in the 1950s and 1960s, but has served as a guiding ideology for successive managers. Even though they were unable to replicate Busby's on-field success, managers such as Docherty and Atkinson provided teams that favoured an attacking and passionate style of play. Thus, even while Liverpool secured a record number of trophies during the 1970s and 1980s, MU largely retained its image as a team that was exciting to watch. Under Ferguson, the team once again became dominant, exhibiting a style of play that featured attack-minded and passionate players, such as Cantona, Giggs, Beckham, Roy Keane, Paul Scholes and Ruud van Nistelrooy.

The second popular perception, of the team as an exemplar of youthful vibrancy, also originates with Busby and his immortal Babes. The legacy of Busby's teams that featured the likes of Duncan Edwards and George Best, through Norman Whiteside who as a 17-year-old became the youngest ever player to compete in a World Cup Final in 1982, to the modern era of Giggs and Beckham, MU has consistently promoted young, talented individuals who have enjoyed widespread popularity. Of course, this emphasis on youth spreads beyond individual players: Ferguson's teams, very much reflective of the Busby Babes listed earlier, have featured the likes of Giggs, Beckham, Scholes, Gary Neville, Phillip Neville, Nicky Butt, Wes Brown and John O'Shea, players who have either developed through the club's youth scheme or been brought to the club while very young. Thus, even though these players now have international experience, they have all been associated with MU from a young age, and thus promote the imagery of youthful endeavour developed by Busby. No other English team has managed to develop so many young players of such high quality over such a short period of time.

The third facet of MU's image concerns the ways in which individuals at the club have become inculcated into mainstream popular culture. Several sporting celebrities of the late twentieth and early twenty-first century have enjoyed a status previously reserved for music and film stars. However, individuals at MU seem to have enjoyed a place in popular culture that those at other football clubs have been unable to match. Matt Busby and the Busby Babes are the earliest examples of this. The Munich disaster ensured that the individuals that died, such as Duncan Edwards, subsequently gained a legendary status, and those that survived, notably Bobby Charlton and Matt Busby, gained enormous respect, sympathy and public affection. Indeed, as has previously been noted, such sentiments were bestowed upon the club as a whole in the period following the tragedy, leading to a massive surge in the club's popularity.

This popularity of MU was reinforced by the successes of the late 1960s and, in particular, the arrival of George Best. At a time when icons such as the Beatles and James Bond were ensuring that British culture was enjoying a worldwide resonance, the glamorous and talented Best, with his lifestyle more typical of a film star than a footballer, was feted by the media both in Britain and abroad. As a by-product, the status of MU and other players such as Charlton and Dennis Law were similarly elevated beyond that normally accorded football teams or players. While there were individuals such as Robson, Whiteside and Cantona that enjoyed a high profile during subsequent decades, it was not until David Beckham's arrival in the 1990s that a true successor for Best emerged. His on-field performances, marriage to Victoria Adams, appointment as England captain and skilful manipulation of his media image ensured his celebrity status. As with Best, he similarly elevated the place of his club and his teammates to a position that transcends sport.

The final contribution to the development of the club's image that we wish to discuss concerns the recent efforts made to position MU as a sophisticated transnational brand. The decision to partner with a global brand such as Nike rather than the more parochial Umbro is a good example of this. Undoubtedly the £300 million that Nike agreed to pay MU over 13 years played an important part in the decision, but the global presence of Nike was also a determining factor. Chief Executive Officer of MU Peter Kenyon noted that 'Nike has global scope, and as they sell our joint products, they market us as much as we market them. It's an ideal deal' (Heller, 2002). Similarly, the decision to partner with the New York Yankees was described as more of an attempt to develop brand image through an association with a US brand that has a credibility and popularity in the US that MU lacks, rather than an attempt to directly increase revenue (Heller, 2002). Partnerships with such renowned brands, and others such as Vodafone, Anheuser-Busch and Pepsi, are all seen as marketing alliances that allow MU to be positioned as a truly transnational brand.

The Theatre of Dreams concept is similarly an attempt to present MU as much more than an English football club. According to Kenyon, 'our growth potential is in internationalizing the brand. We've already built ManU megastores in Singapore and Kuala Lumpur, and we'll soon open one in Bangkok. In the fall we'll begin opening a string of Reds Cafes, branded family restaurants, which are to spread all across Asia' (Heller, 2002). As these and similar strategic initiatives have been unfurled, including the club's subscription television channel MUTV, so the development of MU into a truly global brand has come ever closer to being realised.

While this global expansion is being widely embraced by club personnel, management should be careful in how they seek to extend the brand into related and unrelated products and services, because even strong brands can be undermined by poorly designed strategies (Doyle, 2001). Thus selecting target areas for expansion that fit into an integrated strategic plan, which takes into account image development across the brand, is necessary. In fact, the (strategic and serendipitous) coherence of the four pillars discussed above is something that has been seen as vital to effective brand development in other settings (e.g. Amis, 2003; Keller, 2000).

Reputation

The reputation of MU somewhat parallels the development of the club's image. Michalisin, Kline and Smith (2000) suggested that reputation concerns the quality of a firm's products and services. They also provided a temporal dimension suggesting that the development of a positive reputation requires the consistent delivery of a high quality product or service over an extended period. This then allows individuals to summarise information about what they can expect from an organisation and construct their responses accordingly (Fombrun, 1996; Olins, 2000; Teece *et al.*, 1997).

In the section above, we noted how particular imagery has been coherently developed around and associated with MU. The reputation of the club has largely been constructed upon the ability of MU to consistently reinforce such imagery over an extended period of time. Thus, the image of a club offering exciting, passionate football delivered by a youthful team, made legendary by the Busby Babes, was retained through Busby's philosophy becoming captured as an ideology that underpinned subsequent teams, even when they were not successful. Clearly Ferguson's teams have not only embraced this philosophy, but have employed it to great effect. Furthermore, the addition of expensive foreign imports such as the Netherland's Ruud van Nistelrooy and Sebastian Verón from Argentina added to the allure of the team and continued its reputation for attack-oriented, exciting football.

There is a similar consistency in the way in which MU has become entrenched as a part of British popular culture. Most evidently because of the Munich disaster, Best's notoriety, Atkinson's flamboyance and Beckham's celebrity, the club has retained the profile of a societal institution with a presence that supersedes football.

In recent years, the club has developed a reputation for on-field excellence and success. The multitude of successes during the 1990s were capped by a memorable European Champions League victory at the end of the 1999 season that brought the club an unprecedented Premier League/FA Cup/Champions League Treble. While the Treble has not been repeated, the club has continued to enjoy success in the new millennium, ensuring that its on-field reputation continues to be enhanced.

As a brand, MU has also benefited from the reputation that it has gained from the businesslike way in which it has been operated, something not always true of publicly listed sporting institutions. According to Nigel Hawkins, an analyst at Williams de Broe, 'United look and behave very much like a traditional business from a corporate point of view. They have a strong brand and they have worked to maximize it by bringing in good people to develop it' (White, 1999: 34). This is important from the perspective of satisfying potential institutional (i.e. non-supporter) investors and thus maintaining a relatively strong share price.

While we have thus far focused on the positive dimensions of MU's reputation, there has also been a more negative aspect to the way in which some of the commercial activities of the club have been perceived. It has been argued that MU's business-driven ethos undermines the game of football (Perry, 2001). For example, it has been suggested that a team so concerned with marketing, commercialisation and other business functions cannot focus primarily on football, which it has been contended should be the primary goal of the club. Edwards, not surprisingly, disagrees:

> Without money you can't do these things, so we are commercial. We do not make an apology for that, as long as we don't charge ridiculous prices or rip people off ... We still hope to be the wealthiest club in the world in ten, 20 years time, but think of the things that it does for you, think of the things that it gets you. Players' wages today are going through the roof, but supporters want the best players, so we have to be prepared to be commercial because we want to afford those players.
>
> (Bose, 2000: xxvi–xxvii)

The club's reputation has been damaged by the rapidity with which the design of the team's kit is altered. Parents of young fans have felt pressured into spending large amounts to buy the latest MU kit. For example, a new kit launched in time for Christmas 2000 was the club's nineteenth in eight years (Perry, 2001). According to Nakra (2000), the ethical behaviour of an organisation greatly affects its reputation. Therefore, this type of blatant commercialisation may be damaging. It is a problem that has been recognised by the club. According to Draper, the brand must be managed differently, 'to avoid accusations of greed and fan exploitation' (Darby, 1999a: 14). Partly to offset these accusations, the club provides high-profile contributions to charities such as UNICEF and several community programmes. This is important because reputation, while extremely valuable, is also very fragile (Hall, 1992, 1993; Petrick *et al.*, 1999). As several firms have recently found, damage to a reputation can be catastrophic: thus Draper and his colleagues are right to be concerned as to how they manage the club's reputation.

From image and reputation to commercial success

The criticisms of fan exploitation notwithstanding, it is not difficult to understand the ways in which image and reputation have underpinned the club's commercial success. As Cornwell *et al.* (2001) might have predicted, effective management of these resources has contributed to the differentiation of the brand and resulted in increased financial income to the club. Our analysis revealed four main pillars that together constitute an image of a developing global brand that is associated with youth, passion and excitement, and able to transcend sport into mainstream popular culture. This combination has developed into a unique image for MU. As this resource is firm-specific and cannot be traded for by a rival, it is potentially highly valuable (Barney, 1991; Noda and Collis, 2001). Thus, we agree with Hall (1993) in suggesting that image can be perceived to be a main ingredient in the recipe of competitive advantage.

Although the concerted attempt to evolve MU into a global brand is relatively recent, the other three characteristics of the brand image have a long tradition at the club. Furthermore, the club's consistency in winning trophies under Ferguson has enhanced an already attractive reputation. This reputation is important because consumers have limited time and money to research from whom or what they are going to purchase a product or service. An organisation that can demonstrate that it can consistently satisfy what a consumer is looking for has a definite advantage over a competitor without such a reputation. As Amis (2003) similarly showed with the Guinness brand, MU has demonstrated an ability (reputation) to deliver a consistent set of desirable attributes to key stakeholders who are willing to invest in an association with the brand. These include 50,000 season ticket holders, 130,000 club members, an estimated 57 million fans worldwide potentially willing to buy club merchandise or extended services, sponsors willing to invest millions of pounds in a commercial partnership, and media companies willing to pay MU both directly and indirectly through league-wide agreements (Terra Lycos, 2002). Consequently, the club is able to affirm its place as one of the most valuable sporting franchises in the world (Heller, 2002).

While image and reputation are clearly important in our understanding of the rise of MU, the effective utilisation of these intangible resources is of paramount importance. Without widespread public awareness of the club's image and reputation, such resources will be largely ineffective means through which to attain an advantage. The widespread raising of awareness of the club stems back to the Munich air disaster. Following the crash in 1958 and the subsequent battle for survival of Sir Matt Busby, MU enjoyed an extended period of sympathy from people across the world, many of whom had little interest in football. As a consequence, many more people were sensitised to MU as a sporting institution (Bose, 2000). The rise of Bobby Charlton as an integral part of England's 1966 World Cup winning side and the exploits of George Best also ensured that MU was heavily covered by the media. It is a similar story with other high-profile individuals associated with the club through to the modern era of Giggs and Beckham and a media industry with a seemingly insatiable appetite for gossip and potential scandal. The development of the Premier League into a globally consumed product has also ensured that MU is seemingly never out of the spotlight. As a consequence, the club's image and reputation have had an impact far beyond that of any other sporting club, certainly in Great Britain and quite possibly the world. Manchester United has capitalised on technological advancements that have expanded the available market place and in so doing, have been able to take commercial advantage.

Conclusion

The development of the image and reputation of Manchester United Football Club is grounded in the club's rich post-war history. This starts with the appointment of Matt Busby as manager in 1945, continues with the Munich air disaster of 1958, success in the European Cup in 1968, the pop culture reputation of the club established in the late 1960s and retained ever since, through to the on-field domination of the English Premier League in the 1990s and the unprecedented Treble of 1999. This has been paralleled by unrivalled commercial growth, international expansion, brand extensions, and sponsorship agreements with transnational corporations such as Sharp, Vodafone and Nike.

Manchester United has been described as the most valuable sporting brand name in Europe (Kleinman, 2001) and possibly the world (Heller, 2002). Our contention in this chapter has been that the value of the brand is largely, if not entirely, derived from MU's image and reputation. With the club's image of a global brand that produces an exciting style of play featuring a youthful cast of players that are able to transcend football into mainstream popular culture, MU has built up a unique image. Its ability to sustain high levels of performance and enhance its image over an extended period has also resulted in a largely positive reputation. This has helped maintain its advantage as one of the world's most widely recognised and valuable sporting brands. According to Edward Freedman, MU's former head of merchandising, 'It's an oil well. Up through the ground gurgles this lovely red-and-white gold. No one's quite sure how or why, but it seems to keep on coming' (White, 1999: 33). Unlike Freedman, we offer an explanation for this phenomenon. The football club has transformed into a full-time business entity, becoming 'a seven-day-a-week, 52-weeks-of-the year international sporting brand – a money-printing machine' (White, 1999: 33). This has taken advantage of the image and reputation, built up over many years. The utility of these intangible resources has resulted in an organisation that appears well placed to sustain its position as the world's most glamorous, and richest, football club.

References

Amis, J. (2003) 'Good things come to those who wait: the strategic management of image and reputation at Guinness', *European Sport Management Quarterly*, 3: 189–214.

Amis, J., Pant, N. and Slack, T. (1997) 'Achieving a sustainable competitive advantage: a resource-based view of sport sponsorship', *Journal of Sport Management*, 11: 80–96.

Amit, R. and Schoemaker, P.J.H. (1993) Strategic assets and organisational rent', *Strategic Management Journal*, 14: 33–46.

Barney, J. (1991) 'Firm resources and sustained competitive advantage', *Journal of Management*, 17: 99–120.

Barney, J.B. (2001a) 'Is the resource-based "view" a useful perspective for strategic management research? Yes', *Academy of Management Review*, 26: 41–56.

Barney, J.B. (2001b) 'Resource-based *theories* of competitive advantage: a ten-year retrospective on the resource-based view', *Journal of Management*, 27: 643–50.

Bawden, T. (1999, 6 May) 'Man Utd aims brand at Asian goal', *Marketing Week*, 22(14): 6.

BBC (2002) 'Cash crisis envelops British football', available online at http://news.bbc. co.uk/sport1/hi/football/2329851 (accessed 20 October 2002).

Black, J.A. and Boal, K.B. (1994) 'Strategic resources: traits, configurations and paths to sustainable competitive advantage', *Strategic Management Journal*, 15: 131–48.

Bose, M. (2000) *Manchester Unlimited*. New York: TEXERE LLC.

Bromley, D.B. (2001) 'Relationships between personal and corporate reputation', *Journal of Marketing*, 65: 316–34.

Buzzell, R.D and Gale, B.T. (1987) *The PIMS Principles: Linking Strategy to Performance*. New York: The Free Press.

CNN (2001, 19 February) 'Man Utd top Europe sports brand', available online at www.cnn.com/2001/WORLD/europe/02/19/manutd.brand/index.htm.

Cornwell, T.B., Roy, D.P. and Steinard, E.A. II (2001) 'Exploring managers' perceptions of the impact of sponsorship on brand equity', *Journal of Advertising*, 30(2): 41–51.

Darby, I. (1999a, 29 July) 'Man United's new signing', *Marketing*: 14.

Darby, I. (1999b, 29 July) 'Man United sets up DM strategy to lift fanbase', *Marketing*: 9.

Deephouse, D.L. (2000) 'Media reputation as a strategic resource: an integration of mass communication and resource-based theories', *Journal of Management*, 26: 1091–112.

Doyle, P. (2001) 'Building value-based strategies', *Journal of Strategic Marketing*, 9: 255–68.

Fombrun, C.J. (1996) *Reputation: Realizing Value from the Corporate Image*. Boston, MA: Harvard Business School Press.

Fombrun, C.J. and Rindova, V.P. (2000) 'The road to transparency: reputation management at Royal Dutch/Shell', in M. Schultz, M.J. Hatch and M.H. Larsen (eds) *The Expressive Organisation: Linking Identity, Reputation and the Corporate Brand* (pp. 77–96). New York: Oxford University Press.

Fombrun, C. and Shanley, M. (1990) 'What's in a name? Reputation building and corporate strategy', *Academy of Management Journal*, 33: 233–58.

Grant, R.M. (1991) 'The resource-based theory of competitive advantage: implications for strategy formulation', *California Management Review*, 33(3): 114–35.

Hall, R. (1992) 'Strategic analysis of intangible resources', *Strategic Management Journal*, 13: 135–44.

Hall, R. (1993) 'A framework linking intangible resources and capabilities to sustainable competitive advantage', *Strategic Management Journal*, 14: 607–18.

Harvey, B. (2001) 'Measuring the effects of sponsorships', *Journal of Advertising Research*, 41: 59–65.

Heller, R. (2002, 8 July) 'Big kick', *Forbes*, available online at www.forbes.com (accessed 17 March 2003).

Itami, H. and Roehl, T.W. (1987) *Mobilizing Invisible Assets*. Cambridge, MA: Harvard University Press.

Keller, K.L. (1993) 'Conceptualizing, measuring, and managing customer-based brand equity', *Journal of Marketing*, 57: 1–22.

Keller, K.L. (2000) 'Building and managing corporate brand equity', in M. Schultz, M.J. Hatch and M.H. Larsen (eds) *The Expressive Organization: Linking Identity, Reputation and the Corporate Brand* (pp. 115–37). New York: Oxford University Press.

Kleinman, M. (2001, 8 February) 'Man Utd tops Euro brand value table', *Marketing*, 5.

Kurt, R. (1998) *Red Devils: A History of Man United's Rogues and Villains*. London: Prion Books Limited.

Maidment, P. (2002, 30 September) 'Manchester United expands its global reach', *Forbes*, available online at www.forbes.com (accessed 17 March 2003).

Manchester United (2002) 'Corporate responsibility', available online at http://www.manutd.com/corporateinformation (accessed 14 August 2002).

Manchester United Annual Report (2001) available online at www.manutd.com/pdf/annualreport2001.pdf.

Manchester United Zone (2002) *Manchester United Legends: Sir Matt Busby.* Available online at http://www.manutdzone.com/legends/MattBusby.htm (accessed 5 August 2002).

McMillan, G.S. and Joshi, M.P. (1997) 'Sustainable competitive advantage and firm performance: the role of intangible resources', *Corporate Reputation Review*, 1(Summer): 81–5.

Mellor, G. (2000) 'The rise of the Reds: an historical analysis of Manchester United as a "Super-Club"', in Murphy, P. (ed.) *Singer and Friedlander Football Review 1999–2000 Season.* London: Singer and Friedlander. Available online at http://www.le.ac.uk/crss/sf-review/99–00/00article4.html.

Michalisin, M.D., Kline, D.M. and Smith, R.D. (2000) 'Intangible strategic assets and firm performance: a multi-industry study of the resource-based view', *Journal of Business Strategies*, 17(2): 91–117.

Nakra, P. (2000) 'Corporate Reputation Management: "CRM" with a strategic twist?' *Public Relations Quarterly*, Summer: 35–42.

Noda, T. and Collis, D.J. (2001) 'The evolution of intraindustry firm heterogeneity: insights from a process study', *Academy of Management Journal*, 44: 897–925.

Olins, W. (2000) 'How brands are taking over the corporation', in M. Schultz, M.J. Hatch and M.H. Larsen (eds) *The Expressive Organization: Linking Identity, Reputation and the Corporate Brand* (pp. 51–65). New York: Oxford University Press.

Perry, B. (2001) 'Playing fair? Vision, values and ethics: a study of the co-existence of big business and football', in Murphy, P. (ed.) *Singer and Friedlander Review 2000–2001 Season.* London: Singer and Friedlander.

Peteraf, M. (1993) 'The cornerstones of competitive advantage: a resource-based view', *Strategic Management Journal*, 14: 179–91.

Petrick, J., Scherer, R., Brodzinski, J., Quinn, J. and Ainina, M. (1999) 'Global leadership skills and reputational capital: intangible resources for sustainable competitive advantage', *Academy of Management Executive*, 13: 58–69.

Piore, A. and Chan, M. (2001, 19 February) 'Love them, hate them', *Newsweek International*, 60.

Porter, M.E. (1985) *Competitive Advantage: Creating and Sustaining Superior Performance.* New York: Free Press.

Sanchez, P., Chaminade, C. and Olea, M. (2000) 'Management of intangibles – an attempt to build a theory', *Journal of Intellectual Capital*, 1: 312–27.

Scraton, P. (2000) *Hillsborough: The Truth.* Edinburgh: Mainstream Publishing Projects.

Simms, J. (2002, 21 March) 'Life brands: lost focus?' *Marketing*, 24–5.

Szymanski, S. (1998) 'Why is Manchester United so successful?' *Business Strategy Review*, 9(4) (page numbers unavailable on electronic version).

Teece, D.J., Pisano, G. and Shuen, A. (1997) 'Dynamic capabilities and strategic management', *Strategic Management Journal*, 18, 509–33.

Terra Lycos (2002, 20 May) 'Terra Lycos and Manchester United enter strategic global marketing agreement; exclusive multi-year online strategic agreement', available online at www.terralycos.com/press/pr_os_20_le_02.html (accessed 9 September 2002).

Wernerfelt, B. (1984) 'A resource-based view of the firm', *Strategic Management Journal*, 5, 171–80.

White, J. (1999, February) 'United's hard sell', *Management Today*, 32–8.

Wood, J. (2000) 'Finance's premier league', *The Economist* (April), available online at http://www.cfoeurope.com/20004a.htm.

Wright, R. W. (1994) 'The effects of tacitness on tangibility on the diffusion of knowledge-based resources', *Best Papers Proceedings*, 54th Annual Meeting of the Academy of Management, 52–6.

Part II
Economy United

4 Why does Manchester United keep winning on and off the field?

A case study of sustainable competitive advantage in professional team sports

Bill Gerrard

One of the major features of English professional soccer over the last decade or so has been the dominance of Manchester United both on and off the field. Since the Football Association (FA) Premier League was formed in 1992, Manchester United has won the championship eight times and never finished outside the top three. In addition, Manchester United has enjoyed considerable recent success in both domestic and European cup (i.e. knockout) tournaments, winning the FA Cup (1990, 1994, 1996, 1999), the Football League Cup (1992), the European Cup-Winners' Cup (1991) and the Union of European Football Associations (UEFA) Champions League (1999). The winning of the Treble of the FA Premier League, FA Cup and the UEFA Champions League in season 1998-9 is unparalleled. Only the similarly dominant Liverpool team of the 1970s and 1980s had previously come close in the season of 1976-7, winning the League Championship and European Cup and reaching the FA Cup Final, only to lose, by a strange twist of historical fate, to Manchester United. Off the field Manchester United has been similarly dominant, recording the highest turnover of any soccer team worldwide most years and considerably ahead of its nearest domestic challengers. Manchester United is listed on the London Stock Exchange and has achieved a peak market value in excess of $1 billion.

An important topic of research in economics, strategic management and other business disciplines is the persistence of competitive success (see, for example, Hay and Vickers, 1987; Saloner *et al.*, 2001). Why do some firms continue to achieve excess returns (i.e. rates of return above the cost of capital) over a long period of time? Excess returns offer a strong signal to existing and potential competitors of profitable opportunities, yet successful business organisations are able to continually withstand such competitive pressure. These successful firms have achieved a sustainable competitive advantage and the sources of this advantage are a matter of considerable academic and business interest. To date the literature has focused on business organisations but the concept of sustainable competitive advantage is potentially applicable to a much wider range of organisations. Professional team sport offers a uniquely attractive research site for the study of sustainable competitive advantage for a number of reasons. First, professional sports teams are involved in both sporting and commercial competition, providing an opportunity to study differences and similarities in how external and internal factors impact on how competitive processes determine sporting and commercial performance. Second, professional team sport is a highly transparent and data-rich industry in which it is possible to observe and measure the performance of key individuals within the organisation without any access requirement. The nature of sporting competition is very amenable to quantification and statistical analysis. Sporting competition occurs in the public domain so that an extensive amount of performance data can be collated independently of the organisation, avoiding issues of commercial sensitivity, data coverage and organisational bias in reporting. In addition, many professional sports teams are organised as companies subject to the usual requirements of regular financial reporting. Finally, the periodicity of performance monitoring is very high. Unlike many industries in which there is little or no direct reporting of production and sales performance beyond that which can be gleaned from the financial statements, professional team sport provides continuous performance monitoring of sporting success by way of match results and player performance. Professional team sport is a very news-intensive industry with a myriad of possibilities for exploring the impact of new information on individual and organisational behaviour. Given the attractiveness of professional team sport as a research site, coupled with the sporting and commercial dominance of Manchester United over the last decade, a detailed examination of why Manchester United has been so successful provides an excellent case study of the sources of sustainable competitive advantage.

/ The basic proposition of this chapter is that Manchester United has achieved a dominant organisational performance in both the sporting and commercial competitive domains as a consequence of accumulating three key strategic resources: playing talent, fan goodwill and organisational effectiveness/The method of analysis adopted is that of quantitative benchmarking. Manchester United's sporting and financial performance, and its stocks of strategic resources, are measured and compared to the performance and resource endowments of a benchmark group of leading English professional soccer teams: Arsenal, Aston Villa, Chelsea, Leeds United, Liverpool, Newcastle United and Tottenham Hotspur. It is shown that Manchester United's recent dominance is strongly correlated with its accumulated stocks of strategic resources.

The structure of the chapter is as follows. The next section explores the concept of competitive advantage in professional team sport. Alternative theoretical approaches to the sources of sustainable competitive advantage are discussed. The resource-based model of a professional sports team is proposed. The following section provides empirical evidence on the recent sporting and financial performance of Manchester United and comparisons with the benchmark group. This leads on to the next section on the sources of Manchester United's competitive advantage with a detailed examination of playing talent, fan goodwill and organisational effectiveness, with particular emphasis on coaching effectiveness, again in the context of benchmark comparisons. By way of conclusion, the final section discusses the problems Manchester United may face in maintaining its competitive advantage in the future.

Competitive advantage in professional team sport

Competition is a process of strategic rivalry. Strategic rivalry implies inter-dependence in the actions and outcomes of a group of organisations. The actions of each organisation are influenced in part by the actions, both actual and expected, of the other organisations. Any improvement in performance by one organisation entails poorer performance by at least one other organisation. Sporting competition provides a classic example of strategic rivalry. Within business competition, strategic rivalry is often most intense in differentiated custom markets characterised by branded products and oligopolistic structures (i.e. markets dominated by a small number of large firms). Organisations possess a competitive advantage if they are able to outperform rival organisations. A sustainable competitive advantage allows an organisation to persistently out-perform its rivals. In the context of business competition, a sustainable competitive advantage implies that a firm is able to generate excess profits (i.e. above the cost of capital).

A key issue in strategic management is the explanation of why some firms are able to achieve a sustainable competitive advantage. Two general approaches are used to explain sustainable competitive advantage: the structuralist approach and the resource-based view.

The structuralist approach emphasises the external context in which firms operate. This approach is an economics-based perspective that explains excess profits as the result of a protected market position. The structure-conduct-performance paradigm, developed by Bain (1956), focuses on three structural characteristics of industries as the key determinants of the conduct and performance of firms: concentration (i.e. the size distribution of firms), barriers to entry and product differentiation. Porter (1980) is a modern exponent of the structuralist approach. His five-forces model highlights five structural drivers of firm performance: rivalry among existing firms, the bargaining power of suppliers, the bargaining power of buyers, the threat of substitute products or services, and the threat of new entrants.

An alternative approach to explaining sustainable competitive advantage is provided by the resource-based view (see Barney and Arikan, 2001, on the origins and development of the resource-based view of the firm). The resource-based view locates the sources of sustainable advantage in the internal context of firms, emphasising the role of strategic resources that are scarce, valuable and imperfectly replicable. It follows that firms earning persistent excess profits have successfully obtained and protected a unique configuration of strategic resources. The resource-based view focuses attention on those intangible resources that are most difficult to replicate. Barney (1991) highlights the importance of tacit knowledge within firms. Tacit knowledge is a form of experience effect, acquired through learning-by-doing and not amenable to systematic codification. By its very nature, tacit knowledge is not easily replicated by rival firms. Berman, Down and Hill (2002) have tested the role of tacit knowledge as a source of competitive advantage using team performance in the National Basketball Association (NBA). Measuring tacit knowledge as shared experience, defined as the appearance-weighted average of the number of years that players have spent with the team, Berman, Down and Hill find that shared experience has a significant positive impact on the number of regular season wins achieved by a team.

The resource-based view has arguably become the dominant paradigm in strategic management. It is now beginning to emerge as an appropriate approach for understanding competitive advantage in sport management, particularly in professional (including intercollegiate) team sports. The nature of the professional team sports industry is such that structural factors are more relevant to the economic performance of a sports league as a whole than the relative performance of individual teams within a league. Sporting competition is not subject to positioning strategies designed to limit competitive threats. A sporting contest is the purest form of strategic rivalry, with a win–lose outcome entirely dependent on the ability of teams to acquire playing resources and to utilise these resources effectively. The resource-based view is the natural paradigm for the analysis of sporting competitive advantage. Smart and Wolfe (2000, 2003) adopt the resource-based view to analyse the role of playing and coaching resources in team performance. Smart and Wolfe (2000) undertake a case study of the Pennsylvania State University football programme and conclude that the programme's competitive advantage derives primarily from the unique historical and cultural attributes of its coaching resources. Smart and Wolfe (2003) focus on the relative importance of playing and coaching resources in major league baseball. Statistical analysis of team performance over the period 1991–2000 shows that playing resources are the key driver of sporting success with little discernible contribution by coaching resources.

The resource-based model of a professional sports team consists of four basic relationships:

1   the team objective function
2   the sporting production process
3   the revenue function
4   the cost function.

A simple but general formulation of the resource-based model can be stated formally as follows:

$$\text{Max } V = V(R{-}C, W) \tag{1}$$
$$W = W(Q, M^{W}) \tag{2}$$
$$R = R(W, F, M^{R}) \tag{3}$$
$$C = C(W) \tag{4}$$

Equation (1) is the team objective function. A team is assumed to maximise ownership value, V. Ownership value depends on both financial performance, $R{-}C$, and sporting performance, W. Financial performance is measured by profit, defined as revenue, R, minus costs, C. Equation (1) captures the performance trade-off within professional sports teams. Team owners may differ in their preferences over sporting and financial performance. Profit-maximising team owners will only derive indirect benefit from sporting performance to the extent that improved sporting performance yields higher profits. By contrast, the sportsman-owner, as defined by Vrooman (1997), derives intrinsic value from sporting performance quite independently of the impact on financial performance. The sportsman-owner is, therefore, prepared to trade off financial performance in order to achieve better sporting performance.

Equation (2) states that sporting performance depends on the stock of playing resources, Q, and the stock of coaching resources, M^W.

Equation (3) is the team's revenue function. Team revenue consists of four principal revenue streams: gate and other matchday revenue, TV and other media revenue, sponsorship revenue, and merchandising and other commercial revenues. All of these revenues are likely to be 'results-elastic', sensitive to the team's sporting performance. Winning teams will attract more fans, both at the stadium and watching on TV, and this, in turn, will have a positive impact on the value of the team's media and image rights as well as the value of merchandising sales and other team products and services. Conversely, teams losing on the field also tend to lose off the field as fans stay away from the stadium, watch the team less on TV and buy fewer team products and services. The size of the revenue streams also depends crucially on the underlying size of the team's fan base. A team's fan base is largely a matter of history and geography. Teams that are based in larger cities and with better historical and/or current records of sporting success will tend to have bigger fan bases. Equation (3) captures all of these effects by stating that total team revenue depends on sporting performance, the size of the fan base (i.e. the stock of 'allegiance' resources), F, and the stock of general (i.e. non-coaching) managerial resources, M^R.

Equation (4) is a simple cost function in which costs depend primarily on the stock of playing resources. This recognises that player wage costs is the single most important cost driver in any professional sports team.

Substituting equations (2), (3) and (4) into equation (1) and simplifying them yields the following reduced-form equation:

$$V = V(Q, M^W, F, M^R) \tag{5}$$

Equation (5) summarises the resource-based view of a professional sports team. It states that the organisational performance of a professional sports team depends on its accumulated stocks of four strategic resources: playing resources, coaching resources, allegiance resources and general managerial resources. This provides the basic theoretical framework for the benchmark analysis of Manchester United. Ultimately the analysis will seek to establish that Manchester United has achieved a competitive advantage in both sporting and financial performance and that this advantage is derived from its accumulation of large stocks of playing, coaching and allegiance resources.

The sporting and financial performance of Manchester United

It is generally accepted that Manchester United was originally founded in 1878 when the dining-room committee of the carriage and wagon works of the Lancashire and Yorkshire Railway Company formed Newton Heath Y and LR Cricket and Football Club. The Football League was first established in 1888 as a professional soccer league with a single division of 12 clubs. Two further clubs joined in 1891. Newton Heath Football Club was invited to join the following year when the First Division was further expanded to 16 clubs and a new Second Division of 12 clubs was created. Newton Heath entered the First Division and played its first league game on 3 September 1892, losing 3–4 away at Blackburn Rovers. Newton Heath finished its first season at the bottom of the First Division but avoided relegation in a play-off (known as a 'test match') by defeating the Second Division champions, Small Heath (now known as Birmingham City). Newton Heath was relegated the following season and remained in the Second Division for the next eight seasons. The club went bankrupt in 1902 and was reformed as a new club, Manchester United, that retained Newton Heath's Football League status and continued to play at Newton Heath's ground at Bank Street, Manchester. The club moved to Old Trafford in 1910 and has remained there ever since (although bomb damage during the Second World War forced Manchester United to play at Maine Road from 1941 to 1949).

Prior to the 1950s, Manchester United achieved little sporting success other than two League Championships and an FA Cup win in the first decade of the century. Indeed, Manchester United languished for much of the inter-war years in the Second Division. The club's fortunes improved dramatically in the immediate post-war period under the manager Matt Busby, appointed in 1945. Manchester United finished as runners-up in the First Division four times in five seasons between 1946 and 1951 and won the FA Cup in 1948. Manchester United eventually won the League Championship in 1952 and then in consecutive seasons in 1956 and 1957 with a team of young players known as the 'Busby Babes'. As league champions, Manchester United entered the European Cup (first established in 1955) in seasons 1956–7 and 1957–8, reaching the semi-finals on both occasions. However, tragedy struck on 6 February 1958 on the return from the quarter-final tie with Red Star Belgrade in Yugoslavia. The aeroplane carrying the team crashed while attempting to take off for a third time in blizzard conditions at Munich airport after a refuelling stop. Eight United players were among the 23 passengers killed, and two other players were never able to play again. One of the dead was Duncan Edwards, widely regarded as the most talented English player of his generation. The tragedy of so many young players being killed created enormous sympathy for the club both nationally and internationally.

It took several years for Busby to rebuild his team but he succeeded, winning the League Championship in 1965 and 1967, and the European Cup in 1968. With players such as Bobby Charlton, Denis Law and George Best, Manchester United became associated with individual flair and a very attacking style. However, Busby's achievements proved difficult to emulate by his successors. Manchester

United's success in the 1970s and 1980s was limited to three FA Cup triumphs in 1977, 1983 and 1985. The club was relegated from the First Division in 1974 (ironically by a goal scored by Denis Law who had joined Manchester City after being released by Manchester United the previous summer) but returned immediately as Second Division champions.

/The current period of success began with the appointment of Alex Ferguson as manager in 1986. Ferguson had established his managerial reputation in his Scottish homeland by breaking the stranglehold of the two Glasgow giants, Celtic and Rangers, to lead the small provincial club, Aberdeen, to an unprecedented three League Championships, four Scottish Cup victories and winning the European Cup-Winners' Cup in 1983. Ferguson's managerial reign at Manchester United produced little success initially until the FA Cup in 1990 and the European Cup-Winners' Cup in 1991. Ferguson won his first English league title in 1993, the first season of the FA Premier League. The rest, as they say, is history with Ferguson's teams winning 12 major domestic and European honours from 1992 onwards, culminating in the Treble in 1999.

Manchester United's sporting historical performance in comparison to the benchmark group is summarised in Table 4.1. With 29 major honours, Manchester United ranks behind only Liverpool in the all-time winners' list. But the historical gap between Manchester United and Liverpool in terms of major honours remains significant, with Liverpool having won three more League Championships and, perhaps more importantly, winning the European Cup on four occasions compared to Manchester United's two victories in the European Cup and the Champions League. Manchester United's dominance since 1992, particularly in the League Championship with eight titles, is matched historically only by Liverpool's 18-year dominance from 1972 to 1990, during which time Liverpool won 22 major honours including 11 League Championships. Manchester United's nearest challenger since 1992 has been Arsenal, with eight major honours including two League Championships. Historically, Arsenal ranks just behind Manchester United in the all-time winners' list, with 25 major honours. Aston Villa ranks fourth in major honours but the majority of these were won before the First World War. Overall, it is clear that Manchester United has achieved a sustained competitive advantage over the last 50 years or so with close to a position of competitive dominance in the League over the last 11 years. Only Liverpool and Arsenal have been as successful with Liverpool's dominance in the 1970s and 1980s remaining the only instance in which Manchester United's current dominance has been emulated and even surpassed.

Manchester United's dominance of the FA Premier League is charted in Table 4.2. Manchester United has amassed 135 league points more than its nearest challenger, Arsenal, the equivalent of just over a 12-point gap every season. Manchester United has never finished outside the top three, winning the Premiership title eight times and finishing runners-up twice. By comparison, Arsenal has won the Premiership twice and finished runners-up on four occasions. Key to Manchester United's success has been its phenomenal scoring rate of over two goals per game. Liverpool, the club with the second best Premiership scoring

Table 4.1 Historical sporting performance

	Manchester United	Arsenal	Aston Villa	Chelsea	Leeds United	Liverpool	Newcastle United	Tottenham Hotspur
Year of formation	1878	1886	1874	1905	1892	1919	1881	1882
Year of league entry	1892	1893	1888	1905	1893	1920	1893	1908
Years in top division	78	86	92	68	88	49	73	68
League championships	15	12	7	1	18	3	4	2
FA Cup	10	9	7	3	6	1	6	8
Football League Cup	1	2	5	2	7	1	0	3
European Cup/Champions' League	2	0	1	0	4	0	0	0
European Cup-Winners' Cup	1	1	0	2	0	0	0	1
Fairs Cup/UEFA Cup	0	1	0	0	3	2	1	2
Major honours, total	29	25	20	8	38	7	11	16
Major honours, 1992–3 onwards	12	8	2	4	5	0	0	1

Table 4.2 FA Premier League performance, 1992–2003

	Manchester United	Arsenal	Aston Villa	Chelsea	Leeds United	Liverpool	Newcastle United	Tottenham Hotspur
Games	430	430	430	430	430	430	388	430
Wins	269	218	166	179	207	181	178	150
Draws	101	119	124	128	110	116	94	116
Losses	60	93	140	123	113	133	116	164
Goals scored	863	683	533	637	704	601	615	569
Goals conceded	394	388	481	489	449	494	467	596
Points	908	773	622	665	731	659	628	566
Goals scored per game	2.007	1.588	1.240	1.481	1.637	1.398	1.585	1.323
Goals conceded per game	0.916	0.902	1.119	1.137	1.044	1.149	1.204	1.386
Points per game	2.112	1.798	1.447	1.547	1.700	1.533	1.619	1.316
Champions	8	2	0	0	0	0	0	0
Runners-up	2	4	1	0	1	0	2	0

record, has scored on average over 14 fewer goals each season. Manchester United has outscored Arsenal by over 16 goals per season. Defensively Manchester United and Arsenal have almost identical records with Arsenal conceding six fewer goals over the 11 seasons.

Manchester United's success on the field is matched by its success off the field. Table 4.3 provides details of the financial performance of the benchmark group in 2002. Manchester United's turnover of £148 million is considerably ahead of its rivals. Chelsea, as part of Chelsea Village, the hotel and leisure complex encompassing the Stamford Bridge stadium, are the only other club with a turnover in excess of £100 million. Both Arsenal and Liverpool, with turnovers of £91 million and £99 million, lag significantly behind Manchester United in their capacity to generate income. The average turnover of the whole benchmark group is £89.8 million. Aston Villa, the smallest club financially in the benchmark group, has a turnover of just under £47 million, only 31.6 per cent on Manchester United's turnover.

Manchester United enjoys the benefits of a virtuous circle of success. Sporting success enhances its revenue streams, allowing the club to spend more on playing talent to achieve further sporting success. Manchester United's financial strength allows it to maintain the highest level of staff costs in the Premiership while achieving the highest level of profitability. In 2002 Manchester United spent £70 million on staff costs, the largest proportion of which was spent on player wages. Arsenal spent £61.5 million on staff costs. Chelsea and Liverpool lagged further behind with staff costs of £57.3 million and £56.0 million, respectively. The average staff costs for the benchmark group as a whole in 2002 was £49.7 million.

Given its financial size, Manchester United is able to maintain one of the lowest wage-turnover ratios in the Premiership despite its high level of staff costs. Manchester United's wage-turnover ratio in 2002 was 47.3 per cent. The benchmark group average was 55.4 per cent and Arsenal recorded the highest wage-turnover ratio of 67.5 per cent. Given its low wage-turnover ratio, Manchester United achieved an operating margin of 22.6 per cent compared to the benchmark group average of 11.6 per cent. Liverpool's operating margin of 14.6 per cent also exceeded the benchmark group average, but both Arsenal and Chelsea performed below average with operating margins of 7.4 per cent and 7.3 per cent, respectively. Only Manchester United and Liverpool were able to generate any significant return on equity. Manchester United paid dividends to shareholders of just over £8 million as well as retaining just under £17 million of profits within the business for future investment. Liverpool paid no dividends to shareholders, retaining the whole of its after-tax profits of just over £6 million.

Manchester United's success has allowed it to reward all of its stakeholders. Fans have enjoyed sporting success, with the considerable investment in playing talent. Shareholders have received regular and increasing dividend payments. Dividend payments have grown by over 14 per cent annually since 1993. Players and directors have also earned high levels of remuneration. By comparison, in most other clubs, shareholders have received little or no dividend payments as clubs have chased the dream of sporting success by spending heavily on playing talent.

Table 4.3 Financial performance, 2002

	Manchester United	Arsenal	Aston Villa	Chelsea	Leeds United	Liverpool	Newcastle United	Tottenham Hotspur	Average
Turnover (£000s)	148,070	91,073	46,724	115,319	99,449	81,503	70,898	65,033	89,759
Staff costs (£000s)	69,999	61,453	30,872	57,251	56,031	53,612	32,055	36,576	49,731
Operating profit (£000s)	33,425	6,780	4,419	8,390	14,496	-7,930	14,755	9,240	10,447
Pre-tax profit (£000s)	32,347	-22,343	-350	451	9,092	-33,875	-3,079	946	-2,101
Dividends (£000s)	8,053	0	882	129	0	0	4,460	0	1,691
Retained profit (£000s)	16,986	-20,562	-1,368	-16,580	6,041	-33,875	-7,539	467	-7,054
Tangible assets (£000s)	130,118	46,430	41,599	179,948	40,937	42,537	93,722	46,306	77,700
Intangible assets (£000s)	82,209	53,060	37,990	60,761	61,232	66,469	53,197	27,741	55,332
Net asset value (£000s)	137,443	72,203	62,105	83,353	51,522	1,394	36,472	37,663	60,269
Net funds/debt (£000s)	933	242	-2,098	-80,715	-20,578	-77,891	-45,245	-7,055	-29,051
Wage-turnover ratio	47.27%	67.48%	66.07%	49.65%	56.34%	65.78%	45.21%	56.24%	55.41%
Operating margin	22.57%	7.44%	9.46%	7.28%	14.58%	-9.73%	20.81%	14.21%	11.64%
Return on equity	18.22%	-28.48%	-0.78%	-19.74%	11.73%	-2430.06%	-8.44%	1.24%	-8.90%

The sporting and financial strength of Manchester United compared to the rest of the benchmark group is summed up well by the balance sheet. Manchester United had total fixed assets of £212 million on 30 June 2002 comprising £130 million of fixed assets, principally the Old Trafford stadium and the Carrington training facility, and £82 million of intangible assets representing the amortised value of the transfer fees on purchased player registrations. Only Chelsea has total fixed assets with a book value greater than Manchester United, mainly due to the value of the land and buildings in the Chelsea Village hotel and leisure complex. However, whereas Manchester United has no net debt, Chelsea has accumulated a net debt of £81 million to finance its investment programme. For the benchmark group as a whole, the average book value of total fixed assets is £133 million with £78 million of tangible assets and £55 million of intangible assets, and £29 million net debt.

In sum, the evidence of Tables 4.1–4.3 clearly shows that Manchester United's sporting performance has been as dominant over the last decade as Liverpool's achievement in the previous two decades. But, unlike Liverpool in the 1970s and 1980s, Manchester United has peaked at a time of unprecedented commercial opportunities for professional sports teams. As a consequence, Manchester United has achieved a massive competitive advantage in commercial terms that reinforces its sporting success. Its huge revenue streams allow Manchester United to invest heavily in both physical and playing assets, with no debt burden and still able to pay significant dividends to shareholders. Manchester United's financial performance is unparalleled in the professional team sports industry.

The sources of Manchester United's competitive advantage

Playing resources

Manchester United's sporting dominance of English domestic soccer over the last decade or so shows first and foremost a sustained competitive advantage in the stock of playing resources. Manchester United's financial strength has allowed the club to outspend all of its domestic rivals consistently over the last decade. For example, as shown in Table 4.3, in 2002 Manchester United incurred staff costs of £70 million, more than £8.5 million more than the next biggest spender, Arsenal. To the extent that the player labour market is efficient in setting relative wage levels consistent with player quality, then total expenditure should provide a rough indication of relative playing squad quality. In this respect Manchester United has a sustained and significant advantage over its rivals.

As also noted above, Table 4.3 shows Manchester United to be substantially ahead of its rivals in the book value of its purchased player registrations. Professional soccer operates a transfer market in which clubs can acquire players under contract to other clubs conditional on payment of a transfer fee as compensation. Since 1998, football clubs in the UK have been required by financial reporting standards to treat player registrations as intangible assets and the associated transfer expenditures as a capital cost. Transfer expenditures are amortised over the length of a player's contract. Hence the book value of a club's intangible assets at any point in time represents the amortised historic cost of purchased player registrations. The book value of a club's intangible assets is likely to significantly underreport the current market value of the club's playing squad for two reasons. First, amortised historic cost may bear little relation to current market value, particularly for young and mid-career players under conditions of high transfer market inflation. Second, the book value of the club's purchased player registrations excludes both free agents (i.e. out-of-contract players acquired without any transfer payment) and home-grown players that have graduated from the club's own youth development programme. The underreporting problem can be very severe. For example, Leeds United's playing squad in September 1991 had an estimated market value of £198 million but a reported book value of £64 million (Leeds United, 2001: 12). In June 2002 Manchester United reported the book value of its purchased player registrations as £82.2 million compared to a benchmark group average of £55.3 million.

Manchester United's competitive advantage in the acquisition of playing talent is detailed in Table 4.4. Over the five-year period 1998–2002, Manchester United incurred net transfer expenditures of £98.9 million, representing an annual average of £19.8 million. The annual average for the benchmark group over the same period was £12.1 million. Over the period, Manchester United spent £30.5 million more than the benchmark group average.

The resource-based view suggests that sustainable competitive advantage depends on accumulating strategic resources that are not perfectly replicable by competitors. In this respect, a large stock of players acquired in the transfer market is not unique. Other clubs can seek to emulate Manchester United by also acquiring talented players in the transfer market. What is unique is Manchester United's competitive advantage in the transfer market arising from its financial resources, which has allowed it to maintain the highest level of net transfer expenditure in the Premiership. Furthermore, Manchester United may have been more exceptional in its capability to successfully integrate new players into the playing squad.

In respect of playing resources, Manchester United's sustained competitive advantage lies not only in its acquisition of new players but, much more importantly, in its ability to develop home-grown talent through its youth development programme. Home-grown talent is a unique strategic resource, not easily replicable by other clubs. Leading clubs such as Manchester United engage in extensive scouting activities both nationally and internationally to identify and recruit the best young talent. Youngsters from as young as 8 years old are trained and coached. By the time the most promising home-grown talent graduates into the first-team squad, these players may have spent anything up to 10–12 years within the club. These players are very experienced in the club's culture and style of play, and may develop a degree of loyalty to the club that may facilitate their retention in future years. The tacit knowledge of how the club does things acquired through learning-by-doing in the club's youth development programme can yield a significant sustainable competitive advantage.

Table 4.5 provides evidence of Manchester United's competitive advantage in the development and retention of home-grown talent. Table 4.5 shows the

Table 4.4 Net transfer expenditure, 1998–2002 (£000s)

	Manchester United	Arsenal	Aston Villa	Chelsea	Leeds United	Liverpool	Newcastle United	Tottenham Hotspur	Average
1998	19,073	2,810	3,039	5,433	9,082	6,200	10,442	7,178	7,907
1999	6,630	5,289	12,064	10,030	28,758	3,418	12,279	12,466	11,367
2000	17,849	7,508	4,722	12,619	4,542	16,156	9,322	16,577	11,162
2001	43,310	973	10,941	14,196	18,531	28,189	8,765	2,117	15,878
2002	12,083	3,164	7,941	29,620	16,657	25,470	10,940	6,894	14,096
1998–2002	98,945	19,744	38,707	71,898	77,570	79,433	51,748	45,232	60,410
Annual average	19,789	3,949	7,741	14,380	15,514	15,887	10,350	9,046	12,082

Table 4.5 Home-grown starting league appearances, 1992–2003

	1992–3	1993–4	1994–5	1995–6	1996–7	1997–8	1998–9	1999–0	2000–1	2001–2	2002–3	1992–2003
Arsenal	40.91%	37.45%	27.71%	24.40%	22.49%	16.51%	15.55%	12.92%	16.51%	17.46%	12.44%	22.21%
Aston Villa	17.53%	12.99%	12.34%	9.57%	10.05%	12.92%	19.62%	13.40%	14.83%	21.05%	31.82%	16.01%
Chelsea	39.18%	28.14%	21.86%	29.90%	24.64%	23.21%	8.13%	8.13%	9.09%	8.61%	8.85%	19.07%
Leeds United	16.67%	19.70%	22.51%	26.56%	19.14%	19.38%	30.62%	42.58%	29.67%	26.08%	42.34%	26.84%
Liverpool	14.50%	19.48%	18.18%	18.90%	22.25%	31.34%	32.54%	33.49%	22.49%	24.40%	23.44%	23.73%
Manchester United	14.50%	8.23%	17.53%	37.80%	35.41%	44.74%	39.23%	37.80%	47.85%	40.43%	45.45%	33.54%
Newcastle United	26.88%	24.46%	16.23%	16.75%	18.90%	10.05%	10.77%	11.96%	13.16%	9.81%	14.11%	15.73%
Tottenham Hotspur	22.94%	31.82%	31.82%	28.23%	34.45%	30.86%	29.19%	31.34%	30.62%	8.61%	13.16%	26.64%
Average	24.14%	22.78%	21.02%	24.01%	23.42%	23.63%	23.21%	23.95%	23.03%	19.56%	23.95%	22.97%

percentage of starting Premiership appearances from 1992–3 onwards supplied by players that are graduates of the club's youth development programme. The annual average for the benchmark group over the whole period is 23 per cent and this has remained very stable over the whole period, despite the greater internationalisation of the player labour market in the 1990s following the Bosman ruling by the European Court of Justice that, as well as establishing free agency for out-of-contract players, also removed all restrictions on the number of foreign players from other European Union countries that clubs could sign and field. Manchester United's record in producing home-grown talent was significantly below average in the first three seasons of the Premiership. However, from season 1995–6 onwards, Manchester United has had phenomenal success in producing home-grown talent. Whereas other Premiership clubs have averaged 1–2 home-grown players in their starting line-ups, Manchester United have averaged 4–5 home-grown players. Manchester United's sporting success has been founded on a group of exceptionally talented youngsters – principally Ryan Giggs, David Beckham, Paul Scholes, Nicky Butt and Gary Neville – who have made their way together from schoolboy trainees to first-team regulars and full internationals. There are few parallels in the modern era of such a talented and successful group of players emerging together from a club's own youth development programme. Although Arsenal began the period with a relatively high number of home-grown players, this has not been maintained and, indeed, with the appointment of a French coach, there has been ever greater reliance on acquired foreign players, particularly top French international players. Liverpool's home-grown starting appearances have fluctuated around the benchmark average. Leeds United produced an outstanding crop of home-grown talent in the late 1990s but some of these players became peripheral as the club turned to the transfer market to increase its playing strength. Although David Beckham has now been transferred to Real Madrid, Manchester United continues to have a significant home-grown presence in its starting line-up. John O'Shea, a defender, was at the time of writing the latest youngster to establish himself as a first-team regular.

The strategic importance of a significant home-grown presence in the first-team squad represents another example of the role of tacit knowledge effects identified by Berman, Down and Hill (2002) as key driver of team performance in the National Basketball Association (NBA). Berman, Down and Hill found a statistically significant association between team performance and shared experience where shared experience is defined as the average number of years with a team weighted by the total number of minutes on court during the season. Tables 4.6a and 4.6b provide evidence of experience effects in the Premiership for the benchmark group for seasons 2000–1 and 2001–2. Four measures of experience and skill are provided. Average age, calculated as the average age at the start of the season weighted by the number of starting league appearances during the season, provides a measure of general experience. Average career scoring rate, calculated as the player's scoring rate per league appearance over his playing career up to the start of the season weighted by the number of starting league appearances during the season, provides a measure of a key skill. Shared experience

Table 4.6a Experience effects on team performance, 2000–1

	Manchester United	Arsenal	Aston Villa	Chelsea	Leeds United	Liverpool	Newcastle United	Tottenham Hotspur	Average
Average age	26.98	28.32	28.17	28.14	25.39	24.60	26.01	26.40	26.75
Average career scoring rate	0.150	0.127	0.122	0.156	0.134	0.137	0.125	0.123	0.134
Shared experience	122.21	136.29	74.86	65.70	37.78	57.44	54.29	55.12	75.46
Continuity	0.722	0.739	0.571	0.251	0.582	0.125	0.617	0.218	0.478
Points	80	70	54	61	69	68	51	49	62.75
League position	1	2	8	6	3	4	11	12	5.88

Table 4.6b Experience effects on team performance, 2001–2

	Manchester United	Arsenal	Aston Villa	Chelsea	Leeds United	Liverpool	Newcastle United	Tottenham Hotspur	Average
Average age	27.40	27.16	27.08	26.88	25.48	25.95	26.04	28.82	26.85
Average career scoring rate	0.171	0.134	0.107	0.139	0.134	0.156	0.156	0.145	0.143
Shared experience	117.30	103.38	65.26	43.35	58.34	92.18	70.99	59.24	76.26
Continuity	0.563	0.487	0.049	0.468	0.313	0.652	0.359	-0.019	0.359
Points	77	87	50	64	80	66	71	50	68.13
League position	3	1	8	6	2	5	4	9	4.75

is the equivalent of the Berman, Down and Hill variable, defined as the total number of league appearances for the club weighted by the number of starting league appearances during the season. Finally, the continuity variable is the correlation between the number of starting league appearances in the current season by each player making at least one starting or substitute league appearance and the number of starting league appearances for the club by the same players during the previous season.

As can be seen in Tables 4.6a and 4.6b, the average age of Manchester United's players is close to the benchmark average, suggesting that there is little or no advantage in the total experience of its playing squad. However, Manchester United's playing squad in both seasons ranks significantly above the benchmark group average in respect of average career scoring rate, shared experience and continuity. In 2000–1 Manchester United and Arsenal had the two squads with the most shared experience and the highest degree of continuity relative to the previous season. The clubs finished first and second in the league, respectively: Manchester United's superior attacking abilities, yielding 79 goals to Arsenal's 63 goals, seemingly provided the crucial difference. In season 2001–2, Manchester United finished third in the Premiership, the only time that the club has failed to finish in the top two, despite collecting only three points fewer than the previous season. Although the level of shared experience was similar to that in the previous season, there was considerably less continuity in the starting line-up between the two seasons. Arsenal and Liverpool finished above Manchester United but had even less continuity. The success of Arsenal, collecting 17 points more than the previous season, seems to lie in being able to effect a reduction in the average age of the team (Arsenal's squad had the highest average age in 2000–1) while maintaining a relatively high level of shared experience. Liverpool, on the other hand, appear to have gained the benefits of greater shared experience. While a detailed econometric study is required to investigate the structural relationship between experience effects and team performance, the evidence of Tables 4.5, 4.6a and 4.6b suggest that a major source of Manchester United's sustained competitive advantage in the sporting domain has been its development of a group of highly talented home-grown players who have contributed to a high level of shared experience and continuity that rival clubs have been unable to match over a sustained period.

Allegiance resources

A key driver of Manchester United's commercial success is the size of its fan base. Table 4.7 provides evidence of average league attendances since 1920. As can be seen, during the inter-war years Manchester United's average attendances lagged behinnd most of the benchmark group, reflecting the relative lack of sporting success, with a significant period outside the top division. After the Second World War, as Manchester United's sporting performance improved, so too did its gate attendances. From the time of the Munich tragedy in season 1957–8, Manchester United has been the most popular club in England in terms of gate attendances

Table 4.7 Average league attendances, 1920–2003

	Manchester United	Arsenal	Aston Villa	Chelsea	Leeds United	Liverpool	Newcastle United	Tottenham Hotspur	Average
1920–1 to 1928–9	26,568	30,004	29,739	32,190	30,732	18,552	31,414	29,031	28,529
1929–30 to 1938–9	22,005	41,061	34,635	32,121	26,722	17,223	25,717	28,814	28,537
1946–7 to 1956–7	42,632	47,868	36,586	42,305	40,527	25,927	46,950	44,149	40,868
1957–8 to 1967–8	45,377	34,935	27,335	34,230	40,270	26,736	33,275	43,954	35,764
1968–9 to 1979–80	49,088	35,188	30,153	30,480	45,497	33,118	30,384	32,604	35,814
1980–1 to 1991–2	42,216	30,198	22,952	18,697	35,910	20,869	22,105	28,032	27,622
1992–3 to 2002–3	53,726	35,806	33,042	29,768	40,669	35,358	39,511	31,629	37,439
1920–1 to 2002–3	40,972	36,447	30,498	31,189	37,590	25,727	32,722	34,133	33,660

even during the long period of Liverpool's dominance in the 1970s and 1980s. Since the start of the Premiership, Manchester United has averaged league attendances at Old Trafford of nearly 54,000. This average has been severely restricted by capacity constraints. Manchester United expanded its stadium capacity from 45,000 in 1992 to a current level of 67,600 but games remain sold out with substantial excess demand for tickets. By comparison, Liverpool and Arsenal have ground capacities of 38,000 and 44,000, respectively. The average gate attendance for the benchmark group as a whole since 1992 is 33,660. Both Arsenal and Liverpool operate at full capacity and have well advanced plans to build new stadiums. But, until these plans are realised, both clubs will be at a very significant commercial disadvantage. Furthermore, gate attendance is only one measure of the size of a club's fan base/All indications are that Manchester United has a huge advantage over its domestic rivals in fan allegiance amongst those fans who do not regularly, if ever, attend home matches/ It has been claimed that Manchester United has over 3 million fans in the UK and tens of millions worldwide. What is undoubtedly true is that Manchester United's fan base far exceeds all of its rivals and it will take a long period of sporting and marketing success for any of these clubs to close the gap significantly.

Coaching resources

/The other major source of Manchester United's competitive advantage is its endowment of coaching resources./Manchester United's current team manager, Sir Alex Ferguson, was first appointed in November 1986, after a very successful stint as manager of Aberdeen. Ferguson's stint is the longest by some distance of any Premiership manager. The next longest serving Premiership manager is Arsène Wenger at Arsenal, appointed in September 1996 nearly 10 years after Ferguson's appointment. Ferguson's Premiership experience and success rate is unequalled. As can be seen in Table 4.8, Ferguson has managed Manchester United for all of its 430 Premiership games with a points-per-game ratio of 2.11. Wenger has been in charge at Arsenal for 258 Premiership games with a points-per-game ratio of 2.00. The performance gap between the two managers since Wenger's appointment is the equivalent of 30 league points. In these seven seasons of head-to-head rivalry, Ferguson has won five Premiership titles to Wenger's two. Ferguson and Wenger are way ahead of the benchmark average in terms of both Premiership games in charge and points per game.

There is a very clear link in professional team sport between team performance and managerial tenure (see, for example, Scully, 1995; Dobson and Goddard, 2001). Successful teams tend to have long-serving managers. The causal relation-ship is clearly two-way. More successful managers tend to be retained whereas less successful managers tend to have their contracts terminated early. Successful managers acquire considerable tacit knowledge, building up their experience with individual players and the club organisation and culture. However, it is very difficult to precisely disentangle the impact of the manager on team performance. Indeed, as Dobson and Goddard (2001) point out, empirical studies of managerial

Table 4.8 Managerial performance

	Manchester United	Arsenal	Aston Villa	Chelsea	Leeds United	Liverpool	Newcastle United	Tottenham Hotspur
Number of managers since league entry	17	19	23	21	15	22	23	24
Average tenure (years)	5.24	5.16	4.52	4.14	6.00	3.35	4.22	3.92
Current manager	A. Ferguson	A. Wenger	D. O'Leary	C. Ranieri	G. Houllier	P. Reid	B. Robson	G. Hoddle
Date of appointment	Nov-86	Sep-96	May-03	Sep-00	Jul-98	Mar-03	Sep-99	Apr-01
Premiership games, current club	430	258	0	109	190	8	146	84
Premiership games, all clubs	430	258	145	109	190	215	146	251
Premiership points per game, current club	2.112	1.996	–	1.706	1.758	1.625	1.658	1.310
Premiership points per game, all clubs	2.112	1.996	1.786	1.706	1.758	1.274	1.658	1.315

efficiency in English Premiership soccer have found radically different estimates of Ferguson's performance, largely due to the problems of properly controlling for the amount of playing talent at his disposal. (Interestingly, Wenger is generally found to be one of the most efficient managers.)

Table 4.8 supports the strong link between playing success and managerial tenure. Within the benchmark group, the most successful clubs have the longest managerial tenures. Historically, as shown in Table 4.1, Liverpool, Manchester United, Arsenal and Aston Villa have won the highest numbers of major honours. These clubs have also historically had the longest average managerial tenures. Liverpool has had 15 team managers over its history, which gives an average managerial tenure of 6.0 years. Manchester United ranks second behind Liverpool in managerial tenure with 17 managers during its entire history, representing an average managerial tenure of 5.2 years. By contrast, the least successful club in the benchmark group historically, Leeds United with only seven major honours, has changed manager every 40 months compared to the benchmark average of 55 months per managerial tenure. There is also a clear link between current managerial experience in the Premiership and team performance. Within the benchmark group, the managers with the longest tenure at their club tend to have the best points-per-game record. The two managers with the lowest points-per-game ratio, Glenn Hoddle and Peter Reid, have short tenures with their current clubs. Hoddle is currently managing his fourth Premiership club while Reid is at his third Premiership club. The one exception to the tenure–success relationship is David O'Leary, now manager at Aston Villa. At his previous club, Leeds United, O'Leary achieved a points-per-game ratio of 1.79 that ranks only just behind Ferguson and Wenger. The reasons for the termination of O'Leary's appointment at Leeds remain obscure, although the club directors have publicly stated that it was due to his failure to qualify for the UEFA Champions League. Suffice to say that, in the season following O'Leary's sacking, Leeds United narrowly avoided relegation and his successor, Terry Venables, was sacked and replaced by Peter Reid before the end of the season.

Glory, glory Man United?

Manchester United's sporting and financial performance since the formation of the FA Premier League has been unique. Liverpool achieved a similar degree of sporting dominance in the 1970s and 1980s but without any comparable commercial success. Manchester United's success is in part a product of the times. The greater commercial opportunities available during the current economic boom in the industry have allowed Manchester United to achieve a virtuous circle of sporting and commercial success that has accelerated the widening of the competitive gap.

Manchester United's sustainable competitive advantage has arisen from its resource endowment. Its financial strength has enabled the club to acquire top players in the transfer market. But the club's sporting success has been ultimately due to the unique ability of the coaching staff, headed by Alex Ferguson, to identify and develop home-grown talent, and then deploy the available home-grown and acquired playing talent to achieve effective team performance. The tacit knowledge of its playing and coaching staff is the basis of Manchester United's sporting success. The size of its fan base, due to its large-city location and its history of past success and personal tragedy, has put Manchester United in a unique position to maximise the revenue potential created by its current sporting success.

To what extent Manchester United's competitive advantage is sustainable in the longer term is a matter of speculation. The size of its fan base will always give the club a significant revenue advantage over its domestic rivals. However, Manchester United's ability to continue fielding a team that can dominate the Premiership is more problematic. The current crop of home-grown talent, at the time of writing, is exceptional and will be difficult to replicate in future years. Manchester United will also have to deal with the succession problem of how to replace their current manager when he does eventually retire, as well as replacing the current team as players also move on or retire. Manchester United's financial strength will always allow it to acquire top playing talent but whether or not the future coaching staff will be able to deploy that talent as successfully as the current coaching staff is not assured. Liverpool has struggled in the last decade to emulate the success of the previous two decades. Similarly, Manchester United struggled for over two decades to recapture the glory of the Busby era of the 1950s and 1960s. Manchester United will continue to be one of the top European soccer clubs by virtue of its enormous endowment of allegiance resources, but history suggests that it will be difficult to replicate the same degree of sporting dominance.

References

Bain, J.S. (1956) *Barriers to New Competition*, Cambridge, MA: Harvard University Press.

Barney, J.B. (1991) 'Form resources and sustained competitive advantage', *Journal Of Management*, 17: 99–120.

Barney, J.B. and Arikan, A.M. (2002) 'The resource-based view: origins and implications', in M.A. Hitt, R.E. Freeman and J.S. Harrison (eds) *The Blackwell Handbook of Strategic Management* (pp. 124–88), Oxford: Blackwell Publishers.

Berman, S.L., Down, J. and Hill, C.W.L. (2002) 'Tacit knowledge as a source of competitive advantage in the National Basketball Association', *Academy of Management Journal*, 45: 13–31.

Dobson, S. and Goddard, J. (2001) *The Economics of Football*, Cambridge: Cambridge University Press.

Hay, D. and Vickers, J. (1987) *The Economics of Market Dominance*, Oxford: Blackwell.

Leeds United (2001) *Leeds United plc Annual Report 2001*, Leeds: Leeds United plc.

Porter, M.E. (1980) *Competitive Strategy: Techniques for Analyzing Industries and Competitors*, New York: Free Press.

Saloner, G., Shepard, A. and Podolny, J. (2001) *Strategic Management*, New York: John Wiley & Sons.

Scully, G.W. (1995) *The Market Structure of Sports*, Chicago: Chicago University Press.

Smart, D.L. and Wolfe, R.A. (2000) 'Examining sustainable competitive advantage in intercollegiate athletics: a resource-based view', *Journal of Sport Management*, 14: 133–53.

Smart, D.L. and Wolfe, R.A. (2003) 'The contribution of leadership and human resources to organizational success: an empirical assessment of performance in major league baseball', *European Sport Management Quarterly*, 3: 165–88.

Vrooman, J. (1997) 'A unified theory of capital and labour markets in major league baseball', *Southern Economic Journal*, 63: 594–619.

5 Trouble at the mill

Nike, United and the Asian garment trade

Andrew Ross

It was only a matter of time before Nike came knocking at Old Trafford's door. Manchester United had fashioned itself as the top dog in the course of a decade when football's cachet soared along with the revenues of the elite clubs. After an initial failed bid, in 1996, to buy out licensing rights over the club's kit, the sportswear giant succeeded six years later. By winning the United contract, in the biggest sports sponsorship deal in history, Nike made its most portentous bid to capture the one truly worldwide sports market it does not yet dominate. Phil Knight had forged his commercial empire on the basis of the overseas appeal of American sports, or in global games with elite constituencies, like tennis and golf. When basketball's overseas penetration levelled off in 1994, the company's rate of growth could only be sustained by getting into the global football market. In 1997, its overall North American and Asian sales began to slump, and Nike reaffirmed its decision to hitch its corporate future to the football wagon. The sport's blend of fanatical clubbability and lifestyle expressionism, its relentless expansion into emerging markets, spearheaded by the revenue-crazed policies of the International Federation of Football Associations (FIFA), and its increasing gentrification offered the most fertile ground for the kind of super-tribalism to which commercial branding aspires.

As part of the deal with United, which began in July 2002 just as the World Cup ended, the company paid almost half a million dollars to Manchester United plc for exclusive rights to sponsor the club's clothing, manufacture and sell its merchandise – which covers the entire lifestyle spectrum, from bed linen to hard liquor and ketchup. Also thrown in was the right to operate the worldwide retail business, which accounts for a huge portion of the club's income. A wholly-owned subsidiary was set up to run the licensing and retail operations, and Nike won majority control over its board.

In effect, the company bought unfettered access to the world's most successful football megabrand. For United to fulfil the 13-year contract, the team must stay in the Premiership, and, more significantly, achieve a European competition place every season. If revenues exceed a certain target, the club receives a half share of additional profits too. Needless to say, United also benefits greatly from its association with the biggest sports brand of all. In signing with Nike (it also enjoys a big sponsorship deal with Vodafone, garnering $50million over four years), dered its long-standing relationship with Umbro, a Manchester company. Although Umbro is no slouch in the global football market (it sponsors England's national side, along with top club teams like Chelsea and Celtic), the switch neatly illustrates the transition from local ties to multinational affiliations. By the mid-1990s, United had become a byword for trading a community-minded regional identity, so cherished by football purists, for the 'imagined community' of its global faithful – imagined, in turn, by the club's directors as an 'emerging market'.

Second only to the Dallas Cowboys in the net worth of its franchise, United's runaway success in building value through global branding is without parallel in the sporting world. Executive decisions had openly driven the mercurial rise of 'Gold Trafford'. Beginning with the 1992 recruitment of Edward Freeman, a merchandising wiz enlisted from Tottenham Hotspur, and continuing through the reign of Peter Kenyon, recruited from Umbro, the club's corporate policy was that 'we must treat the fan as a customer'.[1] As a result, it was decided to expand the club's revenue stream far beyond gate receipts. Within a few years of Freeman's arrival, revenue from Old Trafford ticket sales accounted for less than half of the plc's commercial income, even though the ground was one of the biggest in the United Kingdom (UK). The strategy of converting fans into customers was aimed at the 20 per cent of all British fans who say they support Manchester, and at the estimated 54 million active fans worldwide. Indeed, United now has fan clubs in 25 nations, TV deals in 135, its own cable subscription channel (MUTV) and fashion label (muct), and a megastore (plus two other stores) at Old Trafford that is possibly Manchester's number one visitor attraction. With its licensed merchandise and paraphernalia flying off the shelves all across Asia, the club's only major holdout market is the United States (US) – a little problem that was supposed to be addressed by a joint marketing deal with the New York Yankees, though little has come of it.

As a publicly traded company since 1991, United's first responsibility is to its shareholders, and so its corporate exploits have not always endeared its management to home fans. Yet many of them hold stock in the plc, and they have learned to have their say when executive decision-making appears to favour the business of selling replica kits over the competition for glory on the field. This scepticism has served fans well in their protests against two high-profile business names: Rupert Murdoch and Nike. The Nike deal got off to an especially bad start because it was announced to London stockbrokers and investment bankers before fans (the club's part-owners if they are shareholders) and Umbro (the former licensee) even got an inkling of the contract negotiations. Shareholders United (SU), a collective of stockholders ('who care more about their club than their dividends') expressed their outrage to management at making a deal with the leading paymaster of global sweatshops. The club's customer charter, they pointed out, explicitly opposes the exploitation of child labour, and forbids United from doing business with suppliers that employ children, or indeed any workers under illegal conditions: '[Manchester United] will not knowingly buy goods from any supplier or manufacturer who does not comply fully with the labour, safety and other relevant laws of the country of manufacture ... No orders will be placed from suppliers employing child labour under the age allowed in the country concerned.'[2]

SU evolved from a group called Shareholders Against Murdoch which was founded in 1998 to fight the planned takeover of the club by Rupert Murdoch's satellite operator, BSkyB. Its own parent was the Independent Manchester United Supporters Association, initially formed out of contempt for overzealous stewards telling fans they had to stay seated while watching matches. The anti-Murdoch campaign mobilised top lawyers, economists, journalists and academics in publicising the media baron's more unscrupulous deeds and protesting the growing influence of television over the game.[3] The result was so effective that the Blair government referred the case to the Monopolies and Mergers Commission (MMC) which blocked the bid on the grounds that the takeover was anti-competitive in the media market, that it was contrary to the public interest, and would 'damage the quality of British football' by exacerbating the gap between rich and poor clubs.[4] En route to its victory, Shareholders Against Murdoch had waged 'the most sophisticated football campaign that there has ever been,' dealing a highly public rebuff to the power of United corporate board members who had approved the deal.[5]

The Murdoch campaign was the most highly visible attempt by fans to exercise some homegrown control over the wave of corporate money-spinning, and the TV revenue in particular, that had fuelled the football industry during the 1990s boom. As football rose in the ranks of global industry, its corporate development followed the familiar template established by the globalisation of the economy: vast rewards for the investor and celebrity professional class, and starvation wages for the apparel-producing sweatshop class; diversification of product and extensive subcontracting of labour and services; expansion into emergent regional markets around the world; the aggregation of corporate media power and private ownership; and the rise to primacy of branding. In fact, the globalisation of sport as a whole, brokered by the regional development policies of powerful organisations like FIFA and the International Olympic Committee (IOC), and culminating in the commercial cornucopias of the World Cup and the Olympics, tells us virtually everything we need to know about the impact of modern capitalist economics.[6]

In this new business model for football, fans increasingly have complained about being sidelined, cast either as loyal consumers of replica kits and other merchandise, or as showbiz extras required to be colourful and vocal in their role in the lucrative spectacle of televised football. Their participation in fanzine culture and independent supporters' associations offers a chance, however marginal, to take a more active role in shaping the destiny of a game with the deepest of working-class roots. Shareholder power is a step further, and rests on the claim that the game, and the club, rightfully 'belongs to us'. The immediate goal behind the creation of SU was to encourage and facilitate supporters to buy shares so that they could influence decision-making: its 'long-term aim is to deliver ownership of the club (through Manchester United plc) to its loyal supporters'. Ironically, this form of pressure is rooted in the same overheated soils of privatisation that germinated the recent corporate career of business-class football.

When I first spoke to him in the autumn of 2002, Oliver Houston, SU's press officer, was quick to declare that, far from being an anti-Nike group, the organisation plays an important role in share-buying and dividend-sharing for its members. To a large degree, then, the members feel that their investments are affected by decisions that may compromise 'the independence and integrity and reputation of the club'. It is in this role as an interested party that the organisation sees itself protecting the club from adverse business decisions. For example, Houston pointed out that 'there is a get-out clause in the contract for Nike if United drop out of the Premiership, but no get-out clause for the club if Nike is exposed for employing child labour.' In addition, his members were all too aware that 'Nike is renowned for interfering in football matters', most notably, and notoriously, in the case of the sponsorship deal with the Brazilian national side, and so they feared the consequences for United. Their guardian-like concern for the club extends to dismay at the actions of its directors, who introduced the clauses in the customer charter not long before the Nike contract was announced. While there are 30,000 shareholders in the club, only 20 per cent of the shares are owned by individuals, with perhaps only 1 or 2 per cent in the hands of the small shareholders who are members of Shareholders United. Though its takeover move was thwarted, BSkyB was, until recently, still the largest shareholder in the club, with 9.9 per cent. Nonetheless, Houston insisted that his organisation has a good deal of influence over larger institutional investors and fund managers, not to mention press relations that generate headlines.

Even so, the group's campaign against the Nike contract was hardly powerful enough to move United's directors to action. In fact, it took the best part of a year before the plc's director, Peter Kenyon, met with SU representatives at all. In the course of the meeting, in October 2002, Kenyon confirmed that there had been no second thoughts on the Nike deal. He also expressed the plc's opposition not only to putting a supporter's representative on the board, but also to scheduling the annual general meeting (AGM) for a weekend date when small shareholders could attend. SU had put resolutions to that end on the agenda of the 2002 AGM, whose slogan turned out to be the ponderous but stunningly accurate: 'Manchester United, not just a football club ... but a global brand'. At season's end, a proposed meeting between Nike representatives, plc directors and SU remained unscheduled, and SU had not as yet been permitted to view the Nike contract. Jonathan Michie, the chair of SU, acknowledged that the organisation's successes overall had been 'pretty limited', beyond getting the directors to acknowledge its existence.

United had long been criticised for exploiting its fans by issuing new strips almost every year. The first Nike strip was introduced in the autumn of 2002, only 15 months after Umbro's last – a gold kit to celebrate the club's centenary year. Yet the Nike outfit quickly established itself as the best-selling kit so far, in a year when record profits were posted by the club (profits, before player trading, for the six months until 31 January 2003 showed an increase of 32 per cent). Largely as a result of its booming business in soccer (its soccer revenues rose 24 per cent, to $450 million, in 2001), Nike returned to double-digit profit growth in fiscal 2002, with its net income rising 12 per cent, to $663.3 million.[7] Counterfeits of the Nike strip were available in Bangkok months before the rollout, and were being worn around Old Trafford almost as quickly. Better-quality fakes were soon being produced by the East End sweatshops used by the official retailers. Almost indistinguishable from the real thing, and selling for half the price, they attracted the attention of United's hit squads, and reminded fans of the club's outrageous mark-ups. Earlier in the year, the Office of Fair Trading had taken legal action against United, Umbro, the FA and several retailers for fixing the astronomical price of retail kits.[8]

By mid-season, the blue 'away' shirt had sold out, and Nike chose not run up more in order to create demand for the next kit. Even so, it was alleged that the company had not been happy with the first year of merchandising profits. Reportedly, its revenues were less than the upfront annual licensing fee it paid United. The deal had resulted in further friction with SU when some overseas members of fan clubs were 'converted' into members of the merchandising subsidiary. But by the end of the first season as Nike's brand bearer, the buzz generated by SU's campaign had dissipated, with little apparent impact on the consumption patterns of supporters, ever eager to fork out money to show their brand loyalty. Compared to the success of the campaign against the Murdoch takeover, and despite the fact that Nike was as much a villain in the public eye as Murdoch had been, the complaints against Nike came nowhere near to catching the imagination of the club's most influential supporters, let alone its vast fan base.

For one thing, it had been a done deal, unlike the Murdoch bid, which required an all-important interval before approval. In addition, rumours about new takeover bids now commanded greater attention, along with a campaign to rescue the game from the scheduling priorities of TV paymasters and restore it to its traditional 3 p.m. weekend slot.[9] Nike's public relation (PR) machine, trumpeting its 'continuous improvement' of labour conditions, had helped to persuade some doubters. When all is said and done, concerns about the club's association with child labour had not amounted to much compared to the undeniable appeal of the combined superbrand of Nike and United. If nothing else, this was a reflection of the difficulty many supporters now had in distinguishing the club's success on the pitch from the plc's success. United not only regained the English Premiership title in 2003, but also finished the season with a bill of fiscal health that was streets ahead of other clubs in the League, many of whom were on the verge of bankruptcy. The disparity underlined the degree to which raw capital resources are able to buy the kind of success on the playing field that fans crave. Financial superiority clearly brings the trophies home. The same story applied to the other members of the continental elite such as Real Madrid, Barcelona, Juventus, Bayern Munich and AC Milan, who virtually dominated both their national leagues and the European Champions League. Unlike in the business world, where competition is aimed at burying rivals, every football team depends on the competitive survival of others. The professional sport now faces a parlous future as the gap between the tycoon clubs and the rest of the field widens yearly.

Brand protectionism

Despite Nike's efforts, by any means necessary, to counter the damage caused by exposé after exposé, the swoosh is now indelibly associated with the image of children slaving around the clock for a pittance to produce shoes that can retail for $150. Because of its history and corporate strategies, Nike has been a textbook illustration of the logic of the multinational free trade corporation – from its origins as a distributor of Japanese knock-offs of Adidas running shoes, to its career as a contractor in Korea and Taiwan – and then, when wages in these countries rose, its enthusiastic participation in the 'race to the bottom' in countries under authoritarian rule like Indonesia, Vietnam and China, where half a million of the company's workers earn a famously subminimum wage. Ever since the late 1980s, the company has been saddled with the taint of sweatshops and has spent large amounts of money in lavish PR moves to cleanse its brand.[10] Nonetheless, the bad publicity is likely to have played some role in the flagging sales (down 11 per cent) of the mid-1990s, and provided some part of the impetus to penetrate the football market. But any illusions that the move to this new sport would give the company a clean slate were quickly dispelled.

Concern about the sweatshops behind 'the beautiful game' had ignited earlier in the decade when the first exposés of child labour in Pakistan's football-export industry came to light. At that time, Adidas monopolised the trade. In the US, the issue exploded in 1996 when Nike, the first major American contractor, was caught red-handed by prizewinning journalist Sydney Schanberg, who posed as an exporter to write about the brutal conditions under which children laboured to stitch 35 million footballs a year in the production centre of Sialkot. In a widely-cited *Life* magazine article, he described the arduous working day of Tariq, a 12-year-old 'who earns 60 cents a ball, and it takes most of a day to make one'. A village factory foreman offered Schanberg 100 stitchers for the price of the debt incurred by their masters, who had bought many of them as children from their parents.

> I tell Afral Butt I'll consider his offer of bonded workers, but first I need one of the Nike balls for my engineers to test. No problem, he says, selling me one for 200 rupees (roughly $6). That's what it cost to make a quality football ball in Pakistan, in labour and materials, with a profit thrown in – just $6. In the US, these balls sell for $30 to $50. More than half the nine million football balls imported into the US each year come from Pakistan and all enter the country tariff-free. The words 'Hand Made' are printed clearly on every ball. Not printed is any explanation of whose hands made them. For the rest of that day in Pakistan, I keep thinking: Someone actually offered to sell me 100 men and children for less than $200 apiece. In effect, I would have owned them.[11]

The article was accompanied by stark illustrations, one of them a photograph of a three-year-old stitcher, whose hands were so tiny she could barely handle the scissors. Combining her labour with that of her mother and her three sisters earned the family 75 cents per day.

With advance knowledge that its labour practices would be highlighted in Schanberg's *Life* article, Nike launched the first of a long series of counter-strikes by announcing a plan with a subcontractor to centralise the stitching process and eliminate child labour from its village operations. The International Labour Organisation (ILO) soon entered into an agreement with the Sialkot Chamber of Commerce and Industry and the United Nations Children's Funds (UNICEF) to regulate the industry, with the goal of ending the use of village children. Along with Reebok, Adidas, Mitre, Wilson, Puma and other leading brands, Nike signed on, consenting to disclose its stitching locations and submit them to routine inspections by a group of ILO-recruited monitors. FIFA gave the agreement its seal of approval, and formulated its own good code of conduct, based on the core conventions of the ILO (freedom of association and collective bargaining, no forced labour, no child labour, no discrimination in employment, no excessive hours, the right to one day off per week, and a wage sufficient to cover basic needs). To date, FIFA is the only major sports federation to address the issue of sweatshop labour in the sporting goods industry.

Monitoring of production facilities is notoriously difficult, however, and in June of 2002, another flare-up forced FIFA to issue a denial that World Cup balls were being produced in south Asian sweatshops. Taking a leaf from Nike's book of non-accountability, Keith Cooper, FIFA's Communications Director, told a news conference: 'We are responsible for organising the World Cup, we are not responsible for the labour conditions in factories.' The football stars who command huge salaries and handsome sponsorship fees are also 'not responsible'. Like Nike's stable of US icons – Michael Jordan, Bo Jackson, John McEnroe, Tiger Woods, Andre Agassi, Allen Iversen, Monica Seles, the Williams sisters – their deafening silence on the topic is the glue that keeps the entire celebrity/branding/sweatshop system of the sports goods industry from unravelling. In the run-up to the World Cup, exposés of labour violations behind the leading soccer brands continued to surface, most notably in China's Guangdong Province, far from the monitor's eye, where the Hong Kong Christian Industrial Committee found egregious conditions in factories producing for Adidas, Puma, Wilson, Umbro and Diadora. While quality control for hand-sewn balls was very strict, passing through 10 inspections before finishing, the corresponding regulation of conditions in the workplaces barely existed. Manufacturing processes unique to soccer-ball production exposed workers to industrial and health hazards – heat poisoning and burning, chemical contamination – in addition to the usual sweatshop diet of underpayment, exhaustion from long hours and restrictions on personal freedom.[12] In the wake of these and other reports, pressure on FIFA came through the Clean Clothes Campaign and the Global March Against Child Labour, which ran a highly visible campaign to remind the world football authority of its commitment to Fair Trade monitoring and regulation.[13]

Over time, the ILO/FIFA monitoring system has offered companies a blessing unforeseen in the original agreement. They can act to protect their brand property by notifying the ILO monitors about counterfeit balls if they do so in the name of combatting child labour. Football clubs have followed this example by alerting government watchdogs about sales of counterfeit replica kits. In the UK, the Office for Fair Trading and the Ministry for Consumer Affairs work in conjunction with the World Trade Organisation and Interpol to hunt down the pirate producers, and rely on tips from the merchandising directors of football clubs to carry out their work. These agencies act in the name of three principles:

• to stem the loss of tax revenue to the black market
• to combat the sweatshop labour exploited by counterfeiters
• to protect the intellectual property rights of companies and clubs.

Since counterfeit items are invariably produced in an additional run at the factory that makes the official goods, the principle of protecting labour is a dubious one. By contrast, the cause of protecting the brand is a huge boon to producers and marketers of the replica kits that carry a retail mark-up comparable to that of a Nike sneaker. Several years ago, Doug Hall, the loose-lipped vice chair of Newcastle United Football Club, got himself into hot water by boasting to a tabloid reporter: 'We sell 600,000 shirts a year. Every shirt costs £50, but the shirts cost only £5 to make in Asia.'[14] His comment was condemned for its casual assumption that fans are easily bilked, not because it exposed the club's reliance on substandard Asian jobs for a large part of its income.

In this respect, Manchester United is, once again, in a league of its own. Now that the team officially has a brand mark instead of a club crest, 'Manchester United' is trademarked, and can be legally protected against all efforts to use the name on non-official goods. The result is often a vicious circle. For example, the club's aggressive moves to build its brand in the Asian market has compromised its own extensive garment operations in the region. Increased demand for kits inevitably encouraged local pirates who are often the same contractors used by the club. United set up its own counterfeit detection unit, and its investigators cooperated with Thai police in hundreds of raids on Bangkok sweatshops, confiscating millions of dollars of goods. Again, the club's directors can seize the high ground by claiming that their war on counterfeiters is also a crusade against labour exploitation. In truth, the primary reason for the flourishing of black market production is that a considerable profit can still be made even after undercutting the jumbo mark-up that the plc imposes on the official replica kits.

The Asian connection

The association of the name of Manchester with prized garments is hardly new in Asia, nor is the business of speculating about the worth of Asian markets a recent matter in the northern English city which served as the home of the Industrial Revolution, and was itself the mother of all sweatshops in the nineteenth century. In fact, the reputation and wavering fortunes of Manchester cotton have been linked with south Asia for hundreds of years, and this latest twist is an ironic consequence of that history. Any explanation of the rise of Manchester from obscurity to its zenith as the prime manufactory of British industry and commerce is incomplete without accounting for the eradication of the Bengali textile industry, along with the creation of a plantation system in India to maintain a cotton supply for the mills of England's 'Cottonopolis' that would compete with the product of US slave labour.

Indian handicraft manufacture had long dominated the international textile trade. Bengali muslins, in particular, were much prized among the Arabs, Greeks and Romans of the ancient world. In medieval times, India's manufacturing skills bore comparison with, or surpassed, the European equivalents in textile, ironwork, shipbuilding, glass and paper. By the seventeenth century, ginghams, chintzes and calicos from Bengal were the height of fashion all over Europe, and, in due time, the commercial preeminence of these exports began to pose a threat to the livelihood of rising domestic industries at that time.[15] A moral panic ensued about the potential ruin of national economies. Wearers of Indian-made cloth were reviled, and physically assaulted, for being unpatriotic, and politicians were bombarded with appeals for protective legislation to promote their native industry. In spite of its passion for laissez-faire trade, the British government passed a 10-percent import duty on Indian imports in 1685, doubled the tariff five years later, and passed a law shortly thereafter, banning the wearing of silks and calicoes and imposing fines on offenders. Legislation in 1700 and 1720 went further, banning all imports of printed, painted or dyed fabrics.

After the 1757 conquest of India, the East India Company concentrated on profit from the textile export trade by squeezing the local handloom weavers whom it had brought under rigid contractual control. The Company's lucrative trade from their handicraft products continued to thrive in the face of the competition offered by Lancashire's mechanisation of spinning and dyeing. The cheapness of the Manchester factory product still could not compete in many markets with the superior quality of Bengali products, and so commercial war had to be waged through other means. In 1813, the East India Company's trading monopoly was ended, and the import duty was raised to 85 per cent while British goods were taxed at only a fraction of that duty on entry into the subcontinent. In 1840, members of the Select Committee of the House of Commons heard a witness cite the opinion of J.F. Shore, a retired East India Company administrator:

> This supersession of the native for British manufactures is often quoted as a splendid instance of the triumph of British skill. It is a much stronger instance of English tyranny, and how India has been impoverished by the most vexatious system of customs and duties imposed for the avowed object of favouring the mother country.[16]

Such sentiments were often on the lips of those, like Shore, who had seen, first-hand, the devastating impact on Bengali industry.

The mills' supply of US raw materials was hit hard in 1861–3 by the 'cotton famine' generated by the Civil War, and Manchester merchants lobbied hard for the India Office to develop a sustainable crop as an alternative source of supply to Confederate cotton. The campaign pitted the rising power of the northern parvenu capitalists against the rule of aristocratic politicians like Lord Palmerston and Sir Charles Wood, the first Secretary of State for India. The requests of the Manchester men went against the grain of laissez-faire policy, and foundered initially on the poor state of transport and communications in the Indian interior. Yet several factors conspired to break the deadlock. Free trade, it was conveniently decided, was not particularly applicable to Indian trade; the prospect of vast areas of 'underdeveloped' agricultural land was too much of a revenue bonanza to ignore for long; and cotton cultivation, in particular, was perceived to be an effective way of settling the interior with Europeans. These arguments were made by the Empire's 'friends of India' in the name of mutual benefit, to the industrialist and to the Indian peasant alike. In the same vein, scientific improvement of agriculture and the introduction of freehold tenure were pronounced to be the potential source of rich rewards for the *ryot*.[17] Just as Bengal had been bled dry by the East India Company (in 1835, the company's director reported that 'the bones of the cotton-weavers are bleaching the plains of India'), the wealth of the subcontinent's labour would soon flow into the bank accounts of British planters, industrialists, speculators, and colonial officials as India became the 'milch cow of the Empire'.

From the late 1830s, duties on the import of raw cotton from India were abolished, and by the 1870s, Anglo-Indian trade had begun to resemble the classic colonial pattern. Bengali's export textile industry had been laid low by repressive taxation and legislation, and the indigenous cotton staples that supplied it for centuries were now replaced by low-grade high-yield seeds grown specifically for Lancashire machines. Textiles bearing the name of Manchester flooded the international markets once dominated by Bengali goods. Dacca, ironically known as the 'Manchester of India', had long since been decimated: it lost 70 per cent of its population between 1800 and 1839. (In 1757, Robert Clive had described the textile capital as 'extensive, populous and rich as the city of London.'[18]) Most of India's precolonial manufacturing industries had been purposely ruined, and deurbanisation had set in. British capital would now be invested in extractive industries and in a plantation economy (indigo and jute proved even more lucrative than cotton) which made India a massive exporter of raw materials and importer of manufactured goods from England. To ensure this arrangement, all native attempts at manufacture and processing of textiles had to be successfully suppressed.

The standard textbook account of the Industrial Revolution attributes Manchester's ascendancy to a series of famous inventions – steam power, the flying shuttle, the spinning jenny, the throstle, the water frame, Crompton's mule and the power loom. In fact, technological innovation was probably not the key cause for the region's emergent economic power. Manchester merchants and industrialists prospered at the direct expense of the Indian craftworkers whose manufacture could not be beaten by fair trade, and who had to be reduced to serfdom by colonial imposition so that British industry would have cheap, raw materials for its mills and new markets for its own export trade. As a result, the fate and fortunes of both regions were inextricably linked. It was fitting, then, that the Indian independence movement was launched with a boycott of Manchester imports, and that Gandhi's spinning wheel became the most powerful symbol of anti-colonial economic resistance.

In the half-century after Indian independence, the regional patterns of production and trade would be restructured. By the late 1960s, the burgeoning garment export trade in east Asia and south Asia once again posed a threat to domestic industries in the developed countries. Domestic protection, while it was promoted, was no longer viable, however, not when multinational companies could have favourable access to cheaper labour overseas, and thereby compete in the cutthroat export market to the West. As mills in the North closed shop, the global sweatshop came into being, and quickly concentrated itself on the low-wage floors of Asia. When Manchester's name finally reappeared on goods, it was no longer to designate the place of manufacture. It was as a logo, in the form of United's football crest, that the name sustained its newfound fame, with Manchester claiming the lion's share of the profit, just as it had once been. However much transformed, the ties with Asia appeared to be as strong as ever.

In their heyday, Manchester's merchants profited, at a distance, from the destitution of Bengal's handloom weavers and the enslavement of Africans who supplied King Cotton from the American South. But they had to physically share their city with the working men and women who formed the world's first industrial proletariat. Marx and Engels largely formed their picture of industrial labour from the appalling working and living conditions of these mill workers. 'In a word,' Engels wrote in his famous account, *Conditions of the Working Classes in England*, 'the workers' dwellings of Manchester are dirty, miserable, and wholly lacking in comforts. In such houses, only inhuman, degraded and unhealthy creatures would feel at home.'[19] In Engels' case, his knowledge came from close observation of Manchester's streets and factories, where he had been sent to work as a manager at his father's own mill in Salford.

Liberal reformers of the era shared Engels' humanitarian concerns for the conditions of the Lancashire labourer, but their sympathies were rarely extended to the Indian plantation workers whose exploitation was the basis of the domestic industry. Manchester free-trade radicals like Richard Cobden and John Bright, who waged war against the Corn Laws for immiserating urban workers, were also at the forefront of the campaign to develop the Indian cotton supply. In that capacity, they paid lip service to the overtaxed plight of the *ryot*, but primarily as a rhetorical vehicle with which to push the local trade agenda of the Manchester industry. When public anxiety about the sweatshop conditions of the Asian labourer surfaced again a century and a half later, a large part of it was fuelled, as before, by concern about the loss of domestic jobs.

So, too, it was focused on the wretched circumstance of teenage women and children in the export processing zones of the offshore garment industry. Engels himself had paid particular attention to the gendered division of factory labour inside the Manchester mills. After the spinning and weaving machinery is installed, 'practically all that is left to be done by hand,' he noted, 'is the piecing together of broken threads, and the machine does the rest.' Since 'this task calls for nimble fingers rather than muscular strength' it is lowly paid 'women and girls alone who work the throstle spindles.' Women, aged from 15 to 20, but rarely any older than that, also dominated the power-looms, 'among the mules,' and 'in the preparatory processes,' while children were to be found everywhere, mounting and taking down the bobbins, and squeezing between machines to gather up discarded material.[20] The manufacturers denied that these patterns of employment existed, and that they were displacing higher-priced men from their livelihoods. Engels' moral condemnation of female factory work still has echoes in contemporary anti-sweatshop literature. In 2001, for example, the National Labour Committee (NLC) surveyed the working conditions of hundreds of thousands of young women employed in Dhaka's export garment factories, producing for the likes of Nike and Reebok, and Wilson. Compared to other countries they had visited, in Bangladesh they found 'the greatest level of exploitation the NLC has ever seen'. Descendants of the Bengali weavers, the Dakha women were 'trapped in abject misery'. Malnourished and abused, they toiled for up to 18 hours a day in overcrowded, unsanitary workplaces: 'By the time they reach 30, most workers leave of their own accord, worn out, exhausted, sick and penniless – or management forces them out so they can be replaced with another crop of young teenage girls.'[21]

Manchester and Dakha had changed their roles. One can only imagine what Engels would have made of a visit to the Old Trafford megastore. In that most peculiar of emporiums, fans of a football club with origins as a factory worker team pay exorbitant prices for cheaply produced goods that are sewn and glued in Asia by the same class of women and children who toiled in the original 'workshop of the world'. Many of the goods are tagged with 'Made in Bangladesh' and 'Made in China', the same countries that were once forced to import machine-made cottons and yarns from Manchester, after the decimation of the Bengali textile industry, and after the gunboat diplomacy that opened China's treaty ports to British concessions in 1842. Economic history can boast few examples with a more profound or ruinous irony.

Notes

1   Alex Fynn and Lynton Guest, *For Love or Money: Manchester United and England – The Business of Winning* (London: Andre Deutsch, 1999), pp. 41–2.
2   See Article 1.6, Manchester United club charter.
3   United had almost been sold to Robert Maxwell, another media tycoon, in the mid-1980s, at the time he had acquired Derby, Oxford and Reading. But the media, at that time, only covered the game. By 1998, Murdoch represented a media complex that funded the game.
4   See the articles by Peter Crowther, Nicholas Finney and Adam Brown on the MMC's decision to block the bid in S. Hamil *et al.* (eds) *Football in the Digital Age: Whose Game is it Anyway?* (Edinburgh: Mainstream, 2000); and A. Brown and A. Walsh,

Not for Sale: Manchester United, Murdoch, and the Defeat of BSkyB (Edinburgh: Mainstream, 1999).

5 Mihir Bose, *Manchester Unlimited: The Rise and Rise of the World's Premier Football Club* (London: Orion, 1999), p. 291. Bose's book presents the most detailed account of the takeover bid. Spearheading the anti-Murdoch campaign were Michael Crick and David Smith, who had authored the first book to capture the disgust of fans with the brash commercialism of the club's directors: *Manchester United: The Betrayal of a Legend* (London: Pelham Books, 1990).

6 Toby Miller, Geoffrey Lawrence, Jim MacKay and David Rowe, *Globalization and Sport: Playing the World* (London: Sage, 2001); John Sugden and Alan Tomlinson, *FIFA and the Contest for World Football: Who Rules the Peoples' Game?* (Cambridge: Polity Press, 1998).

7 Stanley Holmes and Christine Tierney, 'How Nike got its game back', *Business Week* (4 November 2002).

8 'Scum Airways', *The Observer* (17 November 2002).

9 With its stock price in the doldrums, or underpriced, fears of another takeover were rife at the end of 2002. Senior city bankers floated a financial plan to turn Manchester United into a mutual organisation owned solely for the benefit of its fans. Ownership would be in the hands of a mutual trust, whose director would be elected partly by supporters. By the spring of 2003, two Irish turf magnates, J.P. McManus and John Magnier, had steadily increased their holdings through their offshore company, Cubic Expressions, to 10.37 per cent, making them the largest shareholders in the club, and triggering a fresh round of takeover rumours.

10 Jeff Ballinger has been the veteran Nike watchdog, producing invaluable research on the plight of the company's Indonesian workforce. Only under intense public pressure did Nike issue a 'Code of Conduct' and take steps to justify its refusal to take responsibility for the brutal labour practices of its subcontractors. See Jeff Ballinger and Claes Olsson (eds) *Behind the Swoosh: The Struggle of Indonesians Making Nike Shoes* (Upsala: Global Publications, 1997). In other Asian countries, Vietnam Labour Watch, Hong Kong Christian Industrial Committee, Asia Monitor Resource Center, China Labour Watch and Global Exchange have all applied monitoring pressure through their exposés of the company. With the help of No Sweat, the UK anti-sweatshop organisation, SU was able to host one of the best selections of Nike watchdog resources on its website, at http://www.shareholdersunited.org. For other web resources, see 'Academics studying Nike' at http://cbae.nmsu.edu/~dboje/nike/nikemain.html. However, the Nike campaign no longer seems to be an active interest on the part of SU. There is no mention of it on SU's refurbished website.

11 Sydney Schanberg, 'Six cents an hour', *Life* (June 1996), pp. 38–48.

12 Hong Kong Christian Industrial Committee, 'Report on the working conditions of soccer and football workers in mainland China' (Hong Kong; Hong Kong Christian Industrial Committee; revised version, May 2002). Over the years, the Clean Clothes Campaign has brought pressure to bear on sportswear giants like Adidas and, along with Global March Against Child Labour, took on FIFA, through their Euro 2000 and World Cup 2002 campaigns. See http://www.cleanclothes.org.

13 The World Cup 2002 campaign is summarised at http://www.globalmarch.org/world-cup-campaign/.

14 *News of the World*, 15 March 1998.

15 Edward Baines, *History of the Cotton Manufacture in Great Britain* (London: Fisher, Fisher and Jackson, 1835) especially Chapter VI.

16 Lajpat Rai, *England's Debt to India: A Historical Narrative of Britain's Fiscal Policy in India* (New York: Huebsch, 1917) p. 135. Horace Wilson points out in his notes to James Mill's *The History of British India*: 'Had not such prohibitory duties and decrees existed, the mills of Paisley and Manchester would have been stopped in their outset and could scarcely have been set in motion even by the power of steam. They were

created by the sacrifice of Indian manufacture.' Quoted in Noam Chomsky, *Year 501: The Conquest Continues* (Boston: South End, 1993), p. 14.

17 The story of the campaign for an Indian cotton supply is told in detail by Arthur Silver, *Manchester Men and Indian Cotton, 1847–1871* (Manchester: Manchester University Press, 1966). Also see Arthur Redford, *Manchester Merchants and Foreign Trade 1794–1939* (Manchester: Manchester University Press, 1956), 2 Volumes.

18 Cited in Chomsky, ibid., p. 12.

19 Friedrich Engels, *The Condition of the Working Classes in England* (1845), translated and edited by W.O. Henderson and W.H. Chaloner (Oxford: Basil Blackwell, 1958), 'The great towns', p. 75.

20 Ibid., p. 158.

21 National Labour Committee, *Bangladesh: The Struggle to End the Race to the Bottom* (New York: NLC, 2001), p. iii.

6 Misers, merchandise and Manchester United

The peculiar paradox of the political economy of consumption

Carlton Brick

> Less than a month after thousands of youngsters pulled on their favourite club jersey at Christmas, the men who run the club ordered the Red Devils to trot out in blue at Southampton. Loyalty doesn't seem to be enough any more; rather it is exploited to make us pay more ... Which brings me to my fear that the values that make soccer the people's game are being eroded.
>
> (Tony Blair, quoted in *The Guardian*, 11 September 1998: 22)

Whilst the global explosion in the consumption of replica team merchandising may have filled the coffers of manufacturers, sponsors and club superstores alike, there is an argument that it has brought only problems for sport, corrupting and corroding the authentic and communal identities that have been nurtured by the ties of history and tradition. Such a claim has a particularly embittered resonance within the cultures of English professional football, and Manchester United undoubtedly its most celebrated *bête noire*. This chapter examines the issue of consumption within the political economy of English soccer. It focuses upon the ways and means through which the replica shirt functions within particular fan cultures surrounding Manchester United as a signifier of (in)authentic loyalty.[1] Key within these discourses are the themes of conspicuous nonconsumption. Žižek (2001) draws attention to the 'miserly' nature of capitalism, whereby abstinence and self-denial become dominant market motifs. These are strong themes within cultures of Manchester United fandom. The chapter locates these themes within broader discourses of modern anti-capitalism, and ideologies of consumer regulation. The chapter concludes that the politicisation of consumption within English football is premised upon a conservative demand for restraint, which corresponds with, rather than resists, the dominant ideology of contemporary capitalism.

The cultural politics of value

The replica shirt has been a notable feature of the commercial maturation of English football. This chapter investigates the competing politics of value (Appadurai, 2000: 6) that are played out through the consumption of football merchandise. Within a rapidly commercialised and commodified culture, commodities are produced as a source of symbolic (sign) value, rather than as use or exchange values (Baudrillard, 1998, 2000). In this sense commodities are no longer produced simply for exchange, but take on and become the embodiments of emotional and aesthetic values that transcend traditional conceptions of the capitalist market. In turn commodities are imbued with cultural significance by which social relationships and identities are constructed and demarcated. It is the central argument of this chapter that a dominant expression of the consumption of English football is mediated through a contested politics of value – between pecuniary value and emotional/aesthetic value. Furthermore the war of values is dominated by an ideology of temperance and frugality. These forms of consumption utilise the commodity (the replica shirt) as markers of inauthentic and excessive consumption and provide a vivid example of the contemporary form of commodity fetishism. Marx (1983: 76–87) suggests that whilst the commodity appears as a straightforward and seemingly trivial thing, it reveals itself as a profoundly complex and contradictory network of relationships. Via the theoretical standpoint of dialectical materialism, Marx outlined how, through the capitalistic production of commodities, actual social relationships between humans manifest themselves and appear as their direct contradiction, the paradoxical (anti-social) relationship between things. Žižek (1989: 24) has elucidated the importance of this theory, noting the tendency towards 'misrecognition' that arises out of the fetishistic nature of the commodity. The act of 'misrecognition' that the theory of commodity fetishism exposes (Žižek, 1989) – that active social relationships between humans appear as the passive relationship between things in commodity form – does not take place solely in the 'relation between things' but also occurs in the 'relation between men': passive relationships between things assumes the appearance of the active relationship between humans. This can be seen in the ideological and intellectual 'cultural turn'. For example, the anthropologist Appaduari (2000: 3) equates the commodity with human sociability, suggesting that commodities '... like persons have social lives' and '... can characterise many different kinds of thing, at different points in their social lives', In essence, within capitalistic forms of production (of meanings) the social relationships between humans not only *appear* as though they are relationships between things in commodity form, but *actually* are relationships between things in commodity form.

The act of misrecognition embodied within commodity capitalism lies at the heart of the political economy of consumption in English football and the discursive contestations of fandom played out through the clash of values (pecuniary and the aesthetic/emotional). This misrecognition operates at two levels. The first concerns the overestimation of the role played by the manufacture and sale of club merchandising (such as the replica shirt) as an exchange value (source of profit) and as a use value. The second act of misrecognition concerns the unquestioned assumption that the cultural politics of consumption, or more accurately the politics of anti-consumption, offers a legitimate point of resistance to the processes of commodification and capitalistic accumulation.

Merchandise United: misrecognising exchange value

As a corporate entity, Manchester United has gained a reputation as a ruthless exploiter of its consumer base. Referred to in some quarters as 'Merchandise United', the club has in recent years seemingly embarked on the cynical production of a veritable rainbow of team strips and a plethora of branded 'tat'.[2] There are four points of misrecognition pertinent to the themes of this chapter. First, misrecognition of the role of the replica shirt and merchandising as an exchange value within the economy of football. Second, a misrecognition, especially within official discourses, of the use value of the replica shirt/merchandising within cultures of fandom – it is generally assumed that there is a linear relationship between the commodity and fan loyalty, i.e. the purchase of a replica shirt signifies loyalty to a particular club by the consumer. This reading is undermined by dominant fan cultures surrounding Manchester United. The third and fourth aspects of misrecognition relate to wider questions of the commodification of culture and the forms of resistance to these processes. I will look at each of these points of misrecognition in turn.

There has been a tendency to overestimate the importance of replica shirt and merchandising sales in the accumulation of revenue by clubs. But, this said, it should be noted that as a concept the exchange value of the commodity retains a particular discursive significance within the contestations of football culture.

Szymanski and Kuypers (2000: 39) have noted the recent expansion in football-related video market and leisurewear, of which the replica kit is an integral element. In 1996 Manchester United topped domestic replica shirt sales, shifting about 850,000 units – some 250,000 more than any other club and 350,000 more than England. This unprecedented position might suggest that this is an important avenue of revenue for the club. Whilst merchandising and the replica shirt may appear to have played a key role in the economic transformation of English football, commentators urge caution. According to Dempsey and Reilly (1998: 277), diversification and increasing commercial activity via merchandising are relatively safe ways for football clubs to accrue profit. It is initially less demanding of capital investment (as compared to the building of hotels, conference centres and stadium upgrades etc.), with costs being underwritten by a clothing manufacturer who pays for the right to produce the products. As a result, the club actually takes the smallest cut of any sales revenue: 8 per cent, compared to 22 per cent taken by the manufacturer, 22 per cent by factory costs, and the largest slice of 32 per cent going to the retailer. Even the state takes a bigger slice than the club,:16 per cent in value-added tax (VAT) (Szymanski and Kuypers 2000: 72). Figures are based upon the sale price of £37.99 for a Reebok Liverpool shirt).

The income generated by Manchester United through merchandising, £11.4 million (for the year 2002) accounts for only 7 per cent of overall turnover. Despite popular prejudice, gate receipts still account for the majority share of Manchester United's income, comprising 39 per cent of total turnover (Manchester United plc 2002: 1). Furthermore, whilst the merchandising market may be a relatively cost-effective area for generating income, it is an extremely volatile one, and contrary to common belief it is not a market area that will just simply go on growing (Dempsey and Reilly 1998: 278–9). For the year 2002, Manchester United's club turnover increased by 13 per cent on the previous year to £146.1 million. At the same time merchandising turnover fell by almost £8 million on the previous year's figures. Similar trends can be seen at other clubs such as Newcastle United, another club explicitly associated with the sale of the replica shirt. Reasons for this relative decline in merchandising income are related to the peculiarities of the market itself. Dempsey and Reilly (1998) contend that the relatively low base and short time span within which the merchandising industry has developed has resulted in an overestimation of the consumer base for such products, and an underestimation of 'customer resistance'. Football consumers will not go on buying everything and anything that has a club badge stamped on it.

'That shirt is everything, wear it with pride':[3] misrecognising use value

It is to the issue of 'customer resistance' and its relationship to notions of supporter loyalty that I now turn. Whilst as noted above the replica shirt has been misrecognised as a source of income, its value as a site of contestation sits at the heart of the narratives of contemporary fan subjectivity. In December 1999, the Football Task Force reported that:

> ...[The Football Task Force] believes that merchandising is an issue [that] demonstrates the balance to be struck by football clubs in their relationships with their supporters. Merchandising has been a success because supporters have wanted to buy their clubs' products and wear them proudly. They are an expression of support and loyalty.
>
> (Football Task Force, 1999: Para. 6.4)

Such sentiments are echoed elsewhere in the official socio-political discourse of modern football:

> The temptation to exploit what is essentially a monopoly position has not always been resisted. Football supporters do not shop around like casual buyers. Parents do not tell their children that they cannot have the Tottenham shirt they want but must settle for an Arsenal one because it is on special offer.
>
> (Smith and Le Jeune, 1998: Para. 2.10)

For soccer officialdom, the replica shirt conveys a fairly straightforward and unproblematic relationship between the consumer and the club – one of unremitting loyalty and devotion (which is subsequently exploited by the club). The mono consumptive loyalty of the fan is echoed in academic sociological and economic accounts. King (1998: 141) compares the consumptive practices of fans of pop bands with those of football clubs. The football fan:

... shows remarkable monomania. Most fans of pop bands own records of other bands or see other bands playing, while the dedicated football fan of a football club will exclusively attend matches of that club and purchase only that club's merchandise.

(King, 1998: 141)

But the relationships assumed within the monomanic consumption of merchandising, suggested above, are undermined by actual consumer practice within fan cultures. It is not the case that the so-called 'dedicated fan' will exclusively attend matches of that club and purchase only that club's merchandising. For example, the Bayern Munich flags, shirts and scarves worn by fans of Liverpool prior to the European Champions League Final between Manchester United and the German club in 1999, is informed by their dedicated allegiance to Liverpool and the voracity of their rivalry with Manchester United within the (sub)cultural capital of Liverpool fandom. Nor can it be taken for granted that the wearing of a team's shirt should be interpreted as a sign of committed loyalty and support.

Within the folklore of contemporary football, Newcastle United supporters have the reputation for being amongst the most loyal and most passionate. This passion is manifest in the wearing of the Newcastle United replica shirt. Within Manchester United fan cultures, Newcastle fans' consumption of club merchandising is read, not as a sign of loyalty and passion, but as their opposites. The Manchester United fanzine, *United We Stand*, frequently refers to the supporters of Newcastle United as 'Geordie Muppets'. This 'muppetry' characterises Newcastle United fandom as the unreflexive and atavistic consumption of contemporary football, dependant upon commodities (the replica shirt) as the sole and soulless expression of loyalty.

'Bandwagon-jumping, glory-hunting twats ... sod off'?[4]

It is not only rival club fandoms that Manchester United fanzines decry as commodity dependent. Similar spleen is vented upon sections of Manchester United support itself. Terms such as 'day trippers' and 'glory hunters' have become a shorthand by which forms of conspicuous consumption are decried as wanting, disloyal and illegitimate. The greatest act of disloyalty to United is to shop at the showpiece club megastore, the unrepentant monument to the part of the club that has sold its soul to the lure of global lucre:

Is there anyone who still doesn't get some sort of feeling or emotion stirring up inside of them as they approach the ground? I doubt it very much, unless you are carrying 47 mega-store bags and sporting a painted face, complete with jester's hat, whilst complaining that the club should run courtesy buses from the mega-store directly to your turnstile or lounge entrance.

(*Red Issue*, 32, April 2000: 27)

In its January 1999 issue, *Red Issue* carried a full colour parody of the merchandise-buying, 'so-called' United fan on its inside cover. It shows a photograph of a United (non)fan wearing a white away replica shirt, holding in each hand a Manchester United megastore carrier bag. Significantly, a third megastore carrier bag is pulled over the (non)fan's head, rendering him/her featureless, unidentifiable and obscure – a faceless consumer, more of a product of the club's marketing strategies than the deeply and historically informed emotions of 'authentic' fandom. This ersatz, atavistic and success-based consumption of the club brand is portrayed as the antithesis of the loyal matchgoing Red.

Desire, excess and frugal fandoms

Mickey, a 30-something season-ticket holder from Manchester, and match-going regular for some 20 years, resents the club's courting of a geographically distant but affluent consumer:

> ... my wish is that more local people should be given access to tickets by the club. You can't even go to the ground, walk to the ground and buy a ticket. It's all postal applications. It's hopeless. It's annoying when it's your local club and you've got to apply and stand the same chance of getting a ticket as someone from the southeast or Norway and elsewhere, who spend most of the day in the megastore.
>
> (Mickey, personal interview, March 1999)

Whilst Mickey constructs the reorganisation of the club's ticketing operations as discriminating against the local fans in favour of distant consumers, it is actually the formal non-discriminatory nature of these procedures that sits at the heart of Mickey's objections, and those of many fans like him. Access to match tickets at Manchester United is conducted through postal and Internet applications, whereby members can apply for tickets (due to frequent oversubscription, a ballot is usually held). This most recent season (at the time of writing), substantial changes have also been made to the way in which tickets for away games are allocated. Previously, away tickets went on sale to season-ticket holders, based on attendance at away games. The system now operates a new loyalty scheme whereby applications for away tickets (usually 2000 for Premier League games) are entered into a ballot. Entry into the ballot is determined by the season-ticket holders' regular attendance at home league games. The club estimates that there are some 18,000 season-ticket holders who meet the criteria, and argues that it is much more just and transparent, allowing supporters previously out of the away-ticket loop to overcome the catch 22: denied access to away tickets because they haven't attended away fixtures (via official formal routes). Such mechanisms cut across the 'traditional' privileging of 'local' consumers, but rather than privileging of a 'distant' consumer, there has been an actual formal democratisation of access to Manchester United.

Each application is equal, there is no privileging of geographical locale – each fan has the same formal equality of access and exclusion. Using the notion of 'autocolonisation', Žižek argues that global capitalism reformulates the relationships between the colonising functions of capital and the nation state. Within this reformulation, there is at a formal level at least a potentiality towards the 'democratisation' of what have been previously particularistic identities within the market place:

> ... with the direct multinational functioning of Capital, we are no longer dealing with the standard opposition between metropolis and colonised countries; a global company, as it were, cuts its umbilical cord with its mothernation and treats its country of origin as simply another territory to be colonised ... the new multinationals have exactly the same attitude towards the local population as towards the [non local] population.
>
> (Žižek, 1999: 215)

It is this equality, implicit in the new global consumer market, which feeds the popular disquiet towards the commodification of sporting culture, which finds expression and solace in the myths of exclusion and authentic particularism. Whilst supporting United since the age of 12 (1988–9), Tony, a Londoner, only began to attend games on a regular basis during the late 1990s. Whilst issues of money, income, travel and parental influence (Tony comes from a nonfootballing family) have undoubtedly influenced Tony's pattern of support, he offers a striking counter to the assumed favouritism of the club's new ticketing arrangements against the local fan base implied by Mickey. In the following, Tony places emphasis on networks of 'knowing' and the difficulties of negotiating and becoming part of such networks. For Tony, his geographical distance from Manchester exacerbates these problems rather than resolves them:

> I started going regularly the season of 1999–2000, because obviously before that I had no means of knowing about the membership scheme, and basically, finding out about how to get tickets. Obviously it's different for a London club like Chelsea, Tottenham or someone like that. The problem with United is that there are certain ways of finding out. It's not easy to find out unless you know somebody or know somebody who knows somebody, you know. You can't just go like that. You ring up the club and it's all recorded info. The only people you can actually speak to are in the mail order shop. You can become a member but that's no guarantee of actually getting to see United.
>
> (Tony, personal interview, July 2000)

The subsequent efforts made by Tony to 'find out' and become a part of the networks of 'knowing' have become the core elements of his fandom:

> I became a member at the end of 1999–2000 season. Yeah, but it's much more than that. I've always wanted to be a member, but it's about becoming involved.

> Like pushing yourself, making an effort to find out, making the time, really pushing yourself to get yourself into a position where you can get tickets, start planning how you're going to get to Manchester. It's not like you can just go down to the ground, is it? Tickets, transport all have to be planned.
>
> (Tony, personal interview, July 2000)

Via an opposition to the erosion of his formerly privileged position as a local consumer, Mickey constructs a notion of the loyal supporter reflected in the United fanzines – predicated against the conspicuous consumption of United as a branded product:

> I'm probably one of the supporters they [Manchester United plc] hate because I go to Old Trafford [on match days] and drink in the local pubs. We get the Metro down there, go in, have a sing song and a few beers, a laugh, and then after the match go back to the pub. That's all we do. We don't buy any of the commercial stuff, shirts and all that. I don't wear a [replica] shirt, a scarf, badge or anything like that. I haven't bought a programme for years. None of the lads do. I don't even buy refreshments at the ground, always outside if I have to. I follow the team, I don't particularly follow the club.
>
> (Mickey, personal interview, March 1999)

According to Tony, on the other hand, his consumption of Manchester United merchandising is a reward for the time and dedication he has shown in becoming an 'active supporter':

> For a while I didn't buy stuff. But mainly I always get the end-of-season video. I've got a few shirts. I've started buying them more now, because I'm more of an active supporter now. I wasn't going to games, I wasn't bothering to buy the shirt.
>
> (Tony, personal interview, July 2000)

The time, dedication and loyalty that both Mickey and Tony devote to Manchester United are expressed in seemingly oppositional ways. Mickey's fandom consciously shuns the commodified aspects of modern football, such as merchandising and the replica shirt. Tony consciously embraces these aspects, as symbolic manifestations of his dedicated support and love for his club. Whilst seemingly oppositional, both positions express fundamental consistencies. Both are entirely conspicuous in their unswerving devotion to Manchester United. Furthermore, the notions of abstinence and self-denial that run through Mickey's – and the United fanzines' – conceptualisations of an authentic support (and which I would argue are consistent with the sensibilities of more generalised expression of the post-Hillsborough fan movement) express the same desires and excesses embedded in the consumer-orientated fandom of Tony. Whilst Mickey's fandom might be conceptualised as thrifty or frugal, and rhetorically opposes the 'excessive' and atavistic hedonism of the commodity-orientated subjectivity of the new consumer, the desires that inform his frugal consumption are consistent with, and as excessive as, those of the consumerist 'hedonism' of a merchandise-buying fan like Tony. This relationship expresses what Žižek (2001) refers to as the 'paradox of the Miser'. It is this paradox that sits at the heart of football's contemporary political economy. Žižek (2001: 40) suggests:

> The paradox of the Miser, however, is that *he makes an excess out of moderation itself*. That is to say: the standard description of desire focuses on its transgressive character: ethics (in the premodern sense of the 'art of living') is ultimately the ethics of moderation, of resisting the urge to go beyond certain limits, of a resistance against desire which is, by definition, transgressive – sexual passion which consumes me totally; gluttony; destructive passion which does not stop even at murder ... In contrast to this transgressive notion of desire, the Miser invests moderation itself with desire (and thus with a quality of excess) ... And it is only *this* desire, the very anti-desire, that is desire *par excellence*.
>
> [original emphasis]

Žižek adds that this paradox finds its most explicit expression in contemporary consumer capitalism:

> This basic paradox enables us to generate even phenomena like the most elementary marketing strategy, which is to appeal to consumer's thrift: is not the ultimate message of advertising slots 'Buy this, spend more, and *you will economize*, you will get extra free!'? ... The embodiment of this surplus is the toothpaste tube whose last third is differently coloured, with 'YOU GET 30% FREE!' in large letters ... In capitalism the *definition* of the 'proper price' is a *discount price*. The worn-out designation 'consumer society' thus holds only if one conceives of consumption as the mode of appearance of its very opposite, thrift.
>
> (Žižek, 2001: 44, original emphasis)

The themes of abstinence and self-denial that inform particular expressions of resistant soccer fandom mirror this tendency. This frugal sensibility is predicated upon the excessive desire to consume football in its most Spartan and basic forms as possible. The more frugal the consumption, the greater and more excessive the expression of love, loyalty and devotion. Within this discourse, the excess of '... consumption is only allowed in so far as it functions as the form of appearance of its opposite' (Žižek, 2001: 46). That is, as a non-consumption.

Towards a critique of the new temperance

There are wider political inferences to be drawn from the explorations into football's consumer culture outlined above. As noted, a prominent expression of this culture is a particular anti-consumptive stance that espouses the ethos of abstinence and temperance. The demand for consumptive temperance and consumer restraint has become synonymous with the rise of the modern anti-capitalist and anti-globalisation movements in recent years. Jeremiad tales of the evils of rampant consumerism, such as Naomi Klein (2001, 2002), Kalle Lasn (1999) and George Monbiot (2000), top the bestseller list. Their core argument is that the state should forcibly restrain individual consumers and the corporations that sell to them. There is nothing new in the attempt to mobilise the notion of temperance as a point of political agitation and resistance, but the new temperance movement bears little similarity to the aims and ideologies of their historical forebears of the nineteenth and early twentieth centuries. Fissures of difference emerge when considering the respective movements' relationships to notions of the public and political spheres.

Whilst the temperance movement of the nineteenth and early twentieth centuries has been characterised as particularly conservative and puritan in its outlook, as suggested by Wagner (1997), there can be little doubt that the key dynamic behind the movement was the wider struggle for political emancipation and social change that shaped the late nineteenth century's political landscape. It was via the temperance movement that women forced their way into the public arena of political debate (Zollinger Giel, 1995; Tyrell, 1991). Indeed the temperance movement in the United States contributed much to the struggle for racial egalitarianism (Fahey, 1996). In a British context temperance echoed similar emancipatory demands sitting at the ideological heart of the Chartist movement, repeal of the Corn Laws and the demands for Home Rule in Ireland (Malcolm, 1986). In contrast, the temperance of the social movements of the twentieth century is characterised by an explicit retraction of the public domain. Indeed some advocates of consumer restraint argue that the slide into the consumerist and commodified hell that now characterises modern living is a direct consequence of the expansion of the public domain. In her essay 'The new politics of consumption: Why Americans want so much more than they need', Juliet Schor argues that the social and inspirational emancipation of women and subsequent entry into the American white-collar workforce during the 1950s and 1960s resulted in the collapse of community and neighbourhood, paving the way for the mass consumerisation of social relations (Schor, 2000). Far from echoing the demands for temperance of the past, the retreat from the social that characterises the modern anti-consumption sensibility degrades the concept. In a Platonist sense, temperance, the virtue of moderation and self-control, should not only be adhered to by individuals but also by the state in its actions.

State regulation is an implicit demand of the modern advocates of anti-capitalism. Indeed contemporary anti-capitalism's conceptualisation of the state is more Hegelian than Marxist, seeing it as a neutral and emancipatory (although temporarily corrupted) force, sitting above and beyond the interests of global capital, rather than as the prime mechanism through which the interests of capital are achieved. The demand for the state regulation of excessive behaviours and actions is echoed in the world of English soccer. Whether it be the criminalisation of 'abusive' spectator behaviour, or the regulation of the game's economic and commercial development, there is an unprecedented emphasis placed upon the need for restraint – apart from that it is the state who is given free reign to corral and police an ever-expanding domain of social activity. The cultures of soccer fandom that have emerged in a British context in recent years, of which the discussion of Manchester United provides a vivid example, offer salient illustration of the fundamental paradox that lies at the heart of contemporary global capitalism. Via the notion of temperance, radical postures of resistance are struck against the increasingly commodified experience of soccer culture. But these postures resemble little other than illusory myths, as they mirror exactly the ways in which contemporary capitalist cultures operate. This is the tragic paradox of English football's political economy of consumption – positions of resistance, in all eventualities, are positions of acquiescent compliance.

Notes

1 The interviews used in this chapter are drawn from an ethnographic study of Manchester United fandom and the consumption of English football. Interviews were carried out between January 1999 and May 2000. In the interests of respondent confidentiality, names have been changed.
2 Hunter Davies, *The Guardian*, 4 April 1994.
3 John Sadler, *The Sun*, 18 March 1998.
4 *Red News*, 57, 1998.

References

Appadurai, A. (ed.) (2000) *The Social Life of Things*, Cambridge: Cambridge University Press.
Baudrillard, J. (1998) *The Consumer Society: Myths and Structures*, London: Sage.
Baudrillard, J. (2000) *Death and Symbolic Exchange*, London: Sage.
Dempsey, P. and Reilly, K. (1998) *Big Money, Beautiful Fame: Saving Football From Itself*, London: Nicholas Brealey.
Fahey, D.M. (1996) *Temperance and Racism. John Bull, Johnny Reb, and the Good Templars*, Lexington: University Press of Kentucky.
Football Task Force (1999) *Football: Commercial Issues*. A submission by the Football Task Force to the Minister for Sport, 22 December 1999, London: Football Task Force.
King, A. (1998) *The End of the Terraces: The Transformation of English Football in the 1990s*, London: Leicester University Press.
Klein, N. (2001) *No Logo*, London: Flamingo.
Klein, N. (2002) *Fences and Windows*, London: Flamingo.
Lasn, K. (1999) *Culture Jamming*, New York: HarperCollins.
Malcolm, E. (1986) *Ireland Sober, Ireland Free: Drink and Temperance in Nineteenth Century Ireland*, Dublin: Gill and Macmillan.
Manchester United plc (2002) *Not Just a Football Club*. Annual Report, Manchester: Manchester United plc.
Marx, K. (1983) *Capital: A Critique of Political Economy*. Volume 1, London: Lawrence and Wishart.

Monbiot, G. (2000) *The Captive State: The Corporate Takeover of Britain*, London: Pan.

Schor, J. (2000) 'The new politics of consumption: why Americans want so much more than they need', *Boston Review*, available online at http://bostonreview.mit.edu/BR24.3/schor.htm/.

Smith, Sir John and Le Jeune, M. (1998) *Football: Its Values, Finances and Reputations.* Report to the Football Association, London: Football Association.

Szymanski, S. and Kuypers, T. (2000) *Winners and Losers: The Business Strategy of Football*, London: Penguin.

Tyrell, I. (1991) *Woman's World, Woman's Empire: The Woman's Christian Temperance Union in International Perspective 1880–1930*, Chapel Hill: University of North Carolina Press.

Wagner, D. (1997) *The New Temperance: The American Obsession with Sin and Vice*, Boulder, CO: West View Press.

Žižek, S. (1989) *The Sublime Object of Ideology*, London: Verso.

Žižek, S. (1999) *The Ticklish Subject: The Absent Centre of Political Ontology*, London: Verso.

Žižek, S. (2001) *Did Somebody Say Totalitarianism? Five Interventions in the (Mis) Use of a Notion*, London: Verso.

Zollinger Giele, J. (1995) *Two Paths to Women's Equality: Temperance, Suffrage and the Origins of Modern Feminism*, New York: Twayne Publishers.

7   Red and black

Inside Manchester United's underground economy

John Sugden

Association Football's[1] world governing body, the International Federation of Football Associations (FIFA), estimates that, through legitimate commercial activities alone, globally the game it oversees generates in excess of US$250 billion, a sum greater than the gross national product of many medium-size countries and equivalent to that of the biggest transnational companies (Sugden and Tomlinson, 1998). The UK's share of this market is immense, with the English Premier Division alone generating in excess of $15 billion. Manchester United, the League's flagship commercial enterprise, is the richest club in the world, with an annual turnover in excess of $150 million (Boon *et al.*, 2000). Between them, David Conn's *The Football Business* (1997) and Tom Bower's *Broken Dreams* (2003) exposed English football's pernicious, but nonetheless legitimate, enterprise culture. This chapter provides an insider-based resumé of football's other business – it's extraordinarily lucrative underground economy.

Unaccounted for, in the shadows of the world's most popular game and beyond the control of the world's richest clubs, there is a huge, illegitimate commercial culture. Counterfeit replica kits and related 'snide' clothing (as the insiders call faked designer apparel), all manner of unapproved football memorabilia, unlicensed catering operations, the ticket touting industry, and the independent travel business, are the main features of this black and grey market. This essay centres on the activities of a group of Manchester grafters – people who make their living working the black economy – whose gang the author gained access to and tracked between 1998 and 2002.

A note on method

What follows is based upon a more extensive piece of work that provided the basis for the book, *Scum Airways: Inside Football's Underground Economy* (Sugden, 2002). This is a study of a deviant subculture in the classic social anthropological/ ethnographic and interpretative traditions evidenced in the work of figures such as Becker (1963); Maurer (1964); Polsky (1967); Parker (1974); Willis (1977); and Robins (1984). It also draws heavily on the investigative tradition. Classic subcultural studies by Robert Park and his contemporaries in the Chicago School in the 1920s and 1930s were in part dependent upon the methods of investigative and muck-raking journalism. In the 1960s and 1970s, Jack Douglas at the University of California retrieved this tradition, arguing that any valid critique of what is really going on must go beyond passive observation and embrace the investigative (Douglas, 1976: 12).

To get at multiple truths, direct observation necessarily goes beyond gazing at the surface. Douglas's research strategy is based upon the assumption that everyday social life has a tendency to be duplicitous: that individuals and groups construct and present images of who they are and what they do that can mask underpinning social realities (Douglas, 1976: 55). His view of the nature of social life is framed by his experience of researching relatively microscopic, albeit 'deviant', sub-cultures. However, his basic principles can be taken to apply to all walks of life. He does not believe that all people are fraudulent all of the time, but he does maintain that even the most trivial areas of social interaction can be distorted through combinations of misinformation, evasions, outright lies and stage management or 'front'. He argues that social research must account for this and advocates mixed methodologies that are simultaneously 'cooperative and investigative' (Douglas, 1976: 56) – that is, methodologies that take note of self-generated and freely given legends, but that also subject such 'official histories' to scrutiny from a multitude of vantage points.

If Douglas's arguments are relevant for studies of the everyday, they are even more important when it comes to researching marginal areas of social life where secrecy and deception are key principles (Sugden and Tomlinson, 2002: 12–14). In such circumstances not only is it necessary for the researcher to adopt an investigative position, it may also be required that the investigator undertake a participant role that is at least partially covert. It was with these principles in mind that the author entered the world of the Manchester grafters.

The grafters' game

Big Tommy's nickname is without irony. At 6 feet 4 inches and 23 stone (322 lbs), he is a big man. He used to be a lot heavier, weighing in closer to 30 stone (420 lbs). Despite dieting, he's still more bouncy castle than brick outhouse, and his ample gut constantly struggles to escape the confines of his trousers. Tommy's in his early forties, but his round, fresh face makes him look closer to 30. This deception is reinforced by a high-pitched voice, making his broad Manchester accent sound as if it belongs to a minor soap opera star. In this realm, *Only Fools and Horses* merges with *The Sopranos* around football. It is a gathering place for ticket touts, counterfeiters, con men, petty thieves, drug dealers, hooligans, neo-Nazis and a few even more serious criminals, some of whom are all of the above.

Penetrating this world is difficult. Understandably, its gatekeepers are suspicious of outsiders, as many of their activities are at best marginal to the law and sometimes illegal. In this case, I made my breakthrough in Marseilles in 1998 when I inveigled my way into Big Tommy's gang as they enjoyed a rare day off from their World Cup ticket-touting activities on a small island off the French coast (Sugden 2002: 17–31). Even on the inside, early understanding is hampered by a coded language or tout-speak: a mixture of back slang, cockney rhyming slang, market-stall tic-tac, and the touts' own invented gibberish. Tickets are 'briefs' or 'bits', the latter being the general term for any commodity or unit of gear up for sale, whether it is a ticket, a T-shirt or a sleeve of 200 cigarettes. 'Cat' is short for category and is associated with the range and calibre of tickets available. Any counterfeit good, from forged tickets to fake replica shirts, are known as 'snides'. Firms are hooligan gangs made of 'the Lads' – hooligan generals and their foot soldiers. Terms like 'pony', 'monkey', 'wonna', 'carpet', 'chink' and 'rouf' are used to talk about different prices. Making a good profit is often referred to as 'having a good drink' or 'having a good butty'.

As well as the distinctive lingo, everybody in this trade seems to have nicknames. Collectively they refer to themselves as 'grafters', 'spivs', 'swag-workers', and the obvious 'touts'. Then there are individual pseudonyms: Rat; the Short-arm-typist; Jimmy the Mac, Rocket, Fat Vinnie, Lardy Les, Tunes, Sailor, Alehouse, Porno Kev, and, of course, Big Tommy. Using nicknames and coded language protects the gang's anonymity and means that they can negotiate prices with one another – usually via mobile phones – in front of punters without them having the faintest idea of what the mark-up is likely to be. Big Tommy is a key player in and gatekeeper to this grafters' subculture. He is not some latter-day Fagan who rules this rogues' gallery, but the deals he does, places he goes to and wheels he sets in motion guarantee that sooner or later he will rub shoulders with all of them.

Big Tommy grew up in north Manchester's Cheetham Hill where he was born in 1962, beneath the brooding shadow of Strangeways Prison, in a street of terraced houses squeezed between the city centre's commercial and business districts and the factories, warehouses and industrial parks to the north. He was born in the 'never had it so good' 1960s, but grew up in one of the most traumatic periods in the northern capital's rich social and economic history. In his childhood he witnessed the final decline of Manchester's Victorian industrial infrastructure, as one by one the mills and factories closed down around him. In his teenage years the Thatcher years were on the horizon. The deindustrialisation of Britain accelerated so that by the time he left school the factories, mills and engineering works where generations of working-class kids had served their apprenticeships as turners, weavers, mechanics and cabinet makers had all gone.

By the time he was 15 the neighbourhood had degenerated and was well on its way to becoming key turf in the city's combat zone. 'Those days,' remembers Tommy, 'all the kids were at it, mainly for fun, messing about, but 15 out of 20 of them would grow up to be villains.' Like most of his mates, Tommy left school at 16 with no formal qualifications and little or no prospect of getting a decent job. Tommy was always clever, but in a street-wise rather than scholarly fashion. He landed and lost a series of low-paid, semi-skilled and unskilled jobs, interspersed with periods on the dole. But in Manchester, Tommy's generation of working-class kids refused to lie down and passively accept their roles as Thatcher's sacrifice to monetarism. Not when, only a few miles away, in Manchester's regenerating city centre, they could see a parallel generation of

Yuppies getting richer and richer on the back of their misery. Where extravagance and affluence are found shoulder to shoulder with depression and poverty, something has to give. The friction between the rich and the poor in Manchester generated a creative, survivalist energy that sparked its own youth-cultural revolution. This revolution moved in many directions, simultaneously feeding a divergent, entrepreneurial culture. Its clearest and loudest expression came in the music and dance industries. In the 1980s the city earned its reputation as Madchester, a name that reflected its image as a boom–bust, happening, frontier city

Manchester became a national leader in popular culture. It dominated the rock-and-roll scene and was the home of post-punk, superstar bands like Joy Division, Simply Red, the Smiths, the Happy Mondays and Oasis. The development of its Gay Village meant that Manchester rivalled Brighton as the gay capital of Britain. With the Hacienda at its hub, 1980s Manchester also boasted the best nightlife in the country and became the epicentre of the rave and acid-house dance scene. This was a culture of youthful hedonism and consumption towards which a generation of unemployed grafters from the city's run-down council estates were drawn like wasps to an open jam pot. To hell with life on the dole or the minimum wage in a biscuit factory; what was an orgy of consumption for many could be a good business opportunity for a few others. There were T-shirts to be knocked up and knocked out at rock concerts; raves and acid house parties to organise and supply with ecstasy; and there were other, harder drugs to be bought and sold. As Dave Haslam, a former disc jockey at the Hacienda Club argues, the new-era Spivs were drawing on a rich heritage, 'These young creative characters continue to draw strength from their own self-belief and the city's traditions of DIY [do-it-yourself] youth culture. Perhaps there still lingers in them the spirit of the old street hustlers, amateur Houdinis, and hawkers living on in the modern-day grafters in Salford, Manchester and beyond, selling a bit of this, pushing stuff, moving in' (Haslam, 2000: 261)

Madchester's golden period, its so-called 'summer of love' was short lived. The City earned a darker reputation as possessing one of Britain's most vibrant and violent drug cultures and in time challenged London and Liverpool as a centre for armed robbery, gang warfare and murder. The old school of Manchester hard men gave way to a new generation of desperate young men brought up in the unforgiving terraced streets and estates of Moss Side, Cheetham Hill, Salford, Broughton and Collyhurst. The infamous and influential Quality Street gang was replaced by more ruthless gangs such as the Pepper Hill Mob, the Doddington, the Gooch and Moss Side. At the same time the currency of control changed as the authority of muscle gave way to the power of the machete, Browning and Uzi. Madchester became Gunchester.

It is not the case that football fans, hooligans, touts, ravers, fashion designers, musicians, DJs and drug dealers are all different people living in discrete, sealed off worlds. Many of them are the same people and most of them come together in the pubs, clubs and, most significantly, on the terraces and in the stands (Redhead, 1993; O'Connor and Wynne, 1996). In their own ways, Old Trafford and Main

Road were as central to the communication network that underpinned the vibrancy of Madchester as the Hacienda Club. It was in and around football that young people met and shared experiences and ideas. It was in this milieu that football's underground economy was cultivated.

Football, the cement of his life, offered Big Tommy an alternative to a career in serious crime. He had played the game as a youth, but when he was 16 he got a hiding from a bouncer outside a Manchester nightclub and ripped the ligaments in his right knee, ruining what had been a promising amateur career. Instead of playing, like so many other young men in the late 1970s and 1980s, he became a fixture at Old Trafford's Stretford End, where he rubbed shoulders and eventually joined up with the top hooligans in United's elite fighting firm, the Red Army. Today most of United's top Lads, as Big Tommy calls them, can trace their pedigrees back to this self-styled golden era of hooliganism. Big Tommy refers to these punters as the 'Lads', hard-core, 30-something, hooligan-hedonists. His use of the term 'Lads' differs from that employed in anthropologist Tony King's (1998) study of fan culture at Old Trafford. In King's work, at least in part, the Lads are portrayed as working-class heroes who from the terraces lead popular resistance to the Club's total commodification. While there is an element of this in and around Manchester United, mixed within are more sinister and violent groups of supporters. It is these people to whom Tommy refers when he talks about the Lads.

As part of the reimaging of Manchester United plc in the 1990s, the role of the club's fans in the serious hooligan wars of the 1970s and 1980s has been airbrushed out by the public relations people. The records clearly show that when it came to hard-core hooliganism, the Red Army were up there with best, or worst Firms (hooligan gangs), depending upon your perspective, and were role models for those that followed in the 1980s, such as Chelsea's Headhunters and West Ham's Inner City Firm. Even though the punishment was later watered down to a fine, it was United's fans, not Liverpool's, who sparked English football's first European ban when they rioted in the streets of St Etienne after a Union of European Football Associations (UEFA) Cup game. What is less well-known today, at a time when hooliganism has become a much more strategic affair, and when serious hooligan incidents have tended to be underreported in the media, is that Manchester United's Firm are still very active. Most of today's top men can trace their pedigrees back to hooliganism's self-styled golden era. Some have continuously been involved. Others are born-again hooligans, having come back to it after raising families, building careers, and/or flirting with the drug and dance club scene. Some not only control and coordinate much of the contemporary violence that still permeates football, but they are also the main movers and shakers in the football black market and other related illegal enterprises. Tommy is one of these 30-to-40-something terrace legends and he has used this experience skilfully as a springboard to launch his business ventures.

Tommy's conversion to full-time grafting did not happen overnight. Every week when he went to games he saw people hanging around grounds all around the country buying, selling and swapping match tickets. In the 1980s Tommy started doing a few tickets as a sideline to his more focused hooligan activities.

He managed to make enough money to fund his devotion to following his club and made a little spending money to boot. Big Tommy went global in 1990 when he travelled with the England supporters to Italia 1990. Using locally honed touting skills he managed to fund his whole trip, living well, seeing all the England games and keeping his hooligan hand in with the odd ruck with the Ingerland boys. Tommy returned to the United Kingdom (UK) with £500 in his pocket. Rather than blowing it as he might have done a few years before, he reinvested it in 20 tickets for United's early season encounter with Arsenal. Tommy made another good profit that once more was ploughed back into his fledgling business. Big Tommy began to realise that, rather than being a means to an end, touting could become an end in itself. While he would go on being an ardent Manchester United supporter, he now began to view his affiliation with his 'the Reds' more and more as a business relationship.

By this time Manchester United plc were well on the way to becoming the world's richest football club with a reported annual turnover of more than £100 million (Bose, 2000). As United prospered so too did Big Tommy and the rest of Manchester's football grafters. New-era fans had more disposable income and didn't mind disposing some of it on tickets at double the face value or more. Gradually Tommy built up his contacts and squeezed his way into Old Trafford's touting network. If you moved in the right circles, there were always ways and means to get your hands on tickets. Tommy's tickets came from many sources, including players and their agents, corrupt officials and security staff at the clubs, multiple applications to membership schemes, phantom season tickets and sometimes legitimately through getting up early (or paying somebody else to) and standing in the rain at the ticket office on those rare occasions when tickets actually went on public sale.

Working from an office at home, in the early 1990s Tommy set up his own ticketing agency which prospered until 1994 when buying and selling-on tickets (touting) was made illegal in the UK. This legislation forced the Big Man to shut down the legitimate side of his business, putting him back onto the black market and into the snide rag trade. When Manchester United opened their chain of replica kit, souvenir and memorabilia stores, Big Tommy and gangs of other Manchester grafters likewise went into business making and selling fake gear. It is estimated that globally the trade in counterfeit goods generates around £250 billion. As much as £60 billion of this circulates in Europe. The UK accounts for approximately £8 billion of this black economy and is viewed as the counterfeiting centre of Europe. Trading Standards guess that as much as 10 per cent of all clothing worn in Britain is fake and a huge slice of this market is in sporting goods. Because of its global popularity Manchester United is a key target of the counterfeiters. In 1999 the club's anti-fraud team seized fake replica shirts worth more than £2 million – and they were only the ones that they found. But as fast as they seize them the grafters source more from sweatshops in Leicester or from the Far East. (The snide-trade is not without its comic moments, and spelling can be a problem. When after the 1998 World Cup Final, Manchester United signed up Frenchman Fabien Barthez, one of Big Tommy's grafter mates immediately printed hundreds of snide T-shirts and goalkeepers' tops with 'Bartez' on the back of them.)

The people who are responsible for policing this trade in counterfeit gear work from a small office tucked away in a flat-roofed red-brick warehouse next to Old Trafford's north stand. Manchester United no longer have a club crest, they have instead a Brand Mark that cost the club more than a million pounds to register. Before this, street hawkers had been able to trade legally in goods that bore Manchester United's crest, claiming that this was a badge of affiliation and loyalty. Now that 'Manchester United' is a trademark, such trade is outlawed.

Angela is the club's Trademark Manager and Elaine is her assistant. A photograph of a bare-chested David Beckham adorns the wall above the two women's desks. Pinned to a display board in the corner are what look to be home-and-away copies of Manchester United's then new Nike team shirts. In 2002 the club abandoned its longstanding relationship with Umbro in favour of a multimillion pound deal with Nike. One of the unwanted by-products of the marriage of the brand name of the biggest football club in the world with the globally sought-after Nike 'swoosh' was a dramatic boom in the counterfeit market for the latest shirts.

The shirts on Angela's wall in May 2002 were in fact snides. The public launch of the real thing was not scheduled until the following June. Angela explained how, back in February, they had organised a closed showing of the new kit for the press. No cameras were allowed, but the next day artist's impressions of the new shirts appeared in the tabloids. Less than two weeks later the first counterfeit shirts appeared on the streets of Bangkok. Not long afterwards they were being worn in and around Old Trafford. 'Those who buy them like to think that they are genuine and have come out of the back of a factory in Taiwan,' explained Angela, 'but look closely and you can tell they're fake. Anyway the real ones are being made in a factory in Morocco.'

Manchester United has five hit squads that operate around the ground on match days closing down counterfeit traders and confiscating their material. They pay particular attention to grafters that they see on a regular basis, but there are not many of them. Just like drug dealers, the main players do not sell the product themselves; they have a series of runners who do that for them. Rarely do they use the same ones on consecutive weeks. However, Angela and Elaine recognise that most of the snide shirts are sold well away from the ground. 'It is getting more and more difficult to control. It used to be that we could get intelligence of container loads of the stuff coming into the country that we could then grab with Trading Standards and police at the port of entry or some warehouse,' explained Angela. 'Now it tends to come in by the vanload. They just drive up to the back of a factory or club and let it be known that they have some gear to sell which they do out of the back of the van in the car park. It's costing the club millions.'

At first the counterfeit merchandise was cheap and its poor quality reflected this. But it was not long before the grafters began to source their materials from the same Far East sweatshops used by the official retailers. Soon their snide replicas were virtually indistinguishable in style and quality from the real thing, and selling at less than half the price. For the impoverished mothers of fanatical kids from Manchester's run-down estates, according to Big Tommy, the grafters were viewed like Robin Hoods, while the club itself, as it churned out yet another away kit at £40-plus per shirt, was regarded as a 'robbing bastard' – a view, it seems, shared by the Office of Fair Trading who in 2002 took kit manufacturer Umbro, the Football Association (FA) and big clubs like Manchester United to court for unfairly fixing the price of replica shirts.

The Far East is where more than 90 per cent of the world's counterfeit produce comes from, and, as one *farang* (Westerner) put it, 'Bangkok is the bootleg capital of the world.' The working motto of Thailand could easily be 'You design it, we'll copy it.' Anything from suits to sophisticated pieces of computer technology can be found and purchased on Bangkok's counterfeit market. The emergence of so-called designer fashion – the kind of apparel for which the display of the company logo is at least as important as the quality of the fabric and costume design – has given a huge boost to Bangkok's renowned counterfeit rag trade. Nowhere is this expansion more evident than in designer sport and leisure wear. Alongside longstanding top-range labels like Ralph Laurent and Hugo Boss, there has grown a huge market in polo-shirts, T-shirts, sweatshirts, tracksuits and replica football shirts bearing names like Puma, Umbro, Nike and Adidas.

Mike is Adidas UK's Trademark Production Manager. A considerable proportion of his job is dedicated to identifying fake products. Mike is a kind of snide detective, who works alongside Trading Standards, Her Majesty's Customs and Excise and the police tracking down and eradicating the counterfeiters. This is now recognised as such a huge problem for the sportswear industry that companies like Umbro, Nike and Adidas work closely together within the framework of the ACG (Anti-Counterfeiting Group) in a collective attempt to stamp out the illegal use of their labels. In the case of the snide football gear, they also work closely with the big football clubs.

Mike explained that there is no limit to the ingenuity and cheek of the counterfeiters. 'Anything we make, almost before it's on the clean market, they've copied it and it's being knocked out in street markets and pubs and clubs up and down the country.' Sometimes the fakers will go so far as to produce goods that Adidas and its competitors do not even make themselves. I remembered one of my first encounters with Freddie in Manchester when I was trying to track down Big Tommy. He had Hilfiger watches for sale at a time when Hilfiger did not produce them themselves. 'There seems to be no end to their cheek,' Mike told me, 'I've seen mobile phone covers, watches, jewellery, the lot all with our logo on. The worst I've ever come across is a set of Adidas knuckle-dusters!'

The main counterfeit market, though, remains in sports clothing. 'Ten years or more ago', explains Mike, 'most of this gear was produced domestically in sweatshops in the north and midlands. Then the quality wasn't up to much – cheap and cheerful – and you could spot a snide a mile away. Nowadays 80–90 per cent of it is produced abroad, almost all of it in the Far East in countries like Indonesia, Singapore, China, the Philippines and Thailand where most of it comes from.' Now not only is there more of it, but also it is of much better quality. In the beginning most of the stuff used to be straightforward copies. A grafter could take a particular shirt to a Thai tailor and ask him to copy a couple of hundred. The tailor would take his best guess at the design and quality of material and produce an order of forgeries that would look fine from a distance but that would not usually stand up to closer scrutiny. Today, however, they don't just fake the deign and the logo, but they also use virtually identical materials, so much so that some of the better stuff cannot be detected as counterfeit by look and feel alone.

Emulating banknote security devices, several leading companies have gone so far as to have holograms embedded within their products, making them more difficult to reproduce. Difficult, but not impossible, as the counterfeiters them-selves are conversant with the latest computerised textile techniques. Mike tells me that investigators now use computer technology to scan and test samples of suspect produce, 'but even the computers can't spot the difference between the best fakes and the real McCoy'. At the 2000 Sydney Olympic Games such was the concern of the organising committee over counterfeiting that they used DNA taken from the saliva of an unnamed leading athlete and incorporated it into a special ink to be used in all official products sold at the games. Officials could then distinguish the real from the fake by using hand-held scanners.

The problem is that all it needs is for somebody who works in the factory where the genuine article is being produced to steal the design and the specifications of a given item, and an identical product can be manufactured in another sweatshop around the corner. More sophisticated organised criminal gangs steal the latest product from international trade fairs and sometimes have large quantities on the market before the genuine article is released. In 1999, for instance, a Chinese gang stole Reebok's prototype DMX shoe from a display stand. The counterfeit shoes were on sale in Eastern Europe and Russia within weeks, long before their official release by Reebok.

To add to the difficulty of the task facing the snide detectives, these modern counterfeiters also replicate the products' labelling, tagging and packaging down to the smallest detail. They have even gone so far as to replicate the paperwork that is used to support the manufacture and distribution of legitimate merchandise. In one particular case the only way the snide detectives identified a shipment of 5,000 items as counterfeit was when they checked back through the chain of paperwork and discovered that this was a limited edition and Adidas had only produced a 1,000 of them in the first place. These counterfeiting operations are now so thorough, Mike tells me, that some major high-street retail outlets have been conned into buying large quantities of counterfeit produce.

In the Far East the counterfeit market serves three types of customers. First, and of least importance to Mike and the rest of the snide detectives, are ordinary tourists who go to places like Bangkok on holiday and pick up a new wardrobe for themselves and faked gifts for their friends and relatives. Then there are lone carpetbagger grafters like Billy, Alehouse, Nick and their mates who visit Thailand for a bit of rest and relaxation and come home with a couple of suitcases jam-packed with snide CDs and computer games and fake replica football kits. The latter, Mike explains, can be picked up for less than £2 in Thailand and peddled back in England in the usual places for £20–25. If Billy can pack 200 shirts in a couple of holdalls and turn them around in Manchester's pubs and clubs he stands to earn himself a cool £4,000.

This kind of one-man smuggling is more of an irritation to the big sporting goods companies than a serious problem, particularly when compared to the third type of customer, those big-time crooks who buy in bulk and shift in big volume. This is where the boundaries between the counterfeit textile business and organised crime become very blurred. Some of the techniques used to shift counterfeit gear from the Far East and penetrate the UK market are exactly the same as methods used by the drug cartels to move narcotics around the world. To counteract this the snide detectives have to deploy the same techniques as the drugs squad, including using undercover agents. Mike told me the details of one big operation that the detectives had managed to infiltrate. The operation was organised by a Thai family from their base in Geneva. In Thailand 300,000 fake Adidas units (the term used for any product) were run up and packed into a container before being driven to Singapore. From Singapore they were shipped to Rotterdam's free port area and held in a bonded warehouse for several weeks, out of the reach of Dutch customs, before being shipped on to Spain. According to Mike, a corrupt Spanish customs official cleared the cargo after which it was sent back to Holland. Spain is in the European Union (EU) and goods cleared by customs in one EU country are generally waived through by customs officials of another. Thus it was relatively easy for the shipment to be freighted from Holland to the UK and taken to Manchester for distribution. In another case, customs intercepted a consignment of counterfeit apparel that had been shipped from Holland to Liverpool in flower boxes.

The UK is one of the biggest markets for counterfeit sportswear, alongside Japan and the United States of America (USA). In the UK the main centres for import, manufacture and distribution are in the north and midlands with Manchester and Leicester being the most important cities. It is mainly from there that much of the snide gear that ends up on market stalls or in pubs and clubs in Liverpool, Leeds and Glasgow comes from. Through his work for Adidas, Mike knows the main players in this network very well and describes most of them as likeable rogues. 'For them,' Mike tells me, 'it's not wrong, it's just part of a way of life that has been going on for generations. They think that they're just doing a job like anybody else. Some of them even send me Christmas cards!'

This is one of the many problems faced by the snide detectives when trying to bring such people to justice. Neither the grafters themselves, nor the majority in the communities they provide for, see that there is anything wrong with what they do. On the contrary, it is viewed more as a public service than as a crime. I once sat in a pub in north Manchester waiting for Big Tommy and Billy and within 15 minutes had been offered for sale cigarettes, football shirts, meat joints and a set of German steel carving knives. This was obviously business as usual and nobody batted an eyelid. It was rumoured that in some neighbourhoods in Merseyside, the grafters operated like milkmen, delivering contraband booze, cigarettes and perfume to the doorstep.

This kind of trade is also attractive not just because of the huge profits that can be made, but also, much to Mike's lament, because the punishment for getting caught is usually very light. Get caught with a couple of kilos of heroin at Bangkok's Don Muang Airport and, if you're lucky, it is 10 years in the notorious Bangkok Hilton, as the city's squalid high security prison is known. The authorities' approach to the snide market is considerably less strict. It is not in the interests of the faltering Thai economy for them to crack down on the counterfeiting industry as it keeps people in work and brings money in. Get caught with a suitcase full or even a container load of the latest Manchester United strips and the worst that tends to happen is that you have your gear confiscated.

Sanctions are not much more severe at the UK end. Customs will seize and destroy such contraband, but often do not prosecute. Officially, counterfeiting and smuggling are criminal offences that can be punished with 5–10-year custodial sentences, but rarely are such cases brought to trial, and when they are the maximum sentences have been between 12 and 18 months. It is much more usual for culprits to be cautioned and sent away with a £50 fine. Mike complains that most of the big fish that he is after can afford expensive lawyers who often advise their clients to demand a trial at the crown court. They know full well that the prospect of a long and complex trial that eats far into the court's already stretched budget is not appealing for the authorities. Thus, charges in such cases are often dropped. When they do get into court the usual defence of accused traders is that of due diligence. They claim to have taken all reasonable precautions to make sure that the stock that they imported was genuine. The standards of counterfeiting are now so high, defence lawyers argue, that often the likes of Adidas and Nike themselves cannot easily detect fakes of their own products. 'What chance does my client, a humble market trader, have, Your Honour, when the companies themselves find it hard to tell the difference between fakes and the real thing?'

Eventually I suggest to Mike that because legitimate brands use child labour and sweat shops, buying fake gear that is produced in similar conditions does not trouble the consciences of too many consumers. I also put it to him that one of the problems with getting the authorities or anybody else to see these kinds of activities as criminal is that the real product is oversold and overpriced. Aggressive marketing and the constant changing of kits and related designer sportswear styles puts an unreasonable burden on less well-off families who have to cater for the sport- and fashion-hungry appetites of their children. If the likes of Billy, for instance, can supply a counterfeit Manchester United shirt which in all detail is an exact copy of the real thing, then surely he is providing a community service?

Not surprisingly, Mike rejects the 'Robin Hood' argument. For a start he argues that the genuine product is of a higher quality. He also believes that it is unfair that companies like his should spend millions developing a high-quality product only to see the counterfeiters produce inferior versions for sale on the black market. Mike also contends that this kind of trade is not only illegal and damaging to legitimate business, but it is also almost seamlessly connected to other, more sinister kinds of organised crime: 'Some of the most violent and experienced criminals in the country have realised the huge fortunes that can be made from counterfeiting.' To reinforce his point, he offered several examples. One involved a major seizure of counterfeit goods at a warehouse in West Yorkshire.

One evening, Trading Standards officers, along with police posing as warehousemen, took delivery of the four wagon-loads of counterfeit sportswear that they had been tipped off to expect, and arrested the drivers. They were about to shut down the operation when a fifth wagon, unrelated to the first four, pulled up at the gates blaring its horn. The driver had been held up in traffic on his way up from London and seemed desperate to have his cargo unloaded that night. Thinking that they had nothing to lose, the police duly obliged and when they opened up the container they discovered that it too was packed with counterfeit gear. When this driver was arrested he showed signs of wild panic, unusual for a relatively low-key, snide gear bust. Eventually he broke down and explained to police that he was driving for a London mob that, amongst other things, peddled drugs around the city's casino gambling circuit. He was meant to drop off the snide gear in Yorkshire, get paid off then drive across the Pennines to Liverpool and use the money to pay for a consignment of heroin and cocaine that was badly needed in the Smoke's casinos. According to Mike, using the profits from the clothing black market as a grubstake for drug dealing and other more serious felonies was not unusual.

Counterfeiting can have even more sinister connections. Mike claimed that in Northern Ireland, loyalist paramilitaries control both the counterfeiting and drugs markets and use them to finance their terrorist campaigns. Angela, Manchester United's Trademark Manager, shares Mike's views on this. She once went to a market in Ulster and had to be protected by heavily armed police as she searched for fake Manchester United gear. The Royal Ulster Constabulary (now the Police Service of Northern Ireland) had warned her that she would be at serious risk from the paramilitaries if she attempted to investigate them alone. Mike's and Angela's views are supported by the National Criminal Intelligence Service (NCIS) who estimate that 60 per cent of the organised crime gangs involved in counterfeiting are also drug traffickers.

In another, different kind of case, Mike told of a bust on a sweatshop in the heart of Leicester's Asian community. Early one morning he was with police and customs as they broke down the door of an ordinary looking terraced house. Once inside they found it had been extended backwards to accommodate dozens of sewing stations and rack after rack of counterfeit designer clothing. About to leave, one of them heard a noise coming from the attic. When they investigated its source they found 20 illegal immigrants cramped in the roof space. It turned out that since their illegal entry into Britain they had been held in the house and used as slave labour in the sweatshop. This was justified as a somewhat indeterminate means of paying for their illegal journey into the country. 'So you see, this is not a victimless crime,' claims Mike, airing a view shared by the UK's Consumer Affairs Minister, Kim Howells, who asserts that 'Counterfeiting is often the tip of the criminal iceberg. There are links between counterfeiting and organised crime and it is often used as a means of laundering money gathered by drug dealers.'

Spivving tickets and flogging swag is hard work, high risk, unpredictable and, for the most part, illegal. By the time he was in his thirties Big Tommy was looking to extend and stabilise his business interests around football. The opportunity was provided by UEFA and their media and marketing partners with the makeover of Europe's Cup competitions and the birth of the Champions League. The innovative European competitions gave Big Tommy a new structure within which to deploy all of his hard-come-by streetwise skills, catering for the travel needs of a new generation of migrant fans. Now at least six, and potentially more, British clubs participate in league and knockout games in Europe. Most clubs have official ticket allocation and travel schemes, either run by themselves, as is the case with Leeds United, or by favoured commercial partners, like Travel Care or Miss Ellies, who sort out Manchester United's travel. Many fans reject such schemes because official one- or two-day trips are expensive and usually not long or flexible enough to permit the kind of sightseeing mini-breaks, doubled up around football, that lots of today's supporters prefer. Others travel independently out of protest. There are thousands of fans who are ardent supporters of their teams but sworn enemies of their club as a commercial entity. They feel alienated and disenfranchised by the increased dominance of those in business suits over those in tracksuits and choose to turn their backs on official schemes of any kind. Then there is the hooligan element that is neither welcome on official trips nor attracted to them. This is Big Tommy's core market.

Getting started, he used his old hooligan connections at Manchester United to cultivate and cater for a market of fans who always travel abroad with their teams, not simply for the football, but equally importantly for thrills and spills of being abroad with like-minded groups of middle-aged men behaving badly. For these punters, an enhanced schedule of European and global football provides regular opportunities for a series of what amounts to extended stag parties in some of the world's most exciting cities. Big Tommy is sensitive to the Lads' particular requirements and arranges his trips accordingly: plenty of time for binge drinking; local knowledge of the red-light districts; and tickets in the home supporters' end. Amsterdam is the Lads' favourite European venue, and when Manchester United played a post-season friendly in Bangkok one firm took the opportunity to provide a week in Pattaya, the seediest seaside sex tourist hangout in South East Asia. In the past these groups of fans had to go it alone, getting hold of tickets, finding transport and booking accommodation. This is where Big Tommy and the independent football travel business come in. Beyond the reach of UEFA, the English FA and individual clubs, Big Tommy has put together quite an operation. He block-books flights and, if demand is sufficiently high, charters whole planes. He arranges hotels and acquires tickets for targeted matches abroad. The independents rarely get an allocation of tickets from the clubs who generally disapprove of and despise them. Tommy likes to posture as a businessman, but he is still an experienced and knowledgeable tout who skilfully works the local underground ticket market in places like Munich, Madrid and Milan to garner enough briefs for his clients. The grafters also have used a number of ingenious ruses to get themselves and their customers into grounds without tickets. Forging media and VIP passes is a favourite. One grafter boasted about how he regularly smuggled punters into Barcelona's Nou Camp stadium by paying off the security guards to the players' car park. On another occasion he provided stolen Champions League camera crew vests and VIP passes to get a group of Leeds fans into Anderlecht's ground in Belgium where they watched the game from the seats reserved for the players' wives. So long as you do not mind who you're sitting next to, Big Tommy or one of his associates will get you there and get you in – making nonsense of UEFA's policy on fan segregation.

Big Tommy is by no means the first ex-hooligan to exploit knowledge of the Lads and their needs and appetites in the service of the travel business. Foremost among these was 'Icky's Luxury Coaches' operated out of Tunbridge Wells by Steve Hickmott, then the self-styled leader of Chelsea's top firm, the Headhunters. Icky was a legend during these hooligan heydays. His coach convoys would terrorise the country on match days, avoiding the police and turning up out of the blue to confront other firms when they least expected it. Icky's activities were brought to an abrupt end when he was dragged out of bed in a dawn police raid and arrested for hooligan-related offences. Based on evidence gathered during a police undercover operation, Hickmott was tried at the Old Bailey, found guilty and sentenced to 10 years' imprisonment, by some distance the longest ever jail sentence given for hooliganism. Icky served two-and-a-half years before he was released after it was revealed that the police had tampered with some parts of the evidence that was used against him. Hickmott now lives in self-imposed exile in Thailand, running a bar in Pattaya's red-light district called the Dog's Bollocks (Ward and Hickmott, 2000).

Big Tommy found himself working in a crowded market, but, just as he had done with the tickets, he managed to elbow his way in. After a few successful trips his reputation grew and he built up a steady following. The Big Man's timing couldn't have been better. Just as he launched himself as a serious player in the travel business, United had their best ever run in the Champions League, ending in a famous victory over Bayern Munich in Barcelona. United had not performed on such a stage since the era of Charlton, Best and Law. There was a whole generation of supporters that had not been alive to witness the Reds' last European Cup triumph. Every man and his dog wanted to be in Barcelona to experience the culmination of United's attempt at the Treble. Estimates vary, but as many of 60,000 Manchester United supporters went to Barcelona and a few thousand went with Big Tommy.

The money he made from the Reds' European triumph plus the handsome grub stake he had creamed from working the tickets at the World Cup in France 1998 gave the Big Man further scope for investment and development. Like all good capitalists, Tommy was shrewd enough to know that he would have to expand into other markets to survive. In London, the market around Arsenal and Chelsea, the only clubs in the capital with a reasonably predictable European pedigree, was already monopolised by the London spivs, and the scousers had Liverpool's firms well covered. It came as a godsend for Tommy when David O'Leary took over a young Leeds United side and took them into Europe. Leeds' official travel company is owned by the Club and when they first qualified for Europe there were no established independents challenging their monopoly. Leeds has more than its fair share of dissident fans and a significant number of Lads. Neither constituency was particularly enthusiastic about travelling with the officials. It promised to be a ripe market for the Big Man.

When Leeds qualified for Europe Big Tommy went to Elland Road to make contact with some of the Leeds Lads that he knew through his Manchester United hooligan days. At first Leeds firms were reluctant to travel with Big Tommy because of his reputation as hard-core Manchester United. It is usual for anybody who does not support Manchester United to profess a hatred for them; Leeds' enmity, however, is in a league of its own. The Leeds fans routinely refer to Manchester United and its supporters as Scum and profane songs and chants about them, including irreverent references to the 1958 Munich air disaster, are regularly aired at Elland Road. Some supporters even go so far as to have 'Munich '58' tattooed on various parts of their bodies. But Big Tommy's prices are hard to beat and a handful of Leeds Lads took a chance and went with his company to Prague when their team played Sparta. They came back mightily impressed after a cheap and cheerful, hassle-free trip during which they had been put up in the Renaissance, the Czechoslovakian capital's top five-star hotel, a better hotel than the one that the players were staying in. Since then, whenever Leeds plays in Europe, Big Tommy takes hundreds, sometimes thousands, of Leeds Lads. 'Aye,' belly-laughs Big Tommy, 'but because they know we're Man U, even though they travel with us, and enjoy themselves, they still call us Scum Airways.'

Big Tommy chartered an aircraft and took a planeload of Leeds fans to Istanbul for the ill-fated Galatasaray game in 1999. Kevin Speight and Christopher Loftus, the two Leeds fans who were stabbed to death before the game, were Big Tommy's customers. Billy, Big Tommy's right-hand man at the time, was the courier for the trip. He was in the bar with the victims when the trouble started. 'The Lads weren't causing any trouble,' he recalls. 'Just having a few beers and a bit of a laugh. Then the Turks came. Some of them were tapping on the windows with those long kebab knives, challenging us to come outside.' When they did eventually leave the bar, Galatasaray fans attacked them. According to Billy, the Turkish police did nothing to protect them. On the contrary, they set about the Leeds fans even as two lay bleeding to death on the pavement. Most of the Leeds fans were blissfully unaware of what had happened. Billy had the harrowing task of ringing around the hotels the next morning to let all the people on the ITL package, most of whom were close friends of Kevin and Christopher, know what had happened. Tommy and Billy went to the funerals in Leeds and, some time later, Big Tommy organised and gifted holidays for some of the grieving relatives.

This was a low point for the Big Man but he has since bounced back, adding teams like Leicester and Newcastle to his overseas portfolio. He has also broken into the England market, once more combining his skills as a ticket tout and a travel operator to put together packages that are attractive to those who don't want to or aren't allowed to travel with the official England travel club. As his business has developed, while he still has a huge soft spot for the Lads, he has endeavoured to make his football travel packages more attractive to 'straight members' – as he calls law-abiding fans. Big Tommy craves respectability and as owner of what is now the second-largest independent football travel business in the country is more than halfway to achieving it. He lives in a comfortable detached house with two cars in the driveway in a sought-after residential suburb in north Manchester and is a stand-up member of the local Round Table.

Conclusion

There is a body of evidence that suggests city-based entrepreneurial criminal activity – that is, crime that has money-making as its prime motivation – has been on the rise since the 1990s. Taylor (1999) argues forcefully that this is related to a process that he refers to as the 'marketization of social relations'. Amongst other things this process has led to a loosening of the traditional boundaries between petty and organised crime at the local level. Taylor explains, 'I have also been concerned to display the link between competitive "market society", the production of new and heightened forms of social marginality – involving structures of disadvantage across a range of different markets of opportunity – and the consolidation and development of different local "economies of crime"' (Taylor, 1999: 228). According to Taylor, post-Fordist societies, those dominated by consumerism and a free-market ethos, create multiple differentials between varieties of rich and poor while at the same time generating incentive and opportunity for a wide variety of grey and black economic activity. A key point made by Taylor is that much of this activity, at least at street level, is not popularly believed to be criminal (1999: 231).

Taylor may well have been describing the activities of Big Tommy and the rest of the Manchester grafters. None of them are particularly well educated in any formal sense, but they are clever and streetwise nonetheless. According to their own legends, they are local Robin Hoods who, in and around the football entertainment industry, have created and exploited an alternative economy using innovative and flexible business skills which, in other walks of life, might have entitled them to some kind of award. Big Tommy, for instance, works the ticket market like a Wall Street commodities trader, shifts stocks of snide gear like a Harrods buyer, and moves hundreds – sometimes thousands – of people around Europe with the sophistication of Thomas Cook. As a young man he looked and learned as a class of Yuppies made themselves fortunes playing the stock market and his beloved Reds reinvented themselves as Manchester United plc to become the richest club in the world. In a classic playing out of Robert Merton's model of deviancy, with legitimate avenues to a share of these riches blocked, Tommy's adaptive response to the 'strain to anomie' was to become an innovator – that is, he found other, less legitimate routes to the same culturally prescribed goals. The Big Man is not the first and will not be the last to graft his way to wealth and status. Occasionally when Arsenal are in town for the Man U game he takes along a former Gooner (Arsenal) hooligan and once mortal enemy to the game. His guest and now friend runs the biggest independent football travel business in the UK and owns luxury holiday homes in the Caribbean. As they sit in their executive box trading fables about past hooligan wars and counting their money, Mrs Thatcher would surely be proud of them.

Note

1   Hereafter simply referred to as football.

References

Barnes, T. (2000) *Mean Streets: A Journey Through the Northern Underworld*, Bury: Milo.
Becker, H. (1963) *Outsiders*, New York: The Free Press.
Boon, G., Philips, A. and Hann, M. (2000) '20 richest clubs in the world', *Four Four Two*, 65, January: 68–74.
Bose, M. (2000) *Manchester Unlimited: The Money, Egos and Infighting Behind the World's Richest Football Club*, London: Texere.
Bower, T. (2003) *Broken Dreams, Vanity, Greed and the Souring of British Football*, London: Simon and Schuster.
Conn, D. (1997) *The Football Business: Fair Game in the 1990s*, Edinburgh: Mainstream.
Douglas, J. (1976) *Investigative Social Research: Individual and Team Field Research*, Beverly Hills, CA: Sage.
Haslam, D. (2000) *Manchester, England: The Story of the Pop Cult City*, London: Fourth Estate.
King, A. (1998) *The End of the Terraces: The Transformation of English Football in the 1990s*, Leicester: University of Leicester.
Maurer, D. (1964) *Whiz Mob: A Correlation of the Behaviour Pattern of Pickpockets*, New Haven: College and University Press.
Merton, R. (1957) *Social Theory and Social Structure*, Glencoe: Free Press.
O'Connor, J. and Wynne, D. (eds) (1996) *From the Margins to the Centre: Cultural Production and Consumption in the Post-Industrial City*, Aldershot: Arena.
Parker, H. (1974) *The View from the Boys*, Newton Abbot: David and Charles.
Polsky, N. (1967) *Hustlers, Beats and Others*, Chicago: University of Chicago Press.
Redhead, S. (1993) *Rave Off: Politics and Deviance in Contemporary Youth Culture*, Aldershot: Avebury.
Robins, D. (1984) *We Hate the Humans*, Harmondsworth: Penguin.
Sugden, J. (2002) *Scum Airways: Inside Football's Underground Economy*, London: Mainstream.
Sugden, J. and Tomlinson, A. (1998) *FIFA and the Contest For World Football: Who Rules the Peoples' Game?*, Cambridge: Polity.
Sugden, J. and Tomlinson, A. (2002) *Power Games: A Critical Sociology of Sport*, London: Routledge.
Taylor, I. (1999) *Crime in Context: A Critical Criminology of Market Societies*, Cambridge: Polity.
Ward, C. and Hickmott, S. (2000) *Armed for the Match: The Troubles and Trials of the Chelsea Headhunters*, London: Headline.
Willis, P. (1977) *Learning to Labour: How Working-Class Kids get Working-Class Jobs*, London: Saxon House.

Part III
Embodied United

8   Where did it all go right?

George Best, Manchester United and Northern Ireland

Alan Bairner

Tuesday 18 March 2003: The Red Devil Bar

A smaller than usual crowd has gathered for a Manchester United Champions League game. United have already qualified for the quarter-finals, a fact not lost on Sir Alex Ferguson who has chosen to give a number of his younger players a taste of European competition. The result is predictable enough. A good performance by the relatively inexperienced United team but victory for the hosts, Deportivo de La Coruña. The low-key atmosphere offers more opportunities than normal to look around. Manchester United memorabilia cover the walls. Amongst the icons, one image is more remarkable than most – that of George Best, whose face looks down from the centre of the gantry circled by the inscription, 'The Red Devil Bar – The Best'. But what, one might ask, is strange about George Best's image being displayed in a bar named in honour of Manchester United? Only the fact that Best grew up on the other side of this deeply divided city. This is Belfast, not Manchester, far less Salford. On the walls of the Falls Road, on which the pub is situated, the images are those of dead Irish republican hunger strikers, not Protestant footballers who spent most of their careers playing for English clubs. This is a city where heroes tend to divide rather than unite. It is also a city where sport reflects the divisions that operate throughout the wider society and where football is commonly a major indicator of who one is and where one is from (Sugden and Bairner, 1993; Bairner, 2002). But Best's enduring appeal appears to cross the divide, as does that of Manchester United. Or so it would seem.

This chapter examines the status of George Best as Northern Ireland's greatest sporting celebrity. It discusses the extent to which Best was a product of the society in which he grew up. It also outlines the relationship between Manchester United and the Irish and notes the degree to which this has been articulated in terms of perceptions of United as a Catholic club. Against this, the chapter concludes by considering how far George Best's iconic standing was a significant factor in permitting the club to attract substantial support from both of Northern Ireland's main traditions.

It is only since the start of the new millennium that academics and intellectuals have turned their attention to George Best. That they have done so at all tells us more about the celebrity status of David Beckham and a handful of other superstars than about Best himself. As Cashmore (2002: 102) notes in his study of Beckham, 'no other footballer of the time got remotely the same kind of attention as Best'. He states quite categorically, however, that 'even George Best, who sprang out of the Beatlemanical sixties culture and became the first athlete to be given the same kind of attention as a pop star, wasn't subject to the elaborate scrutiny and saturation coverage afforded subsequent sports celebrities' (Cashmore, 2002: 9). One such figure is Paul Gascoigne, writing of whom Giulianotti and Gerrard (2001: 135) claim: 'Best's celebrity celebrated the new working-class dream of individualism, easy consumption and spectacular mobility.' It is hoped that this chapter reveals that there has been rather more to Best than that and also that he is easier to understand than one might initially imagine or want to believe. It is tempting for academics to look for complexity even when common sense may hold the key. Thus, Giulianotti and Gerrard (2001: 135) write that 'Gascoigne's postmodern stardom embraces all ungrounded signifiers, and assembles a stream of reversible images and contradictory events that brook no meta-narrative.' This reads suspiciously like an analysis penned by people who have never enjoyed the experience of simply spending an entire day getting absolutely rat-arsed with their mates. The examination of George Best which follows is arguably more empathetic.

George Best was unquestionably one of the greatest ever footballers. He was also a celebrity who attracted widespread media attention. Perhaps even more interesting is the fact that, at least at the time of writing, Best is still alive. He is an alcoholic. He has been close to death saved only by a liver transplant. Best is also an Ulster Protestant.

About a boy

In her study of David Beckham, Julie Burchill (2002) makes much of the player's upbringing. She notes that his father was a gas fitter, his mother a hairdresser, that they married in Hoxton, east London, honeymooned in Bognor Regis and then returned to their terraced house in Leytonstone. According to Burchill (2002: 27):

> ... in this simple sentence we can see a wealth of poignant detail, a snapshot of an age about to pass as surely as that of the steam train: the handsome young couple, both proud of their trades (soon to be outstripped by call centres and McJobs), with high hopes and modest dreams (replaced by low expectations and Lottery fantasies), marrying in a place now overrun by art hags and ponces, holidaying in a thriving seaside town now surviving courtesy of the DHSS, returning to take out a mortgage in an area now gentrified beyond all recognition, and where a terraced house would certainly be beyond the pocket of a hairdresser and a gas fitter.

Out of this social context, the character of David Beckham was formed. 'Ancient and modern both; that was the Beckhams, and that is Beckham to this day' (Burchill, 2002: 28). As with Beckham, so it is with George Best. In no small measure, the boy simply became the man.

As George Best (1991: 5) records in his first autobiography written with Ross Benson, he was born in Belfast on 22 May 1946 'into a solid, working-class family, Protestant by religion, decent and honest in its beliefs'. Joe Lovejoy (1999: 9) similarly writes that 'George Best was born into a solid working-class background, Presbyterian *for those interested in such details*' (my emphasis). Only someone who is relatively unfamiliar with the labelling that dominates Northern Irish society could imagine that these facts might conceivably be without interest. The question, 'What are you?', is regularly asked even if not directly as people negotiate their relations with 'the other sort' with countless different objectives, ranging from the romantic to the murderous. Lovejoy (1999: 15) describes the Bests as a religious family 'in an entirely non-political way' and as Free Presbyterian without 'any of the bigotry associated with Ulster sectarianism'. This is slightly at odds with Best's own account. In his later autobiography, Best (2002: 32) asserts, 'Religion has never bothered me and there is no way you could ever call my family bigots.' However, he adds, 'If you were a Protestant, you joined the Orange Order, as I did, and my dad and grandad both had spells as master of our local lodge.' The fact is, of course, that not all Ulster Protestants join the Orange Order, a point that is forcefully made in Sam Hanna Bell's novel, *The Hollow Ball* (1961), which revolves around the life of a young footballer (Bairner, 2000). Indeed, Best (2002: 33) admits that, even in his childhood years, the Orange Order's Twelfth of July demonstrations constituted 'a sectarian festival'. Furthermore, although George Best grew up in the years before the troubles, he was conscious from an early age of those sectarian tensions that lay just beneath the surface of an apparently peaceful society, which would come to the fore with deadly consequences in the late 1960s.

Indeed, Best cites sectarianism as one of the reasons why, having passed his eleven-plus examination, he subsequently left Grosvenor High School and completed his education instead at Lisnasharragh Intermediate. According to Best (2002: 32), he was constantly subjected to sectarian abuse on his journeys to and from grammar school because 'Grosvenor High School was in the middle of a Catholic area and the kids from the other schools, like the Sacred Heart and places like that, knew from my uniform that I was Protestant'. It should be added of course that Best also lists other factors that made his short stay at Grosvenor an unhappy one. These included having to travel some distance to his new school, no longer being with his old friends from the Cregagh estate where he lived and above all, one surmises, the fact that rugby union as opposed to soccer was the sport of preference at his new school. Best (1991: 14) writes, 'In an indirect way it was Belfast's religious barriers that made me into a soccer player.' Whilst this may be something of an exaggeration, it is undeniable that the young Best grew up knowing that in Belfast and in Northern Ireland more generally religious affiliation mattered.

Arguably, religious differences were less important during George Best's childhood than they have subsequently become. As he notes, 'The troubles had not started and on the Cregagh estate, the vast, sprawling council estate where I was brought up, Catholic and Protestant lived side by side and no one gave much thought to that' (Best, 1991: 13). He recalls that his mother's best friend was a Catholic. Yet, as he puts it, even then 'everyone knew where they belonged' (Best, 1991: 14).

Identity matters

Of course, the conflict in Northern Ireland has never been solely or even primarily about religion. National identity also matters. In this respect, Best's story is similar to that of so many people who have grown up in the pro-British tradition of Northern Ireland but have become largely indistinguishable from other Irish people in the eyes of outsiders. His former wife, Angie Best (2001), refers repeatedly to his Irishness – 'this little Irishman' (6), 'this drunken little Irishman' (19), 'the Irish charm' (19), 'the wild Irish charms' (19) and 'the charming little Irishman' (56). As Best (2002: 302) recalls, that was also the perception of the Metropolitan Police officer who arrested him in 1984 on a drink-driving charge and addressed him as 'You little Irish wanker. You Irish scum. Another piece of Irish dirt' (Best, 2001: 326).

Best has contributed to this particular reading of his identity, describing himself in Michael Parkinson's (1975: 61) biography as 'a mad Irish sod'. Burchill (2002: 8) confirms this view, comparing Tom Jones with Best and commenting that 'Above all, these Celtic princes drank for Wales and Ireland respectively'. Others have referred to Best's Irish, and Celtic, ancestry in more analytical terms. For example, Parkinson (1975: 57) quotes that doyen of sports journalists, Hugh McIlvanney, who comments on Best,

> I suspect that deep in his nature there is a strong self-destructive impulse. The Celts, whether Irish, or Welsh, or Scots, whether sportsmen or artists or politicians, have always been pretty strong in the self-destructive department. If hell did not exist the Celts would have invented it. Sometimes I think they did. With George Best I have frequently had the impression that he felt uncomfortable when things were going too well.

Parkinson (1975: 7) also pursues this line of inquiry when he suggests that 'People who like theories about genes will be interested to know that Anne Best [Best's late mother] is of pure Irish stock but Dick Best's family were immigrants from Scotland.' One might question the very notion of pure Irishness contained in this statement. In other respects, though, Parkinson's comment brings us closer to a more complex truth about Best's identity. Whilst the Ulster Protestant can be dismissed in England as just another Irishman, in Northern Ireland itself, his perceived identity is unlikely to be either Celtic or Irish. Even those Ulster Protestants who do want to celebrate their Irishness recognise the problems. Belfast librarian John Gray expresses the dilemma, 'My imagined identity is Irish, and my desired identity is Irish, but I am very specifically Northern Irish' (McKay,

2000: 71–2). On the other hand, 'When I go to England it is not exactly a foreign country, but it is not my country' (McKay, 2000: 71). Caught betwixt and between, in matters of identity as in so many other ways, the Ulster Protestant community has come to regard itself as what David Dunseith has called 'an embattled minority' (McKay, 2000: 26). It is to this community that George Best owes much of his identity. Unlike most members of that community, however, George Best possessed the talent to represent Northern Ireland at the level of international sport.

Country matters

For many Northern Irish Protestants, the very existence of a 'national' soccer team is a matter of huge significance. It demonstrates to the world that Northern Ireland exists as a distinct entity. It is not just a part of Ireland, nor is its identity wholly subsumed within Britain. Although Catholics have always been willing to play for the 'national' team, they have arguably done so with far less of a sense of real belonging than that which has characterised the involvement of Protestants both as players and as fans. In that respect, however, George Best's links to his parental culture are weaker than they might have been. According to Lovejoy (1999: 163), 'Northern Ireland rarely saw the jewel in their crown in its best light.' In part this was because of the rival demands of club and country, a situation replicated in later years, albeit in relation to a different national team in the career of Ryan Giggs. In both cases it may also have been felt at times that there was little point wasting their immense talents on teams that were incapable of enjoying international success. As Lovejoy (1999: 157) writes of Best, 'By accident of birth, a player on the same plane as Pelé and Cruyff was condemned to scratch around with the no-hopers of Northern Ireland, and missed out on all the major tournaments.' This is a harsh judgement, not least because Northern Ireland have managed to qualify for the World Cup Finals on three occasions both before (1958) and after (1982 and 1986) George Best's all too short international career. Yet Best (1991: 69) himself has contributed to this analysis by claiming that:

> Playing for Northern Ireland was recreational soccer – there was hardly any pressure on you because you were not really expected to get a result unlike the Brazilian or the Italian or even the English teams are – and the way Manchester United is.

Lovejoy (1999) appears to support the view expressed by former Northern Ireland player, Derek Dougan, and on occasions by Best himself that the latter's career might have gone on longer had he been able to play for a more successful international team. Cynics, on the other hand, might argue that, as self-confessed advocates of an all-Ireland national side, neither Dougan nor Best were sufficiently committed to the Northern Irish team and all that it represents in the minds of Ulster unionists. As Best (2002: 302) puts it, 'I have always believed that the two associations should have got together and formed one national team.' He believes that politics and money have stood in the way of such a development, adding,

'The hangers on and the officials of the two Associations are too frightened of losing their freebies and their status.' It would be wrong, however, to infer from comments like this or from Best's regular absences from the Northern Ireland team that he has ever turned his back on his place of birth. Furthermore, his affection for Northern Ireland and its people is largely reciprocated.

No place like home

George Best remains phenomenally popular in Northern Ireland. Whilst the rest of the United Kingdom, and indeed the rest of the world, now hear of him intermittently, he continues to make regular appearances on BBC Northern Ireland and on Ulster Television. In addition, at the beginning of 2003, Northern Ireland's most widely read local newspaper, the *Belfast Telegraph* (2003), published a special edition that contained not only extracts from Best's recently published autobiography but also articles written by *Telegraph* football writers. A much bigger audience naturally saw the BBC's *This Is Your Life* programme first broadcast on 6 March 2003 and featuring George Best for the second time in its long history. Even on this occasion, however, much was made of Best's popularity back home with an appearance from local comedian, Patrick Kielty, and a tribute from television presenter, Eamonn Holmes, who posed the question, 'Who wouldn't want to say that they come from the same place as George Best?' This might well have begged the additional question in the minds of some viewers, 'Who would want to say that they come from the same place as Kielty and Holmes?' but let that pass. The overwhelming majority of Northern Irish people are either proud of Best – a genuine superstar who originated from their small part of the world – or, at worst, tolerate him as a charming rascal who never quite grew up. It is a role that Best has been happy to play.

For the benefit of Michael Parkinson (1975: 92), Best commented, 'I'm daft as a brush.' Whannel (2002: 113) indeed refers to Michael Parkinson's promotion of Best's 'Jack-the-lad insouciance'. Lovejoy (1998: 282) adds, 'To say that he is unreconstructed is like suggesting that Hugh Hefner may have had eyes for more than one woman.' There is, of course, a darker side to this aspect of Best's personality to which we shall return. But it is undeniable that his reputation as a likeable rogue has stood him in good stead with his Ulster public and with a wider audience. It is worth noting, for example, that in his study of media sport stars, Whannel (2002) situates Best among the 'pretty boys' rather than the 'bad boys'.

Best himself is all too aware that the people of his native city and of Northern Ireland more generally have been kind to him. Despite never having been offered a testimonial game by Manchester United, Best was thus honoured at Windsor Park in Belfast on 8 August 1988 with a match played in front of 25,000 and producing gate receipts of £110,000. It came at a particularly low point in Best's life and he commented, 'The people of Belfast saved me. They have given me the means to sort out my finances, and my life' (Lovejoy, 1999: 338). Moreover, the love affair was by no means one-sided. As his former wife confides, Best thought romantically about his birthplace: 'Every now and then he would surprise me with a poem he'd written, or a piece of prose about his life in Belfast' (Best, 2001: 59). Despite all the eventful years that Best spent away from Belfast, it is not inconceivable that the clues to understanding his inner being are to be found in his upbringing in that city.

Being George Best

Whilst recognising the dangers of over-theorising the blindingly obvious, I propose to argue that George Best is most easily understood by reference to his Ulster Protestantism, understood both theologically and politically. Describing the travails of certain sports stars, Whannel (2002) makes reference to Critcher's (1979) use of the concept of 'dislocation' to describe soccer stars for whom remaining working-class was not an option but who nevertheless sought to resist incorporation into a middle-class way of life. According to Whannel (2002: 51), 'George Best is the archetypal dislocated football hero whose talent, personality and background were insufficient to withstand the pressure, both on and off the field.' Best's dislocation, however, was not rooted solely in an inability to negotiate rapid social mobility; he was also dislocated both spatially and, it will be argued, culturally. Like many other players in the years after the abolition of the minimum wage, Best was faced with the problem of dealing with unaccustomed wealth. But he was also a young labour migrant who had left behind family and friends in the quest for sporting success. In the opinion of his former wife, 'George was too young at the age of fifteen to go off to Manchester United; I think he should have been made to finish school' (Best, 2001: 57). Indeed his first visit to Manchester lasted only one night before homesickness set in (Best, 2002). Had he decided not to go back, both English football and Manchester United would have suffered; one can only speculate, though, on the consequences for Best himself, just as one can only refer speculatively to another possible source of his dislocation – the fact that he found himself separated from his parental Ulster Protestant culture.

The Calvinism of Ulster-Scottish Presbyterianism is a difficult influence to shake off. At its most sinister, it is the world of R.L. Stevenson's *Strange Case of Dr Jekyll and Mr Hyde*, that Manichean creation of which George Best is arguably a modern incarnation. As his first wife recalls, 'When he was drunk, George could go either way – nastiness and meanness, or flirtation – but when he was sober he was quiet and withdrawn' (Best, 2002: 58). He is clearly capable of jealous rage as his second wife, Alex, acknowledges; she also admits that their relationship has been punctuated by instances of domestic violence (Lovejoy, 1999: 354–8). Whannel (2002: 113) refers to Best's 'objectification of women'. Indeed, according to Whannel (2002: 127), Best's faults and failings are such that his life 'has been transformed into a moral homily – a warning, like a nineteenth-century moral tract, concerning the dangers of giving way to emotion, desire, hedonism and alcohol'. As will be argued later, Best's chosen way of life has not led to universal condemnation. But it has clearly been at odds with the basic precepts of his parental culture.

Growing up in a good-living and God-fearing Protestant family has led many a young man (and woman) to use alcohol to overcome personal diffidence, with highly unpredictable consequences. In this respect, Best has more in common with his fellow Ulster Protestants, rock star Van Morrison, who includes Best in a list of exiled Irish geniuses in his song, *Too Long in Exile*, and former world snooker champion Alex Higgins, also 'a product of his time and upbringing in Protestant Belfast' (Borrows, 2002: 17), than with the English-born football players along with whom he has traditionally been categorised. Another Ulster-born Protestant, poet and critic Tom Paulin, comments, 'It was bizarre to grow up in a statelet that had no future. The root of it all is Calvinism. The sense of being persecuted and a member of an elect minority, feeding its persecution complex' (McKay, 2000: 296). One of the more damaging results of this condition has been a lack of ease with ideas and an increasing inability to present an articulate defence of core beliefs.

According to Angie Best (2001: 7), 'George has an amazing brain, but he was never given the opportunity to use it.' This comment is uncannily similar to one made to Susan McKay by Shankill-Road-born artist, Dermot Seymour:

> Being a Protestant, for me, is like having no head, in the sense that you are not allowed to think. It is hard to hold an individual thought about anything ... Out of that inability to think comes a lot of bizarre extreme behaviour, like the Shankill Butchers.
>
> (McKay, 2000: 302)

It would be highly invidious to compare George Best with the psychopathic killers who terrorised Belfast in the 1970s. But his behaviour was, at times, undeniably bizarre and extreme.

The footballer whose life most closely parallels Best's was also a Protestant, albeit a Scottish one. The late Jim Baxter's playing career peaked in his mid twenties and he died in 2001 at the age of 61 having already received a liver transplant. According to his biographer, Baxter suffered from a 'peculiarly Scottish trait that ate away at him over the years: the capacity to self-destruct, which has damaged so many of the nation's sporting giants' (Gallacher, 2002: 5). A player of immense talent, an iconic figure for Rangers and for Scotland and a trendsetter in his time, Baxter's greatest problem, according to Gallacher (2002: 36), 'was hiding from reality'. The realities that confronted George Best when he first went to Manchester were his social class, his place of origin and his Ulster Protestantism. Each was to contribute to his dislocation. But arguably it is his religio-cultural background that tells us most about the manner in which he sought to exorcise his personal demons. The second half of this chapter will argue that this also helps us to understand the magnetic attraction of Manchester United for people in Northern Ireland.

Manchester United and Ireland

Wolverhampton Wanderers was the English club with which Best identified when he was growing up in Belfast (Best, 2001). This statement contains within it three important insights – first, the widespread Northern Irish interest in English football even as early as the 1960s; second, the standing of Wolves at that time; and, finally, the fact that Best, like many Ulster Protestants, had chosen to eschew one of their main rivals, Manchester United, widely perceived, then and in some quarters even now, to be a club with strong Irish Catholic connections.

In the words of John Scally (1998: 11), 'Manchester United have excited Irish soccer fans like no other team.' Celtic fans might challenge this assertion and there are indeed more Celtic supporters' clubs in Ireland than Manchester United ones. One should bear in mind, however, that given its origins in Glasgow's Irish immigrant community and its subsequent success, Celtic is virtually the only Scottish-based team that could command the support of Irish Catholics. Amongst English clubs, on the other hand, the choice would superficially appear to be much greater. Thus, the fact that there are around 80 official Manchester United supporters' clubs in Ireland (43 of them in Northern Ireland) is impressive evidence of the club's popularity (www.unitedmanchester.com/sport/mufc-supporters-Irish.htm).

Scally (1998) seeks to explain the Irish obsession with Manchester United by referring to the history of the Irish diaspora in the city of Manchester itself. He notes that by 1841, one tenth of the city's population was Irish. Furthermore, 'Whilst most Irish immigrants were anxious to protect their national identity in foreign fields, they were also anxious to blend in their new environment' (Scally, 1998: 42). By the 1870s, one important way of doing this was to play and watch association football. Thus, 'Football was a badge of identity which enabled Irish immigrants to consider themselves as Mancunians' (Scally, 1998: 46). It was 'the battery that drove Irish immigrants' imaginative lives and dared them to see themselves in a very different light – as pillars of the Manchester community' (Scally: 48). The club to which most of then turned was Manchester United, whose ground was owned by a Catholic family, the De Traffords. In addition, according to Scally (1998: 45), 'From the very beginning, Irish players were at the heart of United's playing staff.'

Arguably, Scally (1998: 98) goes too far when he asserts that 'Anyone who is Irish Catholic in Manchester is expected to support Manchester United, who have always being (sic) perceived as the Catholic team ...'. His attempt to ascribe the preference of the Gallagher brothers – of Oasis fame – for Manchester City to their father's refusal to give in to 'the tyranny of conformity' (Scally, 1998: 98) makes rudimentary sense. But it does not negate the fact that Irish Catholics and people of Irish Catholic ancestry do support City. United's Irish connection is nevertheless secure and Scally documents in loving detail the list of Irish-born players who have played for the club, both before and after George Best. Until the 1950s, however, many of these had been Irish Catholics. There had also been a succession of Catholic managers, including most famously Sir Matt Busby, whom

Scally transforms into an honorary Irishman as well. Based on the fact that the legendary manager's maternal grandfather had emigrated from Ireland to Scotland, Scally (1998: 12) argues, 'Of course, Busby was an Irishman – at least more so than many who have lined out for the boys in green [i.e. the Republic of Ireland] in recent years.' Undeniably, Busby was a devout Catholic and became particularly close to some of his Catholic players, most notably Pat Crerand (Lovejoy, 1999), another Scot of Irish ancestry, and his assistant Jimmy Murphy, Welsh-born but with an Irish immigrant father (Risoli, 2001).

Manchester United and Northern Ireland

Despite Manchester United's outwardly Catholic image, however, much is made of its integrative potential by both Scally (1998) and Chris Moore (1999), who has written on Manchester United's Northern Irish connection. With reference to support for the club in Ireland, Scally (1998: 12) writes, 'What is particularly remarkable about this obsession is that in a country where ecumenism has been so absent, this passion is shared by northern Protestants and southern Catholics alike.' Moore (1999: 12) adds, 'Speaking of my Irish friends who also follow United brings me around to the fundamental purpose of writing this book, *United Irishmen*. When it comes to the Red Devils, Ireland *is* United' (Moore's emphasis).

The fact is, though, that over the years, many Ulster Protestants have rejected Manchester United as the English club of choice. Noting that snooker player, Alex Higgins, is a United fan, Borrows (2002:123) comments that this is unusual 'for a Belfast Protestant'. In fact, it is not at all unusual for Belfast Protestants, and Ulster unionists more generally, to support Manchester United but the author was provided with graphic evidence of the intensity of hatred felt towards United in some sections of the Protestant community whilst teaching a group of loyalists inmates of the Maze prison in the 1990s. A number of prisoners arrived for the class wearing Manchester City shirts and, when asked about their reasons for supporting City, proceeded to rhyme off a series of 'facts' which proved, to them at least, that United remains a Catholic club. But there is more to the unionist community in Northern Ireland than loyalist paramilitarism. There are Manchester United supporters' clubs in numerous towns that are overwhelmingly Protestant and unionist – Bangor, Larne Newtownards and Portadown to name but a few (www.unitedmanchester.com/sport/mufc-supporters-Irish.htm). The question is – to what extent was George Best a major factor in making the club respectable in the eyes of his fellow Protestants?

George Best was by no means the first Ulster Protestant to play for Manchester United. Indeed, two such players – Harry Gregg and Jackie Blanchflower – were involved in the 1958 Munich disaster. Blanchflower was so seriously injured that he never played again. Gregg became one of the heroes of the rescue efforts. It is worth noting in passing that Gregg was the product of a mixed marriage, having a Protestant father and a Catholic mother (Gregg, 2002). Nevertheless, he was a brought up as a Protestant, as was Blanchflower, although this did not prevent the latter from being given the last rites in the wake of the Munich crash (Scally: 1998). It was the Catholic tradition that dominated the club during Best's great years – Busby, Murphy, Crerand, Stiles, Law and the southern Irishmen, Shay Brennan, Tony Dunne and, briefly, Johnny Giles. Indeed, Eamon Dunphy, who spent a short time at the club, believes that it was Busby who had actually given Manchester United its Catholic identity. According to Dunphy (cited in Scally, 1998: 90), 'Matt identified character with Catholicism, and he believed that character was the key to success in professional sport.' This was surely an alien environment for a young Ulster Protestant to find himself in. It is true that Best was to be followed to Old Trafford by an eminent group of players whose backgrounds he shared. These included Jimmy Nicholl, Sammy McIlroy, David McCreery, Tommy Jackson and Norman Whiteside. It is Best, however, who continues to stand head and shoulders above the rest, and not only in the eyes of Ulster Protestant Manchester United fans. By the end of the 1990s in a poll conducted by a supporters' magazine, he was voted second in the all-time list of Manchester United greats with only Eric Cantona ahead of him. But the fact that he is 'one of theirs' has inevitably been an added source of pride for his co-religionists. That said, his origins did not turn Northern Irish Catholics against him or the club that he played for. What is the secret then of Best's ecumenical appeal?

The Best factor

First, he was a footballing genius. Even the most blinkered fans of other English clubs would find it difficult to deny that Best was one of the most talented performers of all time. Second, the fact that Best has always been less strongly identified with the Northern Ireland team than with Manchester United means that he has never been turned into an icon purely of unionist sport.

Third, Best grew up in Belfast before the troubles and had left his native shores long before the end of the 1960s when the simmering tensions of which he himself had been aware reached boiling point. Despite those tensions, the 1950s were a relatively tranquil period in Northern Ireland's turbulent history. As Patterson (2002: 183) notes, 'Attitudinal change was in part a reflection of important social developments. The post-war improvement in living standards meant that the arrival of the "consumer society", while not displacing traditional fixations, drained them of some of their emotional centrality.' Best reflected on this when confronted with the violence of the 1970s. He writes, 'The streets were no longer full of kids kicking a ball about but of British soldiers and tanks' (Best, 2002: 173). One of his cousins was killed, caught in crossfire and almost certainly struck by a British army bullet. Yet in many ways this was a world from which Best had managed to escape. Had he been growing up a decade later, who knows how things might have turned out? But as it has transpired, Best has found it relatively easy to speak and write about Northern Ireland in ways that would please even the most exacting of community relations activists.

This leads to a fourth aspect of Best's transcendent appeal. He comments, 'Creed and colour have never been an issue for me. I just believe in each to his own, unless that involves hurting someone else, which is wrong whichever religion or political dogma you believe in' (Best, 2002: 34). With specific reference to his birthplace, he suggests, 'You would have to be pretty naïve to come from Belfast and believe that there is only one religion doing wrong and it is not the one you believe in. There is good and bad on both sides and it takes two to make a war, which is what we've had in Northern Ireland for all these years' (Best: 2002: 233). Best received death threats during his playing career, purportedly from republicans. Loyalists, on the other hand, offered to help him to escape from the open prison to which he was sent in 1984 for a drink driving offence aggravated by assault on a police officer (Best, 2002). He declined the offer and has consistently avoided becoming embroiled in the ethno-sectarian divisions that have dominated life in Northern Ireland since the formation of the state. Indeed, as recently as December 2000, he gave his support to a cross-community project in Kilkeel, County Down, and emphasised once more that 'No matter what colour, shape, size or religion it doesn't matter' (BBC News Online, 2000).

It is also important to recognise that in this respect Best has practised what he preached. At the personal level many of his closest friends in football have been Catholics, including Pat Crerand, the late Shay Brennan and Denis Law. Moreover, in terms of sports policy, his call for an all-Ireland national team appears ecumenical in the extreme. His personal association with Catholics also leads us to a fifth, final and arguably far more contentious theory about Best's personal appeal which derives, perhaps surprisingly, from his drinking.

It is difficult to argue this point without appearing to suggest that Ireland is a nation of drunks: undeniably, though, Best's drinking habits, while explicable in part in relation to his Calvinist upbringing, certainly brought him into contact with a way of life more commonly associated, at least in its relatively guilt-free manifestation, with Irish Catholic society. Much has been made of David Beckham's transgressive power – 'new man' and 'gay icon' (Burchill, 2002; Cashmore, 2002; Whannel, 2002). But Best has also behaved transgressively by taking the stereotype of the Ulster Protestant – 'haudin' it in' – and turned it on its head. Whilst many Ulster Protestants, even those in the public eye, might appear repressed, wary of strangers and anally retentive, Best increasingly defied the stereotypes. Time and again, he, and also for that matter Alex Higgins, have beaten the Catholic Irish at what has traditionally been regarded as their own game, and imitation, as they say, is the sincerest form of flattery. Furthermore, comparing Best with Alex Higgins in terms of fielding difficult questions at sportsmen's dinners, the latter's biographer comments, 'Best also had charm enough to deal with the situation, whereas Higgins felt compelled to lash out' (Borrows, 2002: 334).

The spirit of George Best is at work when members of many of Northern Ireland's Manchester United supporters' clubs set off for Old Trafford. According to Scally (1998: 13), for many Irish fans, the stadium possesses a 'sense of mystery and religious calling'. But for the cross-community groups that travel with supporters' clubs such as those from Omagh and Portstewart, the religion being practised is vastly different from those that they experience on a daily basis. In a society where many institutions as well as places of residence are segregated along the lines of religious difference, here is a faith that can cross the divide. Similar observations could almost certainly have been made in connection with Northern Irish support for other English clubs, although not of course for Celtic and Rangers. What makes support for Manchester United somewhat different, though, is the club's traditional image. The fact that the latter has long since ceased to matter, except in the eyes of the more extreme, owes much to developments at Old Trafford whereby the club abandoned tradition in favour of consumer capitalism. But it also owes something to George Best.

Conclusion

Many of George Best's difficulties in life are almost certainly linked to his working-class, Ulster Protestant background. He has been socially dislocated in at least three ways – from his class, from his place of birth and, at a symbolic level, from his parental culture. On the other hand, the fact that he was a Protestant meant that it became less likely that his fellow Ulster Protestants would continue to view Manchester United as symbolically Catholic. In addition, by avoiding taking overtly pro-unionist positions and by acting in transgressive ways, Best did nothing to alienate Irish Catholics from the club with which he spent the most successful years of his career. People support football teams for a variety of reasons and it would be absurd to suggest that George Best was the sole factor that attracted fans in Northern Ireland to Manchester United. Catholic nationalists already had good reason to support the club and inevitably there were Ulster Protestants who, just like thousands of people from throughout the United Kingdom, were first enthused by United in the wake of the Munich disaster. Nevertheless, it would be equally foolish to underestimate the extent to which George Best was instrumental in consolidating and adding to the massive support for Manchester United in Northern Ireland.

Postscript

Back in the Red Devil Bar, most of the drinkers have gone home and the barman confides that he is a Manchester City supporter. He also expresses some dismay that the extensive televised coverage of Champions League games has interfered with his plans to show more films in the bar. As for George Best, he points to the image behind the bar and says, 'He would never come here because of where it is.' Divided cities, it would seem, always have their limits.

Acknowledgements

This chapter could not have been written without the insights provided by countless conversations with Manchester United supporters from Northern

Ireland. Special mention must be given to Derek Lyons, Colin McKenna, John Rooney and Martin Tabb and also to Sean O'Connell, an Irish Catholic Mancunian who opted for City. I owe the idea that 'haudin' it in' is the quintessential characteristic of Ulster unionism to my good friend Alan Black, mine host of the Edinburgh Castle in San Francisco and purveyor of Scottish culture, good sense and first-class fish and chips.

References

Bairner, A. (2000) 'Football, society and the literary imagination: Sam Hanna Bell's *The Hollow Ball* and Robin Jenkins' *A Would-Be Saint*', *Kunnskap om idrett*, 4: 30–43.

Bairner, A. (2002) 'Sport, sectarianism and society in a divided Ireland revisited', in J. Sugden and A. Tomlinson (eds) *Power Games: A Critical Sociology of Sport*, London: Routledge.

BBC News Online (2000) 'Best support for cross-community project', 19 December. BBC News Online available at http://news.bbc.co.uk.

BBC Television (2003) 'This is your life', 6 March.

Belfast Telegraph (2003) 'The Best of times: reflections of a genius', 20 January.

Bell, S.H. (1961) *The Hollow Ball*, London: Cassell.

Best, A. (with N. Pittam) (2001) *George Best and Me: My Autobiography*, London: Virgin Books.

Best, G. (with R. Benson) (1991) *The Good, the Bad and the Bubbly*, London: Pan Books.

Best, G. (with R. Collins) (2002) *Blessed: The Autobiography*, London: Ebury Press.

Borrows, B. (2002) *The Hurricane: The Turbulent Life and Times of Alex Higgins*, London: Atlantic Books.

Burchill, J. (2002) *Burchill on Beckham*, London: Yellow Jersey Press.

Cashmore, E. (2002) *Beckham*, Cambridge: Polity Press.

Critcher, C. (1979) 'Football since the war', in J. Clarke, C. Critcher and R. Johnson (eds) *Working Class Culture*, London: Heinemann.

Gallacher, K. (2002) *Slim Jim Baxter: The Definitive Biography*, London: Virgin Books.

Giulianotti, R. and Gerrard, M. (2001) 'Evil genie or pure genius? The (im)moral football and public career of Paul "Gazza" Gascoigne', in D.L. Andrews and S.J. Jackson (eds) *Sport Stars: The Cultural Politics of Sporting Celebrity*, London: Routledge.

Gregg, H. (with R. Anderson) (2002) *Harry's Game: The Autobiography*, Edinburgh: Mainstream.

Lovejoy, J. (1999) *Bestie: A Portrait of a Legend*, London: Pan Macmillan.

McKay, S. (2000) *Northern Protestants: An Unsettled People*, Belfast: Blackstaff Press.

Moore, C. (1999) *United Irishmen: Manchester United's Irish Connection*, Edinburgh: Mainstream.

Parkinson, M. (1975) *Best: An Intimate Biography*, London: Arrow Books.

Patterson, H. (2002) *Ireland Since 1939*, Oxford: Oxford University Press.

Risoli, M. (2001) *When Pelé Broke Our Hearts: Wales and the 1958 World Cup*, Cardiff: St David's Press.

Scally, J. (1998) *Simply Red and Green: Manchester United and Ireland – A Story of a Love Affair*, Edinburgh: Mainstream.

Sugden, J. and Bairner, A. (1993) *Sport Sectarianism and Society in a Divided Ireland*, Leicester: Leicester University Press.

Whannel, G. (2002) *Media Sport Stars: Masculinities and Moralities*, London: Routledge.

9 Under the skin of Manchester United

Knowing footballing bodies

Eileen Kennedy

On 25 June 2001, Channel 4 broadcast a documentary about the ups and downs of the career of George Best. The documentary was called 'George Best's body', and throughout the programme x-ray images appeared in a split-screen format alongside shots of Best in action. For example, whilst discussing Best's excessive drinking, the screen showed images of Best in a bar alongside an x-ray image of an upper torso, inviting us to speculate on Best's liver. When Best's relationships with women were profiled, the x-ray image was of a pelvis, and when the documentary talked about Best developing deep vein thrombosis, the x-ray panned down to the lower leg.

A recurrent motif appears to connect media representations of Manchester United footballers: the attempt to model the interior of body and mind. Reporting on George Best's liver transplant on 31 July 2002, the *Mirror* newspaper edged a double-page spread with close-up photographs of Best, drink in hand, toasting the camera, one for each year between 1967 and 2000. At the centre of the spread, a diagrammatic representation of the mechanics of a liver transplant asked the reader to imagine what was going on inside Best's body.

The bodies of Manchester United footballers seem to hold a particular fascination for the public. Extraordinarily intimate newspaper images following the disaster at Munich airport in 1958 showed footballers' injured bodies, in all their vulnerability and mortality, laid up in hospital beds. Going back further still, the original club drew its players from among Lancashire and Yorkshire Railway workers in the nineteenth century. These fit, industrial bodies were uniquely visible as a workforce, already on display to the new travelling classes. The gaze of the contemporary media on the bodies of celebrities like Best, Beckham and Keane may be different from the perspectives of the past, but it retains an intimate relationship with their bodies, often wishing not to stop at the surface of the body, but to go deeper, to go inside.

Footballers suffer from largely invisible injuries – tears and strains on the inside that do not show on the surface. Nevertheless, the camera gets as close as possible. Shots of Beckham's physical and emotional distress following his highly publicised foot injury during the Champions League quarter-final against Deportivo de La Coruña in 2002 focused on his pained facial expression as he was carried off the pitch. Both the *Mirror* and the *Sun* featured diagrams of the broken bone, which, in the case of the *Sun*, was a particularly interesting computer-generated image of a foot with bones visible inside.

The bodies of Manchester United footballers are made known to us in many ways: the player's body is described in numbers (age, weight, height ...) as is the performance of that body (appearances with club, goals scored with club, international caps, international goals ...). We see them perform on the pitch and explain their performance off it. Perhaps the waxwork of Beckham at Madame Tussauds presents the ultimate in the desire to get to know the player: *Goal!* [The exhibit] offers the possibility of experiencing the tension of Beckham's World Cup qualifying free kick against Greece at Old Trafford as the floor pulsates in time with Beckham's pounding heartbeat.

Recently, Roy Keane has been the object of attention for a range of media. The Channel 4 documentary 'Inside the mind of Roy Keane' (7 January 2003) assembled a host of 'expert' commentators (including a psychologist) to explain Keane's behaviour, and pasted extracts from his autobiography read in an Irish accent over images of Keane on the football pitch and in daily life. The result was a sense that Keane's inner thoughts were being broadcast aloud.

While the physical experiences and emotional states of other Manchester United players are being made available to us, the opportunity to see inside Roy Keane's head is at the time of writing held out as the ultimate prize. The cover of the DVD Roy Keane: As I See It promises sensation as 'Keane tells it how it is'. One of the more interesting segments of the film shows Keane in action on the pitch, while other players describe his temperament, accompanied by discordant, twangy Irish folk music, its apparently deliberate unevenness signifying the disarray of Keane's mental state. The association of his behaviour with his Irishness is underlined by the commentary 'It's tough on the foreign players'.

Roy Keane featured on the cover of *The Observer* newspaper's *Sport Monthly* supplement in September 2002. Staring straight ahead, he holds a dead bird's head in front of his face, its beak framing his right eye. The skull of the bird has caved in to reveal decaying brain matter, making an evocative connection with the title of the magazine's feature story which foreshadowed the Channel 4 documentary, 'Inside the mind of Roy Keane'. The text below the image suggests that Keane is A Man Possessed and promises 'his most candid interview ever'.

The desire to know what makes Keane tick is interestingly framed within the culture of consumption in the advertisement for *Guardian Unlimited*'s online DVD hiring service. The advertisement shows an envelope addressed to Roy Keane, Home Dressing Room, Old Trafford, Manchester, on top of which is placed the DVD of the Robert De Niro film, Taxi Driver. This speculation on Keane's taste in movies asks us to enter a complex network of identification and consumption practices to consume the fantasy of Keane's consumption habits.

This parade of representations suggests that it is the interior of Manchester United footballers' bodies that is of peculiar interest to the inquiring eye of the media, a view made ever more possible as new technologies become increasingly common place. In many ways, these images of Manchester United players evoke the explorations of the potential of new media in contemporary art. For example, the artist Mona Hatoum's installation, Corps Etranger, offers a way of thinking about the relationship between the gaze and embodiment. This installation, which featured in the Tate Gallery's exhibition of artists' work short-listed for the Turner Prize in 1997, takes the form of a cylinder, inside which, on the floor, is projected an endoscopic video image of the artist's body being explored internally. This artwork raises questions about the relationship between embodiment and the gaze, combining feelings of repulsion and fascination, familiarity and strangeness. As a form of self-portrait, the artwork raises issues about representation, the body and gender as well as playing on the implications of the title, '*corps etranger*' (strange/foreign body).

The relationship between embodiment, gender and the gaze is, then, one that has been the focus of previous investigation. Yet these representations of Manchester United footballers do not obviously correspond with the conclusions of those investigations. For example, Morgan has observed that 'women tend to be more embodied and men less embodied in social scientific, popular and feminist writings and representations' and that this may be seen 'as reflecting the well-known ideological equation between women/men and nature/culture' (2002: 407). Similarly, classic literature exploring gender and the gaze in a cinematic context (Mulvey, 1975) has associated masculinity with the gazing subject not the object of the look. Nevertheless, there does exist a literature that seeks to explore representations of male bodies in magazines and on film, and it will be interesting to explore this literature with a view to making sense of these peculiar representations of footballers' bodies. To this end, this chapter will consider Manchester United footballers' bodies in three interrelated ways: as subject to scopic penetration, as spectacle and as abject bodies. It will show how anxieties about class and masculinity are played out on the bodies of the footballers and argue that the complexity of these representations can be accounted for by the presence of an uneasy, middle-class male gaze.

Inside the visible of Manchester United

In an article exploring discourses of masculinity in new Australian men's magazines, Cook (2000) makes some observations about the way men's bodies are represented that could illuminate the politics of the representation of Manchester United footballers. Research previously undertaken in 1995 (Cook and Rudge, 1996) had uncovered ambiguous codings within the press coverage of men's health issues, finding 'representation of even the archetypically tough and resistant body (manual workers, sportsmen) overshadowed by penetrative, diagnostic technologies (x-rays, cancer screening)' (2000: 171). Four years later, Cook argues, fully developed genres of new-masculinity representations have emerged. The 1995 research revealed pressure to replace the traditional image of Australian masculinity (rough and tough, big and bulky, strong and invulnerable) with a 'cooler masculinity of rationalised and planned physical fitness' (p.172). For Cook, this move had 'clear class implications' (p.172) as the hegemony of working-class manual labour and rural independence gave way to the 'slimmer and trimmer executive masculinity of the body-beneath-the-suit' (p.172).

Cook (2000) finds a conflict in discourses of masculinity within the 'reports of regimes such as diet control, regular prostate screening, or various invasive surgical techniques used for high-masculinity sports-related injuries such as knee reconstruction or tendon repair' (p.172) found in the Australian press. Cook refers to the work of Easthope (1986) and Foucault (1994) to argue that authoritative scientific discourse has been culturally associated with masculinity, as has 'the unquestionable right to scope and scalpel penetration of the body's surface' (p.172). This invasive, regulatory gaze discovered by Foucault has been seen to have intensified with the development of new visualising technologies, Cook maintains. Yet, if the medical gaze has been associated with a 'powerful masculinity', then it has traditionally been seen to be the female body upon which it has exercised its rights 'to examine, define and surgically penetrate' (p.172). However, in the representations Cook analyses, it is the unwilling flesh of male bodies that is subject to inspection by this invasive, masculine, medical gaze.

Cook considers three sites of representation of the male body: bodybuilding magazines, men's skin-care commodity marketing and the surfing magazine, *Waves*. In each site, Cook finds a range of compensatory textual strategies to deal with the conflicting gender codings of the representations. For example, while the body is represented as a mechanistic cyborg in the bodybuilding press, partitioned into its constitutive muscle groups, Cook finds that the 'extension of claims to scopic medical penetration of the body's interior, has led to an exteriorization of the anatomical detail, which inscribes "soft" tissues onto the body's "hard" surface' (p.174). Similarly, the 'Slash of the month' feature in *Waves* magazine (in which readers send in photographic evidence of gruesome wounds sustained in the pursuit of surfing) are described as 'trophy images: accounts of pain as its own inverse', refocusing attention onto 'the ultimate invulnerability of those very individuals who have reported the wound' (p.182). The bodies that Cook finds in this literature are cyborg bodies 'of silvery liquid' with a capacity to melt or disassemble, reform and reconstitute, which, she argues, is still a form of masculinity. Following Eco and Easthope, Cook suggests that by the body's 'very capacity for transformation, it is overtly phallic' (p.183).

There is a correspondance between the representations Cook describes and the invasive, medical imaging of the bodies of Best, Beckham and Keane. Cook points to a clash of competing forms of powerful masculinity within the representations in her analysis. Similarly, the powerful, active bodies of men playing for (arguably) Britain's premier club, engaged in Britain's most popular sport, and thereby representing what may be to many the ultimate in masculinity, are subjected to the lens of another, contrasting version of masculine authority. The 'clear class implications' Cook observes are similarly unavoidable within the gulf between the masculinity of the medical gaze and the masculinity of the gazed upon.

Yet, while the bodies of Manchester United footballers are laid bare for the x-ray eyes of the media, there is no exteriorising strategy to compensate: the injuries of the players remain irresistibly interior, hidden. The regularity of accusations of fakery is testimony to the invisibility of the complaints that mysteriously take the player further out of sight for a period of convalescence. There is something very particular about the representations of celebrity Manchester United footballers that demands explanation.

Previous attention to the representation of the 'star' has focused on Hollywood cinema (Dyer, 1987). The insights of film theory, particularly in its attempts to explore the spectacle of masculinity on the big screen, may be useful in illuminating the specificity of these sporting celebrities. It is to film theory, therefore, that we turn next.

Masculinity as spectacle

Just as Laura Mulvey's now classic article 'Visual pleasure and narrative cinema' (first published in *Screen* in 1975) has formed a starting point for many discussions of cinematic images of women, theorists interested in analysing representations of men in film also tend to begin with Mulvey's account (for example, Cohan and Hark's edited collection, 1993). The reason for this interest is the way Mulvey appears to theorise away the possibility of anything other than femininity as object of the gaze. The representations under analysis here, however, are of Manchester United footballers. Professional football is an occupation that for many connotes the ultimate in masculinity, but one which simultaneously involves the presentation of male bodies for the consumption of other men. Manchester United Football Club's massive commercial and global success means that, perhaps even more than for any other club, the experience of Manchester United is a fundamentally mediated one (see Brick, 2002, for a discussion of how even those fans most likely to define themselves as authentic eschew the stadium experience for that of the pub). It is, therefore, interesting to explore Mulvey's account of the gendering of the gaze and its object in relation to representations of Manchester United footballers.

Drawing on psychoanalysis, Mulvey (1975) points to the scopophilic pleasures of cinema. The first of these pleasures she understands as a controlling and curious gaze which takes other people as objects. This is an active look, and as such is gendered masculine, and its object of investigation is the female figure that connotes 'to-be-looked-at-ness'. Secondly, cinema offers the opportunity for the spectator's narcissistic recognition/mis-recognition of the ego ideal on the screen, allowing for identification with the central character of the film's narrative. The function of the woman in the narrative is to make things happen, to be the bearer of meanings, rather than the maker of meanings. Upon her the male gaze can project its fantasies. However, recognition of sexual difference in psychoanalytic accounts is a traumatic event – the female becomes associated with lack which evokes the threat of castration in the male. The masculine unconscious, therefore, offers two responses to obviate the experience of anxiety that the sight of the female can produce. The first involves reenacting the original trauma, through investigating and demystifying the woman, and solving the problem by devaluing, punishing or saving her. There is a sadistic pleasure in this voyeuristic look which lies in first ascertaining guilt and then punishing or absolving the crime. The second involves a complete disavowal of castration, by fetishising part of the represented female figure so that the threatening image becomes comforting. 'The fetishistic gaze is captivated by what it sees and does not wish to inquire further, to see more, to find out' (Ellis, 1982, cited in Neale, 1993: 17).

Whilst generally acknowledging the importance of Mulvey's article for an understanding of the relationship between gender and the gaze, there has been plenty of time since its initial publication for critics to take issue with aspects of her argument. Consideration has been given to films where spectacle and drama appear to be structured around the look, not at the female, but at the male figure. Neale (1993) cites Willemen's analysis of Antony Mann films in this regard:

> The viewer's experience is predicated on the pleasure of seeing the male 'exist' (that is walk, move, ride, fight) in or through cityscapes, landscapes or, more abstractly, history. And on the unquiet pleasure of seeing the male mutilated (often quite graphically in Mann) and restored through violent brutality.
>
> (Willemen, in Neale, 1993: 13)

The anxiety associated with the female figure as object of the gaze has similarly produced the look at the male figure in these representations, Willemen argues. Neale (1993) furthers this point, in reference to the anxiety engendered by the sight of the wounded male body in Peckinpah's Westerns:

> The threat of castration is figured in the wounds and injuries suffered by Joel McCrea in Guns in the Afternoon, Charlton Heston in Major Dundee, and William Holden in The Wild Bunch. The famous slow-motion violence, bodies splintered and torn apart, can be viewed at one level as the image of narcissism in its moment of disintegration and destruction.
>
> (Neale 1993: 15)

It is difficult not to see the connections between Whannel's account of the media's cyclical punishment, redemption and celebration of David Beckham (2001) and the sadistic voyeurism that Mulvey says characterises one response to anxiety brought on by the gaze. The disciplinary discourse aimed at Roy Keane can be seen to be of the same order, as can the painstaking detail of the media's documentation of Best's descent into alchoholism and his salvation through surgery.

As for fetishisation as a second strategy to avoid anxiety, on 12 April 2002, a magnified image of gigantic proportion dominated the front cover of the *Sun* newspaper: Beckham's foot. Along with the headline, 'Beck us pray', the text accompanying the image exhorted readers to 'Lay your hands on David's foot at noon and make it better' in an effort to heal the broken metatarsal that threatened to keep Beckham from playing in the 2002 World Cup. The invocation of religion and iconolatory in this representation, along with the obvious attempt to disavow anxiety, intensified the moment of fetishisation of Beckham's body part: 'help mend Beckham's broken foot – and revive England's World Cup hopes'.

The association of anxiety with the spectacle of masculinity is a regular theme within discussions of cinematic representations of the male. Yvonne Tasker (1993), in her discussion of action cinema, makes reference to Dyer's analysis of stardom, suggesting that its central paradox is its instability 'constantly lurching from one formulation of what being human is to another' (Dyer, 1987: 18). For Tasker, 'the territory of the star image is also the territory of identity' which ultimately reveals itself to be as unstable as stardom, a 'process of the forging and reforging of ways of "being human" in which a point of certainty is never ultimately arrived at' (1993: 233). An inevitable part of this process is 'the ongoing formulation and reformulation of ways of "being a man"' (233–4) and it is this uncertainty that is played out in the action movie. As masculinity is seen to be a performance, it becomes denaturalised and 'anxieties to do with sexuality and difference are increasingly worked over the male body and its commodification as spectacle' (1993: 237). Referring to Lacan's concept of male parade 'in which the accoutrements of phallic power, the finery of authority, belie the very lack that they display', she suggests that, within these films, the muscularity of the male bodies functions like a costume, ironically, to veil a lack of power.

Film theory might also be useful in exploring the power relations involved in making somebody the object of the gaze. Hark's discussion of the film Spartacus considers the way in which the 'permission to become a spectator demarcates the master from the slave' (1993: 155). By making spectacles of others, situating them on the side, not of the seeing subject, but the inhuman object, Imperial Rome was able to enforce its power over those it dominated. Within the binaries of culture, masculinity is more usually associated with the human side, the seeing side. However, in films like Spartacus, and arguably in representations of footballers, masculinity is bound up with embodiment, the animal rather than the human, the side more usually associated with femininity. Gender confusion is the inevitable result of exposure to the gaze.

Abject bodies?

June 2002, and *Marie Claire* magazine announces 'Man on cover alert!'. Fuss (1992) has suggested that the address of images of women in women's magazines is a complex process, creating a tension between having and becoming the female image in the female reader. While these magazines are ostensibly aimed at a heterosexual female readership, Fuss suggests that they engender what she calls a homospectatorial gaze. The first man on the cover of *Marie Claire*, was, of course, David Beckham. While even Spartacus refused the dehumanising gaze of his owner in his most intimate moments, Beckham announces 'I'm an animal in bed.' The spread inside the magazine has an extreme close-up image of Beckham's face and neck (a shot Fuss describes as typical of images of women in these magazines, and one that suggests a vampyric address), his gaze directed towards text on the facing page that details the ways he is offered for consumption by the reader: 'father, lover, Becks, icon, hero'. The article itself continues to trouble gender categories, by having Beckham discuss his nails and acknowledge 'I sound like a girl, don't I?'

There is much in this article that can be said to destabilise and denaturalise notions of gendered identity. If women's magazines regularly offer images of women for the consumption of women, revealing a complex and shifting process of sexual identification, what happens to Beckham's masculinity as he stands in for the usual female on the cover is anyone's guess. Butler reports the sentiments of a lesbian femme who liked her boys to be girls, 'meaning that "being a girl" contextualises and resignifies "masculinity" in a butch identity' (Butler, 2002: 49), arguing that it is 'precisely this dissonant juxtaposition and the sexual tension that its transgression generates that constitute the object of desire' (p.49). Butler goes on to suggest that, similarly, heterosexual or bisexual women may prefer their girls to be boys. Perhaps that is the case here.

Creed (1993), in her analysis of horror films, suggests that by mixing categories like dead and alive (vampires) or animal and human (werewolves), monsters belong to that order of things that 'disturbs identity, system, order', which Kristeva has characterised as abject (Kristeva, in Creed, 1993: 121). Central to Kristeva's theory of abjection is society's requirement that the abject be expelled in order to maintain acceptable forms of subjectivity. However, 'a crucial aspect of the abject is ... that it can never be fully removed or set apart from the subject or society: the abject both threatens and beckons' (Creed, 1993: 121). The monsters Creed describes, in their moment of monstrosity, take on the characteristics of female bodies: changing shape, bleeding, becoming penetrable, giving birth. In this way, and because femininity is associated with the abject, Creed suggests that monsters are feminised.

Abjection offers a way of understanding the complexity of the representation of the Manchester United footballers' bodies discussed here. Their exposure to scopic penetration and the spectacle puts them on the side of the feminine, yet their embodiment of superhuman agency (in their finer moments) indelibly marks them with high masculinity. As such, the abject quality of these bodies 'beseeches, worries and fascinates desire' (Kristeva, in Creed, 1993: 121). Every condemnation of Keane's tackle on Haaland requires it to be reinspected, each voice of concern at Best's profligate past needs a picture to show it all again.

The body of another footballer that has been similarly pored over, criticised and analysed is that belonging to Paul Gascoigne. While revered for his ability to display artistry on the pitch, Gascoigne has been reviled for his boorishness, characterised as incapable of controlling infantile bodily drives, yet he demonstrates the ultimate autonomy of adulthood in making his body bend to his will. Horrocks (1995) has observed an underlying tension within the gender identity of players like Gascoigne:

> ... the body/spirit split is mapped onto dualities within class and gender. The working-class male is seen as corporeal, gross, eructating: the middle class is more spiritual, more refined but looks with envy and a certain excitement at the physical carnival enacted by men such as Gazza. Gazza's body and

personality become a text which is alienated from him, in fact becomes public property, upon which can be inscribed various messages.

(Horrocks, 1995: 163)

The ambivalent relationship with these abject bodies is filtered through the lens of class, in Horrocks' account. An observation such as this demands a reexamination of the class dynamic involved in the way these footballers' bodies have been positioned as objects of the gaze.

Fergie decks Becks and mocks Sven: how the tale was told

On Monday 15 February 2003, news began to emerge via the *Sun* that Alex Ferguson and David Beckham had been in a post-match altercation the previous Saturday (which had seen a 2–0 win by Arsenal and put Manchester United out of the Football Association [FA] Cup). Apparently, Ferguson kicked a boot across the players' dressing room, which struck Beckham above his left eye. By Tuesday, the papers were full of pictures of Beckham unashamedly sporting a wound visually enhanced by its dressing of Steri-strips placed 'X-marks-the-sport' style over his eyebrow, as well the Alice band that pulled his hair back, exposing the injury for all to see. The *Metro* (a free sheet aimed at London's tube travellers) offered a vision of 'Beckham: The inside story on THAT injury' in the style of a 'Roy of the Rovers' cartoon depicting the dressingroom scene, the boot at point of impact and Beckham's contemplation of his wound: 'Hey, what other colours do these butterfly stitches come in?' The *Sun*, meanwhile, offered a cut-out-and-keep guide to making your own Steri-strips, with the injunction to 'Band it like Beckham' for those whose identification with the footballer might prompt the adoption of a similarly stylish battle scar.

Media interest in the story continued all week, but by the weekend the news had shifted from Ferguson and Beckham to Ferguson and Eriksson. The Sunday papers of 23 February had switched their interest from Beckham's brow to the allegations Alex Ferguson had made that the England manager, Sven Goran Eriksson, had intended to break his contract in order to take over as manager of Manchester United if Ferguson had stood down.

The new story was discussed in both the tabloids and the broadsheet newspapers, papers traditionally considered to address different segments of the British public distinguished by class and education. Yet, despite the omnipresence of the story, a glance at the style of the reporting across the range of tabloids and broadsheets reveals a distinct difference in approach, one that might be related to the class dimension of the newspapers' address. Among the broadsheets, the story had a double-page spread in both the *Observer* and the *Sunday Times*, and two-thirds of a page in the *Independent on Sunday*. The tabloid papers, the *News of the World*, the *People* and the *Sunday Mirror*, all featured the story on their back page, with between three and five pages of coverage inside. In the broadsheets, the story appeared to be principally about Ferguson, while in the tabloids, it was Eriksson's behaviour that was the centre of the story.

The *Observer* alerted readers to the story with a headline and picture on the front pages of both the main news section and the inside sport section. Each picture digitally combined images of the major players in the story. On the main section cover the image presented a grim-looking Ferguson as if flanked from behind by Eriksson and Beckham, who appear to be looking accusingly towards Ferguson. The image on the sport section showed only Eriksson and Ferguson, again with Ferguson in front and Eriksson's stare piercing the back of Ferguson's head.

The main story, under the headline 'Fergie's here to stay', characterises Ferguson as passionate and manipulative, suggesting that his motive was not only to 'embarrass' Eriksson but 'because he does not want to make way for Eriksson, nor anyone else for that matter'. The accompanying photograph is of Eriksson and Ferguson, in side profile, their gazes meeting, with Ferguson pointing his finger at Eriksson in an assertive, if not aggressive, gesture.

At the bottom of the double page runs 'Bootgate', 'The story behind the story', a trawl through the tabloid reporting of the boot-to-head incident over the course of the last week. Placed at this significantly low point on the page, the column adopts the nickname intimacy of tabloid-speak to tell of 'Becks', 'Giggsy and Keano', 'Fergie' and the boot. Bordering the main spread, another article speculates pessimistically on the length of Keane's remaining career in Premier League football, describing a 'routine operation' ... 'to have his hip examined and scar tissue removed'.

The broadsheets all characterise Ferguson and Eriksson as opposites in temperament. The *Sunday Times* conceives of Eriksson in its readers' language of stocks and shares while describing Ferguson as having a 'volcanic temper'. In the face of this volatility, Eriksson appears dispassionate and objective, if still the outsider: 'When Eriksson departs, it will not be because of anything Ferguson has said. More likely it will be because he dislikes media intrusion here, he now appreciates that club versus country is a debilitating English disease ...'. The contrast between Ferguson's spoken words and the language of the broadsheet is keenly made in the *Independent on Sunday* as an extract from the famous interview ('They'd done the deal all right ...') is inserted into an otherwise extremely literate article. For the *Observer*, Eriksson's composure (described in the *Independent on Sunday* as a 'lack of visible emotion') makes him, in spite of his actual nationality, typically English. In the *Observer*'s version of Englishness, Eriksson is 'the Iceman, England the country of manners'.

In the tabloids, however, the story centres not on Ferguson and the attempt to see inside his mind for motive and future intention, but on Eriksson's apparent disloyalty to the England team. The back page of the *People* has an image of Eriksson in side profile, his hands clasped over his mouth, forefingers resting on his lips, which gives the impression of evil contemplation as he leans into the accompanying text, which declares, 'Sven. He's lost the plot, he's lost our trust.' Inside, a story sets the record straight about the Ferguson–Beckham rift by giving 'the facts' of the encounter, which turn out not to be as colourful as we might otherwise have thought, thereby salvaging Ferguson's reputation somewhat. The *Sunday Mirror*, in contrast to the broadsheets' use of 'Fergie', refers only to Ferguson as 'Sir Alex Ferguson' who 'suggested in an interview last week that the Swede shook hands with United's board'. The *News of the World* are similarly intent on this respectful mode of address while describing both Eriksson and the Manchester United board as 'treacherous' and therefore deserving of each other. Interestingly, the same photograph used in the *Observer* appears also in the *News of the World*, but this time the heads of Eriksson and Ferguson are separated by the text of the article and its accompanying headlines, which leave little doubt as to the paper's affiliation: 'Sven's United shame' opposite 'Sir Alex Ferguson opens his heart to the sport of the world'. The *News of the World* even has a different slant on Keane's future, countering the pessimism of the *Observer* with 'Keano to play for five more years.'

Class, gender and the gaze

Manchester United FC is a global phenomenon, with media interest in the players no longer confined to the back pages of tabloid newspapers. The bodies of the footballers are regularly subjected to both a voyeuristic and fetishistic gaze, and the sadistic inquiry of the voyeuristic scopophilia that surrounds them is not even content to rest on the surface of the body, but wants to see inside the minds and bodies of the players. Despite their masculinity, their spectacular bodies appear to evoke the same anxiety that the sight of women's bodies arouse, since the media use the same strategies to contain it. Confusion as to their rightful place within the hierarchy of gender and the gaze produces the fear and fascination that surrounds the abject.

To recall Cook's (2000) analysis of new man imagery, however, is to add another dimension to the story. The 'clear class implications' of the move away from the bulky, combative bodies of the labouring class to the 'cooler masculinity of rationalised and planned physical fitness' (p.172) is also observable within the power dynamic of the media's gaze on the footballer's body. While similar approaches to the imaging of the footballer's body are discernible across the range of media, irrespective of its class connotations, the more sustained attempt to probe the interior of the players' minds and bodies appear in publications like the *Observer Sport Monthly* and within sports documentaries broadcast on Channel 4. Arguably, these media are engaged in cultivating an address to a middle-class male audience and in so doing reveal a particular relationship with the working-class bodies of the footballers that are the subject of the magazine articles and television programmes. A desire for intimate knowledge of these bodies is evident, but the possibility of identification appears problematic. The coverage of the Ferguson/Beckham/Eriksson triangle by the broadsheets is revealing in this regard. The *Observer* reports in its 'Bootgate' article that 'New Man versus Old Man' is a hot topic at the *Observer*'s Tuesday news conference'. The *Observer* itself appears on the side of the new men, with their cooler, middle-class, rationalised masculinity, identifying with the gaze of Beckham and Eriksson drilling into the back of the old-style, working-class Ferguson, in their front page collage advertising the story within.

Foucault (1977) has made us aware of the relationship between power and knowledge. To turn another person into a spectacle is to assert power over them. Yet the bodies of Manchester United footballers display a more immediate power in their control of their physicality that is the substance of the spectacle. This is not a static picture, however. The struggle between these two positions of power is regularly played out in the media, as these powerful bodies are opened up and gazed upon, and the institution of sport science appears intent on taking control of the performance into its own hands.

From the spectacle that the powerful bodies of railway workers would have provided for the middle-class rail passenger in the nineteenth century to the contemporary media celebrity, the tensions between class, gender and the gaze have followed Manchester United throughout its history. Manchester United footballers' bodies continue to worry and fascinate desire.

References

Brick, C. (2002) 'Fandemonium: the discourse of authenticity in the FA Carling Premier League', unpublished PhD thesis, University of Surrey Roehampton.

Butler, J. (2002) 'Performative subversions', in S. Jackson and S. Scott (eds) *Gender: A Sociological Reader*, London: Routledge.

Cohan, S. and Hark, I.R. (eds) (1993) *Screening the Male: Exploring Masculinities in Hollywood Cinema*, London: Routledge.

Cook, J. (2000) 'Men's magazines at the millennium: new spaces, new selves', *Continuum: Journal of Media and Cultural Studies*, 14(2): 171–86.

Cook, J. and Rudge, T. (1996) *Masculinity, Risk-taking and Men's Health and Safety*, Adelaide: University of South Australia and Workcover South Australia.

Creed, B. (1993) 'Dark desires: male masochism in the horror film', in S. Cohan and I.R. Hark (eds) *Screening the Male: Exploring Masculinities in Hollywood Cinema*, London: Routledge.

Dyer, R. (1987) *Heavenly Bodies: Film Stars and Society*, Basingstoke: Macmillan.

Easthope, A. (1986) *What a Man's Gotta Do: The Masculine Myth in Popular Culture*, London: Paladin.

Foucault, M. (1977) *Discipline and Punish: The Birth of the Prison*, London: Penguin.

Foucault, M. (1994) *The Birth of the Clinic: An Archaeology of Medical Perception*, New York: Vintage Books.

Fuss, D. (1992) 'Fashion and the homospectatorial look', *Critical Inquiry*, 18: 713–37.

Hark, I.R. (1993) 'Animals or Romans: looking at masculinity in Spartacus' in S. Cohan and I.R. Hark (eds) *Screening the Male: Exploring.Masculinities in Hollywood Cinema*, London: Routledge.

Horrocks, R. (1995) *Male Myths and Icons: Masculinity in Popular Culture*, London: Macmillan.

Morgan, D. (2002) 'You too can have a body like mine', in S. Jackson and S. Scott (eds) *Gender: A Sociological Reader*, London: Routledge.

Mulvey, L. (1975) 'Visual pleasure and narrative cinema', *Screen* 16(3): 6–18.

Neale, S. (1993) 'Prologue: masculinity as spectacle. Reflections on men and mainstream cinemea', in S. Cohan and I.R. Hark (eds) *Screening the Male: Exploring Masculinities in Hollywood Cinema*, London: Routledge.

Tasker, Y. (1993) 'Dumb movies for dumb people: masculinity, the body, and the voice in contemporary action cinema', in S. Cohan and I.R. Hark (eds) *Screening the Male: Exploring Masculinities in Hollywood Cinema*, London: Routledge.

Whannel, G. (2001) 'Punishment, redemption and celebration in the popular press: the case of David Beckham', in D.L. Andrews and S.J. Jackson (eds) *Sport Stars: The Cultural Politics of Sporting Celebrity*, London: Routledge.

Media

'George Best's body', 25 June 2001, Channel 4.

'Inside the mind of Roy Keane', 7 January 2001, Channel 4.

The *Mirror*, 31 July 2002.

The *Mirror*, 11 April 2002.

The *Sun*, 12 April 2002.

Roy Keane: As I See It, 2002, Bombo Sports and Entertainment Production.

The *Observer Sport Monthly*, September 2002, no. 31.

The *Metro*, 18 February 2003.

The *Sun*, 18 February 2003.

The *Sunday Times*, 23 February 2003.

The *Independent on Sunday*, 23 February 2003.

The *Observer*, 23 February 2003.

The *News of the World*, 23 February 2003.

The *Sunday Mirror*, 23 February 2003.

The *People*, 23 February 2003.

Marie Claire, UK Edition, June 2002.

10 'Cute with vague feminist gender shift'
Posh and Becks united

Pirkko Markula

This chapter is about Victoria Beckham, also known as Posh Spice from the pop music group Spice Girls. Why write about her in a book about Manchester United when she is not even a football fan (and her footballing husband is no longer with the club)? She says herself: 'My interest in football is limited to David. I don't watch the ball, I watch David. If the two coincide, then fine' (Beckham, 2001: 5). I don't support either, but like Victoria I surely watch David, the world's best footballer and a handsome man, if he is on television. Neither one of us really cares about football, but we are, nevertheless, quite closely connected to it. Victoria through her marriage to David Beckham, me through my work as a sport sociologist in the United Kingdom (UK), where football is the self-acclaimed king of sports. We have more things in common, as it turns out: rather than sports people, we are trained dancers. What are we doing in this book, then? Victoria herself finds academic interest in her rather incomprehensible, like when in a Devon pub, 'A woman came up to me and said that her daughter was doing media studies at university studying me and David. I mean, how weird is that? The world was going mad' (Beckham, 2001: 336). My university is in Devon and obviously I am among those weird university people. I suppose her world of pop stardom and fame is equally strange and artificial to me: artificial nails, artificial hair extensions, artificially enhanced voice, artificial lifestyle. Why *not* write about her life then? After all she, with her pop star lifestyle, was the most famous woman associated with Manchester United Football Club during David Beckham's long reign there until his transfer to Real Madrid. So much so that she continues to evoke very strong feelings among the football community. Victoria described the attention she receives: 'Posh Spice. Who everyone knows wants to take their precious Golden Boy away from Manchester United, everyone knows who she is, the most hated woman in England, that's what I've been called. Nice' (Beckham, 2001: 4). How can a particular footballer's wife be so hated? In this chapter I aim to understand the otherness she feels within the football world. I am particularly interested in applying a feminist interpretation of Gilles Deleuze's theory of becoming-woman that lifts devalued otherness to the centre of analysis. This can offer us, Victoria and me, a positive site for the redefinition of female subjectivity within/through football.

Becoming-woman: Gilles Deleuze and feminism

Unlike Jacques Derrida, Michel Foucault or Jacques Lacan, Gilles Deleuze has not been very widely quoted by feminists. One reason is, perhaps, the relative inaccessibility of Deleuze's phantasmagorical world of rhizomatics; another, as some feminists assert, is his depoliticisation of women's struggles. This does not mean, necessarily, that Deleuze's philosophy is entirely unsuitable for feminist analyses, however, as there have been some applications of his theory to analyses of women's condition in the world (e.g. Braidotti, 1993, 1997; Grosz, 1994b; Fraser, 1997).

Deleuze aims to expose philosophy as an ontology of a unified subject and then, together with Felix Guattari, develop a new, transgressive way of understanding 'the subject'. According to Deleuze, theoretical assumptions of psychoanalysis, semiotics and Marxism are based on the ontology of a unified subject that seriously limits our capacity to understand the world and ourselves. Such an ontology is limiting, because it visions humans as functional, organised 'organisms' open to interpretation of their significance and subjectification. For Deleuze, this locks the analysis of the forces embodied in humans, animals, things, or the world into a narrow frame:

> ... you will be organised, you will be an organism, you will articulate your body ... you will be signifier and signified, interpreter and interpreted ... You will be subject, nailed down as one, a subject of the enunciation recoiled into the statement.
>
> (Deleuze and Guattari, 1987: 159)

Furthermore, the insistence on a unified subject results in a world of 'molar' unities such as classes, races and sexes that form and stabilise identity (Grosz, 1994) that are organised based on divisions of dualistic, oppositional difference such as men/women, black/white, other/self. Therefore, the ontology of a unified subject has led to the stratification that creates inequalities in society. To overcome the limitations of a unified subject and to radically refigure the notion of identity, self and difference, Deleuze introduces his world of rhizomatics.

Through the notion of the rhizome, Deleuze conceptualises difference beyond the great 'illusions' of representation such as a stable identity based on a definition of dualistic difference. Rhizome refers to a worldview that is not grounded in one 'root': one truth, one identity, one reality. He contrasts the rhizome to an image of a tree that, supported by one major root, is supposed to grow tall. 'Nature doesn't work that way' (Deleuze and Guattari, 1987: 5), he concludes, but as a rhizome. Nature multiplies through particles, it is heterogeneous, but connected, yet in unstructured ways.

> Rhizome as subterranean stem is absolutely different from roots and radicles. Bulbs and tubers are rhizomes ... The rhizome itself assumes very diverse forms, from ramified surface extension in all directions to concretion into

bulbs and tubers ... Rhizome includes the best and the worst: potation and couchgrass, or the weed.

(Deleuze and Guattari, 1987: 6-7)

In the rhizomatic world, subjects and objects are a series of flows, energies, movements, strata, segments, organs, intensities. They are fragments capable of being linked together or severed in potentially infinite ways other than those which congeal them into identities. Deleuze labels the linkages between the heterogeneous, disparate and discontinuous fragments as assemblages that can be ideas, things, human or animate. These assemblages are not permanent linkages, but they are endlessly experimenting, aligning and realigning, mutating and metamorphosing into new ways of existence. Therefore, assemblages do not produce a permanent identity, but are nomadic and made rather than found or natural. As a result, identities become multiple instead of fixed and formed in a constant process of assemblage, they become molecular instead of molar.

In contemporary society, the signs for redefinition of a molar subjectivity into a molecular one rest in marginalised groups, in minorities and in devalued otherness such as womanhood. It is important to emphasise, however, that Deleuze's nomadic and processual understanding of identity does not assume that, just because one belongs to a minority, such as womankind, one is born with a capacity to break out from the limitations of a fixed, molar identity. On the contrary, the process of becoming molecular is always 'made', not natural or 'unconscious'. Ultimately, all identities will be broken into a field of molecular trajectories and we will turn 'imperceptible'. However, Deleuze uses the notion of becoming-woman as a medium in the process of becoming-imperceptible.

A woman, usually conceptualised as a passive, devalued but necessary operator of the phallocentric system of majority/sedentary/molar, turns into the figurehead of Deleuze's becoming/minority/molecular/nomadic (Braidotti, 1997). In Deleuze's view, becoming-woman does not mean turning physically or even symbolically into a molar identity of woman, but rather becoming-woman means different things for men and women. For men, 'it implies a de- and restructuring of male sexuality, of the forms of genital domination, bringing into play the micro-femininities of behaviours, the particles of another sexuality' (Grosz, 1994a: 177), and thus inviting into play the multiple forces suppressed under the forms of domination. Deleuze is not equally clear what becoming-woman means for women, but feminists such as Elizabeth Grosz (1994a) theorise that it involves the destablisation of the molar, or feminine, identity by questioning the coagulations, rigidifications, impositions required by patriarchal power relations. This process then disengages the segments and constraints of the molar entities of woman or feminine to reinvest into other particles and flows, speeds and intensities. As Rosi Braidotti (1997) summarises: during the process of becoming, one peels off 'stratum after stratum, the layers of signification that have been tattooed in the surface of our body and ... in its psychic recesses and the internalised folds of one's sacrosanct "experience"' (p. 78). Furthermore, for Braidotti, becoming-woman is necessarily an embedded and embodied process: 'the process of becoming is like the patient task of approximating, through a series of adaptations, the raw simplicity of the forces that shape one's embodied intensity or existential temperature' (p. 68). Therefore, becoming-woman involves specific movements, specific forms of motion and rest, speed and slowness, points and flows of intensities. It is always multiple as it engages in the movement or transformation from one thing to another. This process occurs in a space that Deleuze labels the Body without Organs (BwO).

As I stated earlier, Deleuze defines 'organism' – our understanding of the physical body as a hierarchical, organised, functional entity – categorising identity into molar entities and aims to go beyond such narrow conceptualisations with his concept of BwO. BwO is regarded neither as a locus for consciousness, as in psychoanalysis, nor an organically determined entity, but is rather the body before it became an organism: a surface of speeds and intensities before the body is stratified, unified, organised and hierarchised (but not a blanket for rewriting or remapping the body – not a representational body). Because BwO is neither inhabitable nor representable (Fraser, 1997), it is not important what BwO is, but how it functions, what its affects are, what it produces: 'the linkages it establishes, the transformations and becomings it undergoes, and the machinic connections it forms with other bodies, what it can link with, how it can proliferate its capacities' (Grosz, 1994a: 165). BwO, therefore, is a discontinuous, nontotalisable series of processes, organs, flows, energies, corporeal substances and incorporeal events, speeds and durations and, as such, represents the dismantling of molar identities as the prevailing social order. BwO always exists in a relation and, therefore, the self and identity are displaced as the locus of political change (Braidotti, 1997; Fraser, 1997). How, though, does feminist research rest on such a concept as BwO?

The most defining feature of Deleuze's philosophy is the idea of an identity in flux. For feminism, this is a somewhat problematic starting point, because an identity, that of a woman, is the founding concept in the struggle against oppression. Deleuze does not necessarily advocate the abandonment of women's fight for better conditions because, as Braidotti (1997) points out, the world is not Deleuzian quite yet. But Deleuze might help feminists explore more radical forms of women's 'resistance': radical forms of molecular becoming that will break the oppressive stratification of the molar identity, woman. Therefore, the first task is to expose the molarity of the feminine identity. For a feminist researcher this means a radical reconceptualisation of how to analyse femininity. To attempt an analysis of the molecular, a Deleuzian has to abandon the idea that feminine is a representation, a sign of ideology. If femininity is not a symptom, a product of patriarchal culture, what is it? Moreover, how is it possible to live without an identity? Molecular might not necessarily mean no identity, but perhaps, more closely, an idea of femininity as a series of micro-femininities that are constantly in the process of becoming through micro-processes, intensities and flows. This reorientation shifts the focus from an individual and identity to a new meeting point in the BwO. Now individuals or micro-intensities connect directly, not through the mediation of systems of ideology or representation, but through assemblages or trajectories that intersect in the BwO.

This is a subject whose embodiment is a process of perpetual becoming (Braidotti, 1997). Therefore, a Deleuzian analysis does not require a total dissolution of identity, a complete destabilisation and defamiliarisation of identity; but rather micro-destratifications, and intensifications of some but clearly not all interactions (Grosz, 1994a). What does this mean for my analysis of Victoria Beckham?

Following a Deleuzian anti-essentialist philosophy, I cannot read Victoria Beckham as a representation, a signification of femininity shaped by ideology or discourse. So what do I do instead? I follow Braidotti's (1997) advice and plan to explore possible radical forms of molecular becoming by analysing a series of media texts of Victoria Beckham, hoping to find cultural illustrations of becoming. To achieve this, I somehow have to shift the focus from her identity and representational body into interactions that intensify into assemblages and turn the molar femininity into a nomadic, molecular process of becoming. Somehow, I have to look for a BwO that creates lines of flight between her and others. Somehow, I have to reconceptualise her body from an organically determined entity into a performing, processual becoming-woman.

Victoria Beckham: becoming-woman

In the Deleuzian vision, marginalised groups, particularly, embody signs for redefinition of molar categories and, thus, can guide the process of becoming molecular. There is, however, nothing seemingly 'minority' in Victoria Beckham. She is white, young, thin, wealthy, happily married to a famous man and a mother of two healthy children. But such classifications, for Deleuze, are, or course, molar identities that limit the bodily forces into unbreakable categories. Instead of reading her as a representation of femininity shaped by dominant ideologies, I aim to read her identity pragmatically: what she can do. Therefore, femininity, instead of being a limitation, is looked at as a positive; as a constant process of becoming-woman. It is comprised of micro-femininities that break down the molar category of woman.

I aim to look at Victoria becoming-woman through the lens of popular media texts. It is evident that the media tend to capture their subjects into molar categories, but, as Braidotti (1997) argues, we should also detect grids of possible lines of becoming across such texts. Such grids might become more visible through media texts over which Victoria has some control herself, such as her autobiography *Learning to Fly* and a TV documentary 'Being Victoria Beckham' created simultaneously with the book. Therefore, my main focus in this chapter is on these two texts.

The process of becoming-woman involves a reconstruction of the body as a Body without Organs. When the body is freely amenable to flows and intensities, it becomes a BwO which might be something that neither Victoria nor I are ready for. I ask, however, what is the thing or idea that breaks down the gendered definitions of the feminine subject and creates a grid for possible lines of becoming in Victoria's autobiographical texts? What are the assemblages that intensify connections between individuals and create a process of becoming-woman (and challenge the molar femininity)? The first step in this process is to detract my focus from what her body is. It is no longer relevant to read her body to be something else, like a representation of ideology, despite the great temptation to analyse her thin, young, sexy, fashionable, heterosexual, reproductive body as the penultimate representation of a patriarchal definition of femininity. In order to trace the process of becoming, the focus has to switch to what Victoria's body does. This can further lead to tracing the possible assemblage of microfemininities that demonstrates Victoria's process of becoming-woman. Such trajectories can also make visible trajectories that link her with other subjects (David) or things (Manchester United) to create molecular processes of becoming-woman and ultimately signal to a direction of a Body without Organs. And what does Victoria do?

Becoming-woman: the performing body

As long as she can remember, Victoria wanted to dance, to become a dancer. Her family remembers that she was always dancing, going to dance classes since she was three years old (dancing in this context is not defined more clearly, but seems to refer to performing in musical productions). After seeing the film Fame, Victoria decided to take her dancing 'more seriously' and she enrolled in the local dance school. There she is remembered as a little girl with stars in her eyes and 'something magic in her' (ITV, 2002); she is credited for hard work, but, curiously, not for her dancing ability. One of her teachers states: 'There are lot of people, I'm being quite honest here, with more talent doing less than Victoria is doing' (ITV, 2002). Victoria, regardless, aimed for a professional dance career and enrolled in a training course at the Laine Theatre Arts in London. Despite her hard work, Victoria's dance career did not blossom. She feels that it was not necessarily her ability – what her body can do – but the way her body looked: too fat. Victoria's teenage insecurity about the way her body looked surfaced during her dance training where the emphasis was on the body shape of the dancers. She recalls:

> It was always the very tall leggy beautiful girls who would start off the finale, and we'd all join on the line, high-kicking all the way back … And I'll never forget the last dress rehearsal. I was standing, at the back of course, and Betty Laine came up to me and said: 'You're so fat I'm going to have to fly you in. I'm going to have to get you in on a crane because you're such a roly-poly.'
> (Beckham, 2001: 52)

Even today, regardless of her successful modelling career, she is extremely conscious about her body shape. It was not until the Spice Girls that her performing ability was recognised. Victoria herself, however, does not consider the Spice Girls much of a dancing act, but notes that it was easy for her, a trained dancer, to perform the choreography. Therefore, if her body's looks is a source of great insecurity, her determination, her ambition and her hard work, have helped her to succeed and today she says: 'I love what I do, I HAVE to perform.' She has learned to fly. Curiously, David continuously refers to her as a singer, never as a dancer.

Singing, of course, is what Victoria is known for now. However, she does not talk a lot about her musical training. She says:

> Because I'd been on the dancing course rather than the musical theatre course at Laine's, I hadn't done a lot of singing but I've always been able to belt something out ... I didn't want to showcase my voice, I wanted to showcase my personality.
>
> (Beckham, 2001: 55)

Generally, her singing ability is treated with suspicion and she is often accused of 'lipsynching' rather than using her own voice. However, performing with the Spice Girls gave her all the confidence she was lacking. Her successful career was launched as a member of a group of girls that one music critic described as 'a highly stylised, high-concept team who epitomised the notion of "strength in numbers"' (McCormick, 2002: 25). Victoria, however, characterises the Spice Girls as a group of 'loud, gutsy, ruthless workaholics' (Beckham, 2001: 83). In addition, being a Spice Girl meant constant performance, on and off stage. As each of the band members was baptised with a nickname by Peter Lorraine, editor of the *Tops of the Pops* magazine, Victoria's public persona as 'the classy one, the cool one who wore Gucci' (Beckham, 2001: 117) earned her the title 'Posh.' And a special character came with it. While Victoria confesses that she'd 'been playing a Little Madam ever since I could talk' (p.108), performing Posh gave her the confidence to shop on Rodeo Drive in Los Angeles and tell the shop assistant she already has everything; or to read out half-time scores of the other premiership games in the middle of Old Trafford and make a mockery of it. Despite her confidence as Posh Spice, Victoria's attempts at a solo career have not been as successful. One music critic summarises: 'During the few "live" appearances she made to promote her solo material it was evident that she was actually miming, which hardly displays much confidence in her own vocal abilities' (McCormick, 2002: 25). After her first album was considered a flop, her record company, Virgin, dropped her, but Victoria has recently signed a new contract with Telstar for £1.5 million (Gent, 2002). With her determination and ability to perform, Victoria seems to continue to fly. As she states herself: 'I'm not a diva and I never set out to be a pop singer, I set out to be a performer, and that's what I do best, entertain people' (Beckham, 2001: 364). How can Victoria's performative body be located within Deleuze's framework of becoming-woman?

Victoria's performativity can be understood as a type of microfemininity: a trajectory that forms part of the grid that enables her feminine body to proliferate its capacity and engage in the process of becoming-woman. Microfemininities can also establish a grid of molecular becoming where different subjects engage in refiguration of molar identities. Performativity, I argue, creates a trajectory that links Victoria and David together and enables a different line of flight to emerge in a grid of becoming.

In a Deleuzian rhizomatic world, subjects, rather than locked into stable molar unities, are capable of linking together in trajectories that allow a constant experimenting, realigning and redefinition of identity. Victoria redefines herself in her performing body that simultaneously assembles with other subjects in her process of becoming. David is, naturally, closely connected to such a process as a subject with a highly performative body. Obviously, there are differences between Victoria's and David's bodily performances. David is famous because of his ability as a football player. Everyone, including Victoria, recognises that. Victoria is never credited for being a very good dancer or a very good singer, but she does want to be taken seriously. And with hard work, she has, indeed, become a very good performer, but she never takes anything for granted:

> And sometimes it's made even harder for me because David so obviously does have ability to back it [his fame] up ... it's quite hard for such an insecure person as I am, going out with someone like David. OK, people might sometimes be bitchy about him but the bottom line is no one can criticise him for what he is famous for.
>
> (Beckham, 2001: 368)

However, their ability to perform is the assemblage where their trajectories meet to create a possibility for BwO that shatter both the molar femininity and molar masculinity. Nowhere is this clearer than in their performative style. Victoria is well known for her fondness of designer clothing, particularly Gucci, but while the common joke is that Victoria dresses David, he seems genuinely, if not more, interested in fashion and style than Victoria. Of course, for David, it is easier to break out from the rather narrowly defined masculine style by wearing the well-publicised sarong, designer suits or constantly changing hair styles and colours. When they appear together, the effect of their performative style magnifies: all cameras focus on them, guaranteeing instant attention. Victoria is not unaware of their impact as a couple:

> The sheer fuss that everybody made around us ... quite astounded me. And it did feel really weird, because I've never had that before and David doesn't get that when he's on his own. I'm not saying we don't both get a lot of attention individually, but it's nothing compared with what happens when we're together. It's kind of crazy, people go to pieces around us.
>
> (Beckham, 2001: 367)

Their style, self-described as over the top, is further exemplified by their extravagant parties. Their lavish wedding in 1999 in a Luttrellstone Castle in Ireland was documented by OK magazine who already, two years before the wedding took place, paid £1 million cash for exclusive rights to report the event. For David, that paid for the wedding; for Victoria, that also took care of the security as OK magazine paid to keep the wedding protected from other media. According to their wedding coordinator, Peregrine Armstrong-Jones, the event took ten months to organise and a cast of over 300 to prepare it for the 225 guests. The theme was romantic 'Sherwood Forest' and Victoria describes the wedding: 'We wanted it to be as romantic as possible, with me and David as the prince and princess of the fairy tale that got married and lived happily ever after' (p.247). She also points out that it was not a star-studded wedding and she certainly did not originally mean it be as 'big' as it was but, as is common with wedding preparations, she got simply carried away; however, 'a lot of – a helluva lot of it as always with me – was totally tongue in cheek' (p.247). Nevertheless, the idea of the Beckhams as the 'New Royalty' becomes another trajectory in the grid connecting the Beckhams' performative bodies.

As Victoria, 'like all little girls', had imagined her wedding to be a fairy tale, she as a princess and David as a prince, the wedding was held in the castle, with them wearing crowns and sitting on thrones. She also remembers, when trying on her wedding dress, watching Sophie Rhys-Jones and Prince Edward getting married on television: 'The press were making such a meal out of the comparisons – which one was the wedding of the year and which one was the most royal' (p.244). The theme continues in an advertisement for Walkers Sensations crisps where Victoria appears with Gary Lineker (who promotes Walkers) as the King. Her character is a spoiled Queen who wears a replica of the crown from the famous Beckham wedding. Victoria herself says that she enjoyed the way the advertisement 'poked fun' of her and David's extravagant style: 'That's why I did it. I think that people can laugh and joke about things and so can I. It's very tongue-in-cheek and I really enjoyed it' (Rimmer, 2002: 57).

The Beckhams further cemented their glamorous, 'outrageous high camp' style in their farewell party for the England 2002 World Cup team at their home, commonly referred to as 'Beckingham Palace', in Hertfordshire. The party, reported to have cost 'a six-figure sum' (Kasper, 2002), followed an oriental theme and was arranged in a marquee in the grounds of their mansion. The guest list included, of course, football players but also other athletes and media and entertainment celebrities. The invitation, where the guests were instructed to wear diamonds, already predicted the style of the event. Victoria and David both claim the intention was to be over the top, but, as David says, 'We always do things like that' and Victoria justifies it: 'That's how we like to do things, and everyone invited to the party is excited because it's an occasion, very glitzy. At the same time there's a serious message behind it' (Kasper, 2002: 82). The serious message was to raise funds for the National Society for the Prevention of Cruelty to Children (NSPCC), one of the couple's favourite charities, in an auction that did, indeed, result in £400,000 (Kasper, 2002: 76).

While the Beckhams are often viewed as living a life of the rich and famous 'in a glass house' without the worries of 'normal' people, they don't see themselves as out of touch with the world. Victoria explains that 'We don't really do the whole celeb thing, all the parties, that's not us.' They like to live a normal family life and often publicly emphasise that family and their children are the most important things in the world. In addition, Victoria and David want to give an impression of having a very loving, supporting and close relationship. In many senses they can be considered to be the modern Royals, wealthy and glamorous, but still having a sense of everyday life. As David Furnish, Elton John's partner and one of the few celebrity friends the Beckhams have, comments: 'For many people in this country, they are living the celebrity dream, they really are Mr and Mrs Everyday suddenly gone famous' (ITV, 2002). The Beckhams also engage actively in charity work and a particular instance seems to emerge as another trajectory in the grid that allows the performative bodies of the Beckhams to proliferate into yet another molecular microfemininity. Their connection with a little girl called Kirsty Howard can be analysed as part of a process of becoming-woman.

Becoming-woman: the little girl

The Beckhams are involved in the process of becoming-woman by challenging the molar categories of femininity and masculinity through an assemblage of a high-camp, performative style. Their style loosens the rigidifications of molar femininity by offering a glimpse of a possible, refigured identity. Deleuze offers an additional type of microfemininity that further expands the limits of a molar category woman: a figure of little girl – a figure that Deleuze lifts as a privileged personage of resistance.

According to Deleuze, the little girl is not a sexual fantasy of pure innocence nor a romantic or representative figure, but as 'the site of a culture's most intensified disinvestments and recastings of the body' (Grosz, 1994a: 175) it is the figure of resistance. The girl does not refer to age or 'virginity', but 'is defined by a relation of movement and rest, speed and slowness, by a combination of atoms, an emission of particles' (cited in Grosz, 1994a: 175). As a figure, it is not yet limited by the molar categories of the world and therefore it embodies the life before the body as an organism. Therefore, she is 'the reconstruction of the body as a Body without Organs, the anorganism of the body, is inseparable from a becoming-woman, or the production of a molecular woman' (cited in Grosz, 1994a 175). For Deleuze, the girl is in between dualisms (such as men/women; young/old); a type of abstract line of flight that never ceases to roam upon the BwO. Therefore, anyone can become 'a little girl' and resist the molar categories limiting our bodies. I will now map what possibilities Victoria and David's performative bodies have to deepen their process of becoming-woman with a trajectory to a small girl's performative body.

Kirsty Howard is a 6-year-old girl who, as a result of a heart problem, is permanently attached to an oxygen cylinder. Kirsty is terminally ill and she is the face for a fundraising campaign for her hospice, Frances House children's hospital, in Manchester. She has so far raised over £1 million for her cause and has saved the hospice from financial collapse. Kirsty's favourite footballer is David Beckham. They first met during an unforgettable England World Cup qualifying match against Greece in Old Trafford stadium in 7 October 2001, when the Football Association had invited Kirsty to be the mascot for the game. As with Victoria, it was love at first sight. Kirsty and David entered the stadium hand in hand, Kirsty connected to her oxygen tank by tubes running from her nose. She, like David, walked confidently, beaming with 'a massive smile', as David describes her. At the very last minute of the game, David made history by taking a spectacular free kick that enabled England to go directly to the Cup. Later he attributed some of his success to Kirsty who had 'definitely inspired' him to go through the game. Kirsty became a famous face and David a hero. Obviously they both performed well and, like Victoria and David, together made their performance even more spectacular. What did Kirsty do to achieve this? Could Kirsty be part of becoming-woman of the Beckhams? Of Victoria's becoming-woman?

Celebrities who have met Kirsty during her fundraising campaign note that she embodies some irresistible appeal. It is her big eyes, but also her extraordinary charm, bravery and constant smile, that give her an unusual performative radiance. Rather paradoxically, it is her illness that creates her as a performative, brave, amazing little girl and somehow her bravery multiplies David's athletic bravery and performative radiance. Since their first appearance together, David and Victoria have become the main celebrity figures of Kirsty's fundraising campaign. What is Victoria's connection with Kirsty? Do their trajectories meet in the process of becoming-woman? Their performances are marked by at least one notable difference: nobody hates Kirsty whereas Victoria evokes plenty of abuse from football fans and the media. What, then, can be the assemblage that intersects their performative bodies?

Victoria's connection to Kirsty begins, of course, through David who after his first emotional and inspirational encounter with Kirsty aspired to do something for her cause. Victoria, as a mother, feels most touched by the spirit of Kirsty who, despite her terminal illness, really impacts people ('really pulls your heart out'). While Victoria here is depicted predominantly in the role of the mother and Kirsty as a charming child living through her illness with extraordinary grace, from a Deleuzian perspective their performative bodies, when linked together, can project a type of microfemininity.

Kirsty, who fits the molar categories of young and girl, is not automatically 'a young girl' in a Deleuzian scheme. However, the way her body performs can lift her out of the molar categories reserved for her and engage her into a process of becoming-woman. Kirsty's public performances definitely defy the way we think about illness and children. She is not a little adult, but in all its simplicity, her performance touches people who meet her: her smile, her genuine enjoyment of life, her unpretentious and charming manner when she greets people. It is worth mentioning here that Kirsty has two healthy, beautiful and charming sisters who often accompany her, but do not get the same attention (if any) as Kirsty. It is interesting, then, that a terminal illness creates a context where a girl's performance turns into a trajectory of becoming-woman. In many ways, this conclusion is quite disturbing and several feminists have been alarmed by the concept of 'little girl' as a figurehead of women's resistance.

Deleuze's 'little girl', as the product or effect of becoming-woman, is disconcerting because, even as an abstraction, it seems to deny the process of maturation from women who are constantly changing in orientation and direction. Will such a conceptualisation infantilise women and perpetuate the molar category of woman instead of moving us toward molecular femininity? Women's illness, in this context, might reproduce an asymmetry of the molar gender relations instead of breaking it into microfemininities. While little Kirsty is admired for her spirit, Victoria, who also suffers from an incurable condition, polycystic ovaries, is seldom celebrated for her bravery. Granted, unlike Kirsty's illness, Victoria's condition is not terminal, and its symptoms – irregular or absent periods and consequent infertility, adult acne, excess weight – while quite debilitating in the molar world of femininity, are rather embarrassing and a source of shame. Victoria copes with her symptoms very well, but still suffers from irregular eating patterns that started with her undiagnosed weight gain. An adult woman's illness is not cute, and in the case of Victoria it seems to place her firmly within the molar category of woman. Her body weight is under constant public scrutiny and she is labelled either Porgy Posh or Skeletal Spice, but never seen as having quite the perfect (molar) feminine body. On the contrary, her confident, distinctive style is under constant criticism from football fans and the media. Through this style, however, Victoria can let the 'girl' continue on its flight and challenge the molar categories reserved for femininity in the culture that surrounds her. Her 'being a girl', her microfemininity, is embedded in determination and a rather artificial, high-camp style that tends to annoy and provoke instead of being admired and accepted.

Conclusion

A Deleuzian analysis, which focuses on possible radical forms of molecular becoming embedded in an active body, reveals Victoria Beckham's high-camp performative style as a microfemininity that breaks down the molar category of woman. At least, it has threatened the football supporters' molar category of woman as Victoria refuses to adopt the traditional role of quiet and invisible footballer's wife. While Victoria creates this trajectory in her own right, when it meets with David's performance, the effect of their bodies multiplies to challenge the gendered asymmetries of today's culture. In this sense, Victoria is in a process of becoming-woman, a process that she will most likely deny herself, as it is not her intention to reject 'traditional' femininity. On the contrary, it is not surprising that someone so famous for teetering on high-heeled shoes and wearing tight skirts describes her style: 'What I love more than anything is things that make women look like women. That's why I love corset tops really sucky, sucky, that push your boobs up, hold your waist in and flatter your hips. I like women to wear make-up, do their hair and wear tight sexy clothes' (Beckham, 2001: 352). But then again, it is not the look of the body that Deleuze is interested in, because that limits the analysis within dualisms of unfeminine/feminine or feminine/masculine. Therefore, while Victoria's looks set her firmly within a molar category of woman, her body's ability to perform a style can create a microfemininity that allows for a redefinition of her identity. It is obvious that Victoria's performance is supported by her privileged position as a wealthy woman that allows her to challenge traditional femininity in ways not accessible to everyday people. Her wealth, however, is not a result of a particularly privileged background, but rather a bizarre example of today's entertainment capitalism that has, in its twisted ways, initiated a possible breakdown of its own molar categories.

As Manchester United, more than any other football club, embraced a role in the entertainment industry – Victoria's performative field – what would have happened if they created an assemblage with Victoria's trajectory? Would their performative bodies have radiated new trajectories to break down further cultural categories? Possibly, in ways similar to David and Victoria's double effect, Manchester United could have received unexpected and double positive attention. With David Beckham's departure to Real Madrid, Manchester United seems to be a source of somewhat negative attention. In the meantime, Victoria has to be allowed to perform her style – and can Victoria's becoming-woman benefit and expand football? It can, by challenging the limiting molar categories, but football has to simultaneously engage in the process of becoming-woman and that, as Victoria can testify, seems an unlikely direction. Then again, perhaps Victoria, by performing with David, had already involved football in a grid of becoming-woman?

References

Beckham, V. (2001) *Learning to Fly: The Autobiography*, London: Penguin Books.

Braidotti, R. (1993) 'Discontinuous becomings: Deleuze and the becoming-woman of philosophy', *Journal of British Society of Phenomenology*, 24(1): 44–55.

Braidotti, R. (1997) 'Meta(l)morphoses', *Theory, Culture and Society*, 14(2): 67–80.

Deleuze, G. and Guattari, F. (1987) *A Thousand Plateaus: Capitalism and Schizophrenia*, London: Continuum.

Fraser, M. (1997) 'Feminism, Foucault and Deleuze', *Theory, Culture and Society*, 14(2): 23–37.

Gent, H. (2002) 'Kidnap ordeal changes the Beckhams' lives', *Heat*, November: 12–13.

Grosz, E. (1994a) *Volatile Bodies: Toward A Corporeal Feminism*, Bloomington, IN: Indiana University Press.

Grosz, E. (1994b) 'A thousand tiny sexes: feminism and rhizomatics', in C.V. Boundas and D. Olkowski (eds) *Gilles Deleuze and the Theatre Of Philosophy*, New York: Routledge.

ITV (2002) 'Being Victoria Beckham'.

ITV (2002) 'When Kirsty met David', *Tonight with Trevor McDonald*.

Kasper, R. (2002) 'David and Victoria Beckham grant Hello! an intimate interview', *Hello!*, 21 May: 76–95.

McCormick, N. (2002) 'Why the hits have eluded "Posh"', *Telegraphview*, 6 March: 25.

Rimmer, A. (2002) 'Victoria Beckham', *OK!*, 2 May: 50–60.

Part IV
Local United

11 'Manchester Is Red'?

Manchester United, fan identity and the 'Sport City'

Adam Brown

It was the small hours of 25 February 2001. A 'conga' of around 300 Manchester United fans made its way drunkenly around Manchester city centre and then headed south down Oxford Road towards Manchester City's Maine Road ground. There was a sizeable police escort with a helicopter overhead. Over and over again the delirious, dancing fans kept singing, to the Piranhas' tune 'Tom Hark': '25 years, 25 years/25 years ...'. The song was a mocking reference to the time elapsed since City had won a major trophy. It had been celebrated by United fans that night at a 'Silver Anniversary Party' in the city centre originally, cheekily, and covertly, booked for Maine Road's corporate 'Silver Suite'. The party was cancelled on the day, when the club and police discovered the real reason for the social function. The next day, Maine Road had had a paint job: a huge '25 years' was emblazoned across the gate to the ground's away section, known by City and United fans alike as the 'Gene Kelly stand', a reference to its open air nature and 'the frequency in this city,' as one City fan put it, 'to see fans singing in the rain'. Alongside the ground, in Kippax Street, 'Guvnors RIP [rest in peace]' and 'ICJ' were sprayed on the sides of the terraced houses – the former referring to one of City's 'hooligan firms' of the 1980s (Francis and Walsh, 1997); the latter to United's 'Inter City Jibbers' firm of the same era (Kurt and Micheas, 1997).

A few weeks later and United are playing City at Old Trafford, with City on the point of relegation. Outside the pubs near United's Old Trafford ground, fans soak up the drink and the sun, and heads turned skywards, toward the drone of a small plane. As eyes focus, a banner is visible flying behind the plane reading 'MCFC – REAL CLUB, REAL FANS'. A few minutes later and City fans inside the ground are taunting United supporters with: 'Do you come from,/do you come from,/do you come from Manchester?/Do you come from Manchester?' The song is a jibe relating to the popular belief that many of United's supporters live elsewhere in the United Kingdom (UK) or abroad. However, these examples also appear to demonstrate the importance of collective local identification, belonging to the city, notions of authenticity in football fandom, relationships of success and local pride and of a desire for an essentialised notion of previously existing social configurations in football.

In an age when football has arguably become detached from its sense of place, when the game's globalisation means that Manchester United are able to claim upwards of 50 million fans worldwide,[1] and where allegiances of the young are less likely to be forged through kinship or familial bloodlines, these events came as a stark reminder of football's enduring local meanings for some fans. They raise questions about the place of sport and football in the 'post-Fordist' city and the endurance of local rivalries within an increasingly globalised sport. It also raises issues about the role of, and relationship between, fans, clubs and their urban locality within football's increasingly commodified form.

These questions formed part of a one-year research project in 2001-2, 'Sport, governance and the city', funded by the UK Economic and Social Research Council and undertaken by Dr Derek Wynne[2] and myself at the Manchester Institute for Popular Culture, Manchester Metropolitan University. This research had two principle foci. First, the relationship of the city with sport, and in particular the new ways in which sport was being used as part of economic and social regeneration strategies in Manchester. Second, the role of football in two respects – its relation to these new city processes; and the relationships between the two professional clubs, their fans and the city.

Although the focus here is predominantly on the latter of these two areas of inquiry, it is worth noting some factors relating to the first, not least because this provides the urban and sporting context in which the construction and contestation of football culture in Manchester is played out.

A brief methodological note: the phenomena and events discussed here focus around initiatives and processes which have been propagated and intensified, initially at least, by a specific group of Mancunian Manchester United fans. These are predominantly male (though not all),[3] aged 20–50, and mostly living and working locally. They concentrate around particular organisations – e.g. those that produce United's fanzines, the Independent Manchester United Supporters' Association (IMUSA) – and particular habits, such as travelling to away games, pursuing a hedonistic experience and showing an active participation (such as signing) during matches. They include some of those identified by King (1998: 148) as 'The Lads' and, although there is not space to engage critically with these terms further here, fall into a category which Giulianotti (2002: 31) might (problematically) call 'traditional/hot' supporters, with significant independence from the club.

I have, in some ways, a close, local knowledge of this constituency of fan and have known some of those involved through my regular attendance at Manchester United games over the preceding two decades. My position in relation to these has been changing and at times overlapping – first of all as a fan, then as a fanzine writer, as a supporters' representative and as a researcher. This has given me a knowledge of both these fans and the issues discussed here – and has allowed me privileged access – which extends my knowledge beyond the timescale of the research project itself. It is not, however, without other methodological concerns which I hope to discuss more fully in future publications.

However, it must also be noted that the contested expressions of local identity I will discuss now extend beyond this group in a number of individual and collective actions, and the discourses operate on multiple levels – from verbal, face to face; to the printed word in fanzines and on banners; to the Internet where local contestations occur in a 'virtual' sphere. Further, they are discourses which are now shared – with more limited 'knowing' – by people locally, nationally and internationally, and by people who may not even be football fans.

Manchester's sporting context

Manchester has been a site for the participation of citizens in football since it was understood as a folk game. Walvin (2000: 18) reports that authorities banned the game five times between 1608 and 1657 and even appointed 'football officers', demonstrating that football's relationship to the locality has been problematic for some time.

It was in the industrial age when the city's mass participation in the modern form of football took off. In this regard, the role of Manchester as the 'shock city' of the industrial revolution (Briggs, 1959) and the 'workshop' of the world cannot be ignored. This context meant that the city had a place where the mass working class took up new and rationalised forms of leisure, as old folk forms died out due to the time and place constraints of late nineteenth-century capitalism. Alongside other industrialised towns in Lancashire and urban areas such as Liverpool, the northwest rapidly became a hotbed of football (Holt, 1992; Walvin, 2000; Russel, 1997).

It can be argued that the relationships discussed here between the city and sport would not be possible without this legacy. The nature, size, economy, geography, industrialisation and demographics of Manchester form a cultural and social reservoir on which contemporary football in the city 'floats'; and it is part of the 'structure of feeling' of the city (Taylor et al., 1998). As such, understanding that football culture – which as we shall see is fiercely contested and divided – is important in understanding the contemporary post-industrial city.

In line with the changing nature of the city – pre-industrial, modernist, post-industrial – local authorities have had a changing relationship to football and sport. This goes from bans on folk sports, to the provision of the Victorian swimming baths, parks, pitches and areas for play – based on notions of 'rational recreation' – that are interwoven into the fabric of the city, to the pursuance of new uses for sport, since the mid-1980s, as part of attempts to combat industrial decline. This has included: bidding for and attracting major sports events to re-image the city; building new facilities; and using events and developments to lever in additional revenue, particularly relating to combating social exclusion.[4]

Manchester is certainly not unique in this regard and these developments must be seen within the rise of competitive cities (Castells and Hall, 1994); the problematic use of culture for economic and social ends (Brown et al., 2000); and the wider use of sport to redefine cities (Essex and Chalkley, 1998: 192; Henry and Salcines, 1998); and problems with this approach (Lensky, 2002). However, the Manchester context provides new nuances to these experiences, and the nature of football in the city relates closely to that.

Of principal concern to us was Manchester's staging of the Commonwealth

Games and the city's building of the Sport City complex, which includes the City of Manchester (CoM) stadium, built with £130 million Sports Lottery money. Manchester City's occupancy of that stadium is assured under a SportEngland National Lottery agreement, and is the most obvious example of how football is being drawn into these new sports agendas in the city. It is a development which has itself become intertwined in Manchester's contested football fan culture.

Manchester United have been used in marketing literature about the city, especially through the Marketing Manchester agency, something which it has been argued produces 'brand awareness' of Manchester around the world. However, within the city's approach to football there has been no extensive attempt to develop a football tourism strategy and few attempts to develop any area of work relating to football fans or consumption, except when there have been large numbers of visiting foreign fans.[5]

These issues illustrate the changing local policy and sports context, in which relations between fans and the two clubs have developed, and contested the *cultural* sporting space. That division challenges some of the institutional discourses about Manchester as 'Sport City' and problematises some 'football policy', as with other cultural sectors (Brown *et al.*, 1998). This is evident in a number of examples. Manchester City Council has not introduced football-related 'welcome' signs at the airport or train station because of fears of vandalism from one or both sets of fans (Phelan, 2002). Discourses attempting to create civic pride in relation to football – such as the calls for the 'whole city' to 'join in celebration' in a 'joint' footballing triumph following United's Treble and City's Division Two play-off victory in 1999 (*Manchester Life*, June 1999) – fail both practically and symbolically because they don't take account of deep divisions within football cultures.

The CoM stadium is perhaps the most pertinent example in terms of the contrast between its widespread approval and the culture, beliefs and identities of some local United fans. Several fan contacts from East Manchester, where the stadium is located, reported a collective understanding to refer to it as 'Johnson's Wireworks' – a reference to the large factory which stood once on or near the site. The closure of the factory was, along with the closure of England's largest deep mine pit in the same area, significantly responsible for the social malaise and economic downturn which has blighted East Manchester since the 1970s (*Manchester Metro News* 22 August 2003)' a malaise which it is hoped will be combated by the initiatives of which the stadium is the physical and theoretical centrepiece.[6]

As recently as September 2003, the United fanzine *Red Issue* (No. 69) enclosed a mock rent book for the tenants of the city's newest 'council house', by then the commonly accepted term of abuse for the CoM stadium. It is notable that at times the use of 'Wireworks' displays a nostalgia for the past, in line with these fans' nostalgia for their 'golden age' of football. However, this is contingent and at times it is also a pejorative term belittling the new stadium as a dirty factory. The use of 'council house' picks up on common vernaculars demeaning those who don't own their own home, and these also therefore contrast with institutional discourses of social inclusion. Such symbolic contestations and playful tactics might be seen as counter-hegemonic in challenging the prevailing vernacular and local policy. They provide an alternative narrative to the dominant discourses promoting civic pride about the development.

Clubs, fans and the symbolic conflict in the city

Comparing and contrasting the clubs

Distinctions and rivalries between United and City have existed long before the Premier League and these continue to inform fan cultures. However, the clubs' relationship to the city and especially the fan expressions, which will be discussed below, cannot be separated from the contrasting fortunes of the two clubs in the Premier League era.

Manchester United have dominated the league, winning eight out of 11 titles, including two Football Association (FA) Cup Doubles and one European Cup Treble. The club is rated as the richest in the world and its stock market valuation soared to £1 billion (www.FT.com, 2 October 2000) and is currently around £650m (Independent, 1 April 2004: 45). Although the club experienced serious turmoil in 1998–9 when it was the subject of an unsuccessful takeover bid by BSkyB (Brown and Walsh, 1999; Hamil et al., 2000: 64; Bose, 1999), it has remained financially stable and continued to post record profits despite the sport's reported financial turndown (Banks, 2002). Their Old Trafford stadium holds 67,500 fans, the largest capacity in England.

Manchester City have experienced a much less successful and more tumultuous time since 1992, despite finishing above United in the two seasons preceding the formation of the league. Relegated to Division One in 1996, they sank to Division Two in 1998, before 'yo-yoing' to the First Division (1999), Premier League (2000), First Division (2001) and finishing ninth in the top division in 2003. However, the club has also experienced 17 changes in manager in 20 years and four chairmen in the last 10, two of whom were ousted by fierce fan campaigns (Shaw, 1998). Although in 2002 the club moved to a new stadium which had added only £20m in debt and appeared to be on a more stable financial basis (Manchester Evening News, 14 September 2002), by 2004 the club was facing increased debts of over £100m (Independent, 10 April 2004) and fighting for its Premier League status.

However, whilst I would not want to understate the contrasts, I would not want to overstate them, either. The same era has seen both clubs, to different degrees and at different times, move away from associational, not-for-profit modes of governance to more corporate ones based on profit maximisation. Both have also experienced conflict between fans and the club, and at neither do supporters enjoy any degree of policy-determining role, despite new consultative structures. Of particular interest in the discussion which follows is that at both clubs the collective fan–club relationship is changing to a customer–company one.

Yet senior executives have offered very different characterisations of the clubs. Manchester United's Peter Kenyon and David Gill both talked of the need to 'monetise the global fan base', to ensure that Manchester United remained in 'number one spot' in football *and* business terms, and of the need to 'develop the sporting brand' that is United. By contrast, former chief executive Chris Bird at City talked of the need to 'create unity and stability' and claimed, 'We're still a *community-based football club*, that has got strong Manchester roots, that is determined not to become a middle-class football club.'[7]

It is notable here that these contrasting conceptualisations of the clubs are linked to the fan bases of each in different ways. Those fan bases, however, are also changing within the developing local, national and global football context (and broader society). The lack of emphasis on the local on the part of United executives contrasts with a resurgent Mancunianism among some of the club's hard-core local supporters.

Indeed, both clubs in the 1990s experienced serious fan–club conflict. However, on one hand City fans – who ousted chairman Peter Swales in 1994, and campaigned against Francis Lee in 1998 (Shaw, 1998: 59) – criticised club policy on the grounds that City were not fulfilling their potential as a football powerhouse, and that it needed to be a more modern and successful business (Shaw, 1998: 61). On the other, United fans have attacked their club for ignoring its local fans and pursuing an overly aggressive business policy. Between these polarities may lie a 'hidden' similarity, however, in the search for an 'ideal type' of pre-Premier League club configuration.

The BSkyB takeover battle at United was responsible for a significant 'politicisation' of the fan base, involving, as it did, representations to the government, shareholder issues and submissions to the Monopoly and Mergers Commission (IMUSA, 1999; Shareholders United, 1999; Brown and Walsh, 1999). As such, in terms of the range of issues tackled and concern with a wider football-policy agenda, the depth of understanding and political affiliations made nationally by IMUSA in particular, it can be convincingly argued that United's fan formations include a politicised organisation and fan base of a type which is largely absent at City.[8]

Physical and economic relationships to the city

Fans' interactions with the city operate at a number of levels, and descriptions of them are, of course, prone to generalisations and essentialisations. However, it is possible to identify different kinds of interaction. There is a physical interaction: individual United and City fans live, work and consume in the city, but they also impact as a collective, especially on match day, and this regularly has a significant effect on the activities of the city's authorities. Issues of transport, crowd and event management and policing are all important elements of the organisation and regulation of the city on match day because of the presence of large groups of fans. Whilst at times this raises issues of maintaining public order, far more common are issues associated with the everyday practices of match day. These include the economic impacts of supporters, something beyond the scope of our research yet something which others have suggested elsewhere is significant (Southern *et al.*, 2000).

Symbolic relationships and the city

For our research, some of the most interesting relationships between football supporters and the city are the symbolic ones, which demonstrated significant cultural conflict, especially over issues of locality. Although the characterisations made by club officials contrasted sharply, it is perhaps those of some local fans about their own club/fans, and 'the other', which show the sharpest division. In interviews, on Internet message boards and discussion fora, in fanzine articles and in the songs and chants of both sets of fans, there are widespread and negative portrayals of 'the other' in the locality. Indeed, although rivalry – and especially local rivalry – is part and parcel of football (Giulianotti, 1999: 17), it is the extent to which this centres on a sense of owning or belonging to the city which was a key interest.

The stereotype of Manchester United fans upheld by many City supporters contrasts the local, northern, Manchester-based City supporters with southern, globally-located and non-Mancunian United fans. This classic stereotype seeks to make illegitimate the place of United followers and indeed the club in the city of Manchester. This is reinforced by the fact that United's ground is within the boundaries of Trafford Metropolitan Borough (itself a creation of boundary changes in 1974), not Manchester City Council. Although this perception existed as long ago as the 1960s, it is the success and size of the club in the 1990s which has concentrated this line of symbolic attack.

Associated with this 'not belonging' to Manchester, City fans align other definitions of United fans, along: class lines (City – working class, United – middle class); lines of loyalty (City – loyal and long standing, United – fickle and 'new'); lines of performance as fans (City – passionate and participatory despite 'failure', United – quiet unless winning); relationship distinctions to the new football context (City – anti-commercial, United – merchandise-obsessed). In this, City fans' construction of themselves at the start of this chapter as 'real fans' belonging to a 'real club' aligns notions of what it means to be an 'authentic' supporter with coming from the locality. This also involves the alienation of 'the other' from the city as (in one familiar song) the 'Pride of Singapore', a reference to United's international fan base.

It is also noteworthy that this stereotype is often evident in the national media and is shared by fans of many other clubs. This reflects the increased level of animosity toward United and its fans in the Premier League era, due in no small part to the club's on-field success. This tendency of 'neutrals' to favour City, or any other team United may be playing, is referred to by United supporters as 'ABUism' and those who perpetrate it as 'ABUs' – 'Anyone But United'.

As for Manchester United supporters, among the particular constituency of locally-based fans I have identified there has been a growing antipathy toward such attacks on their legitimacy as fans *and* as Mancunians. Furthermore, in the period at the end of the 1990s when United and City rarely competed together due to City's relegations from the Premier League, these United fans rediscovered the pleasures of a very local rivalry.

The '25 years' party described above is part of a broader symbolic attack by some Manchester United fans on their neighbours. This includes a series of stunts around the 25th anniversary such as 'Happy 25th Birthday' banners hung from bridges all around the M60 motorway encircling Manchester, and the 25th celebrations must be seen within discourses of 'success' and 'size' between the two sets of fans. The tendency of fans, players and officials at City to refer to the club as 'massive' (http://www.football635.com, 2001), has been ridiculed by United fans in a series of pranks.

One of those involved, a United fan known to us, called BBC Radio 5 Live's 6:06 programme (4 December 2000) and fooled the presenter and City-supporting copresenter Susan Bookbinder that he was a City fan, Bert. He then regaled them with declarations about the size of the club ('massive, huge') and even, bizarrely, the manager's head (also, 'massive'). In a lengthy call, the word 'massive' was used 17 times. This itself picked up on a song in which the (supposed) claims to grandeur made by City fans were denigrated. The song had hundreds of verses,[9] each to demonstrate the naivety of City's pretensions, and *Red Issue* produced a calendar with a different verse for each day of the year (*Red Issue* 39, December 2000).

The fact that Manchester United fans displayed a concern with City *at all* is noteworthy, given that at no time since the early 1990s have City challenged United for honours on the pitch. Given the globalisation of United, the success of the team and a business plan which targets a Champions League quarter-final place as *a minimum*, we can see here a rejection of dominant discourses about and by the club by targeting City. This can be seen as a (re)emergence or (re)construction of imagined fan communities creating cultural difference to the 'other' (Appadurai, 1996). Aspects of these processes have been described elsewhere as 'glocalisation' (Robertson, 1992).

I am not inferring here that all Manchester United fans or all Mancunian ones are part of this development. Indeed, at the away European quarter-final against Deportivo de La Coruña in 2002, a group of male fans in their fifties, and from Manchester, derided their younger counterparts around them: 'You're fucking obsessed with them [City]! You shouldn't be singing about them – we're in the European Cup quarter-final for fuck's sake. [...] they're irrelevant!' (author's notes).

Whilst these older fans are critical of the younger fans' approach, animosity to City is still present. *Other* older fans – especially those who had experiences watching United play at Maine Road, post-war – have expressed a support for United alongside a desire to see City, as 'the other Manchester club', do well, something also identified in some historical studies (Mellor, 1999: 36).

For those supporters I have identified as intensifying the local rivalry, however, there is a rejection of the notion that civic pride should override support for your club. These fans' response to attacks on their credibility are based around a set of juxtapositions (see Table 11.1).

Table 11.1 Mancunian United fans' distinctions of themselves and City fans

Manchester United fans	Manchester City fans
From the city – Manchester	From the 'sticks' – Stockport
Success/contenders	Failure/comedy/crisis club
Big club	Small club
Modern	Out of date
Realistic, knowledgeable	Deluded
Street-smart/intelligent	Gullible/stupid
Fashionable/Cosmopolitan	Unfashionable/parochial
Repertoire of songs/atmosphere	Few songs/sullen
Large, successful fighting 'firm'	Incompetent/disorganised 'firm'
Antagonistic to England	'Little Ingerlander'

We see here a multi-faceted strategy in which United fans attempt to combat both the negative characterisations of them made by Manchester City fans, and those made by other fans and the media. However, it is also in part a rejection of their own club and its commercial development. Whilst one might think that this diminishes the impact of the reassertion of the importance of the local within Mancunian United fandom, the nature of the complaints with the club relate closely to issues of who and what they think Manchester United should be; and being part of the locale features strongly.

As such, there is a blurring between a promotion of their own locality and attacks on their club's policies, including demands to reintroduce standing areas at football to aid access for local young fans (IMUSA, 1998); and to prioritise local (especially young) fans in the supply of tickets. Other examples of how this (fluid, contingent) constituency of United fans has promoted itself as Mancunian are the banners which adorn the Stretford End: a City 'mileage clock' now (at the time of writing) showing 28 years; 'The Flowers of Manchester' (a reference to the Munich victims); and 'Republik of Mancunia' in appropriate Russian-styled lettering. These messages are reinforced in hundreds of fanzine articles, and songs such as:

> My Old Man said 'be a City fan' and I said 'bollocks, you're a cunt'.
> I'd rather shag a bucket with a big hole in it
> Than be a City fan for just one minute.
> With hatchets and hammers, Stanley knives and spanners
> We'll show those City bastards how to fight ...

This song works on a number of levels: it attacks City and is sung even if not playing them, reinforcing the importance of the local rivalry; it recalls an earlier epoch in which violence was a common occurrence at football, demonstrating another element deemed to be important in the constriction of the 'real fan'; and it reinforces the aggressive masculinity and heterosexuality of those singing it. The song is, of course, often sung by many fans who may rarely if ever have engaged in football-related violence, although we must recognise that, at times, this symbolic conflict and status-jousting becomes a 'real' physical confrontation.

However, this symbolic conflict is heavily informed by the fans' notions of authenticity and what it means to be a 'real fan', itself contrasting with official discourses on fans. For the supporters I have identified, those constructions of authenticity rely in part upon being seen to belong to the locale. What is in dispute between United and City fans, is not what it means to be a 'real' supporter – the criteria are remarkably similar for both sets of fans – but who fits those criteria best. United fans' promotion of this symbolic battle is more pronounced for three reasons. One, they have been subjected to more questions about their legitimacy as fans than City supporters. Two, this most frequently centres on their 'not being local' in a more extreme way than any other club in the UK. Three, their status as legitimate fans is also partly undermined by their own club, its commercial success, and its 'globalising' policies. As such, this forms part of the 'love the team, hate the club' attitude which we and others (King, 1998: 167) have found.

Such positionings can be riddled with paradoxes. In order to demonstrate United's superiority against their rivals, some United fans celebrate the club's size and on-field success, implicitly ('negotiated', tactical and temporary) supporting the club's globalisation. The references to Munich and even the Russian typography described above also 'nod' toward the club's globalisation. This occurs at the same time as celebrating Mancunian roots and criticising the club. It is therefore both a reaction to club policy, which they view as threatening and favouring non-local fans, and to challenges to their status by opposing fans – seeking to reaffirm their 'authenticity' as fans by emphasising their locality.

This extends to a kind of self-policing of other United fans. Supporters from outside Manchester are sometime derided as 'OOTs' (or Out of Towners); whilst those they consider to be 'bandwagon-jumping' (one of the very criticisms made by City fans) are negatively portrayed as 'JCLs' (Johnny Come Latelys). 'Locality' or 'Mancunian-ness' is increasingly restrictively defined, illustrating a conservative, exclusionary tendency (despite other 'progressive' features) within what might be seen as an imagined fan community-construction. Some United fans also employ a 'Mancunian republicanism', reflected most noticeably in antagonism to the national England team.

Similarly, many City fans who highlight their superior status as 'from Manchester' and as a 'real club' appear to be in contradiction when they also told us that they regard their club as *potentially* and *rightfully* as 'big' and successful as United. City fans are also often proud of their fans who come from elsewhere, as a symbol of the club's stature, contrasting with their 'Mancunian' critique of United.

Mapping the fanbases in the city

To explore this issue further, both clubs agreed to let us map by postcode their respective 2001 season ticket databases (Brown 2002).[10] We found that both clubs had a hard core of support in Manchester (defined as an 'M' post code, based on definitions used by interviewees). This is in some ways a difficult definition (Hand 2002), and the differences between definitions of what constitutes Manchester vary considerably.

What we found was that although there were numerically more United fans within an M postcode district (7,856 to 6,678), there was a higher figure for City when expressed as a percentage of the different total numbers of season tickets (29–40 per cent). Both clubs retained strong regional support in the North West of England – 78 per cent or 12,864 (City) and 72 per cent or 19,788 (United). Despite football's modernisation and other 'globalising' trends, hard-core support for both clubs remains strongly regional. Concentrations in the suburbs and hinterlands of Manchester suggest that local support may have been affected by demographic mobility out of the city centre. Yet despite contrasting experiences, patterns of season-ticket holders remain strikingly similar.

The publication of these 'facts' (*Manchester Evening News*, 28 October 2002) itself generated some debate among fans. In this, fans of both sides seized upon findings to justify their claims to 'Mancunian-ness', showing that there are perhaps two 'realities' at play: one, statistics that suggest relatively strong local and regional support for both; two, popular identifications made about each set of fans in which a Manchester habitus is contested cultural capital. This generates its own cultural dynamics and is as central to understanding relations in the city's football culture as where fans actually live.

The enduring nature of these cultural dynamics was demonstrated in a reference to this mapping work at the last Maine Road derby, which City won 3–1, for the first time in 13 years. Before the game, and in the line of TV cameras, a brave (or foolhardy) 19-year-old United supporter entered the second tier of the Kippax stand. He encouraged City fans with some success to start singing 'City 'til I die' and to unfurl a 50-foot banner. This they waved above their heads for a few minutes before they realised that in the bold, blue letters were the words: 'Manchester is Red'.

Concluding remarks

We can see within these playful and not-so-playful confrontations a number of processes.

For some United fans, as we have discussed, the promotion of a 'Mancunian republicanism' in recent years can be seen as defensive: against some of the club's policies, which are seen as 'anti-local'; against the way in which the club's commercial and on-field success has resulted in a national image of United fans as 'inauthentic'; and against the claims of City and other fans that Manchester City, not United, represents and belongs to Manchester.

We can also see, however, that although there is a negative rejection of others, there is also a positive association with Manchester – and especially its other popular cultures (music, fashion) in which great pride is taken. This reassertion of local identity is occurring in a period when the club and its wider fan base has become more global.

In this process, some fans have created an alternative narrative to the official discourses of the club – such as chief executive Peter Kenyon's aim of creating 'One United – club, fans and team'. For some of those fans I have identified, this extends to a fierce critical stance against what is termed 'new football' and the new forms of consumption (seated, televised, etc.).

Such concerns can be viewed as nostalgic, as part of 'invented' traditions and as part of a search for an authentic past which didn't exist – and they are undoubtedly these in part and at some times and contexts. However, they are also genuine expressions of a sense of loss for past experiences – something which has been noted with United fans (King, 1998: 163) and former attenders at live football elsewhere (Williams and Perkins, 1999). At times this expression of loss is *overtly* promoted as the defence of a constituency of United fans and mode of behaviour which they feel is under threat. Indeed, the increased perception of this 'threat' has resulted in a reification of this 'community' itself.

In such discussions there is clearly a danger of overessentialising individuals or groups of supporters. As such it is right to highlight here that in the research we also subdivided fans along lines of formal (e.g. member/non member) or customer (ticket-purchasing) relations to the club. However, even in these relationships, similar issues of local access became evident. What was also notable, however, was that some fans interviewed advocated that the club, for instance, allocate tickets on the basis of 'loyalty' as well as 'locality', when the former might not imply local fans would benefit. Exploring different ways in which people might be members of multiple 'communities' and how this affects their relationship to the club is an area of further research into football's 'communities'.[11]

Within the reassertion of the local, there is also an element of lifestyle choice – as evidenced in the links between a Mancunian United fandom and local popular culture. There was, for some, a desire to be part of a culturally-aware, youth-oriented community; and within this consumption of 'Manchester' and Manchester United, there are also elements of what Polhemus has termed the 'supermarket of style' (Polhemus, 1994: 128). Yet within these expressions of Mancunian pride we can also see a celebratory, fun-seeking motivation; a playfulness which points toward 'post-fandom' as described by others (Redhead, 1997; Giulianotti, 1999). Such aspects also hint at the nature of contemporary cities as 'fun palaces' and 'fantasy cities' (Hannigan, 1999). In its association with violence, this configuration of fans also shows elements of falling into what Giulianotti calls 'voluntary, risk-taking leisure pursuits' (1999: 51). The desire to be connected to the local is even reflected in the 'placeless' Internet: one United website – 'The Snug' – evokes the cosiness of the local pub, and access is strictly guarded.

These factors perhaps sit uneasily with a project aiming to promote a rooted, authentic fandom. Such formations of fans might be seen as expression of what Anderson (1991) has called 'imagined' communities of sharing common values and experiences, and lessons and stories (especially from the past) which tell them who they are. Yet these are very different notions of community to official ones, to those referred to in policy documents (Collins *et al.*, 1999), or, for example, those whom Commonwealth Games-related initiatives targeted.

Yet, however 'imagined', contingent or transitory these fan communities may be, they are ones football has felt the need to engage with – something implicitly recognised as *commercially* important in Kenyon's attempts to bridge the divide between the club and fans. At Manchester United, this has included the creation of a 'singing section'; the introduction of a fans' forum; and the introduction of customer charters and new means of 'communication' with fans. These initiatives have received a mixed reception.

Given broader factors which might mitigate against strong collective expressions of local identity, such as demographic changes like increased resident mobility and the 'flight to the suburbs', as well as the globalising trends within football and Manchester United in particular, the reassertion of this emphasis on locality seems surprising and suggests an association with the rise of sport in the city. The (fluid) formation of local United fandom described can, however, be both unifying and inclusionary, as well as hostile and exclusionary to those it feels are inauthentic.

Football remains problematic for the city in terms of policy and in its creation of everyday problems for city centre management. Yet it is the symbolic ways in which local fan culture divides and expresses itself in Manchester which jars most with official discourses. It is true that the Commonwealth Games was an event in which masses of Mancunians could participate; yet the use of its premier venue is mocked by some supporters of Manchester United, and there is little common sense of belonging, or pride, shared with fans of City.

This demonstrates that although local identity appears strong(er) this is not a new civic pride in which football's fans in the city share equally. Indeed, the expressions of local identity and the reassertion of the importance of the local within Manchester United's fan base, is precisely designed to create and exploit division with others in this urban context, namely Manchester City fans. This culturally contested 'football-scape' contrasts sharply with official 'city' rhetorics; as well as with much of the direction and policies of Manchester United.

Notes

1 Interview with Peter Draper, Group Marketing Director, Manchester United. This estimate was based upon Mori research conducted for the club in 2001.
2 Derek Wynne was lead researcher on this project, yet died tragically and suddenly during it, on 15 January 2002. Issues raised here will be discussed more fully in a forthcoming book publication. I am grateful for comments on this chapter by Tim Crabbe and Gavin Mellor.
3 Interview with United fan, MM. She referred to her friends as 'United's Boot Girls'.
4 E.g. The 2002 Commonwealth Games North West Partnership.
5 E.g. 1997 Champions League semi-final; 2003 Champions League Final; Euro96.
6 Interview with Tom Russel, Chief Executive New East Manchester, March 2002.
7 Interview with Peter Kenyon, former Chief Executive at Manchester United Football Club (MUFC), 28 August 2001; with David Gill, Group Finance Director at MUFC, 2 July 2002. Interview with Chris Bird, former Chief Executive Officer at Manchester City Football Club (MCFC), 7 May 2002.
8 Interview with City fan (PG).
9 'They've got the tallest floodlights in the land/They've got the widest pitch in the league/They've got Curly Watts as a celebrity fan ... cos City are a massive club'.
10 It is important to note that this was an analysis of season-ticket holders *only*. See www.mmu.ac.uk/h-ss/mipc/football.

11 See www.footballanditscommunities.org, new research by the Manchester Institute of Popular Culture, Manchester Metropolitan University and Sheffield Hallam University.

References

Anderson, B. (1991) *Imagined Communities*, London: Verso.

Appaduri, A. (1996) *Modernity at Large: Cultural Dimensions of Globalization*, Minneapolis: University of Minnesota Press.

Banks, S. (2002) *Going Down: Football in Crisis*, Edinburgh: Mainstream.

Bose, M. (1999) *Manchester Unlimited*, London and New York: Texere.

Briggs, A. (1959) *The Age of Improvement: 1783–1867*, London: Longman.

Brown, A. (2002) *'Do You Come From Manchester?': The Location of Season Ticket Holders at Manchester United and Manchester City*, Manchester: MIPC.

Brown, A., Cohen, S. and O'Connor, J. (1998) 'Music policy, the music industry and local economic development', Final Report to the ESRC, 1998.

Brown, A., O'Connor, J. and Cohen, S. (2000) 'Local music policies within a global music industry, *Geoforum Special Issue on Cultural Industries*, July.

Brown, A. and Walsh, A. (1999) *Not For Sale: Manchester United, Murdoch and the Defeat of BSkyB*, Edinburgh: Mainstream.

Castells, M. and Hall, P. (1994) *Technopoles of the World; The Making of 21st Century Industrial Complexes*, London: Routledge.

Collins, M., Henry, I.P., Houlihan, B. and Butler, J. (1999) *Research Report: Sport and Social Exclusion: A Report for the Department of Media, Culture and Sport*, London: DCMS Policy Action Team 10.

Essex, S. and Chalkley, B. (1998) 'Olympic games: catalyst of urban change', *Leisure Studies*, 17, 187–206.

Football635 (2001) 'Massive quotes', http://www.football365.com/redirect.shtml?/content/features/365features/fw_genfeatur_551070.htm.

Francis, M. and Walsh, P. (1997) *Guvnors*, London: Milo.

Giulianotti, R. (1999) *Football: A Sociology of the Global Game*, Cambridge: Polity Press.

Giulianotti, R. (2002) 'Supporters, followers, fans and flaneurs: a taxonomy of spectator identities in football', *Sport and Social Issues*, 26(2), February: 25–46.

Hamil, S., Michie, J., Oughton, C. and Warby, S. (eds) (2000) *Football in the Digital Age*, Edinburgh: Mainstream.

Hand D. (2002) www.users.tinyworld.co.uk/david.hand1/pridemanchester.htm.

Hannigan, J. (1999) *Fantasy City*, London: Routledge.

Henry, I. and Salcines, J.L.P. (1998) 'Sport and the analysis of symbolic regimes: an illustrative case study of the city of Sheffield', Loughborough University, unpublished paper.

Holt, R. (1992) *Sport and the British: A Modern History*, Oxford: Clarendon.

IMUSA (1998) *Redprint for Change*, Manchester: IMUSA.

IMUSA (1999) *Submission to the Monopoly and Mergers Commission*, Manchester: IMUSA.

Johnstone, S., Southern, A. and Taylor, R. (2000) 'The midweek match: premiership football and the urban economy', *Local Economy*, 15(3): 198–213.

King, A. (1998) *The End of the Terraces: The Transformation of English Football in the 1990s*, Leicester: Leicester University Press.

Kurt, R. and Micheas, J. (1997) *The Red Army Years*, Edinburgh: Mainstream.

Lensky, H. (2002) *The Best Olympics Ever? Social Impacts of Sydney 2000*, New York: State University of New York Press.

Mellor, G. (1999) 'The social and geographical make-up of football crowds in the north-west of England, 1946–1962', *The Sports Historian* 19, November: 25–43.

Phelan, L. (2002) 'Manchester Sport City', paper presented to Of the City Seminar, Manchester Institute of Popular Culture, Manchester Metropolitan University, March.

Polhemus, T. (1994) *Streetstyle*, London: Thames and Hudson.

Redhead, S. (1997) *Post-Fandom and the Millennial Blues*, London: Routledge.

Robertson, R. (1992) *Globalisation: Social Theory and Global Culture*, London: Sage.

Russel, D. (1997) *Football and the English: A Social History of Association Football in England, 1863–1995*, Preston: Carnegie.

Shareholders United (1999) *Submission to the Monopoly and Mergers Commission*, London: SUAM.

Shaw, A. (1998) *Cups for Cock-Ups: The Extraordinary Story of Manchester City FC*, Manchester: Empire.

Southern, A., Taylor, R. and Johnstone, S. (2000) 'The midweek match: premiership football and the urban economy, *Local Economy*, 15(3): 198–213.

Taylor, I., Evans, K. and Fraser, P. (1998) *A Tale of Two Cities*, London: Routledge.

Walvin, J. (2000) *The Peoples' Game: A History of Football Revisited*, Edinburgh: Mainstream.

Williams, J. and Perkins, S. (1999) *Ticket Pricing, Football Business and 'Excluded' Football Fans*, Leicester: Leicester University for the Football Task Force.

12 Love thy neighbour or a Red rag to a Blue?

Reflections on the City–United dynamic in and around Manchester

David Hand

I love Manchester United, they are great – I know because I watch them on Sky TV all the time. I once drove past Manchester on my way to a wedding ... but I didn't have time to get to a match ... I love getting together with all my Man United supporter friends here in London to watch old videos of Bobby Charlton and George Best ... I love all of Man United's strips and I have bought them all for sitting in front of the telly ... I once met a couple of blokes from Manchester but they supported a team called City ... it's unheard of someone from London would support City. I can't understand why anyone would support a team that hasn't won anything in years. Some people support a team just because they were born there – they must be mad!

(MCIVTA, 2002)

Any comprehensive coverage of the United phenomenon must eventually emulate the spoof Internet posting above and consider Manchester City. To an extent, the experience of City's supporters in particular is defined (and lived) differentially in relation to what has latterly become the domineering presence of the United Other. The City–United dynamic is, therefore, a highly significant football and, indeed, social issue in Greater Manchester. This chapter aims, then, to reflect upon Manchester City supporters' perceptions of their neighbour from Stretford. Perceptions are vital to the creation and maintenance of an imagined identity and it will be interesting to consider how the identity of United is portrayed in City fans' projects and other cultural products. The data for the study are drawn from a variety of sources including fans' use of colour, terrace chants, contributions to fanzines, e-zines and Internet postings and popular football writing. Additionally, a recent fictional representation of the City–United dynamic, the film There's Only One Jimmy Grimble (Hay, 2000), will be examined for the light it sheds upon the conflictual relationship between the two clubs' supporters. The methodological approach adopted is qualitative and exploratory. The cognitive and affective elements of football fandom are at least as significant as the behavioural and sociological factors which are the subject of other studies (e.g. Waddington *et al.*, 1998). Indeed, given that usually English football fans' interest in the game is so intensely emotional that parts of everyday life itself are imbued with the defining features and qualities of fandom (Jones, 1997), it would seem important to *identify* and *interpret* the ways in which Manchester City fans' projects represent their lived experience as defined by opposition to United. In this way, the deep meanings and values associated with Mancunian football fandom can be ascertained and discussed. To establish the framework in which the City–United dynamic operates, a number of questions will be addressed. How are United – the club and its followers – portrayed by City fans? What forms do these representations take? Most importantly, what are the principal characteristics of the City–United dialectic as it is played out in and around Manchester?

Colour schemes

Colour matters in Manchester. One is either a 'Blue' or a 'Red', determined by allegiance to City or United, and the ways in which these colours are used constitute a powerful if simplistic symbolic code for Mancunians. In City fans' eyes, (light) blue is good, red is bad. Anecdotes are legion, therefore, about City fans' almost pathological aversion to the colour red. In *Maine Road Voices*, for instance, one fan reports his initiation into local colour rituals when, as a youngster, his wearing of a red T-shirt prompted an explosive reaction from his 'Blue' grandfather: 'Don't ever come here again wearing anything red!' (Waldon, 2002: 79–80). Similarly, another fan wryly notes that his father, 'a Blue ... wouldn't eat bacon ... because it was red and white' (Waldon, 2002: 78). Aversion to red is also much in evidence in the banners and flags carried to City's matches by their supporters. Union flags occasionally appear and when they do, the red crosses of Saints George and Patrick are invariably replaced with sky blue ones while a banner that has appeared frequently over the years speaks volumes about the metaphorical associations of the conflicting colours by proclaiming, 'I'd rather be dead than Red.'

The importance of colour in the City–United dynamic is so significant that commercial companies operating in Manchester must demonstrate some sensitivity towards it. In 2001, for example, staff at a branch of supermarket chain Asda were puzzled by the reaction of certain local children who refused to enter Father Christmas's grotto at the store until it became evident the problem derived from Santa's red-and-white attire: Father Christmas was obviously a United follower and, therefore, a bad man. Once a second Santa was installed, this time resplendent in sky blue, peace and harmony were restored to the local community. In similar vein, sportswear manufacturers Le Coq Sportif, City's official supplier, have been careful to ensure that their traditional logo of a cockerel on a triangular red background is always replaced with a blue background on any merchandise or, indeed, publicity connected with Manchester City.

On a wider note, a research opportunity awaits for a thorough analysis of the negative impact that commercial companies' sponsorship of football clubs might have on certain consumers. In other words, how many potential customers are lost because a firm sponsors a rival club? The question is not without merit and companies that have sponsored United over the years, like Pepsi, Nike and Sharp, would be advised to consider it. The story that City fans keep their kitchen knives blunt to avoid having anything Sharp in the house is humorous (and apocryphal) but also carries with it an important commercial message that telecommunications giant Vodafone appears to have acknowledged. Shortly after it began sponsoring United in 2000, posters appeared in Manchester city centre bearing the slogan 'Vodafone supports the whole of Manchester' which might be interpreted as a (failed) attempt to avoid alienating City fans from its products and services.

Chants for the memory

The antipathy between City and United supporters, from which Vodafone rather clumsily tried to distance itself, is also revealed in chants sung by City fans themselves at matches, as is the rather more obvious devotion to all things blue. City fans' theme song is a rendition of Rodgers and Hart's 'Blue moon'. Hodkinson finds the song uniquely appropriate to the long-suffering fans of a football team that has known little success recently, because, 'It is a lament, a torch song for the bruised, the last swig of hope for the sentimental ... a sweet refrain offered to the sky and whatever lies above it' (1999: 8). Alternatively – and somewhat more prosaically – it might well have been adopted simply because it contains the keyword 'blue' in its title.

Fans' chants are, indeed, still an important feature of the English game. Through their chanting, fans verbalise their affiliations, recount their allegiances and, most importantly from the perspective of the present study, affirm facets of their identity, often defined in opposition to that of their rivals. In addition to the familiar chants of 'If you hate Man United, clap your hands' and 'Stand up if you hate Man U', which are current fare the length and breadth of England, other more specifically Mancunian chants may be heard at City matches that offer further insights into City fans' perceptions of themselves and their neighbours. 'I never felt more like singing the blues/than when City win and United lose/Oh City, you got me singing the blues' is, for instance, a chant that lends some credibility to the belief that a United defeat is at least as pleasurable to a City fan as a City victory. Other chants go beyond the confines of performance on the pitch and affirm almost a moral superiority of City fans over their counterparts. 'City, City, the only football team to come from Manchester', for example, is a shorthand operating on two levels that reaffirms a vital element in the definition of the perceived identities of City and United. First, it points to the fact that both City's old home, Maine Road (from 1923 to 2003) and the new one, the City of Manchester Stadium (to which City moved in 2003) are located in Manchester itself whilst Old Trafford is over the border in Stretford in the borough of Trafford and, therefore, outside the boundaries of Manchester proper. Second, the chant draws attention to the perception that City is the local club, a team primarily for Mancunians, whilst United, with its national and global appeal as well as its widespread fan base, cannot be seen as a truly and uniquely Mancunian phenomenon. A moral superiority is thus asserted by the chant's reassertion of City's local appeal. United's being the 'world's premier national and international "super" club' (Mellor, 2000: 151) cuts no ice with the faithful for whom City remains a site for the celebration of local identity and an integral part of the local community.

This facet of the two clubs' imagined identities is often brought into sharper focus by the chanting at derby games between the two teams. Should the chant go up from United followers that 'We're the pride of all Europe', it is frequently met with the rejoinder from City fans: 'You're the pride of Singapore!' The word 'pride' is employed as a hinge upon which the premise of the chanting is turned away from United's recent sporting dominance towards the club's moral deficiencies in not being a wholly locally supported team. The fact that the rejoinder is immediate suggests City fans are well rehearsed in such degradation rituals. However ritualistic the interaction might be, though, it is nonetheless deeply felt and therefore important. Whether United have more followers in Singapore than Manchester is a moot point. That City have supporters' clubs throughout Europe, in North America, South Africa and Australasia might also be factored into the equation, demonstrating, as it does, that City's fanbase, although admittedly not as sizeable, is at least as internationally widespread as United's. Further complexity is added by recent research demonstrating that, at both clubs, about three-quarters of the season-ticket holders actually live in the northwest of England, the local region (Brown, 2002). However, the same research also shows that, proportionally, significantly more of City's season-ticket holders live in Manchester than United's (40.5 per cent versus 28.2 per cent respectively). The reality is complex; the perception, foregrounded by terrace chants, is simple: City is the Manchester club, United is not.

Fan-tastic journeys

The antagonism between City and United is further displayed in fans' projects beyond the use of colour and terrace chanting. In 1995, for instance, the *Manchester Evening News* conducted a poll on United manager Alex Ferguson's future following a trophy-less season in which several crowd favourites had been sold. The majority of voters agreed Ferguson should be dismissed but there still remains the suspicion that the figures were artificially inflated by mischievous City fans participating in the poll. Revenge for the alleged poll-rigging incident, however, was achieved in 2001 when it became apparent that many United followers were joining radio phone-ins pretending to be City fans. Identifying themselves to their co-conspirators by employing the code word 'massive' in their descriptions of City (thereby mimicking and mocking City fans' aspirations for their own club), the impostors severely criticised the Maine Road club and called for the dismissal of the then manager, Joe Royle. The devious campaign's principal target was BBC Radio 5 Live's '606' programme. Sensing his phone-ins were being hijacked, presenter Richard Littlejohn alerted City's chief operations officer, Chris Bird, who, in turn, contacted several other radio stations to request they be more vigilant when vetting callers: 'At first the whole thing just seemed mischievous, but the campaign has gone on too long and is too concerted to ignore,' noted Bird in an open acknowledgement of the success of the project (Soccernet, 2001).

Occasionally, the Mancunian mischief-makers who poke fun at their rivals do so with considerable imagination and creativity. Prior to a 1991 derby, for instance, City fans executed a stunt that was spectacular in the extreme by using funds generated from sales of the first City fanzine, *Blueprint*, to hire a light aircraft to circle Old Trafford trailing a banner with the inscription 'MCFC [Manchester City Football Club] The Pride of Manchester', thereby taunting the United crowd with a reassertion of Mancunian identity that is so central to City fans. Remarkably, 10 years later, before the 2001 derby, the stunt was repeated. This time, the aeroplane's banner read: 'MCFC Real Club Real Fans'. The message was blunt, if, once again, possibly a touch unfair in its sweeping generalisation. Explicitly, City are an authentic football club; implicitly, United are not.

Perpetuating the same theme, another group of City fans has actually recorded a music CD: 'Project Blue Book' decries United's corporate followers, who, according to Roy Keane's infamous outburst, are too busy eating prawn sandwiches to cheer on their team, by referring to them as 'customers' and mocking their club's status as a plc. City fan turned songwriter Pete Boyle claims United followers are frustrated by 'supporting a plc which is more interested in profits than its fans' as well as affirming that City supporters are 'fans of a football club, not customers of a business' (*Manchester Evening News*, 5 April 2001). In so doing, he highlights another of the most important distinctions that is made when portraying the clashing identities of City and United. Rightly or wrongly, City are perceived as a traditional, community-based football club whilst United's projected identity revolves around its status as a global, commercial, money-making company (for further discussion, see Hand, 2001).

The root of all evil?

In reality, of course, the distinction is not so clear cut and the debate would benefit from some nuancing. Manchester City are also, not surprisingly, engaged in a policy that ultimately aims to emulate United's commercial success. City is itself a plc (quoted on Off Exchange Market [OFEX] rather than the Stock Exchange) and was, indeed, the best-performing English club in 2001 in terms of share prices (Sturgess, 2002: 5). Similarly, attracting hefty commercial sponsorship is by no means the sole prerogative of United. The shirt sponsorship deal City secured with electronics giant Brother in 1997 brought in an estimated £1 million a year and was, relatively, the country's fifth biggest deal, only slightly behind United's reputed £1.25 million/annum partnership with Sharp (Szymanski and Kuypers, 1999: 70). Again, City has not been slow to recognise the money-spinning opportunities afforded by the provision of corporate hospitality at their grounds. When Maine Road was redeveloped in the mid-1990s, 48 executive boxes were installed in the Platt Lane Stand and a further 32 in the new Kippax, features which delighted the chair of the board, the late Peter Swales, who regarded them as a vital component in the club's commercial activities (Murray, 1997: 32). Indeed, the new City of Manchester Stadium is similarly well-equipped (with 68 boxes) and reportedly has the best corporate facilities in England. Whether or not prawn is one of the fillings in the sandwiches served at City matches, the club cannot be said in reality to be diametrically opposed to United in its approach to corporate clientele. Finally, City are now even profiting from their acquisition of Chinese international defender, Jihai Sun. Sun's exploits are followed with considerable interest in his homeland and City directors were quick to visit the world's most populous country to promote commercial links. Mirroring United's activities in the Far East, City is establishing retail outlets in Shanghai and Peking while director Chris Bird, regarding China as 'a land of opportunity', anticipates the generation of 'considerable income over the next 12 to 18 months' (*Manchester Evening News*, 21 October 2002).

For all this, still the image persists that it is United and certainly not City which is tarnished by an overzealous concern with money-making activities. For example, when news broke that United had secreted five mobile phone masts inside their Stretford stadium, a newspaper, reporting that local residents had not been directly consulted, once again foregrounded the image of United as a faceless, insensitive, commercial concern. 'Nothing the club does surprises me any more,' lamented one resident, while another railed: 'The club never tell us anything ... It's just all about money with them and to hell with everybody else' (*Manchester Evening News*, 11 October 2002). Furthermore, even neutral observers of the football industry perpetuate these differences in the imagined identities of City and United:

> With its international marketing reach, one might reasonably ask exactly what it is that ties United to Manchester (especially when a majority of Mancunians are said to support the rival club Manchester City) ... United is distinguished as being a club which does not appear to draw its support primarily from its local area. In Manchester itself, it is said that City is the most popular team, but United is supported all over the country. Moreover, in international terms United is probably the most well recognised English football club. In that sense it is like a brand name such as Coca-Cola, Marlboro or Nescafé.
>
> (Szymanski and Kuypers, 1999: 230)

Hodkinson concurs and further extends the dichotomous images by claiming: 'In stereotypical terms, United is your out-of-town hypermarket, faceless, homogenised and shamelessly avaricious, while City is your friendly corner shop, all how-are-you? and nice-to-see-you, love' (1999: 150. Note the pertinent reference to United being out of town). Having noted that a certain amount of stereotyping is at work in depictions of the two clubs, and despite the reality that their commercial strategies are probably now converging (on United's model) rather than diverging, it should be remembered that stereotypes, for all their inherent distortions and exaggerations, are nonetheless usually rooted in objective realities (for further discussion, see Crolley and Hand, 2002). There are, indeed, still examples of the two clubs doing business differently that serve to reinforce the dichotomy already noted. Even when City belatedly accepted the need to develop its merchandising operations, the merchandising manager, Mike Peak, still highlighted City's difference in this respect from that of their neighbours: sales would be maximised by offering customers desirable quality products 'and not, as is the case at Old Trafford, [by] filling up a big warehouse full of products and saying, "there, go on, just buy it"' (Murray, 1997: 80). Again, shortly after United increased season-ticket prices by twice the rate of inflation for all but executive seat holders (BBC1, 2000), City actually froze their 2003 prices even though the club was moving to bigger and better facilities at their new stadium. Similarly, it would be hard to imagine City allocating a full one-third of its tickets for a derby to executive box holders and commercial partners, which is precisely what United did for the last ever derby held at Maine Road (in November 2002, won by City), much to the disgust of the Independent Manchester United Supporters Association (*Manchester Evening News*, 7 November 2002). So, to regard City as a friendly corner shop placing service to the community over a desire to make a profit might well be slightly erroneous in the context of the football industry of the early 21st century but, insofar as United's equally stereo-typical reputation for shameless greed is concerned, the proverb 'there's no smoke without fire' springs to mind.

Zine-age angst

The perception that City are Manchester's authentic local club whilst United's national and global business concerns deny it the right to be regarded as a purely Mancunian football phenomenon, already apparent in fans' terrace chants and other projects, has also been spotlighted by this brief analysis of commercial activities. Not unsurprisingly, it is additionally one of the mainstays of cultural products devised by City fans. The fanzine movement, for instance, is replete with further examples. Irreverent humour and fierce denigration of the local rival are two of the principal features of fanzine culture (Haynes, 1995) and, as such, are frequently in evidence in publications like *City 'till I Cry*, founded by Tom Ritchie in 1998 to offer a view of the world 'that would fit in with our perception of being humorous and idiosyncratic, and with a raging hatred of all things "Man Yoo"' (Waldon, 2002: 111). These traits are ably demonstrated in this fanzine and in its even longer-running homologues *King of the Kippax* (over a hundred issues since 1988) and *Bert Trautmann's Helmet* (from 1989, originally *Electric Blue*). *City 'till I Cry*, for instance, reacted to the news that, during an official visit to Malaysia, the Queen autographed a United football held up to her somewhat unceremoniously by local youths by claiming to have discovered the content of the royal message inscribed on the offending spheroid: 'Why doesn't one naff orrfff and support one's local team?' (*City 'till I Cry*, 13 October 1998). Other examples of this sharp-edged Mancunian humour abound. The preview in *Bert Trautmann's Helmet* of the first derby following City's return to the Premiership in 2000-1 included the remark: 'This Saturday United play their first match in Manchester for four years' (*Bert Trautmann's Helmet*, 15 November 2000), reiterating the fact that United is not actually based in Manchester proper and thereby reinforcing what is seen as a key element in City fans' self-definition: Mancunian status.

It has been noted, however, that the heyday of the fanzine movement has passed (Waldon, 2002: 114–25) and certainly output is not now so voluminous in this area. It could be, though, that what is happening is not a downturn in the production of fanzine-type material but rather a relocation of it from photocopiers and printing presses to the Internet. E-zines, message boards and websites might well be progressively conquering the space previously occupied by fanzines. One City e-zine, for instance, claims over 3,000 subscribers (Manchester City Information Via the Alps [MCIVTA], 2002). There are, therefore, plenty of examples of the dominant themes of the City–United dynamic to be found in cyberspace. The familiar taunt that too many of United's followers are not Mancunians, for instance, is frequently reiterated through spiky humour. 'What have Old Trafford on a Saturday afternoon at 4.45 p.m. and Wormwood Scrubs got in common?' asks one fan: 'They are both full of Cockneys trying to get out' (MCIVTA, 2002). Similarly, another wag announces a spoof newsflash: 'In light of the fact the vast majority of United fans may have missed out on the recent open top bus tour of Manchester, Chairman Martin Edwards today announced a second bus tour around the M25' (MCIVTA, 2002). Examples of the process could be added almost indefinitely. A third poses a question full of irony of United's directors: 'Why not relocate and build a brand new stadium somewhere near London to reward your loyal lifelong supporters with a shorter journey home after matches?' (MCIVTA, 2002), while a fourth reflects on City's departure from Maine Road and suggests that 'our illustrious neighbours [might] like to rent the ground occasionally so they can visit Manchester more than once a season' (MCFC, 2001). Finally, Internet postings also reinforce the perception that many United followers are: transient glory-seekers, 'How many Reds does it take to change a light bulb? None, they all fled at the first sign [it] was failing' (MCIVTA, 2002); not true fanatics, 'What have the moon and Old Trafford got in common? No atmosphere' (BlueView, 2002); or merely armchair supporters (see Figure 12.1).

The vibrant culture of contestation pioneered by fanzines (Jary *et al.*, 1991) is extended to the Internet, then, where City's 'traditional' fans constantly challenge the new forces of commercialism incarnated by United and resist the discourse and practices of media-driven consumerism.

Figure 12.1 From amoeba to armchair: the evolution of the Manchester United fan.

Source: Manchester City Supporters Homepage (2002)

Writing wrongs?

Issues of place, identification with a locality and fan authenticity and loyalty appear as constants in City fans' perceptions as communicated through the new media of fanzines and the Internet. These concerns are also frequently voiced in the older medium of the book market through popular football writing. The vogue that developed in the 1980s for books in which fans reflect upon their lives in football hardly seems to have abated. Manchester City in particular, presumably because of their high-profile trials and tribulations in the last 20 years, have generated a large number of such works, many with something to say about the City–United dynamic. The most celebrated work of this nature is, of course, Schindler's *Manchester United Ruined My Life* (1998). Schindler, a cinema and television screenplay writer who follows in the line of *soccerati* begun by Hornby, author of *Fever Pitch* (1992), presents an eloquent case for choosing City over United. To opt for City might be irrational in view of cold sporting logic but it is a choice based upon the concept of self-definition via difference and distinction. The masses blindly follow United simply because they win. Using the technique of portraying City and United through a series of antitheses that is, in the light of the present study, increasingly familiar, Schindler notes that City are 'Wrong but Wromantic, United ... Right but Repulsive' (Schindler, 1998: 7).

Schindler's work has received considerable attention, though, and it is more illuminating to consider other works that have received less coverage but which, nonetheless, amply reinforce the identity of United as imagined by Manchester City fans. Winstanley's *Bleak and Blue* (1999), for instance, is unequivocal in this respect and is worth quoting at some length for its humorous foregrounding of many of the features of United's identity that have already been identified in other areas. United is:

- not a Manchester team: 'There is a team based in the borough of Trafford that I cannot avoid mentioning' (Winstanley, 1999: 8);
- not a traditional football club: 'Well, to be honest, they are not so much a football team as a renowned financial concern and fashion house' (p.8);
- not necessarily followed primarily by Mancunians: 'The sight of somebody wearing a shirt in their famous colours – red, speckled blue, green and yellow, black, pink with yellow dots, puce and orange stripes, invisible grey, makes me wince. The only comfort comes when the accent of the wearer reveals origins somewhere between 150 and several thousand miles from Manchester' (p.9);
- not a local concern but a national one: Winstanley refers to United throughout as 'The Nation's Team (The World's Team might be more appropriate)' (p.8) both as a euphemism because he is 'heartily sick of seeing their name in print' (p.8) and as an ironic reference to United's national appeal which is itself not viewed positively but rather as a negative example of the way in which football's traditional driving forces of match-going fanaticism and civic patriotism are being challenged by the new imperatives of media-driven consumerism and commercialism;

- not wholly supported by 'real' fans but followed primarily by television consumers: 'The sheer level of publicity ensures that little boys will claim to support *The Nation's Team* because they are the only team they have heard of, and because it's easy. You don't have to leave your living room. You just sit in front of the television, wearing one of your myriad choice of official replica shirts, then you go and unleash your misguided superiority complex on your friends' (p.9);
- not an object of affection under any circumstances: 'They are the enemy ... whoever, wherever and whenever *The Nation's Team* play, I will support the opposition even if [they] located Mussolini in goal, with a back four of Kissinger, Saddam Hussein, Pol Pot and Hitler, a midfield with Thatcher on the right, Stalin on the left, a couple of Radio 1 DJ's ... in the middle, and Rupert Murdoch up front with David Mellor' (p.10).

Another recent text, *Maine Road Voices*, covers similar ground by allowing fans to recollect their memories of supporting City and denigrating United. 'My mother, my uncles, my grandparents and my cousins were all Reds' notes one contributor, '(though all but one uncle and his son were true Reds, that is never went near the ground but had comfy armchairs)' (Waldon, 2002: 86). Others highlight City and United's contrasting characteristics: 'I've always had a sense of humour, despised big heads, preferred blue and have been proud of the city of Manchester, having been born there ... I could only support Manchester City, couldn't I?' (p.87). Is the implication in this act of self-definition that many United followers are humourless, arrogant non-Mancunians? Indeed, so important is the attachment to Manchester and its perceived role in the City–United dynamic that several contributors to Waldon's book cannot bring themselves to use the word 'Manchester' in conjunction with 'United' at all, preferring instead epithets that highlight United's non-Mancunian status such as 'our friends from Salford' (p.24) and 'Stretford Rangers' (p.118).

The latter mirrors the usage of local media and football personalities. For example, *Manchester Evening News* journalist (and former City player) Paul Hince often refers to 'Trafford Rangers' in his columns; BBC Greater Manchester Radio's (GMR) Ian Cheeseman speaks of 'Stretford United' and former City director Ian Niven would speak of 'Stretford Rangers' (Buckley and Burgess, 2000: 28).

The big picture

Finally, it is worth considering a recent fictional representation of the City–United dynamic for the light it sheds upon the conflictual relationship between the two clubs' supporters. In the British film There's Only One Jimmy Grimble, the eponymous hero is a modest schoolboy footballer and City fan, bullied by his peers, who ultimately overcomes his physical and psychological limitations to achieve success on the pitch. The film may be read as a metaphor of the City–United divide because of its director's desire to make Manchester 'a real character' in the picture (Hay, 2000). Indeed, the locations are set in the city and, in fact, in and around Maine Road itself while the soundtrack is largely made up of elements from the famous Manchester music scene.

Grimble is, then, a 'City boy' who describes himself as 'on the endangered species list ... in the heart of the Man U jungle' (Hay, 2000) as he suffers verbal and physical abuse at the hands of rival United followers at his school. His tormentors outnumber him, symbolising the numerical superiority of United followers over their City counterparts; they are all also bigger and stronger than him, reflecting United's dominance in the real world; and, whilst Grimble is shy and modest, the United bullies are confident and arrogant. In one scene, they urinate on Grimble's City holdall, a powerful representation of the attitude adopted by some United followers towards their neighbours from Manchester. Grimble's chief tormentor is 'gorgeous' Gordon Burley, who may be read as a personification of United itself, at least as seen through City eyes: he is popular and photogenic but vain, a skilful footballer but an obnoxious character. Interestingly, his father is an equally repulsive out-of-town businessman who uses his financial sponsorship of his son's school to dictate team selections to the subservient sports teacher, Eric Wirral. Burley senior thus represents the financial clout behind United and the unadulteratedly commercial elements supporting them. Just as the Burleys represent certain facets of United's perceived identity, Grimble's benefactors in the film may be interpreted as reinforcing the contrasting identity of City. Grimble's adult friend Harry is a likeable Mancunian and fellow City fan who is kind and supportive – the complete antithesis of the Burleys – while Wirral is modest and self-deprecating. The latter, who significantly lives on Maine Road, is an ex-City player struggling to cope professionally with his former glories well behind him, a metaphor for Manchester City itself, perhaps, which has known decline on the pitch (but not on the terraces) for some 20 years.

That the film as a whole is constructed on antithesis is further reinforced by the director's use of colour. The clashing colours of blue and red are here employed systematically in a powerful symbolic code that affirms blue as the colour of comfort, safety and right with red being the colour of anger, danger and wrong. Grimble's school team significantly play in sky blue whilst their opponents are frequently seen in red. In the bullying scenes, Grimble's tormentors generally wear red clothing and in one particular scene, Grimble takes refuge behind the safety of a blue car. Grimble's confidant, Wirral, dresses in a blue tracksuit and drives the schoolboy footballers around in a light blue minibus. Harry's anta- gonistic wife is wearing red in a scene where she berates him and, finally, the naturally blue trimmings of Maine Road are colour enhanced to glow with an eerie intensity as the backdrop to Grimble's ultimate triumph on the pitch as he steers his team to victory in the Cup Final there. Reflecting the colour dynamics employed by City fans in their projects, the mutually hostile colours of blue and red are simply but effectively used by the film to represent good and bad in a manner reminiscent of Hollywood's use of white and black in old westerns.

Conclusion

There is substantial evidence to suggest that the attitude adopted by Manchester City fans towards United is not based upon the principle of 'love thy neighbour'. In the context of traditional English football fandom, founded as it is upon civic pride and fierce local rivalries and antagonisms, there is little reason to suppose it would be otherwise. What it has been interesting to isolate and analyse in the present study, however, are the various forms that this antipathy assumes in and around Manchester. Ultimately and not withstanding the full complexity and contradictions of City and United's identities as social facts, it is clear that perceptions of United held by many City fans deliberately polarise the protagonists in the dynamic and, therefore, portray them through a series of antipathic binary oppositions that serve to establish the projected identity of United as the complete antithesis of City. Consequently, the City–United dynamic operates in the synoptic framework illustrated in Table 12.1.

So mutually exclusive are the imagined identities of Greater Manchester's two dominant footballing forces that, once the right choice is made and a commitment established, there can be only total, utter rejection of the Other. At the end of There's Only One Jimmy Grimble, for instance, the hero speaks for all those born with a blue moon rising when he rejects a scout's proposal to join United in favour of 'a better offer' (Hay, 2000). Looking suitably incredulous, the scout enquires, 'What could be better than Man United, son?' To which Grimble heart-warmingly replies, 'Man City!'

References

BBC1 (2000) 'North West Tonight', 13 April, television programme.

BlueView (2002) available online at http://manchestercity.rivals.net/default.asp?sId= 914&stId=7954254&p=2 (accessed December 2002).

Brown, A. (2002) *Do You Come From Manchester? A Postcode Analysis of the Location of Manchester United and Manchester City Season Ticket Holders, 2001*, available online at http://www.mmu.ac.uk/h-ss/mipc/docs/SeasonTicketReport.pdf.

Buckley, A, and Burgess, R. (2000) *Blue Moon Rising*, Bury: Milo Books.

Crolley, L. and Hand, D. (2002) *Football, Europe and the Press*, London: Frank Cass.

Hand, D. (2001) 'City 'till I die? Recent trends in popular football writing', *Soccer and Society*, 2(1): 99–112.

Hay, J. (Dir.) (2000) 'There's Only One Jimmy Grimble', Pathé Pictures, DVD.

Table 12.1 A City–United dynamic synoptic framework

	City positive	*United* negative
Appeal	local	(inter)national
Imperative	community	commercial
Quality	'real'	inauthentic
Personality	humble	arrogant

Haynes, R. (1995) *The Football Imagination: The Rise of Football Fanzine Culture*, Aldershot: Arena.

Hodkinson, M. (1999) *Blue Moon*, Edinburgh: Mainstream.

Hornby, N. (1992) *Fever Pitch*, London: Victor Gollancz.

Jary, D., Horne, J. and Bucke, T. (1991) 'Football fanzines and football culture', *Sociological Review*, 39(4): 581–97.

Jones, I. (1997) 'Mixing qualitative and quantitative methods in sports fan research: *The Qualitative Report*, 3(4), available online at http://www.nova.edu/SSSS/QR/QR3-4/jones.html.

Manchester City Football Club (MCFC) (2001) available online at http://www.mcfc.co.uk/active.asp?article=26551&display=article (accessed January 2001).

Manchester City Information Via the Alps (MCIVTA) (2002) available online at http://www.uit.no/mancity/mcivta/ (accessed November 2002).

Manchester City Supporters Homepage (2002) available online at http://www.uit.no/mancity/humour.html (accessed October 2002).

Mellor, G. (2000) 'The genesis of Manchester United as a national and international "super-club"', *Soccer and Society*, 1(2): 151–66.

Murray, C. (1997) *Attitude Blue: Crowd Psychology at Manchester City FC*, Stockport: MUS.

Schindler, C. (1998) *Manchester United Ruined My Life*, London: Headline.

Soccernet (2001) available online at www.soccernet.com/england/today/news/index.html. (accessed January 2002)

Sturgess, B. (2002) 'City view', *Soccer Analyst*, 3(1): 5–7.

Szymanski, S. and Kuypers, T. (1999) *Winners and Losers: The Business Strategy of Football*, London: Penguin.

Waddington, I., Malcolm, D. and Horak, R. (1998) 'The social composition of football crowds in Western Europe', *International Review for the Sociology of Sport*, 33(2): 155–69.

Waldon, A. (2002) *Maine Road Voices*, Stroud: Tempus Publishing.

Winstanley, C. (1999) *Bleak and Blue*, Wilmslow: Sigma Leisure.

13 Parvenu United

Local rivalries, smalltown boys and city slickers

Alan Tomlinson

The Football League: founders and newcomers

The (English) Football League was founded in 1888, the logical outcome of the standardisation of the association football code, its escalating popularity with the industrial working class, and the incipient professionalisation of the game played and watched by working men. In his analysis of the occupation of football players with elite clubs between 1884 and 1900, Mason (1980) identified a skilled base to the manual occupations of the 67 players in his sample. These players were from Blackburn Olympic, Blackburn Rovers, Bolton Wanderers, Everton, Manchester City, Notts County, Preston North End, Sheffield Wednesday and Sunderland. Amateurs such as solicitor's clerks, schoolteachers, dentists, lawyers and colliery managers were still to be found in these sides, but very much a minority, 16 as against the 51 professionals. The less skilled manual workers included, as Mason lists them alphabetically, 'bone cutter, cotton mill worker, dyer, factory hand, painter, pickle maker, stoker and tape sizer' (Mason, 1980: 90–1). The skilled workers included a master baker, a moulder, a painter, a felt hatter, a coal miner, a bricklayer, an upholsterer, a weaver and a tailor. Clubs advertised for respectable recruits into the ranks of the professionalising game. Professional sport was clearly an attractive outlet for relatively skilled workers, not merely an escape route for the unskilled. And these players flocked to the clubs in the industrial cities of the northwest and northeast of England, the midlands and Yorkshire. Of Mason's nine sample clubs, six were from Lancashire, but as noted above these did not include Manchester United.

The 12 founder members of the Football League were Aston Villa, Wolverhampton Wanderers, West Bromwich Albion (West Midlands), Derby County, Notts County and Stoke (City added in 1924) – East and North Midlands – and Accrington (re-formed as Accrington Stanley in 1919), Blackburn Rovers, Bolton Wanderers, Burnley, Preston North End and Everton (Liverpool). These last six clubs were all from Lancashire but, apart from Everton, not from the big cities of the county; rather, they came from the expanding and in an economic sense booming small towns in the north and the northeast of the county. No Manchester club was of sufficient merit or prominence to warrant the written invitation, in March 1888, from the League's founder (Aston Villa's administrator

William McGregor), as one of the 'ten or twelve of the most prominent clubs in England' that might 'combine to arrange home and away fixtures each season' (Churchill, 1958: 8). Early champions of the Football League, in its first 19 years, were Preston (for the first two seasons), Everton, and then newcomers Sunderland (three times in four seasons, and then for a fourth time), Aston Villa (five times in seven years), Sheffield United, Sheffield Wednesday (in successive seasons), Liverpool (twice), and Newcastle United (twice). Although the clubs of the smaller Lancashire towns were still competing at the top level, there is in this list a discernible swing to the city. Blackburn Rovers were champions in 1911–12 and 1913–14 seasons, Burnley the second season after the First World War (1920–1). And Huddersfield Town, under the great pioneer of modern football management and systems coaching Herbert Chapman, could come out of the blue – or at least the bleakness of the Pennine valleys – and win the title three times in succession from 1924–6. But resources were pouring in to the city clubs, where greater support and spectator revenues could be guaranteed. In the twentieth season of the League, Manchester United outscored its 19 rivals, and conceded fewer goals than any of them, to secure its first League championship. Seven of the founder members were still in Division One of the League in that season, though Bolton was relegated, and Everton, Preston, Blackburn, Sunderland and Notts County were in the bottom half of the table at the end of the season. Only Aston Villa, of the founders (finishing a distant runner-up to United), looked to be a force at the top level. West Bromwich Albion, Derby County, Burnley, Wolverhampton Wanderers and Stoke City were by now in the league's Division Two, albeit all in the top half.

Manchester United – then called Newton Heath – played its first season in the League in Division One, in the season 1892–3 in which a second division was first introduced. Heath/United finished the season bottom of the division, five points behind Accrington. United survived in the division after a series of what were then called 'Test Matches' between the bottom three of the division and the top three of the new division (this system lasted for six seasons). Outright champions of Division Two, Birmingham City, faltered in these pioneering 'play-offs', as we now know them, and Darwen went up to the top division with Sheffield United. Accrington Stanley and Notts County went down. Heath/United (the team was nicknamed the Heathens) hardly operated in any Theatre of Dreams at that time. In a replay against Stoke City after a 1–1 draw, changing for the game in a local pub called the Three Crowns, the team won 5–2 on a mudbath of a pitch, cheered to survival at its unsophisticated North Road ground by a mere 4,000 onlookers. In the following season, the club at least showed consistency, again finishing bottom, five points behind newly promoted Darwen. This time it did not survive, Liverpool (undefeated and top of the second division in its inaugural League season) coasting home 2–0: the Manchester club was to spend 12 seasons in the second division (adopting the name Manchester United in 1902) before climbing back to the top tier for the 1906–7 season.

This review of the vicissitudes of club fortunes in the early years of the English professional game is more than mere trainspotting, or 'anorak statistics', as we have become accustomed to calling a certain mode of knowledge trivia. It is about historical legacies and local and regional cultural affiliations. A century on from when Manchester United adopted its more metropolitan name, three Lancashire founders remained in the top flight: Blackburn Rovers, Bolton Wanderers and the big city club Everton. Preston and Burnley were holding their own in the division below the Premier, the Nationwide League Division One. But financially, competitively and culturally, they were worlds apart in a boom-and-bust, increasingly fragmented football industry and culture.

Local rivals: the football derby game

One of the fascinating characteristics of football support, in terms of fans and their affiliations, is its very flexibility. A follower of Manchester United might jeer an Arsenal star in an encounter at Old Trafford, yet cheer on that same star in an English international match when the outcome will determine whether England competes in a World Cup Final tournament or a European Nations championship final stage. But less flexible than that is local identity, and the rivalry that stems from competition and matches between local geographical rivals. This has become known as the 'derby match'; Cashmore, or one of his 'editorial team', elaborates on the genesis of this term:

> The Derby is the name given to the annual horse race at the Epson Downs, England, and the Kentucky Derby, which takes place every year in Louisville, Kentucky. Over time, the 'Derby' has been used to describe any sporting competition which attracted great interest and, later, to denote soccer games between proximate rivals, or 'local derbies' as they were called ... the soccer derby has a particular asperity, perhaps because of soccer's own violent history and its roots in working-class communities, where neighbourhood status was often tied to that of the local team.
>
> (Cashmore, 2000: 85)

Giulianotti observes that such matches between teams representing 'specific geographical and cultural identities' based upon rivalry and opposition were good box office for the expanding game:

> These 'derby games' promised comparatively large crowds due to the short distances travelled by rival supporters. Culturally, derby matches sold them-selves; rival fans lived, worked and socialized with each other, discussing, joking, and theorizing endlessly on past and future encounters.
>
> (Giulianotti, 1999: 10)

Giulianotti underplays the element of threat to spectators, the spectre of aggression in these local encounters; whilst Cashmore ignores the more festive, bantering side of them. The historical truth lies somewhere in between. Certainly larger crowds would generate a special atmosphere at such matches. In 1894 the first Football League match to be played between the two Manchester clubs took place at Manchester City's ground, Ardwick. In vile November weather, a crowd of 15,000 watched Heath/United win 5–2; later in the season City went down again, away from home, by 4–1. Giulianotti points out that, like Juventus in Turin, United has acquired a global support, whilst 'City gain a dispropor-tionate affection from its citizens' (1999: 12) in Manchester itself. This sense of City as the stalwart community-based side and United as the Fancy Dans of the game was borne out, in a 1960 review of the League's history, by crowd figures and popular nomenclature: against Old Trafford's record crowd of 76,962, City's Maine Road could nevertheless boast 84,560, an English record for a football match in England outside London; and, more importantly, whilst Manchester United became known as the 'Red Devils', the city's Blues were still, into the second half of the twentieth century, 'popularly known as the Citizens' (Churchill, 1958: 119).

But as a review of the early years of the professional game demonstrates, the midland and the northern roots of the Football League (see Tomlinson, 1999: 149–78) ensured that many games were derbies. Local encounters could be fierce. In a game between Burnley and Blackburn Rovers at Turf Moor, in February 1890, the Burnley supporters were outraged at refereeing decisions that disallowed a goal for their side, but allowed one for the visitors. The Burnley players were so upset that they refused to play on, and kept this up for five minutes. The referee had to be smuggled out of the ground and given a police escort to his home. This local shemozzle merited a report in the *Manchester Guardian*. Perhaps the Burnley fans had a point: the referee's brother was also identified, and he was playing in goal for Blackburn Rovers (Mason, 1980: 161). In Birmingham, Small Heath (from 1905, Birmingham, with City added in 1945) and Aston Villa fans developed strong rivalries, and would follow each other's progress and (mis)fortunes. At a first division match against fellow strugglers Bury (Lancashire) in 1896, the Small Heath supporters cheered the announcement of a series of telegrams logging Aston Villa's defeat in the Cup at Derby (Mason, 1980: 231). A hundred years on, such responses are routine at matches when scores are announced at the half-time interval and at full-time. Baiting your nearest and fiercest local rival has long been an established part of the football ritual. Contiguity has been vital to local rivalries and the derby match's momentous symbolic significance. In the Lancastrian roots of the professional game, matches such as Burnley versus Manchester United were derbies with an added edge, as the metropolitan power base of the game was consolidated (just note how within a few years of each other, the two Heaths in the major cities of the north and the midlands metamorphosised into big city clubs by name). This chapter focuses upon particular moments and matches between Burnley and Manchester United, particularly those that, like a single event for the anthropologist looking closely at a contained community, have made explicit the core dynamics of the culture: in the case of the small Lancashire cotton town and the big Victorian city, a David and Goliath dynamic that has sometimes expressed itself in particularly revealing form in this 'derby with an edge'.

Manchester United versus Burnley: power shifts

In December 2002 Burnley met Manchester United at Turf Moor, in a knock-out Football League Cup match. Manchester won, as was widely anticipated, even without some of the club's top stars. The Manchester side's line-up was still very strong, given the squad that the club could sustain on the basis of its economic resources and brand pulling-power. The ground was full and most fans recognised the quality of football and contributed to the excellent atmosphere. United striker Diego Forlan scored in the first half of the game, diluting the drama of the encounter. At the game was Burnley fan and political scientist Lincoln Allison, who compiled the following notes:

> Away fans were surprisingly impressive, every seat taken and singing vociferously – exemplifying the general truth that away fans en masse are a different breed from home fans.
>
> I did enjoy the following exchange: Them (all 4,000+): 'Lancashire, la la la la etc'. Bloke next to me: 'Fuck off back to Milton Keynes'. We (in general): 'You're just a small town in Cheshire' and 'You're just a load of cockneys'.
>
> Also the 7-year-old lad behind me, as Man U came out for a warm-up: 'You're a load of rubbish and yer ground's a cowshed'.
>
> (Lincoln Allison, personal e-mail to author, headed
> 'Contested Identities', Saturday 7 December 2002)

Lacking competitive edge, the game symbolized the historical story of dramatically shifting changes in fortune for the clubs in the later twentieth century. The home Burnley fans turned out for a special occasion and some banter rather than showing any realistic hope of victory. But many fans at the game could recall very different fiercely contested encounters – and Burnley had won the FA Cup in 1914, and the League championship in 1921. The city club had been far from dominant in the earlier phases of the long-standing rivalry.

Heath/United was baptised in the rough waters of these Lancashire heartlands. Its first match in the League was a 4–3 loss to Blackburn Rovers. Heath/United's first home game in its debut 1892–3 season in the Football League was against Burnley, and in retrospect its 1–1 draw looked creditable alongside a series of heavy defeats as the *parvenu* Mancunians plummeted to the bottom position. At the end of season 1896-7, Heath/United contested the play-offs, beating and losing to Burnley, and drawing 1–1 in its home game with Sunderland at the Bank Street ground in Clayton – to which the club had moved in 1893 – in front of 18,000 spectators. But defeats at Notts County and Sunderland kept the club in the lower division, where Burnley joined it. The turning point came a decade on from the club's entry into the League. After the two inaugural seasons in the upper division the club spent 12 years in the second division, though in the ninth of these, a change of name to Manchester United and a move of location acted as the revitalisation and the basis of the creation of a giant, rather than the awakening of any sleeping giant. In season 1901–2 Newton Heath had struggled financially and performed appallingly, finishing in 15th position in the lower division, but at least above Chesterfield, Stockport County and Gainsborough Trinity. For the new season 1902–3 the club was rebranded as Manchester United, bankrolled by new backers, and soon to be newly managed by Ernest Magnall, who at the end of September 1902 moved from his position as secretary at Burnley Football Club to become Manchester United's first successful manager.

All of this went uncommented upon in the Burnley media. The local club had finished modestly in the second division, well above the crisis-ridden Heath/ United, and in the top half of the table, but a place below Glossop North End. A final match of the season against Glossop drew a mere 1,000 spectators, and in the sport commentary (hardly a section) in the *Burnley Express and Clitheroe Division Advertiser* issues at the end of April 1902, there is no mention of the renaming of Newton Heath. Domestic affairs of the sport drew little local reportage, let alone the crisis of one of the worst teams in the League 26 miles away in Manchester. Football matters seemed so low profile in the local consciousness that just a couple of games into the new season in September, when Magnall was attracted to Manchester, it was of no interest to a local sporting press interested only in on-the-field outcomes of matches against Leicester Fosse and Small Heath. The outcomes proved woeful for Burnley that season. The club finished bottom of the division, but the pedigree of the founder status proved a lifeline: the League committee 'elected' third-from-bottom Doncaster Rovers out, and voted in the latest newcomer, the newly-founded Bradford City. Magnall had left for new pastures and the promise of infinitely more resources, and the swift consequences were the rejuvenation of United and the sudden decline of a small-town club. United finished fifth in the division that season, third in the following two seasons, then secured promotion with a second-place finish at the end of the 1905–6 season. It finished eighth in its first season back in the first division, and ran away with the title in 1907–8, winning it again three years later. In this spell Burnley drifted along in mid-table before gaining promotion back to Division One in 1913.

Magnall, a Bolton-born Lancastrian, used the funds secured by the 'new' Manchester United to assemble his sides by ruthless and astute dealings in the transfer market. Magnall's team-building soon paid dividends, United drawing 40,000 for a 1904 Boxing Day victory against promotion rivals Liverpool. A crowd of 40,000 also turned up in 1906 for a 5–1 Football Association (FA) Cup victory over Aston Villa. Magnall would not be short of funds, and could afford to bring in several of the star players from the other Manchester club, City, which on getting into the first division at the end of Magnall's first season at United, had established itself as one of the top teams in the League, but was breaking FA payment rules. Magnall recruited the Welsh wizard Billy Meredith and four other City players, so laying the foundations for the title-winning side. Playing glamorous football, successfully (winning the FA Cup in 1909) drawing regular and massive crowds, United could continue to plan and think ambitiously, and the club invested £90,000 in its new stadium, Old Trafford, opened in January 1910. As Ernest Magnall lifted the trophy in front of 300,000 waiting fans at Manchester's Central Station, serenaded by a brass band's rendition of 'See the conquering hero comes', he must have thought back fondly to the crowds of 1,000 that he'd left behind at Turf Moor. He'd been back there during the successful Cup campaign, when Burnley led 1-0 in a match abandoned in a blizzard, United winning the rearranged tie 3-2. This Cup match, in which second division Burnley ran current Division One champions United so close, has gone down in local football folklore. Even half a century later, when the Burnley-United rivalry was revived by a more expansive local sporting press in the town, the match would be given pride of place in a review of the history of the encounters between the two clubs.

The context of this review was the Munich tragedy of Thursday 6 February 1958. 'Matches between Burnley and Manchester United invariably have given pleasure to thousands over a period of years, and have been enjoyed by spectators and players alike ...' (*Burnley Express and Burnley News*, 19 March 1958: 7), wrote Sportsman, reeling off a list of memorable matches, including that during United's first Cup-winning campaign. Another Cup encounter, in January 1954, has etched itself in the consciousness of Burnley fans. Manchester United was defeated 5-3 at Turf Moor. Burnley defender Tommy Cummings recalls this game against the current League champions, the first of Manchester manager Matt Busby's famous 'Busby Babes':

> Manchester United were one of the top sides and their visits to Turf Moor always guaranteed a big crowd and a good atmosphere. How the events unfolded that day was just fantastic. The Manchester United lads came to meet us afterwards and we couldn't believe it.
>
> (Prestage, 2000: 50)

'A great game and a terrific day out,' recalled supporter Donald Speak (Prestage, 2000: 50). These recollections by player and fan alike do not indicate any deep resentment of the elite opponents, more a sense of pleasure in victory and sportsmanlike respect.

A dignified respect was the response in Burnley to the news of the Munich tragedy. The tragedy was page one news, but not the main story on the Saturday after the crash, in which eight players lost their lives and several more players were injured. Two other stories dominated the top of the front page of the *Burnley Express and Burnley News* on Saturday 8 February. One referred to a 'Textile trade SOS to Minister', a running story on the economic plight of the town's cotton industry. The other was 'Her bacon and egg pie won her a fine suitcase', featuring a photograph of the mayor, Alderman Mrs M.A. Battle, presenting the prize to the lucky winner at Burnley Gas Showrooms. But at least the Munich story was given some front-page space, in which the chairman of Burnley Football Club, Mr R.W. Lord ... said: 'I feel overwhelmed. It is most upsetting news. What a terrible affair. It must be the most tragic happening to hit football.' The piece, entitled simply 'The football 'plane tragedy', went on to recall the respect and warmth at the heart of the relationship between the two clubs:

It was not only that Manchester United are a Lancashire club, but their league, cup and international prowess, and play against Burnley, had won them many admirers in the town and district. Whenever they have been engaged in a European Cup match at Old Trafford, United have had a contingent of supporters from Burnley, where tickets for their games were in considerable demand.

When Mr Frank Hill was manager at Turf Moor, the Burnley players and those of United played each other in friendly golf matches, and a spirit of happy comradeship exists between the clubs. They have found themselves staying in the same hotel when both teams have been engaged in London fixtures, and on occasions have travelled north in the same train.

(*Burnley Express and Burnley News*, 8 February 1958: 1)

The 'spirit of happy comradeship' was to be undermined over the following few weeks, as the spontaneous sympathy for the tragedy-hit club became mixed with a pragmatic survivalist sense of self-preservation. Burnley had returned to the first division in 1947, finishing third in its first season back at the top. The club finished consistently well in the division over the next decade, finishing seventh, seventh and sixth in the three seasons preceding the Munich disaster. It was hardly surprising that bigger clubs would be looking to prise away young Burnley stars to more glamorous clubs and settings. One of the biggest of these stars was Northern Ireland international Jimmy McIlroy. In the New Year of 1958, Sportsman, in the 'Football Notebook', reported weekend stories of McIlroy's dissatisfaction, of the Irishman wanting a move to another club. McIlroy was also heading off to Ireland for an international game against Italy, and rumours were rife that some big Italian club would make an offer to Burnley of such a high transfer fee for the player, of such a scale, that the club would be unable to turn it down. The issue was summarised column: 'If an Italian club came along with a fabulous offer, and the international wanted to go ahead, would Burnley be prepared to part in those circumstances?' (*Burnley Express and Burnley News*, 18 January 1958: 15). The potential loss of McIlroy was a central page one story, and the player was reported as having commented that the contract system caused him some 'uneasiness':

> McIlroy's name has been linked with Arsenal, Tottenham Hotspur and Manchester United, but the only comment has come from Arsenal, whose manager, Mr Jack Crayston, said that McIlroy was a fine player and they would be interested if any move was forthcoming, but they were 'sitting on the fence'.
>
> (*Burnley Express and Burnley News*, 18 January 1958: 1)

Plenty of comment had been forthcoming earlier in the week, though, from chairman Bob Lord: 'You can tell the public that McIlroy is not leaving Burnley. There is not a club with enough money to buy him. We are not making stars for other clubs to take off us' (*Burnley Express and Burnley News*, 15 January 1958: 6).

The McIlroy instance was like a dress rehearsal for Bob Lord's bigger media splash in the days after the Munich disaster. If United was interested in star players before the tragedy, the stricken club was desperate for them afterwards. The assistant manager of Manchester United visited Turf Moor, purportedly to meet up with the trainer of Burnley's opponents on the day, who was being released by Luton to help out back at Old Trafford. The visit generated rumours that he was 'interested' in Burnley's players, including winger Brian Pilkington:

> United's deputy chief stayed on to watch the game but was non-committal about an approach to Burnley for playing assistance.

However, Lord was quick to halt talk of any transfer from Turf Moor. While expressing regret about United's unfortunate position, he pointed out that there was no hope of them obtaining players from Burnley.

> 'United cannot expect to approach a club with the hope of getting their star players,' said Mr. Lord. 'No matter how sorry we feel for them they entered the European Cup knowing the risk and now they should not feel that clubs are obliged to sell their best players on their behalf. Brian Pilkington is not for sale.'
>
> (*Burnley Express and Burnley News*, 19 February 1958: 7)

Lord, widely known as the Burnley Butcher, whose book would later carry the epithet 'Burnley's forthright chairman', was true to form here. Let the big city club sort out its own affairs in a normal marketplace, Lord was saying. He was almost saying too that the tragedy was the club's own fault. The scene was set for a League match the following month that would make all talk of the comradely spirit sound like sanctimonious cant.

Manchester United visited Burnley on 15 March 1958. The build-up in the local press was dignified and respectful, anticipating an 'all-important match' that was also 'vital from a prestige point of view' (*Burnley Express and Burnley News*, 15 March 1958: 7). Burnley had lost its last couple of games, its season was losing its momentum, managers had changed and transfer rumours, exacerbated since Munich, had been unsettling:

> Manchester United have been the focal point of much deserved sympathy since the tragic accident ... Fortunately the Old Trafford club were better placed for reserves than many other clubs (including Burnley for instance) and ... they are making a remarkable recovery, to the delight of their great crowd of admirers.
>
> However United have gone beyond the stage of extended commiseration and are re-building the team. Their young reserves have risen to meet a shattering situation with the bold spirit typical of the club and offer another serious challenge to Burnley who have been wallowing in a 'slough of despond' in their past two matches.

Maybe the very fact that they are entertaining such a team as the great United will be an incentive for much needed improvement.

(*Burnley Express and Burnley News*, 15 March 1958: 7)

Here, in his 'Football Notebook', Sportsman set the scene: 'We are deeply sympathetic to United', he reiterates, 'but they are not in terminal crisis. They have young talent ready to step in, they also', he wrote, 'can buy canny veteran players to fill the gap, and still have some of the top established talent in the land. They have deep coffers, and so it is hardly surprising', Sportsman is implying, 'that they can recover so quickly and successfully, and continue to compete on equal terms at the top level. But they've none of Burnley's stars. Butcher Bob made sure of that. And so these local lads must take the opportunity to show why United might have wanted some of them in the first place.' It's a beautiful piece of writing by Sportsman, respecting the United situation without sentimentality or bogus grief (genuine grief was expressed earlier), telling them that we owe them respect but not favours; and simultaneously goading the Burnley players to get their season back on track by overcoming the fashionable city slickers.

The match generated much controversy. Burnley won 3–0 in front of a crowd of over 37,000 (this was approaching half of the total population of the town). To consolidate his star status, Jimmy McIlroy got on the scorecard. United had a player sent off. The match itself was a stormy, rugged affair, goalless at half time, but turning Burnley's way after United's young player Pearson was dismissed from the field. United's flow and rhythm were disrupted, and Burnley scored their three second-half goals. Sportsman labelled the United players 'angry young men', calling for Matt Busby, on his return, to 'discipline' them 'to the path of great traditions from which they have so lamentably strayed' (*Burnley Express and Burnley News*, 19 March 1958: 7). The United players were condemned for striding 'roughshod over both laws and opponents', for displaying 'an elementary crudeness ... entirely foreign to the cultured football of Old Trafford'. Sportsman acknowledged the quality of United's mix of raw youth and veteran canniness, and especially the flair and fluent movement of the young Bobby Charlton, United's 'star performer with a confidence and skill beyond his years'. But early fouls by Greaves and Crowther, and the introduction of such 'rough stuff' culminating in Pearson's sending off – despite Burnley captain Jimmy Adamson's pleas with the referee on behalf of the United player – led Sportsman to an unambiguous reading of the Manchester players' approach to the game:

They are destroying that feeling of warm-hearted sympathy so freely offered in their facing up to the critical period in their history. The regrettable impression is they were not big enough for such a crisis ... the United youngsters becoming very much like bewildered Babes who have realized suddenly that the world is not all sympathy and adulation but a place of grim struggle and stern justice.

(*Burnley Express and Burnley News*, 19 March 1958: 7)

Match coverage was on the front page of the Wednesday newspaper, with three photographs, and the comment that the match was 'marred by incidents'. At the centre of the controversy was Bob Lord. Sportsman takes up the story, initially in the words of the blunt chairman: 'If incidents of this character are going to be allowed to continue it will not do football any good.' He said that he had learned from a newspaper source that the Football Association had received the referee's report and had called for Manchester United's observations on the match:

> When his attention was drawn on Monday to the allegation made in newspapers that he had said the United team had played 'like Teddy Boys', Mr Lord denied that he had made the remark. The term, he said, had been used, but not by him. 'I know who made it in the first instance but am not prepared to say who is responsible'.
> Mr Lord said that referees and opposing teams were under some difficulty but were trying not to add to United's troubles. However, they should not be provoked.
>
> (*Burnley Express and Burnley News*, 19 March 1958: 1)

The Butcher of Burnley was renowned for his lack of tact (which at times veered into racism). Not only had he derided Mancunians for having too much sentiment for United after the Munich tragedy, he had also once claimed that 'We have to stand up against a move to get soccer on the cheap by the Jews who run television' (Prestage, 2000: 127). David Davies, then a young journalist, who would later become a top executive at the Football Association, once approached him for a comment on a Lancashire League cricket game at the Lowerhouse Cricket Club's ground. He got a curt reply: 'Piss off.' Former barrow-boy turned meat magnate (who do you think supplied the pies at Turf Moor?), Lord was like a music-hall take on the bluff, blunt call-a-spade-a-spade northern self-made man. Hardly cut out for the embryonic era of public relations and media-sensitive sport industry, Lord showed no concern that he might have offended United. Here we have Lord saying that the United players were being favoured in refereeing decisions, and that opposition sides were being asked to treat United differently, in some intangible yet significant way, once the club's fixtures had been resumed. Lord aside, the match and its aftermath revealed a deep undercurrent of rivalry between the clubs, and resentment felt by 'the cotton town kings' (Durkin, 1988, illustration 13 onwards) of the game, at the presumptuousness of the metropolitan giants.

Sportsman was working overtime that week, and in a piece inside the paper, entitled 'United's "shock" tactics big surprise', could talk of the match in the following terms:

> ... the nature of a tragedy, the decline of a cause, and the shaming of a famous name. On this display some members of the gallant young team

risen from the wreck of Munich have a long way to go to be worthy of the rich heritage ...

(*Burnley Express and Burnley News*, 19 March 1958: 7)

United clearly had lost badly, in spirit not merely in the scoreline. Sportsman took up the theme further in his Saturday 'Football Notebook':

There is no doubt that the United match left what one of the Burnley players described as a 'nasty taste'. This was not improved in digestion by the incidents which followed the game and which included the attempts of a Manchester official to continue an 'argument' with a Burnley player, the sending back of refreshments from the dressing room, the discourteous approach of a United personality after keeping directors waiting, and the refusal of an offer to 'make peace'.

(*Burnley Express and Burnley News*, 22 March 1958: 15)

Lord Bob devoted the fifth chapter of his book to this theme, calling it ' "Teddy Boys": The facts' (Lord, 1963: 43–8). Lord goes over the key incidents, recalling the visit of Murphy to Turf Moor, and United's acting-manager's query about the availability for transfer of Albert Cheeseborough and Brian Pilkington:

I had to tell him I could not hold out much hope of those valuable players leaving the club ... It will be remembered that after the Munich disaster it was suggested that other League clubs should help Manchester United with players. We at Burnley were quite prepared to do so, but we were not prepared, if one faces the fact squarely, to wreck our first division side in order to help Old Trafford to regain its feet. Remember that we at Burnley have not the scope surrounding the United in the city of Manchester.

(Lord, 1963: 46)

This was pretty two-faced of the Burnley chairman. He was not really prepared to help United at all, but no doubt felt the need to say that he had been. 'It has often been said that I was unkind to United at the time' (pp.45–6), Lord reflected as he began his defence, and his account was an attempt to calm the waters as well as give his own full account. Of course he was right to hold on to his players. Burnley would be League champions two seasons later, in 1960, and if the club had started to gift players to United the squad would have been depleted in ways that would have made that achievement highly unlikely. Lord recalls 'being spat at by a player in the Old Trafford party who did not actually play in the match ... when I asked at the visitors' dressing-room door to see Mr Murphy. The player concerned is no longer with the United club' (p.46). You soon learned not to mess with Butcher Bob. One employee who had the nerve to beat him at snooker at one of his Saturday night sessions at his masonic lodge came into work on the following Monday morning to find that his cards were waiting for him: the imperious, arrogant Lord had got him sacked (Prestage, 2000: 131). And the

Teddy Boys remark? In 1958 the term was synonymous with hooligan or aggressive thugs, and a rock 'n' roll style that challenged traditional values and established authority. Lord relates his perspective: with him, as he was spat at, was one of his club's co-directors, Frank Kay, who gave Lord permission to reveal that it was Kay who used the term, 'in a quiet, personal aside to me in the passage leading from the board-room to the players' dressing rooms' (p.46). In the end, Lord does not apologise, but throws the blame on the press:

> So what does it all amount to? All this ballyhoo, screaming headlines in the national newspapers, and any number of abusive letters from Manchester people, whose hard-hit club had just been receiving sincere national and world tributes. In plain, John Bull English it amounts to this:
>
> A confidential remark, uttered quietly and personally to me in a private part of our club premises, was overheard by a trespasser, and this trespassing pressman not only seized on it to make a sensational story but apparently gave it to some of his colleagues. Anyway, it appeared in other papers. And Lord had to take the blame, in whopping headlines. Who was the guilty party? Bob Lord? His colleague who made a private comment? Or the trespassing pressman?
>
> (Lord, 1963: 46–7)

Lord leaves us in no doubt. It's the press to blame. No apology here, no rescinding of the Teddy Boy label. Lord acknowledged that over the following months 'the relationship between the clubs improved' (p.47), citing too the long-established rivalry and the 'Stop the game, it's snowing!' match during United's 1909 Cup-winning run. He also knew good box-office, and 'the long memory' of such rivalries would guarantee that 'the United's visits will long continue to pull in the crowds' (p.47). Whilst all this was going on, Sir Matt Busby was still in intensive care in a Munich hospital. For almost a month, Busby was not informed of the fatalities amongst his players and colleagues (Dunphy, 1991: 246). In the long run, Busby bore no grudges. He had been a colleague of Lord's on the Football Association's executive committee, and a long-term friend, and was one of the last visitors to Lord's home as the Burnley man was dying of cancer. The day after Lord's death, in 1981, Busby said:

> This is a great loss to the game itself. Bob Lord was honest and straight and always had to be his own man. I am very sad to have lost such a long-standing friend. Under his direction Burnley reached a pinnacle in British football and he will be long remembered for his devoted service to the game. The Bob Lord stand at Turf Moor is a great tribute to the man and what he helped achieve.
>
> (Durkin, 1988, opposite illustration 82)

Busby knew the football industry inside out, and whatever the expressed strategy of Lord in the 1950s, knew that the abolition of the maximum wage

1960s would favour the rich metropolitan clubs. Star Burnley players such as England and Scotland wingers John Connelly and Willie Morgan would, in the world of the new football economics, soon be on their way to Old Trafford: Connelly for £60,000 in April 1964 and Morgan for £117,000 in August 1968.

Players and fans

Connelly had a marvellous first season at United, in a forward line of Connelly, Bobby Charlton, David Herd, Denis Law and George Best. Between them these players scored 83 of an impressive tally of 89 goals, Connelly getting 15 of them. He played for England 21 times, including in England's opening match of the 1966 World Cup. Going to United was an irresistible move for the St Helen's-born Lancastrian, who recalls his boyhood days watching the post-war game:

> I did follow football, my dad used to take me to odd matches at Liverpool or Everton, either one. I suppose really Liverpool was my team, that I supported because of Billy Liddle, that was my idol at that particular spell.
> (Interview with author, 19 April 2003 – hereafter, personal interview)

Connelly played for United for just two seasons, before moving to Blackburn Rovers in 1966, after the World Cup, and then to Bury in 1970. He always professed an admirable approach to the sport and to his trade, pleased to make his experience available to young players when in the lower leagues towards the end of his career (Football League Review, 1971). Modesty itself throughout his playing days, spending all of his career at Lancashire clubs, Connelly remembers how 'the intelligent training given to me at Burnley' (Graydon, 1962) was well ahead of its time:

> Fantastic, at that particular spell Allan Brown and Bob Lord must have been miles ahead of the time because they – like these blokes have got now, the academies, the Liverpools, the Man Uniteds, these academies – really Burnley had that at that particular spell, obviously not as good as they have now, but at Gawthorpe, in its own way we had – three or four football pitches, an all-weather pitch, little five-a-side football pitches, shooting boards, sprinting tracks – everything. 'Cos I was amazed when I went to United, they didn't have any of that, nothing like that at all, nothing. They only had the Cliff, and all the time I were there, I only went there once, in nearly two years.
> (Personal interview)

Connelly was not alone in his surprise. Noel Cantwell moved from the footballing academy of West Ham United, and was appalled at the lack of professional preparation or tactical sophistication in the United set-up. None of West Ham's 'revolutionary ideas' (Taylor and Ward, 1995: 123) had yet surfaced at Old Trafford, and they created real tensions when Cantwell brought them into United's first-team dressing room (Dunphy, 1991: 268–9). United was not a good place to be on the sidelines, and Eamon Dunphy decided to go anywhere for first-team football rather than stay at Old Trafford in a peripheral role (Dunphy, 1976). There was a lot of pressure at United, and as Connelly remembers, little in the way of systematic preparation. You were just expected to be the best and go out and show that you were. And Connelly slotted into a team of talents that won the title. United could buy big – before Connelly himself, Law from Torino in Italy, Paddy Crerand from Glasgow Celtic, as well as Herd and Cantwell – to place the most outstanding talent available alongside homegrown geniuses Bobby Charlton and George Best. Connelly played for United when crowds could not be accused of lacking passion and commitment, as they have been by the most successful manager in the club's history (Ferguson, 2002); or creating a cultural distance, looking for good wines and delicatessen choices (Keane, 2002) rather than Bob Lord's meat pies. He had good relations with these crowds, and confirmed to me (personal interview) that there was never any hostility expressed towards him when returning to Turf Moor playing for Manchester United. The Burnley fans were realistic. They appreciated the opportunity that one of their own would take to better himself professionally.

There is no standard view of Manchester United held by Burnley fans, and of course there is no reliable or accessible way of gauging a typical fan's or supporter's view. Websites have been a source of illuminating research on followers of particular cultural forms, as demonstrated in Toby Miller's intriguing work on the television series *The Avengers* (Miller, 1997: 145–59). When asking members of a Burnley fans' discussion group (at burnleyfc@yahoogroups.com) how they related to United, the range of responses covered the whole spectrum, from awed respect to obscene invective and venomously expressed hatred. Yet when following the fans' views on players moving from United to Burnley, there was little resentment of United's contemporary status and profile, much more a resigned recognition that in the dire state of the football economy of 2003, for clubs such as Burnley to benefit from free transfers or loan deals was a much preferable state of affairs to any alternative. David May, winner of Premier League honours with both Blackburn Rovers and Manchester United, joined Burnley on a one-year contract in August 2003. May had played only six Premier League games in the previous four seasons for United, though 118 games in all across eight seasons. Andy Braid provided the Web group with the detail on the club's dealings, conducted by manager Stan Ternent:

> David, 33, has signed a deal that runs until the end of the season. He was booed when he captained United in the Worthington Cup tie against Ternent's side last season due to the fact he used to play for their fiercest rivals Blackburn.

This is neutral, objective reportage. Some bantering responses joked about whether David May was connected to musician Brian May, and the rock group Queen, but most expressed a sense of relief that anyone was willing to come to the small-town, economically struggling club. Jo Tomlinson: 'Goodo, a signing! Even though we did boo him last year ...' And THJ:

> Apart from David being a former Rovers guy, the signing makes good sense – if he can stay free from injury. My sources at OT [Old Trafford] tell me he is a stable, honest man and is well thought of by folks at the club. Predict he will captain the side before long.

THJ was proved to be a good forecaster. May was captain when Burnley played Wimbledon at the end of September 2003, on the latter club's inaugural home fixture at Milton Keynes' National Hockey Stadium. In a parody of a crowd atmosphere, the Burnley fans' passionate disapproval of May's dismissal (for two cautions) showed how welcome he was at the club, whoever his previous employee. The fans' acceptance of May, and of Lee Roche, released by United, and Luke Chadwick, loaned by United for the season, was testimony to the dominance of the metropolitan clubs, the Premier elite. In the long history of Manchester United–Burnley rivalry, Parvenu United had come to stay. Burnley was realistic about this, to the extent that it might even soon go by the name of Parvenu Old Boys.

Conclusion

Any lingering resentment or jealousy of Manchester United is understandable and explicable. Bobby Charlton has said of the Munich moment that: 'Before Munich it was Manchester's club, afterwards everyone felt that they owned a little bit of it' (Dunphy, 1991: 249). Manchester City supporters – the 'Citizens' – might dispute this, but Bobby Charlton embodies the truth of his own claim. After Munich, United established a unique brand, despite limited success and even relegation in the years between the retirement of Sir Matt Busby and the ascendancy of Sir Alex Ferguson. And this can be resented, because United has such unrivalled economic power and global prestige that is the envy of its competitors. In some ways this was always the case. In an authoritative history and account of football published in 1960, United is referred to as 'this truly amazing club', whose achievements and performances 'following such a tragic blow' as Munich 'were little short of miraculous' (Fabian and Green, 1960: 385), fitting no doubt the context of an Old Trafford which had held 76,962 for a Cup semi-final between Grimsby Town and Wolverhampton Wanderers in 1939. Burnley had a record gate of 54,775 for a Cup tie against Huddersfield Town (then League champions for the first of their three successive champion-ships), in 1924. The authors, former players for Corinthians and Cambridge University, commented: 'Turf Moor is a good example of a northern ground, rather on the dour side' (Fabian and Green, 1960: 345). The ground has been anything but dour when filled with the atmosphere of a big game. It is the glamour of the big-city club, its swaggering profile, not just its real achievements on the field, that has fuelled the 'derby with the edge' over the years of the

Burnley–United rivalries. This is a kind of relationship no doubt replicated in the relations between United and other Lancashire neighbours – Blackburn Rovers, Bolton Wanderers, Blackpool. It is also symptomatic of the glamour and profile of United that the club is cited as a major example of a fundamental shift in the political economy and cultural industries. In the late 1940s, Manchester Corporation commissioned a film called A City Speaks, covering aspects of the city at work and play. Leisure was a mere appendix in this documentary, coverage of football, leisure and dancing 'tacked on at the end, after the stolid reality of the cotton industry, housing problems, education and health funding, and the structure of local government':

> Fifty years later, you can't even draw a fine line between leisure and business in the city. Football, for instance, has become both big business and one of Manchester's most famous tourist attractions. But Manchester United isn't the only example of the way the city's leisure activities feed into the city's commercial life and leave both economic and physical marks.
>
> (Haslam, 1999: xvi)

Haslam cites, as other examples, cinema complexes and the like. Manchester City Football Club does not offer such a comparable example at all.

Local rivalries have been hugely beneficial for the vibrancy of modern competitive sport. Local, regional and national monopolies are not. There is a realistic recognition of the power of Manchester United by players and fans alike. There are enormous pressures on the club from its public. Steve Coppell has noted that 'United has a unique rapport with the Press,' which is in constant contact with the club, at both local and national levels (Coppell, 1985: 93). But as the success has escalated, and fans' expectations have been raised by the extraordinary triumphs of the 1990s and after, maybe something has been lost. Former Burnley players talk of the passion of the club's fans. Roger Eli, a player at Turf Moor between 1989 and 1994, talked to Lincoln Allison about this:

> Burnley fans seemed to take to me straightaway. Although I'm often described as a utility player, I played centre-half at first and my method was to kick everything that moved. The fans like that. I hardly ever went out at night in Burnley not because of racism, but because the adulation was so embarrassing.
>
> (Allison, 1993)

John Francis, another black player who was at Turf Moor for five years in the 1990s, confirms: 'One night I went into a pub in Burnley and everybody started singing "Super Johnny Francis". They kept it up for ever. It is very embarassing – you don't know what to do' (Allison, 2003. For a published version, see 'Pride and prejudice: the contribution of British black footballers', in *Something to Write Home About: The Magazine of the London Clarets*, No. 156, December 2003, not paginated. The magazine cites its website as http://surf.to/londonclarets).

There are negative sides to this kind of passion, often felt deeply by managers, and exhibited in one extraordinary moment of excess when the wife of one Burnley manager was set on fire at a takeaway restaurant in the town (Ternent with Livesey, 2003). But the passion for the game and the club is deep. Alistair Campbell, former communications director to British prime minister Tony Blair remembers 'everything' about the first afternoon that he watched a game at Turf Moor: 'the crowd, the noise, the smell, the game and the famous claret and blue colours – was magical; I was hooked, and have been ever since' (Ternent with Livesey, 2003: 9). Campbell also observes that 'Burnley was not a flash club. They were rooted in the town ...' (Bull and Campbell, 1994: 10), and many have recognised that, in the words of Liberal Democrat Burnley-born Alex Carlile: 'It was the Clarets that gave Burnley the feel and confidence of a big town' (Bull and Campbell, 1994: 149). In any general history of Burnley (for example, Makepeace, 2000) the football club is presented as vital to the public, civic identity of the town.

Clubs like Burnley – including those revitalised by the spending of fanatical philanthropists such as Jack Walker of Blackburn Rovers, or underpinned by the likes of Reebok such as Bolton Wanderers – will not in the foreseeable future be able to compete with Manchester United. Those days are gone. But sometimes I sit in the parlours of Manchester on match days, tuned in to Sky's live coverage, among devoted United supporters, watching the anxious look on the faces of fans who assume that winning is their club's birthright. There is too much at stake, and the United supporters are humourless throughout. Sitting among them, I cannot help thinking that the English game has lost its soul. When the small-town boys could genuinely compete with the city slickers, you could be assured that there would be a greater drama at play in the everyday rhythms of the football culture. But then I would say that, wouldn't I? I'm from Burnley.

References

Allison, L. (2003) 'Interview with Roger Eli and John Francis 09/09/03, revised 29/09/03'. Unpublished manuscript.

Bull, D. and Campbell, A. (eds) (1994) *Football and the Commons People*, Sheffield: Juma.

Cashmore, E. (2000) *Sports Culture – An A–Z Guide*, London: Routledge.

Churchill, R.C. (1958) *Sixty Seasons of League Football*, Harmondsworth: Penguin.

Coppell, S. (with Bob Harris) (1985) *Touch and Go*, London: Willow Books/Collins.

Dunphy, E. (1976) *Only a Game? The Diary of a Professional Footballer*, Harmondsworth: Penguin.

Dunphy, E. (1991) *A Strange Kind of Glory – Sir Matt Busby and Manchester United*, London: William Heinemann.

Durkin, T. (1988) *Burnley Football Club – A Pictorial History of the Clarets*, Urmston, Manchester: Archive Publications.

Fabian, A.H. and Green, G. (eds) (1960) *Association Football, Volume Two*, London: Caxton Publishing

Ferguson, A. (with Hugh McIlvaney) (2002) *Managing my Life: My Autobiography*, London: Hodder and Stoughton.

Football League Review (1971) 'John Connelly: Interview', *Football League Review*, available online at http://www.geocities.com/Colosseum/Track/6698/profiles/jconnelly.html (accessed 14/01/2003).

Giulianotti, R. (1999) *Football: A Sociology of the Global Game*, Cambridge: Polity Press.

Graydon, J. (1962, May) 'John Connelly: profile', *World Sports*, available online at http://geocities.com/Colosseum/Track/6698/profiles/connelly.html (accessed 14/01/2003).

Haslam, D. (1999) *Manchester, England: The Story of the Popcult City*, London: Fourth Estate.

Keane, R., with Eamon Dunphy (2002) *Keane: The Autobiography*, Harmondsworth: Penguin.

Lord, B. (1963) *My Fight for Football*, London: Stanley Paul & Co/The Soccer Book Club.

Makepeace, C.E. (2000) *A Century of Burnley*. Stroud: Sutton Publishing.

Mallory, J. (ed.) (1977) *Football League Tables, 1889 to the Present*, Glasgow and London: William Collins Sons & Co.

Mason, T. (1980) *Association Football and English Society 1865–1915*, Brighton: The Harvester Press.

Miller, T. (1997) *The Avengers*, London: BFI (British Film Institute) Publishing.

Prestage, M. (2000) *Burnley – The Glory Years Remembered*, Derby: Breedon Books.

Taylor, R. and Ward, A. (1995) *Kicking and Screaming: An Oral History of Football in England*, London: Robson Books.

Ternent, S. with T. Livesey (2003) *Stan the Man: A Hard Life in Football*, London: John Blake Publishing.

Tomlinson, A. (1999) *The Game's Up: Essays in the Cultural Analysis of Sport, Leisure and Popular Culture*, Aldershot: Ashgate Publishing.

Newspapers

Bound volumes of the *Burnley Express and Clitheroe Advertiser* and the *Burnley Express and Burnley News*, consulted in the British Library Newspaper Library, Colindale, London.

Websites

http://hjem.get2net.dk/mufc/about/history – the *Totally* RED *History of Manchester United* (1892–1910). The copyright holder for this site is Jørgen Trankjaer (trankjaer@get2net.dk). I am grateful to Mr Trankjaer for this source, which has provided me with illuminating historical insights and illustrations.
burnleyfc@yahoogroups.com

Interview

Author's interview with John Connelly, Barnoldswick, 19 April 2003.

14 Anfield envy

How the spirit of Liverpool hangs over Manchester United

Grant Farred

It was a good decade to dominate English football, the 1990s. The Premier League was founded in 1992, replacing the old First Division, a move which saw television revenues skyrocket and it made clubs and players, recently freed by the Bosman ruling,[1] wealthier. With the proliferation of satellite, cable and digital TV, the 'beautiful (English) game' became – courtesy of the likes of Rupert Murdoch (and his multitentacled media empire), Barclay Card, and Carlsberg – the truly 'global game' with hundreds of countries tuning in to watch matches beamed from London, the Midlands, Manchester and Liverpool.

For English football, the 1990s also signalled its re-entrance in European club competition, after an absence of five years; it was a painful half-decade for Liverpool fans in particular (because their club was responsible for the ban on the nation's clubs) and English clubs in general. (The five-year ban, imposed on English clubs because of the Heysel disaster in 1984 after horrific violence on the part of English fans who attacked their Italian counterparts in Brussels on a traumatic night that saw Juventus beat Liverpool, expired in 1989.) With the mutation of the European Cup into the Champions League, the very nature of the competition changed. Until that moment, the European Cup permitted only the league winners from all the Union of European Football Association's (UEFA) member countries to participate in a single round (home and away basis) competition, with no group sections. It was luck-of-the-draw stuff, as Liverpool and Nottingham Forest found out in 1978 when, as both highly favoured teams, they were paired with each other for the opening round tie; Brian Clough's Forest team went on to win 2–0 over the two legs. Before the advent of the Champions League, there were no lucrative group sections and no easy pickings in the 'preliminary' rounds which routinely pits major English, German, Dutch and Spanish clubs, who finish third or fourth in their own league, against part-timers or underfunded teams from Scandinavia or Eastern Europe. By the time English clubs were readmitted into Europe, Liverpool, the dominant club of the 1970s and 1980s in both England and Europe, were a side, if not in decline, then precipitously close to it.

The Heysel effect deprived Liverpool of further opportunities to stamp their authority on Europe; the Anfield side had won the premier European title four times between 1977 and 1984, an era that ended with losing to Juventus on the fateful Belgian night in 1985. Heysel robbed the great Liverpool teams of the mid- and late 1980s of the chance to continue their domination of the continent. After the triumphs of 1977, when in Kevin Keegan's final appearance for Liverpool they put Borussia Mönchengladbach to the sword, 1978, in which they became the only English team to repeat a European Cup championship by beating Bruges, 1981, when they bested Real Madrid, and their 1984 victory over AS Roma, Liverpool were well poised for further greatness in Europe. But Heysel changed all that, and then some. Legendary Liverpool players missed out on a European experience that had by the early 1980s become part of the club's folklore. Players such as the magical black English winger John Barnes (who would surely have relished the opportunity to test his skill against the Continentals), his international teammate, Peter Beardsley (a creative striker who with Barnes formed the attacking axis of a massively skilled side and would have excelled as the playmaking goalscorer that he was), Alan Hansen (already an established and senior figure in the side) and Mark Lawrenson (together with Hansen constituting the most adroit pairing in English football who constituted the heart of the defence, defenders who could pass and dribble, sometimes in their own penalty area), the versatile Steve Nicol, the mercurial Irishman Ronnie Whelan, and the hard-running midfield supremo Steve McMahon, all would surely have, at the top of their game in the 1980s and in concert with their talented teammates such as the eccentric goalkeeper Bruce Grobbelaar, and the Irish internationals John Aldridge and Ray Houghton, garnered Liverpool more honours. However, Liverpool have never really recovered from Heysel, or the death of 95 fans at Hillsborough in 1989 in a Football Association (FA) Cup semi-final match against Clough's Nottingham Forest, eventually curtailing not only their European supremacy but also their hold on the domestic game.

Funded as Manchester United are by their plc, their huge Nike and Vodafone contracts, and their insatiable appetite for branding, their dominance of the English Premier League bears a limited imprint: one that bespeaks an economic currency that far exceeds its footballing prowess. Unpalatable as this might be to United fans, they are a club that is more successful at the cash register – where they have made themselves into a stupendously wealthy corporation – than in the (European) trophy room. (Not even remotely as wealthy, having missed out on the marketing bonanza of the 1990s because their success predated the globalisation of the sport, Liverpool fans have taken to dubbing United – with no small amount of class invective – 'The Corporation'[2] (if you can't beat up on 'em, nail 'em for their abominable class politics: make them the unfeeling capitalist class even if your club's paying strikingly similar salaries to its stars). However, unlike United, Liverpool have remained rooted in the community and have resisted the temptation to go the plc route.) Manchester United's financial success became, quite dramatically, a matter of intense speculation when their Chief Executive, Peter Kenyon, suddenly resigned to take up a similar post at Chelsea. With Chelsea bankrolled by new Russian billionaire owner, Roman Abramovich, United 'now find themselves threatened by a rival with huge financial clout'.[3]

While Chelsea may now have the economic muscle and the administrative savvy to challenge United, no one can ignore the latter's record number of Premier League crowns; not even Arsenal's Arsène Wenger would deny Manchester their domestic supremacy. United's financial accomplishments, however, contrast sharply with their relative lack of success in Europe. In sport's terminology, as United's manager Alex Ferguson surely knows but will never publicly admit, almost – as in 'almost getting to the final' – doesn't count. Getting to the quarter-finals and semi-finals are laudable accomplishments but they are really matters for the statisticians and their number-crunching first cousins, the club accountants – on whom the likes of Peter Kenyon and the City keep a sharp eye. 'Almost' can, however, never be mistaken for 'real' – and the pun, as football aficionados well know, is intended – success.

Worse for Ferguson and United, however, is the nagging recognition that one triumph doth not a dynasty make. United may have, in the inimitable musical artist (once again known as) Prince's words, 'partied like it was 1999' at Nou Camp in that year, but, as it stands, that's all Ferguson has to show for himself: a solitary win, in 1999. In European footballing lore, as in any other sport (such as baseball, where United's American partners, the New York Yankees, know a thing or two about dynasties, and, like the Old Trafford outfit, about economic dominance), dynasties are the coin of the realm. Here, as they say, United's money is no good. Win one, as Ferguson has, that's just a win. Two or three, if not in succession but over a five- or six-year period, that's what puts you in rarified company. (Or, four in seven seasons, as Liverpool have done.) In European terms, Manchester United belong to the second tier of the football hierarchy: they are not the elite. Real Madrid, they rule the roost; Bayern Munich, A.C.Milan, Ajax and Liverpool: they're elite. United, to their consternation, with their two triumphs more than 20 years apart, are not.

Their failure to join the elite is the spectre of (unspeakable) frustration that haunts Manchester United, a mad hunger for success that has eluded them – the drive to add to 1999, itself a memorable if slightly fortuitous victory. Money, as the massively overfunded Real Madrid have proved at least nine times (the record they hold for victories in the Champions League and its predecessors), much to United's dismay, can buy you (lots and lots of) success in Europe. So it isn't access to United's horde of cash that separates Ferguson and his club from Real Madrid or Liverpool. This essay is, in part, an explication of Ferguson's failure, a partisan comparison – though there are fair and balanced moments, have no doubt – between the two clubs that have dominated post-1960s English football: Liverpool and Manchester United.

'Anfield Envy' is a complex condition. In its visceral formation, it represents a Liverpool fans' rationale for his or her own club's decade of failure, after their domination of some 15 years. As such, 'Anfield Envy' is a condition that is, at best, a superficial and, at worst, a sadly transparent coding of a Liverpool fan's envy at his or her team's loss of dominance after the Merseysiders' domination of English and European football in the 1970s and 1980s. In some ways it rings as hollow, as only sports-inspired jealousy can, as Fergie's thunderings when he loses in Europe; his rantings and his facile excuses for his defeats to Bayern Munich

(2000) or Bayer Leverkusen (2002) or Madrid (2003). Liverpool fans, who don't get off easy here either because they, and their 'Treble' crown of 2000–1 (mocked as inauthentic by United fans, with some justification) apart, can only think themselves historically superior to Manchester United by citing previous victories. Present Liverpool failures – and there've been too many of those in the post-Kenny Dalglish era – can be made tolerable not only by the successes of the past but by their foes' current 'hardships'. In other words, Bayer Leverkusen's triumph over United is also, however Pyrrhic a victory it might be, Liverpool's. The price of that victory may be great for Liverpool fans, but it is by far the lesser of the evils; and, if truth be told, it's the only currency we have. However, Anfield Envy is also grounded in footballing fact: United's local dominance has never translated into European success. Liverpool's did. This essay is a celebration of that crucial footballing difference. Its one-upmanship is of the variety that only football fans, those whom Old Football would recognise as such, are capable of understanding. After all, what good is success if it doesn't inspire envy in your opponents? What good is history if it can't be used as a blunt cultural weapon?

From meat pies to prawn sandwiches and caviar

If the late-'modern' era of the English game, from the 1960s to the 1980s, belonged to Liverpool, then the postmodern one – the huge increase in player salaries and mobility, the spread of the game through technology, the improvement of fitness regimes, better diets, improved training methods and facilities, the unprecedented marketing of the game and its 'merchandise' (both the club personnel and its accoutrements), and the replacement of the infamously dangerous, raucous and inventive terraces with all-seater stadiums – undoubtedly bears the imprint of Manchester United. Cast in footballing fan metaphor, Liverpool dominated from the declining age of the mythical working-class guy in the cloth cap, which more or less coincided with the moment of Beatlemania (inaugurated by the arrival of the legendary Bill Shankly at Anfield from Huddersfield Town), culminating in the epoch of the cloth-capped fans' grandsons, that generation rendered unemployed by Thatcherism. United rule the era of what their combative skipper Roy Keane, a self-styled Irish working-class hero if there ever was one, disparagingly dubbed – in his description of the new fans at Old Trafford – the 'prawn sandwiches crowd'. Always well-appointed, Keane might have added, in their well-cut Gucci and Armani suits, comfortably seated in their skyboxes way above the crowd. Keane's barb was aimed mainly at corporate executive-types only recently drawn to football by the unprecedented wealth that the game was generating and, an equally important factor, the respectability the sport had accrued.

That is to say nothing of the massive 'cool' quotient newly attached to football from the 1990s.[4] Liverpool, in the famously underachieving Roy Evans years, had their 'Spice Boys'. This group comprised, in no particular order of glamour, Jamie Redknapp (and his singer wife Louise), bad boys Robbie Fowler, Steve MacManaman, and part-time underwear model (and part-time goalkeeper, we

Liverpool fans were convinced, with a vote of confidence or two from Aston Villa and West Ham supporters, I'm sure) David James. (Would Stan Collymore have qualified as a 'Spice Boy' or was he just too far out in left field, apologies for mixing sports metaphors here, to qualify as eligible for any group?) Paul Ince, newly returned to England from Inter-Milan in Italy in 1997, functioned as a sort of marauding captain/overlord (or 'Guv'nor', as he so imperiously prefers to be known) figure for this group of talented 'ballers', to invoke the hip-hop vernacular for cool basketball players (the best-dressed American athletes). Manchester United, in their turn, had Eric 'Karate Kick' Cantona, him of the Gallic flair and the upturned collar (copied without couture-given credit by Dwight Yorke in his United days), Ryan Giggs, and of course United's glamour couple (of whom Ferguson wanted only the footballing half): David Beckham and Posh Spice, a real 'Spice Girl', no less, unlike her male equivalents over in Liverpool who were simply borrowing monikers and trying to make like David who was, first by cultural proximity and then by marriage, a 'real' Spice Boy.

But the Liverpool and United players of that generation had, culturally, a great deal in common. In fact, the Liverpool 'Spice Boys' and their United counterparts seemed to recognise their similarities, so friendly were the players, especially during the build-up to the 1996 FA Cup Final which looked like a 'Spice Boy' club meeting, which Liverpool of course lost. Beckham, Giggs, MacManaman, Fowler, and now Owen and Steven Gerrard, belong to a generation of player far removed from either the 1960s' and 1970s' excesses of George Best (self-destructive genius) or the 'Brut' deodorant commercials of Kevin Keegan (a footballing Mod, if there ever was one). The 'Spice Boys' and their heirs' access to capital and advertising opportunity have made Best and Keegan look like they belonged to the universe of an entirely alien sport – Fowler and Becks made Keegan and Best veritable 'Old Spice' boys (a deodorant that belonged to the days of heavy leather balls and a pay structure euphemistically known as the 'maximum wage').

Following the transformation of the players (and their lifestyles), the breed of fan now populating the stands was similarly, in Alan Edge's terms, distinctly new to the game: 'one's fandom has now acquired a cultish propriety, rendering it the fashion throughout huge chunks of the middle classes where being a football supporter has become an eminently sociable and acceptable preoccupation'.[5] Between Keane and Edge, rarely have a Manchester United player and a Liverpool fan been so simpatico, in such absolute agreement about the deleterious impact of 'middle-' and upper-class support. Prince Harry is, after all, together with Nick Hornby, the world's most famous Arsenal fan. United, of course, have more than simply their 'prawn' people. In fact, so moved by Manchester's triumph in Barcelona was that regarded proletarian novelist Martin Amis that he felt compelled to put pen to paper in a homage to the Nou Camp victory. 'Yes, I was there for the fairytale, glory night on the magic field of impossible dreams,'[6] Amis intones breathlessly, his fingers barely keeping pace with his triumphalist prose as he piles one superlative upon another. Kevin Costner couldn't have said it better as he constructed that hopelessly hyperbolic 'field of dreams'. One can only imagine, now that Chelsea stand expectantly poised for their moment in the New Footballing sun, that Salman Rushdie will offer his own gushing tribute, written no doubt from a secluded box far from the Shed End, to Roman Abramovich's collection of newly acquired multinational millionaires. To reach them all, Rushdie would be well advised to hire a few translators, unless his Spanish, his Italian and his Romanian are up to snuff.

Keane's ire, and Alan Edge's sardonic wit, is aimed at a bunch of 'eminently sociable' supporters attracted by the game's new glamour, its 'cultish propriety,' so different from the dyed-in-the-wool Manchester United, Liverpool, Leeds and Spurs loyalists – passionate, witty, and often outrageous and racist in their cheering – who lived and died with their club's every result. Those belong, like Edge, to the 'broad church of incurable idiocy'.[7] The 'prawn sandwiches' brigade, on the other hand, are fans who don't shout or sing, they're a crowd who don't really understand the game or really have much of an interest in it, fans whose passion is about being seen rather than being heard. In truth, what Keane lamented were all those attributes that made Liverpool's 'Kop',[8] arguably the most famous fans in the world, renowned for their singing and their acid criticism and their passionate commitment to their club's cause, a distinctive and envied bunch. As much as there is an unquestioned veracity in the class politics evinced by the Keane–Edge coalition, there is also reason enough to offer a salutary caution about the unreflective laddish machismo that girds this position.

New Football, its fans (or, more precisely phrased, its new fan base), its ethos, its improved facilities, and its (largely) determined and well-publicised stand against racism has much to laud about it.[9] Furthermore, there was undoubtedly an anti-feminist component to its predecessor as well. Old, Authentic Football represented the values held dear by Keane and Edge: the mythic game that belonged to the white working-class male who stood on the terraces through rain and shine, through victory and defeat, and through too many cold meat pies. Old Football was unapologetically aggressive in its support, always contingent and composed of a potentially violent form of male bonding (which often led to bloody conflict), which was then euphemised as communitarian affiliation and loyalty to the club and its cause (frequently underscored by its own sectarian religious conflict, of which the Protestant–Catholic divide in Glasgow is only the most obvious example). The terraces represented an unreconstructed white masculinity that was hostile not only to opposing fans in general but also to black Britons of any stripe – Caribbean, African, south Asian, and it rarely mattered if you supported the same team – in particular. Everton fans routinely made monkey chants and waved plastic bananas at John Barnes when they played Liverpool. Chelsea fans are so bad on this score that they've been known to boo their own black players. The ethos of Old Football isn't that 'old', as the actions of then-Leeds United players Lee Bowyer and Jonathan Woodgate alleged attack on Asian youths reminded everyone just a few short years ago. Old Football was also viscerally opposed to women, who had far less – if any – access (certainly not of the safe variety) to the terraces in the mythological days that Keane is so nostalgic for. New Football is, slowly and somewhat unsurely, and with less safety in the cheaper seats, creating a place for women, children and even families. There are few football players more committedly working-class than Keane, so it is appropriate – unfortunately, in the light of his well-intentioned politics – that he should be emblematic of the antipathy to the rise of New Football. However, Keane's class identity is perhaps too deeply rooted in precisely the kind of machismo (what other player, let alone Premier League captain, would shove a referee into the advertising boards in a fit of anger?) that made the terraces uninhabitable to black fans and women.

The 'prawn sandwiches crowd' is, from Keane's complicated perspective, the phenomenon that represents the emasculation of Old Football and the 'feminisation' of its successor. Not only are there women now attending football games in historic numbers, not only do women have a moderately successful World Cup of their own, not only do women now have their own leagues and, lord knows, movies about football that cinematise their ambitions (as any one of the millions of teenage girls and older women – as well as the wide assortment of males – who have seen Bend It Like Beckham can attest), but the game's most popular player – or its best marketed commodity – certainly qualifies as 'feminised' by Keane's hardcore standards: David Beckham. The blond-haired London boy who made good at United, him of the rapidly changing, carefully manicured (almost femme) hairstyles, the nifty, trendsetting fashions, and the New Man (and parenting) sensibility. Looking like a member of an American boy band – 'N Sync comes too easily to mind – Beckham's rise to the status of football's global representative, the 'pretty boy' face of the 'beautiful game', symbolises the commercial and aesthetic stakes that Old Football is up against. The cultural loss that Edge and Keane bemoan represents how the class demographics of football's fans is changing, and there is a great deal to be sad about as working folks, families who have been loyal fans for generations, find themselves priced out of stadiums in England by the rich and famous – those whose taste in football fare may be a little too precious and delicate for the tough, combative give-and-take of a Premier League encounter. But Old Football's racism and patriarchal violence are not worthy of nostalgia.

With Roman Abramovich's oil billions, of which he spent over £110 million in just his first few weeks in charge in 2003 (recruiting players from, inter alia, Argentina, Romania, Italy, as well as England), now bankrolling Chelsea, a whole new palate has come to town. Chelsea has always been a club with a split following – the violent, notorious and notoriously racist fans who occupy the Shed End[10] have little in common with the high-end, upscale, fashionable west London crowd who dominate the posh seats; the real difference, however, is that the 'eminently sociable' fade as quickly as Chelsea's league form inevitably does each season, while the Shed fans, with only their annual allotment of hope to lose each season, stay glued to their cheaper seats. But this historic split may soon be irrelevant; there is speculation that caviar and champagne will reputedly soon be on sale at the finer concession stands at Stamford Bridge and the Shed will be compelled into toffydom.

The Abramovich 'diet' will make nonsense of Keane's concerns about (mere) 'prawn sandwiches', reinforcing once again the sentiment that northerners, both east and west, lag far behind the cultural refinement of their southern cousins. Prawn sandwiches might have been deemed elite(-ist) in the cash-rich 1990s, a definitive break with the haute cuisine of meat pies and sausage rolls, that staple of the terraces, but it qualifies as lowly, if not déclassé, early in the new millennium of multinational capital and cosmopolitan managers.

London clubs – especially Chelsea, but Arsenal too have had their share – have always been a magnet for the English game's flashier players – Charlie George, Alan Hudson, Peter Bonetti and 'Bonnie Prince' Charlie Nicholas come quickly to mind. So it marked a natural progression when Chelsea and Arsenal (and Spurs, in the grand old days of the late 1970s) went shopping abroad – and now, in the fitting historical paradox that is global capitalism, find that they got 'shopped', lock, stock and Shed End barrel, as it were, from abroad. Why settle for curmudgeonly, controversial Ken Bates, seldom a man to think before he speaks, when you can have Abramovich, a man who doesn't speak at all (but loves signing autographs, like someone who is a star in his own right, for Chelsea fans outside Stamford Bridge)? He's certainly not English, but it matters not one linguistic jot when he's got – or used to have before he went on that audacious shopping spree – all those euros in his bank account. That Chelsea's foreign legion, among whose first recruits in the early 1990s numbered the dreadlocked Ruud Gullit (first as player then as manager), at the time of writing was still being coached by the under fire Claudio Ranieri, an Italian who has the affable habit of misunderstanding English journalists when it suits him, was entirely predictable. After playing and managing, Gullit was succeeded by another Italian, Gianluca Vialli (there's a trend here, foreigners come to play for Chelsea and end up coaching, even winning trophies, and then being sacked by Bates). However, Chelsea is not the only club to appoint Continental managers. Liverpool and Arsenal are both managed by Frenchmen, with Arsenal's Arsène Wenger more dapperly turned out than his Merseyside counterpart, Gérard Houllier, a man who still looks and even dresses like the schoolteacher he once was.

With their bottomless resources, Chelsea may finally – though holding your collective west London breath is not advised – mount a genuine challenge for the Premier League title. However, while Chelsea chase the elusive pot of gold (the figurative one, since they already have the literal one), Manchester United have other problems.

Native success

Manchester United's manager Alex Ferguson is full of bluster, a man skilled in the art of psyching out and offending, not only opposing coaches and players, but his own charges as well. His ability to get under Kevin Keegan's skin when the former England manager was in charge of Newcastle was the stuff of soap opera, especially when Keegan broke down in public after the needling got too much. There is also, the ex-Geordie manager needs no reminding, the almost farcical way in which his Newcastle buckled under the weight of their own defensive ineptitude – blowing a 12-point lead – and United's resilience, in the 1995-6 season. (The second league encounter between Newcastle and Liverpool provides a synopsis of that season: leading twice in the game, the Geordies conspired to lose a seven-goal thriller. That, in a nutshell, symbolised Newcastle's season: they were exciting and frenetic to watch, and you always knew that their defense, if that is the correct term to describe their woeful marking and hapless tackling, would leak goals at the most inappropriate moments.) Ferguson's battles with Arsenal's Arsène Wenger are so routine as to make them both predictable and boring, although, unlike Keegan, in the Frenchman he has more than met his match. Wenger can give as good as he gets, with better fashion sense and more articulateness than Ferguson, one might add. (But like his United counterpart who, for example, defended Keane when he clattered the referee into the advertising boards, Wenger has the annoying tendency of rationalising the most blatant offenses of his players. We're all aware of his team's astounding capacity to amass red cards season after season, but among his more memorable moments of denial is surely his famous 'I didn't see the incident' response to Sol Campbell's foul on United's Eric Djemba-Djemba in the 2003-4 Community Shield. There were people outside the Millennium Stadium just walking in the street who saw the foul. One would have to add, however, that the United player was by no means innocent in that exchange. It's even possible to feel sorry, if only just momentarily, for the Arsenal defender because Djemba-Djemba's boot was up there for a long, long time.)

Ferguson is so given to feuding that he has succeeded in alienating even the ever-friendly Gordon Strachan, who has not only managed against Ferguson at Coventry and then Southampton, but who, as a combative midfielder, also played for him at Aberdeen, United and Scotland. No small feat, that, giving offensive to Strachan, a manager who has the rare capacity to give an entire interview in English without speaking an intelligible word of the language. In his autobiography, entitled Managing My Life, Ferguson accuses the combative Strachan of a 'cunning streak'.[11]

Of course, Strachan is only one of a number of players to fall foul of Ferguson. Paul Ince, Jaap Stam, Juan Verón ... they all belong to that not-so exclusive club. None of them, however, raised as much publicity as England's king of glamour, David Beckham. The Beckham saga that erupted in the 2002-3 season culminated, in the publication of the midfielder's autobiography (partially serialised in the *Sun* in September 2003), in a series of accusations against Ferguson – stories of Beckham having to be restrained by his teammates, about a blistering verbal attack on Ferguson. Juicy stuff, all of which reveal Ferguson's much-vaunted diplomatic skills. If you can't bend 'em to your will, throw boots at 'em. The by now infamous boot-throwing incident (resulting in stitches above Beckham's eye) and accusations about the 'lifestyle' of the England captain, including criticism of Beckham's decision to miss practice in order to be with his sick child, demonstrates how gifted Ferguson is in the art of ticking off several players: generation after generation. None of Beckham's teammates seem to have had a problem with him. Even the marginally talented Phil Neville (is this guy really an England international? Say it ain't so) hoped until the very end that Becks would remain at Old Trafford. To Beckham's credit, he is the one player to publicly stand up to Ferguson, even if it is only post ipso facto – when he was safely ensconced in Stade Santiago Bernebeau and out of the reach of the Scottish arm and a handy football boot.

However, Ferguson, now 'Sir Alex' from Govan (at what point did self-proclaimed working-class guys take so easily to knighthood? Don't remember Sir Bill Shankly, do you? The Queen wouldn't knight Cloughie, would she?) is the most successful manager in Manchester United's history – and he built a brilliant team at Pittodrie in his Aberdeen days. Jim Leighton in goal, Alex McLeish and Willie Miller in defense, Gordon Strachan wide in midfield, Mark McGhee and Eric Black up front, all combined to make up the one Scottish side capable of challenging the Old Firm monopoly on trophies. In fact, in his Aberdeen days, when he didn't have the kind of cash he has had as United's manager, he may have been at his best as a team builder and a manager. In his 16 years in charge at United he has won the Premier League a record eight times and, of course, he won the Treble in 1999 when United won both major English trophies and the Champions League.[12] Ferguson has exceeded even the achievements of Sir Matt Busby, a Scot who survived the Munich disaster that claimed the lives of eight United players, including the prodigiously talented Duncan Edwards. A redoubtable man, Busby nurtured his famous 'Babes' and, following in the footsteps of his illustrious fellow Scot, Jock Stein of Glasgow Celtic (who managed the first British club to a European Cup victory), he became the first manager of an English team to win the European Cup in 1968. The mercurial George Best, England World Cup winner Bobby Charlton and a young Brian Kidd (later an assistant to Ferguson only to find himself belittled by his ex-boss after he moved to manage Blackburn Rovers), played in Busby's victorious team.

Unlike Busby, Ferguson is rarely gracious in defeat. For all his domestic success, Ferguson has been repeatedly frustrated in his most important goal: the annual quest to add to his one victory over Bayern Munich in Barcelona in 1999 in what has turned out to be little more than tilting at windmills. Don Quixote Ferguson of La Mancha-ster. Appropriate then that his lone success should have come in Spain at the Nou Camp. Don Quixote and Miguel de Cervantes, at least, would have appreciated the irony. So desperate is Ferguson that, after his much-publicised decision to retire at the end of the 2001 season, when success eluded him once again, he renounced his decision and set off on yet another Quixotian adventure across the footballing capitals of Europe. May 2001 had a special resonance for Ferguson and had everything to do with his decision to retire at that particular moment. The 2001 Champions League Final, as every journalist worth his or her salt knows, was scheduled for Hampden Park and Ferguson wanted to bow out in front of his 'native' Scottish crowd. Ferguson is nothing if not a proud Scotsman and he was in search of a poetic finale to a playing career (exclusively in Scotland) and a managerial one that had its roots north of the border. Hampden was to be the crowning glory of his professional life: the player who had 'failed' at Glasgow Rangers (he, of course, has a different, conspiratorial view of events), had been spectacular while in charge at Aberdeen, and failed as a Scotland manager (but he's only one in a long line, to be fair to him), wanted to take his final bow at 'home.'

Except, no one had told the iconoclastic, ex-architect Klaus Toppmoller and his Bayer Leverkusen side about the script. After eliminating Liverpool in a thriller in the quarter-finals, Leverkusen beat United in the semis. Ferguson promptly shelved his retirement plans. But he fared no better the following season when Real Madrid, the gold standard for European football, ushered them out of Europe. Again. (This despite Beckham's efforts, two goals after coming on as a substitute. He'd been in Ferguson's doghouse for lord knows what misdemeanour.)

Ferguson has been repeatedly foiled, been found wanting, as the likes of Real Madrid prove that tactics, technique, skill and the team win the ultimate prize in Europe. Ferguson may have money enough to spend but players such as the massively talented Brazilian Ronaldinho will not play for the Old Trafford side, choosing instead Barcelona over United, frustrating him no end. Domination in the English Premier League, increasingly, will no longer suffice. There are those, proponents of Continental football, who would argue that some of Ferguson's lack of success in Europe may, however, have little to do with him and more to do with the fact that Spain's La Liga and Italy's Serie A demand the kind of football skills that the Premiership, more robust and combative, lacks. Serie A and La Liga, so this version of football reasoning goes (a view not entirely refuted by the English media), are more 'technical' than the Premier League. By which pundits mean something like the following: that players in the Spanish and Italian leagues have elementary control, better ball retention skills, that they have a good (and often very good) first touch on the ball, that they are more 'skilful' – their passing is more adroit, more accurate and more incisive, that they do not boot the ball upfield in the hope that their forwards will run onto it. Continental players, many of whom are not from Europe but Latin America and Africa or, increasingly these days, from Asia, are able to command more time on the ball, they are less likely to be harried into bad passes ... in a word, that possession of the ball, innovation and creativity dominate these leagues.

While there is some merit in this argument that the likes of Manchester City and Newcastle have no talent for the technical aspect of the game, let alone battling Bolton and perennial strugglers Southampton, it is also true that there are teams in the Premiership – Arsenal, Liverpool, Chelsea and United come immediately to mind – who can keep possession of the ball. With the influx of foreign players, the Premier League is evolving. The English sides may not be as adept or as captivating as Real Madrid, but they're a long way from favouring the 'kick first' – the renowned tactic of kicking anything that moves, the ball included, but that's optional – approach that won Wimbledon so many European fans in the 1980s. (Wimbledon? Remember them – Vinnie Jones and his bunch of marauding journeymen?) Arsenal and United certainly play with more élan than AS Roma or Sampdoria. Italian football is technically proficient, but no one ever said it was pretty or easy on the spectator's eye. The 'lag-behind technically' argument, however, is the good news for the Manchester United fans.

Anfield envy

Here's the bad news. When Liverpool won the European Cup, there was never any talk of a discrepancy, of a different 'standard,' between the various leagues. Liverpool was simply the best team. They were better than Borussia Mönchengladbach (Bundesliga – a side that contained the current Scottish manager Berti Vogts, who was run ragged by Keegan on that night in Rome, Rainer Bonhof and the talented Dane Allan Simonsen), they dealt with FC Bruges (Belgium) with a clinical efficiency, they were better than Real Madrid (La Liga), and they were better – if only on penalties – than AS Roma (Serie A). They were probably as good as Juventus on that fateful night in Brussels. But then it really didn't matter. On that night, and at Hillsborough five years later, Bill Shankly's philosophy that 'football isn't a matter of life or death, its more important than that', didn't hold. Football, in this instance, was less important than Scally, as the Liverpool locals are called, lives. As an adopted Scouse, Shanks would have agreed.

To drive the point of Liverpool supremacy home even further: when Liverpool dominated, there were very few 'overseas' players competing in the First Division. Spurs had Argentine World Cup winners Ossie Ardiles and Ricky Villa, and Ipswich had the Dutchmen Arnold Muhren and Frans Thijsen – Muhren later moved to Manchester United. But the number of Continental players in the top flight of English football was miniscule compared to what it is now when clubs can field an entire side without a single English representative: the number of Scandanavians might rival the number of Scots in the Premier League. That wasn't the case just a dozen years or so ago. Consequently, Liverpool players of that era would have had far less regular exposure to and experience of going up against 'Continentals'. They only encountered them, albeit more regularly than any other English clubs, on their European travels. This means that Liverpool was better prepared then than United are now – a team that adapted quicker and a side that lost less. And Liverpool's European campaigners were a better team. Surely you'd rather have Kenny Dalglish than Teddy Sheringham? Who would you choose, Alan Hansen or Jaap Stam (how slow is this guy?)? Kevin Keegan or Ole Gunnar Solskjær? And, here's a no-brainer: Graeme Souness or Roy Keane?

However much such a comparison may gall the Old Trafford faithful, let me offer a sacrilegious (from a Liverpool perspective, that is) explanation: Liverpool's greatest triumphs came not under Bill Shankly, truly a man of the Scouser people, but Bob Paisley, a man who kept his own counsel, quietly. Shanks is rightly installed and deified as the god of Anfield – so shall it be to love and serve Shanks – the manager who made Liverpool the footballing institution it is today. But it was under Paisley that Liverpool conquered Europe, not Shankly. It was, as Shanks himself says, his only regret. Interviewed on the day of his resignation (one of the most painful events in Liverpool lore), he answered in response to that question:

'Any regrets? Aye, just one. Not winning the European Cup.'[13] Unlike his Scottish predecessor, Paisley shunned the spotlight; but he was a master tactician. As the Glaswegian Kenny Dalglish remembers, 'He would look at an opposition team and spot individual flaws in it. He would inform us about their strengths and weaknesses and how we should try to counter them.'[14] Paisley was the supreme strategist – and tactics and football nous, as we well know, is what wins in Europe. Shankly is much admired by Ferguson, his fellow Scotsman. Ferguson acknowledges his awe and reverence for Shankly. It is clearly evident in his autobiography. Recalling preparing for Aberdeen's European Cup tie against Liverpool in 1980, Ferguson is like a schoolboy meeting his football idol:

> Bob Paisley was the all-conquering manager, of course, but Bill Shankly was still around and when Archie Knox .... joined me on a trip to watch Liverpool play Middlesborough at Anfield we were thrilled to meet the great Ayreshireman.
> 'Hello Alex, good to see you – you are doing a terrific job up there,' was Bill's greeting and I was still stuttering my thanks when he went on, 'So you're down to have a look at our great team?' Archie and I, behaving like a pair of groupies, could only mumble an affirmative. 'Aye, they all try that,' said Bill.[15]

The admiration is charmingly obvious in this exchange between the then still young manager of Aberdeen and the legendary Shankly. It was, in addition to that, a bond ideologically cemented by the fact that they were, as Ferguson is all too aware, both self-consciously working-class men with strong trade union sensibilities. They both encountered, Shankly more so than Ferguson perhaps, the devastation of the working class in Lancashire – a fact of working life they both regretted and that bound them, more obviously with Shankly, to their supporters.

Shankly, by his own account and to his deep regret, never triumphed in Europe. Here Fergie the 'groupie' has outdone his countryman from Ayreshire – only 20 miles or so south from the Govan where Ferguson grew up. In the famed Liverpool 'Boot Room', where many a memorable victory was conceived, it was Paisley who understood the value of strategy – of preparing for Europe. Paisley learned from Shankly's failures to translate Liverpool's dominance of English football into European success. It was his careful planning, his painstaking attention to detail, so distinct from Shankly's hubris, and Paisley's humility – he always kept the team in the foreground – that converted Liverpool's European failures into an era of English domination. In Ferguson there is too much Shankly and too little Paisley. And until he learns from his failures, and assembles a good support staff and keeps it intact (how many assistants has he had? Kidd, Steve McClaren, Carlos Quieroz .... a list too long by several), he is always going to be chasing his European tail.

The European Cup is special. Paisley got that. Repeatedly. Shanks's biographer Stephen Kelly talks of the rift that developed between the two men when Paisley took over from Shankly at Anfield. According to Kelly, Shanks was envious of Paisley's success in Europe, believing that his heir had inherited his team and that the European accolades were rightly due to him. Shankly may have had something there. However, it is also possible that he didn't grasp the difference between his managerial style and Paisley's. Europe is about assembling the right mix of players, of preparing assiduously, of executing on those famous winter Wednesday nights; it is about responding, training your players to recognise the occasion, trusting them when things aren't going well, when a bad decision goes against you in a hostile venue, when there's a bad bounce. When luck deserts you. Shanks went close. Paisley went three giant steps (three glittering trophies) further in 1977, 1978 and 1981 making him, very simply, the greatest manager in the history of English football: the 'Manager of the Millennium,' as his (auto)biography is entitled.[16] Never has a biography, 'ghost'-written by John Keith, been more accurately titled. Bob Paisley, native son of Durham in the English northeast, was the first Englishman to lift the European Cup, and is the only manager to have won three European and one European Union Football Association (EUFA) Cup (1976 by beating Bruges in a two-legged final). He won an amazing 13 trophies in nine seasons in charge at Anfield. It is a shadow out of which Ferguson can never emerge: Paisley's years at Liverpool constitute a European dynasty.

Finally, however, Europe is about the players: the manager's role is crucial, but the team's is decisive. Paisley got that. Vicente del Bosque got that – one bad night against Juventus was all it was in 2003, just in case anyone at the Bernebeau is listening. After all, who will forget how Madrid hammered AC Milan at Stade Bernebeau in March 2003, the same AC Milan that was crowned champion that season? Milan has to know that winning the Champions League isn't the same as being the best team in Europe. Real Madrid alone can claim that honour. Paisley grasped Europe because of who he was, but also because of what he wasn't – not articulate with words, a man who didn't have Shanks' quick-wittedness and his sense of the moment, just the right (original) phrase in response to the provocative question. Paisley also understood the demands of European competition because of what he didn't need: constant media attention. Paisley didn't need to be front and centre. His team did. They spoke for him, more eloquently with their style than he could have with his words, in a thick, sometimes awkward, northeastern tongue. So, in a very real footballing way, the Geordie who managed Liverpool to such imperious heights never really needed to speak.

To invoke, however inappropriately, Karl Marx – 'They cannot represent themselves, they must be represented' – Paisley was wonderfully 'represented'. It wasn't only Paisley's tactics that endeared him to his players (as Shanks was beloved by his teams and canonised by Scousers and Liverpool fans the world over. I have a nephew named after Bill Shankly, 19 years after his death in 1981), but it was that he made them the focus of the game. Shankly was a genius. No one could ever have built Liverpool like he did. But Paisley scaled European peaks Shanks couldn't and Fergie never will. Paisley was Shanks' legacy. When Paisley stepped down, he left a team that his successor Joe Fagan could lead to further European glory in 1984. When Joe Fagan stepped down after the trauma of Heysel, Kenny Dalglish took over as Liverpool player-manager and the success continued unabated, with Paisley on hand to quietly 'observe' (they had more than a few conversations about Dalglish's managerial decisions) the success of the now veteran forward he had signed from Glasgow Celtic; Dalglish, perhaps Paisley's favourite son, was ably assisted by the remaining 'Boot Room Boys' (Evans, Ronnie Moran, overseen by a still-present Paisley) even though Kenny had not graduated to the manager's position through their ranks. As they used to say in the 'Boot Room': 'It's the Liverpool way. The team first.' It is a sport's truism that rarely applies but in the case of Bob Paisley, it holds: Paisley proved in and through his European success that it was always 'all about the team'.

As a Liverpool fan, the source of Ferguson's dissatisfaction, and that of Manchester United players and fans the world over, is obvious. Manchester United may have dominated England, but European football has only been dominated by one British club: Liverpool, with their four European Cups. Liverpool belong to the aristocracy. For all their dominance in England, Manchester United will never match Liverpool: the Reds from Anfield belong to a European class to which Fergie and his Manchester Reds do not. Reduced to 'stuttering' by Shankly, Ferguson will never be able to add the moniker 'all-conquering manager' to his resumé. 'Manager of the Millennium' too is a title housed at Anfield. That is a sobriquet reserved for the truly, continentally great. Bob Paisley: the fulfilment of Shankly, the apogean name in British football success. Paisley is the standard by which all pretenders must be judged – and found, one after the other, sadly wanting. He will, like Shanks, always walk with the Kop at his side, but as a manager, Bob Paisley will always walk alone. The diagnosis of the condition that 'ails' Manchester United and their manager can now be revealed. The disorder has an official name: nothing more, or less, than Anfield Envy. Ferguson may reserve his most vitriolic barbs for Arsène Wenger in London, his annual challenge for Premier League supremacy may come from the south, but it is west that he looks, to Merseyside for the real, unspeakable, challenge. By Ferguson's own admission, 'Going to Anfield is like a pilgrimage. It's the derby of all derbies ... it has been an absolute privilege over the years to play at Liverpool.'[17] Although he can never quite bring himself to acknowledge it, there is only one reason that playing Liverpool ranks so highly for Sir Alex: it is 'like a pilgrimage'. He is allowed, on those visits to the hallowed ground that is Anfield, to worship at the shrine of Shanks and Paisley. More importantly, however, and this he must surely know, it is by Liverpool standards alone that Ferguson can be deemed a failure. He cannot but be reminded of it every time he travels those 30 or so miles from Manchester to Merseyside.

It is, however, not only against Liverpool's unmatched history that Manchester United is now struggling. The future doesn't look quite as rosy as it did at the end of the 2002–3 campaign – in which United won their record eighth crown. After overcoming Arsenal's impressive start, and benefiting from the Gunners' abysmal finish, to win the Premiership in the 2002–3 season, it might be possible to mark that moment as the end of an era. For a number of reasons. Although they snatched the title from Wenger's charges, Manchester United can no longer hold the title of the most entertaining team. With the breathtaking skill of forward Thierry Henry (a form he almost never reproduces internationally) and the inventive wing play of Robert Pires (a feat especially noteworthy on a park as narrow as Highbury), Arsenal alone can rightly claim that crown. United are no longer top dogs when it comes to attracting players. Now sponsored by Abramovich, Chelski, as they quickly became known (not so affectionately, by the rest of the Premier League), is the club of the money and the moment in that regard.

United's most important symbol, if not player (the bruising Ruud van Nistlerooy's goals give him that status), Roy Keane, has slowed down so much, is so clearly out of his depth against the likes of Steven Gerrard of Liverpool and Patrick Viera of Arsenal, that he appears to be in the process of collecting the proverbial golden watch for services – gallantly and bravely, it must be said – rendered. But Keane is, without a question, more than a little past his midfield sell-by date. Manchester's most glamorous and financially lucrative player (in terms of replica jerseys bought), Beckham, departed in 2003 for the biggest club in the world for 'Real' glory. With Peter Kenyon's loss, United plc may have lost their most important asset, off or on the field. As chief executive, Kenyon made sure that Manchester's ascendancy was based on their financial clout, and his tenure in west London may signal ominously for the seasons ahead. Why should Kenyon have settled for a prawn sandwich when he was being offered caviar?

As always, however, it may be Liverpool fans that knew that the writing was on the wall for the Old Trafford outfit, that United's moment had come and gone even as they surged toward another championship. In their usual ebullience the Liverpool faithful hung a banner on the Kop when Manchester United visited in the 2002–3 season. It proudly announced our historic supremacy, but it was also uncannily prescient in that it foretold the end of United's local dominance. It read, very simply, 'Always in Our Shadow'. The writing was on the wall, as it were, but Ferguson and his Corporation have never been very attentive to the sagacity of Liverpudlians, have they? Well, they can't say we didn't warn them. Now Anfield Envy is about to become an even more acute condition: Liverpool will always walk, if not alone, then in a company too rarified for Manchester United to keep, in Europe.

Acknowledgements

This chapter is dedicated to my nephews, Shankly and Dudley Farred. To Shanks, named for greatness; to Dudley, who promises to be a ball player. I would like to thank Ben Carrington, friend, fellow Liverpool fan, and part-time semi-pro player, for his careful reading of the essay and the typically smart suggestions he made.

Notes

1 The Bosman ruling was the result of a court case in which Belgian footballer Jean-Marc Bosman sued his national federation after they refused him the right to move from his club RS Liège to the French side US Dunkerque. Bosman took his case to the European court and won – in a landmark case, not only for himself but for all footballers in Europe – the right to move freely when he was out of contract, without his club having the right to receive compensation after his contract expired. Before the Bosman ruling, clubs held the players' registration and so were able to control the movement, the right to seek alternate employment, of their players. It is for this reason that the Bosman case was such a signal event in European sports law. See http:europa.eu.int/comm./sport/key_files/circ/b_bosman_en.html for a fuller account of the Bosman ruling.

2 See Liverpool fan John Williams' *Into the Red: Liverpool FC and the Changing Face of English Football* for a quite balanced critique of United's status as 'The Corporation'.

3 Phil Harlow, 'Is the balance of power switching?', available online at http://news.bbc.co.uk/sport2/hi/football/eng_prem/3091598.stm.

4 In Martin Amis's description, the hippest of the new fans were 'lean, tanned, thirtyish, with cupped mobile, gleaming shellsuit and twinkly trainers' ('The shock of the nou', *Observer*, Sunday 30 May 1999, available online at http:/www.guardian.co.uk/Archive/Article/0,4273, 3869917,00.html).

5 Alan Edge, *Faith of Our Fathers: Football as a Religion*, London: Mainstream Publishing, 1997: 16.

6 Amis, ibid.

7 Edge, ibid., 14.

8 The Kop, which takes its name from the brutal battle of 'Spioen Kop' (which translates as 'spy's head') waged between the British colonial army and the Afrikaners during the Anglo–Boer War (1899-1902), is the name of the world famous Liverpool stand – The Kop. It is the main stand for Liverpool's home fans who are renowned for their amazing singing (their best known anthem is the moving 'You'll Never Walk Alone', the club's official theme song), their quick wit and their abiding passion for the team. Bill Shankly used to say that they could, when they wanted to, 'suck the ball into the [opposition] net' with their passion.

9 See Ben Carrington's essay, 'Too many St George's Crosses to bear', in M. Perryman (ed.) *The Ingerland Factor*, Edinburgh: Mainstream, for a fuller critique of New Football.

10 See John King's trilogy, *The Football Factory, Headhunters* and *England Away*, Reading: Vintage, 2000, for a graphic description of Chelsea fan violence.

11 Alex Ferguson, with Hugh McIlvaney, *Managing My Life: My Autobiography*, London: Hodder and Stoughton, 2000: 222.

12 See Alex Ferguson's *The Unique Treble* for an account of that season (Alex Ferguson, with David Meek, London: Hodder and Stoughton, 2000).

13 Stephen F. Kelly, *Bill Shankly: It's Much More Important Than That*, London: Virgin Books, 1997: 299.

14 Kenny Dalglish, 'Foreword,', in John Keith, *Bob Paisley: Manager of the Millennium*, London: Robson Books, 2001: 1.

15 Ferguson, *Managing my Life*, 172.

16 See Keith, *Bob Paisley* for an engaging portrait of footballing intelligence, modesty and incisive managerial thinking.

17 Ferguson, *The Unique Treble*, 142.

Part V
Global United

15 Manchester, USA?

Toby Miller

When I was growing up I was narcissistically distressed that no-one important had been born in 1958, when I was. The triumphs of Madonna and Michael Jackson in the 1980s changed that. But one thing I had always been able to hold onto before their fame was the 'Munich Air Disaster', however grimly and inappropriately, as a tragic paean to lost youth and an important event of that year. As a child I consumed moving evocations of Duncan Edwards struggling vainly for life, Matt Busby being read the last rites, and Bobby Charlton improbably surviving. These were romantic tales of lost youth, and they were re-romanticised in 1968 when the team won the European Cup, with special resonance for Busby and Charlton and the poetically youthful George Best and Brian Kidd, commemorative substitutes for Edwards and Roger Byrne, who were to move on to their own traumas of dipsomania and drudgery respectively. Manchester United became the world's team, perhaps the first instance of a club losing its localism by accident. Today it claims to have 53 million fans, 4 million of them in the United States (US), and £140 million in annual merchandising revenue. But for all their cosmopolitan renown, 95 per cent of those sales come from Britain and Ireland, and there is a hunger to exploit other markets (Da Costa, 2003; Rawling, 2003).

Transformations

Across the Atlantic, from the 1950s to the 1970s, US baseball's New York Yankees enjoyed years of massive success without trauma, ended only by manager Billy Martin and star Mickey Mantle's excesses and deaths. Both teams shared global fame, ManU by achievement and familiarity, the Yankees by fame rather than scrutiny of their achievement in what was – and remains – a minor, parochial sport. Both clubs went from stellar years from the late 1950s, through disappointments in the 1980s, to triumph in the mid–late 1990s. In the US, the late 1950s had also marked the first loosening of localism in US baseball in a way that left the Yankees as New York's sole major-league representative for some years. Two of the city's three teams, the Dodgers and the Giants, relocated to California with the promise of cheap land and burgeoning radio and television markets. (Of course this did not only signal an end to Gotham's local traditions, as the clearance of Chicano/as and Mexicano/as from downtown Los Angeles' Chavez Ravine was an equally crucial, more physically brutal segment of the transformation.) A decade on from those changes, the two Californicated teams had emerged from the shadows cast by the Yankees, their loss to Brooklyn a matter of regret and resentment amongst the nostalgic, but their location on the left coast heartily endorsed by its denizens. That movement ushered in a new era of team expansions and subsidisation of private ownership by civic boosterism, with ballparks publicly bankrolled and ruling-class threats of relocation underwritten by municipal competition. The era continues unabated 40 years on (Nunn and Rosentraub, 2003).

Meanwhile, sport in Britain was itself undergoing a class transformation between 1958 and the 1990s. Football emerged from a 1970s period of violent white proletarian masculine spectatorship to a more formally governed and ripely commodified era. The 1990s saw expensive, all-seating venues, a new league for elite teams, and TV coverage siphoned onto satellite and away from broadcast television. Football was transformed into middle-class fare in a way that it had not been before. This was not a binary transformation, however, more one of tendency. There are still violent white proletarian masculine spectators, and there have always been peaceful white middle-class viewers, but their relative importance to the sport has shifted.

The present moment for both baseball and football, for the Pinstripes and the Red Devils, is about commodification and alienation as much as internationalism. The latter has led to protests from sectors of the US media who rely on a tiny world that they must understand. A representative reaction is the *Village Voice*'s denunciation of football: 'Every four years the World Cup comes around, and with it a swarm of soccer nerds and bullies reminding us how backward and provincial we are for not appreciating soccer enough' (Barra, 2002).

Many reactionaries embrace such aggression as a classic instance of so-called 'American exceptionalism', whether they are football-loving dust-bowl function-alists or football-loathing Murdoch 'journalists' at the *New York Post* (Trecker, 2003). Of course, other critics, such as Habte Selassie (2002), connect the particular form of US protectionism from football with Cold War scapegoating of immigrants, viewing the rejection of football in the 1940s and 1950s as a rejection of difference. There is ample evidence of equivalent ethnic marking in Anglo-settler societies elsewhere (Miller *et al.*, 2001b), and today, the US is busily racialising football – provisionally relying on Latin American fans to buy tickets for the professional men's game, but remorselessly promoting it to an *angloparlante* white suburbia. So Chicago Fire home games have long been characterised by security guards assaulting people who 'look Mexican' so that *anglo-sajones* will feel like they belong in the stadium (Trecker, 2003). But the right's claims about exceptionalism remain untouched – such shibboleths rarely bother too much with facts, since the provenance of the right is, as ever, power and self-congratulation rather than critique.

Protect me

Still, even *Time* magazine's European business correspondent (Ledbetter, 2002) acknowledges the world-historical extent of cultural protectionism in the US, which applies across the entertainment spectrum (Miller *et al.*, 2001a). Many Europeans regard the level of protection in US sport as akin to socialism, via such quaint anti-competitive transactions as a draft for faux students who have been trained for free in directly and indirectly state-subsidised universities, limits on salaries, revenue-sharing, grounds paid for through taxation, exemptions from anti-trust legislation, no relegation, and limits on cable competition (Ford, 2002). This is a planned, command economy by any other name, one that works efficiently with the recognition that sporting firms need opponents in order to survive. Competition is an end rather than a means, as in other forms of capitalism. Put another way, the US is, as ever in its world of big-state subsidisation of big-idiot private enterprise, practising socialism by stealth via welfare for corporations.

The early twenty-first century clearly shows that the extreme protectionism of the US sports market has run to an oversupply domestically. Networks, cable companies and municipal governments have begun to question the vast subsidies given to the four major professional sports. The bizarre extent of state subsidies to facilities has finally been exposed. Expansion teams are under close scrutiny, and Disney immediately looked to sell the 2002 'World' Series winners, the Anaheim Angels, which they had only bought as a means of 'relandscaping and reinvigorating' the location that houses Disneyland (Goldsmith, 2002). Morgan Stanley predicts that the major TV networks will lose US$1.3 billion on sports between 2002 and 2006. Along the way, the working-class pretensions of these activities – especially powerful in the class claims made against football by supporters of that rather fey activity known as the National Football League (NFL), where gentlemen rest after every 0.0006 seconds of effort – have been eroded (Nunn and Rosentraub, 2003; Beyers, 2002; Solomon, 2002; Hiestand, 2002).

Crisis

Cosseted by these great walls of protection, professional sports in the US has been exceptionally unimaginative in spreading risk and multiplying sources of revenue. So where a club like Manchester United derives a third of its money from ticket sales, a quarter from broadcast rights, a sixth from sponsorship and merchandise, and the rest from affiliated services, US teams rely on spectators and television for three-quarters of their finance (Fisher, 2002). Because of the seemingly endless flow of media funding, US sport entered a speculative bubble, analogous to the dot-com era's 'irrational exuberance' (Shiller, 2000). In barely a decade, overbidding for TV rights, fuelled by Rupert Murdoch's dual ambition of creating a global sporting television service while achieving hegemony in its foundational market, has turned broadcast sport from a prized commodity to a valued loss leader, and finally into a contractual liability. As one commentator puts it, '[t]he US media market is glutted with more sports and entertainment properties than there is ad money to go round' (McCarthy, 2002: 27), during the largest slump in spending on advertising since the Second World War. This has led to an expected US$3-billion-dollar write-down in the value of rights to TV sport paid by US media companies. Such hard-fought deals as NBC's contract for future Olympic Games are liabilities (Chenoweth and O'Riordan, 2002). The problem, however, is not limited only to the US. KirchMedia, the German media empire, was bankrupted by its failure to sell football's 2002 World Cup rights at levels commensurate with the vast cost of purchasing them from the Fédération Internationale de Football Association. When rights are up for renegotiation, television's losses are passed onto sports. Competition for shrinking resources between owners, administrators, coaches, elite players and other fractions of the sporting industries will not be pretty. Meanwhile, the Football League in England is in financial trauma, with the collapse of ITV Digital sending the Nationwide League into collective recession and the top Premier League teams focused more on European than domestic competition. The top sides split between them £180 million a year for overseas television coverage, and United began casting covetous eyes at a separate deal that would maximise their return, perhaps through their own US network (O'Connor, 2003; Wallace, 2003).

This is the background to a collaboration between Manchester United and the New York Yankees. It began with a dispute between the Yankees and Cablevision, a key cable operator in the US. Many people in New York City missed most Yankee games in 2002 because the club declined to sell TV rights to the majority of its matches, preferring to attract advertising to its own network, the Yankee Entertainment & Sports Network (YES). Cablevision retaliated by refusing to carry YES on its system. The issue was resolved prior to the following season, but it led to a dialogue-of-the-deaf, blind date between the Yankees and Manchester United. The YES Network has a link to ManU to screen highlights from Manchester United Television (MUTV), and there has been much talk of synergy between the two teams since the pact was announced early in 2002 (James, 2002). After all, it is clear that they are the two most famous local sports teams of all time, so both could presumably benefit from a connection. The Yankees are world-renowned but world-unwatched, and Manchester United is no doubt covetous of opening up the wealthiest and most protected market in the world – sport in the United States. When the relationship was first announced, it was described as a 'unique alliance of real pioneers'. Two years on, the preferred term was 'an exchange of ideas', in the words of United's marketing director Peter Draper, or, more honestly, '[w]e did not really know what it would be', according to Leo Hindery, head of YES (quoted in O'Connor, 2003). The notion had been to fill Yankee Stadium with red shirts and Old Trafford with blue caps. That has not transpired. The shift from material relations to ideational ones seems like a euphemism for an absence of passion and meaning. Rupert Murdoch's News Corporation refused to grant permission for the rebroadcast of ManU games in New York for months for fear that this would damage Fox Sports World, its US network that shows most of the Premier League contests available on cable in the US. The 2003 British season was the first real trial after respectable ratings for a few games the previous year (O'Connor, 2003) – though quite what it would disclose is far from obvious, given that matches were shown at six in the morning and several days after they had taken place.

I'faith, it had never been clear that this alliance would amount to much. Whilst many Yankee players have come from sufficiently cosmopolitan, sophisticated backgrounds to appreciate football (think of Jorge Posada and Bernie Williams), ManU has not had many players who could do the same for baseball (if you can be bothered to think of Diego Forlan and Juan Verón). The Yankee fan base does include many Latino/as, as does that of ManU. But the resolutely *angloparlante* nature of both clubs' management, administration, media coverage and image does not welcome the kind of outreach required for synergy. Anti-cosmopolitan brutes like Alex Ferguson would, it seems, rather throw a boot than encounter a difference, while YES TV is characterised by blue-collar white-ethnic hosting and obeisance to Watergate Republican George Steinbrenner, the team and network owner. In this sense, a certain cloth-cap traditionalism colours both teams, but with sufficient national differences to keep them apart.

Celebecks

Complicating all this, of course, is the figure of David Beckham. Brute Ferguson's anti-cultural-studies decision to sell Beckham during the 2003 off-season showed the same troglodyte sense of timing as his decision to play Beckham on the bench during European competition the previous season. At the very moment that the player was signing with Real Madrid, his commercial license was being renewed. For despite Japanese and Korean shock and awe at Beckham's spoken tones of a boy-child, and the initial US art-house selectivity of the film *Bend it like Beckham*, the northern summer of 2003 marked his coming to new parts of the world, like some international passport to footballing pleasure. North Asians got over the voice, and North Americans supported the film to the point where it gained wide release. ESPN and other resolutely parochial US sports media suddenly felt the need to headline Beckham, fascinated both by his celebrity and his masculinity.

The idea of the celebrity has existed for centuries, but it gained currency through the 19th century. Democracy and capitalism relied on a notion of publicity that transferred esteem from royalty and religion to commodity value and its embodiment in people. This fleeting fame was criticised for its lack of authentic, lasting value, but it did connote a connection to the popular and played out a series of binary oppositions between public and private, natural and manufactured, apparent and authentic, ideal and average (Marshall, 1997; Gamson, 1994). Some ethnomethodologists refer to the celebrity as a 'personalised stranger', a figure known through media intimacy with the details of her private life rather than through direct human interaction (Watson, 1973: 16, 19 n. 19). This stranger has an aura of intimacy that is generated by a direct address of presenters to audiences and the experience of viewing at home. As Joanne Woodward once remarked of the difference between film and TV: 'When I was in the movies I heard people say, "There goes Joanne Woodward." Now [that I am on TV] they say, "There goes somebody I think I know"' (quoted in McLuhan, 1974: 339). In the case of sport, we have seen the male body come up for grabs as both sexual icon and commodity consumer across the past decade (Miller, 2001). This has been even clearer with the emergence of the 'metrosexual', a term coined by queer critic Mark Simpson (1998 and 2002) and joyfully embraced by Western European, Australian, Latin American and US marketers, with Beckham as its exemplar. The metrosexual was said to endorse equal-opportunity vanity through cosmetics, softness, women, hair-care products, wine bars, gyms, designer fashion, wealth, the culture industries, finance, cities, cosmetic surgery and deodorants, as seen in the US's 2003 summer TV success, *Queer Eye for the Straight Guy*. Happy to be the object of queer erotics, and committed to daily exfoliation and web surfing, the metrosexual was the newly feminised male of the 1990s (St John, 2003; Casqueiro, 2003) who blurred the visual style of straight and gay (Nixon, 2003: 6) in a restless search 'to spend, shop and deep-condition' (*Metrosource*, 2003). Now if there were a serious conjuncture involving the two teams, Steinbrenner would have put his Republican dollars in between Real Madrid and Brute Ferguson to retain Beckham for a joint venture. But that was not happening. The linkage of New York and Manchester was incidental, opportunistic, one of ease and logic rather than planning and deliberation. The result was the loss of celebrity at its height when this would have been the perfect articulation between two businesses and countries. That nothing happened – that nobody seems to have talked about it – signifies the relative insignificance of the YES–ManU venture.

This does not mean that culturalist speculations about the state of football in the US need take this as further evidence of some magic divination about US exceptionalism. It is much simpler than that. Groups of decision-makers at the top of US sports, specifically at its nexus with the media, are very limited and limiting folk. They make no room for athletics, swimming or anything else that is not a world of team masculinity dominated by *angloparlantes*. They hate the increasing dominance of 'their' sports by Europeans and Asians. They eschew investment in and journalistic coverage of any sport that involves real competition. They do not represent the population. They represent an undereducated, undertravelled, undersocialised, politically reactionary media elite – for whom 1958 will remain the year that Madonna and Michael Jackson were born. Brute Ferguson and Watergater Steinbrenner have continued on their entirely separate trajectories. ManU's successful summer 2003 US tour was set up to develop relations with Nike, a key sponsor to the tune of £303 million over 13 years (Trecker, 2003; Rawling, 2003). It had nothing much to do with a baseball team. As for David Beckham, his September 2003 press conference after Real's first European Champions' match provides a fitting epitaph. A Yankees cap covered his latest metrosexual hairdo from the cameras. Or perhaps it was part of it.

Acknowledgement

Many thanks to Dave Andrews for insisting that there was a story here after all.

References

Barra, A. (2002, 9 July) 'Nil and void', *Village Voice.*

Beyers, W.B. (2002) 'Culture, services and regional development.' *Service Industries Journal*, 22(1): 4–34.

Casqueiro, J. (2003, 24 August) 'La Ola "Metrosexual" Irrumpe en la Televisión de Estados Unidos', *El País*: 26.

Chenoweth, N. and O'Riordan, B. (2002, 4 June) 'The sick business of sport', *Australian Financial Review.*

Da Costa, N. (2003, 8 August) 'ManU wants a piece of the pie', *Toronto Star*: B8.

Fisher, E. (2002, 4 June) 'Soccer club's goal is to rule world', *Washington Times.*

Ford, P. (2002, 19 June) 'In business of sport, US one of less-free markets', *Christian Science Monitor.*

Gamson, J. (1994) *Claims to Fame: Celebrity in Contemporary America*, Berkeley: University of California Press.

Goldsmith, J. (2002, 13–14 November) 'Mouse house chief flies with angels', *Variety.*

Hiestand, M. (2002, 30 April) 'Spanning the globe', *USA Today.*

James, S. (2002, 26 March) 'Manchester United – Coming to US TV screens', *Reuters.*

Ledbetter, J. (2002, 4 November) 'The culture blockade', *The Nation.*

Marshall, P.D. (1997) *Celebrity and Power: Fame in Contemporary Culture*, Minneapolis: University of Minnesota Press.

McCarthy, M. (2002, 31 January) 'Bowl, Olympics compete for Gold', *USA Today.*

McLuhan, M. (1974) *Understanding Media: The Extensions of Man.* Aylesbury: Abacus.

Metrosource (2003, September/October/November) 'Defining Metro. Sexuality'. *Metrosource*: 16–17.

Miller, T. (2001) *Sportsex.* Philadelphia: Temple University Press.

Miller, T., Govil, N., McMurria, J. and Maxwell R. (2001a) *Global Hollywood.* London: British Film Institute/Berkeley: University of California Press.

Miller, T., Lawrence, G., McKay, J. and Rowe, D. (2001b) *Globalisation and Sport: Playing the World*, London: Sage Publications.

Nixon, S. (2003) *Advertising Cultures: Gender, Commerce, Creativity.* London: Sage.

Nunn, S. and Rosentraub, M.S. (2003) 'Sports wars: suburbs and center cities in a zero-sum game', in J. Lewis and T. Miller (eds) *Critical Cultural Policy Studies: A Reader*, Malden: Blackwell.

O'Connor, A. (2003, 18 August) 'Sport', *Times*: The Game7.

Rawling, J. (2003, 21 July) 'It is inconceivable that there will be another Wimbledon', *Guardian*: 19.

Selassie, H. (2002, 4 June) 'Warming up to soccer', *Village Voice.*

Shiller, R.J. (2000) *Irrational Exuberance*, Princeton: Princeton University Press.

Simpson, M. (1998) *It's a Queer World: Deviant Adventures in Pop Culture.* London: Harrington Park.

Simpson, M. (2002, 22 July) 'Meet the metrosexual', *Salon.com*, available online at http://www.salon.com.

Solomon, J. (2002, 21 April) 'The sports market is looking soggy', *New York Yimes*,

St John, W. (2003, 25 June) 'Un nuevo modelo de hombre, bien masculino pero sensible, invade las capitales del primer mundo', trans. C. Martínez, *Clarín*.

Trecker, J. (2003, 3 August) 'Manchester United's American tour has been a triumph on the pitch, but the real business was being done off it', *Observer*: 8.

Wallace, S. (2003, 30 July) 'United get teeth into Big Apple', *Daily Telegraph*: 8.

Watson, R. (1973) 'The public announcement of fatality', *Working Papers in Cultural Studies*, 4: 5-20.

16 Memphis United?

Diaspora, s(t)imulated spaces and global consumption economies

Michael Silk and Emma Chumley

In the fin de siècle, we find ourselves in the moment of transit where space and time cross to produce complex figures of difference and identity, past and present, inside and outside, inclusion and exclusion.

(Homi Bhabba, 1994: 1)

Global 'United': football qua boundaries

As Giulianotti (1999) has exhaustively identified, football is *the* global game: it is a cultural practice whose visceral seductive appeal has penetrated popular consciousness from Rio de Janeiro to Reykjavik, Beijing to Bratislava, Melbourne to Madras, Manchester to Memphis – thereby, to some degree, linking the world within a kind of unity-in-football-difference. Although their success has been, at least in some arenas, vastly exaggerated (perhaps a result of on-the-field success at a time of significant transformation within the mediation of world football), Manchester United have sought to capitalise upon, and indeed exploit, the game's global appeal. Manchester United possess transnational characteristics in consumer profile, flexible labour recruitment and the global diffusion of corporate symbolism (Giulianotti, 2002). Far from humble beginnings as Newton Heath LYR (Lancashire and Yorkshire Railways) in 1878, Manchester United have a truly transnational presence, with a large fan base in Europe, Asia and South America (Business Wire, 2002). With a reported 56 million fans in more than 20 markets, Manchester United's communities interact with each other through global hyperspace. As Ben Hatton, Director of Manchester United Interactive, has stated, you can be a United spectator 'whether you're in Dublin, New York or Shanghai' (in Barrett, 2002). Through Manchester United Interactive, the interactive subsidiary armature of the club, the aim is to connect and interact with fans around the world. In conjunction with the new platinum club sponsor, Internet brand Terra Lycos (who join a select group that consists of Anhueser-Busch, Nike, Pepsi and Vodaphone, with, of course, the multiple cross-promotional opportunities that this brings), the objective of Manchester United Interactive, according to Group Managing Director of Manchester United, David Gill, is to:

... significantly extend our global reach and to leverage Terra Lycos's experience as the destination for the world's largest on-line community. This will greatly assist Manchester United in building our own on-line communities to allow our fans to interact with us and each other in their own languages.

(Business Wire, 2002)

The establishment of Manchester United Interactive is a part of the transnational vision of the club. Peter Kenyon, former Chief Executive of Manchester United (he has since become Roman Abramovich's greatest corporate signing, taking on Chief Executive responsibilities for the Chelsea group of companies), has clearly outlined this commitment:

We've enjoyed quite a lot of success here in England, and England is still very important to us. But we knew to grow and keep moving forward, we absolutely had to look beyond our borders. So a lot of our strategy now is figuring out ways to bring the experience of Old Trafford to the rest of the world.

(Fisher, 2002: 1)

The United States (US) is the next big prize on Manchester United's horizon, and the latest British invasion has begun. The club's deal with YankeeNets LLC – the parent group of the Yankees and the New Jersey Nets, and already a Manchester United marketing partner – allows for air-tape delayed games on the new YES network (Fisher, 2002). Further, Manchester United's tour of the US in July 2003 saw sold-out games against Real Madrid and Celtic, a success being exploited in the summer of 2004 with the nine match Champions World Series which pits United against AC Milan, Bayern Munich, Chelsea, Liverpool, AS Roma and Glasgow Celtic. America appears excited about the presence of Global United. Following the success in the 2002 World Cup, the big clubs are interested in building a brand for themselves in North America (Dell'Apa, 2002). Transnational sponsors also express an interest, as Dell'Apa (2002: 9) proposes: 'Sponsors have become more global and less local. Face it, many of the great soccer-supporting companies are based in the US. The multinationals are based here or have significant operations here.' The professional soccer league is clearly excited about the presence of Manchester United, perhaps as a reflection of the unique suburban, consumption-oriented landscape of US soccer (see Andrews, 1999; Andrews *et al.*, 2003). As MLS Commissioner Don Garber has proposed: 'They simply are a massive, massive global brand, one of the most powerful brands out there. Their name signified winning ... the kids are interested' (Dell'Apa, 2002: 9). Perhaps more important than the potential capital gain by already powerful elites is the impact that the presence of a brand such as Manchester United has upon the peoples in any given locale. Consumption of Manchester United in the United States is obviously a different experience than the physical, tangible attendance at the placebound 'Theatre of Dreams' – Manchester United's home, the Old Trafford stadium. Consumption takes place mostly within a global hyperspace, through communications technology, imbued as it is with brand symbolism, mediated representation and global–local logics. Further, consumption takes place by the multi-faceted and complex peoples of the contemporary United States, which consists of a hybrid of nationalities and the intersection of differential class levels. Most notably, and further complicating the historically European origins of the US citizenry, patterns of migration from Latin America accounted for 51 per cent of migration to the US in 2000 (US Census Bureau, 2001).

While there has been some conceptual research regarding the way individuals construct identity through sport (Werbner, 1996; Madan, 2000; Farred, 2002; Giulianotti, 2002; Sugden and Tomlinson, 1998), there has been scant empirical research into how these individuals bond, form allegiance and affiliations, and construct sporting identities within a neo-local place distant from their homelands. Further, there has been no empirical sport research that has focused upon the relationships that form around the presence of 'foreign' media brands within another spatiality. The present study begins to fill the lacuna in this regard.

By placing emphasis on the consumption of Manchester United in the United States, the chapter addresses the allegiances, bonds and affiliations that individuals have with the signs and symbols that form the electronic versions of Global United. As was highlighted in the words of Homi Bhabba (1994) that we used to open this chapter, we are attempting to explore contemporary fluid and complex subjectivities. Through a focus on the supposed decentred subject, we address the places and spaces where ties are severed yet, at the same time, can provide occasion for varied, new or refashioned, forms of collective affiliation. The current research is inherently place-bound in our approach – the majority of our research is based on ethnographic observation and interview data with football communities in Memphis.[1] It is, however, important to consider the reconceptualisations of space within contemporary cultural theorising as a grounding for discussion of the consumption of the hyperreal United in a neo-local place, whilst simultaneously being imbued in a postmodern and hybrid space of consumption.

Reconsidering soccer spatialities: consuming place/s of consumption

Critical scholars have recently begun to interpret the spatiality of human life in much the same way they have traditionally interpreted history and society, or the historicity and sociality of human life (Soja, 2000). Without reducing the significance of life's inherent historicity and sociality, or dimming the creative and critical imaginations that have developed around their practical and theoretical understandings, a reinvigorated critical perspective associated with an explicitly spatial imagination can infuse the study of history and society with new modes of thinking and interpretation. Such reinterpretation can allow for a renewed awareness of the simultaneity and interwoven complexity of the social, historical and spatial dimensions of our lives, their inseparability and often problematic interdependence (Soja, 2000:7), and can vastly aid our comprehension of the spectator identities of Manchester United fans in what Nederveen Pieterse (1995: 63) has called a 'translocal world'.

The inexorable fragmentation of modern life, the widespread belief that 'anything goes' and the apparent loss of a fixed point of societal reference cannot be divorced from latter-day advances in telecommunications, information technology, cybernetic networks and the mass media generally (Baudrillard, 1988). No longer do we inhabit the cornerstone of modernity, the 'Gutenberg galaxy', characterised by the culture of the written word. Rather, we inhabit a post-Gutenberg space centred on the ephemerality of the image. Prominent exponents of critical cultural geography (Harvey, 1989, 2000, 2001; Lefevbre, 1991, 1996; Luke, 1996; Soja, 1989, 1996, 2000; Sassen, 1998, 2001) have thoroughly interrogated the extent to which transnational global communications networks have wrought profound changes on the nature and experience of spatiality. Within this literature, it is frequently asserted that the advent of an invasive global media culture has compressed, and effectively dismantled, the boundaries of sport and time that framed modern existence. Global media and commnications systems can be thought of as processes in the construction of a new 'postmodern geography' (Morley and Robins, 1995) that has had a disorienting and disruptive impact upon political–economic practices, the balance of class power, as well as upon cultural and social life (Harvey, 1989). The creation of a decentred global hyperspace has undermined previously solid (albeit fragile) allegiances and affiliations and has meant that identity has become a site of contestation and struggle (Morley and Robins, 1995). Perhaps more than ever before, a strategic awareness of this collectively created spatiality and its social consequences has become a vital part of making both theoretical and practical sense of our contemporary life worlds at all scales, from the most intimate to the most global (Soja, 2000). In opening up our ways of considering spatiality, we can consider some of the cultural tendencies which are associated with a late capitalist mediated modern consumer culture and the (looser) agglomeration of (sporting) bonds within it (Featherstone, 1995).

These recontextualisations of contemporary life clearly challenge the great modernist narratives that juxtapose the polyarchic, 'fixed' community (whether identified by class, race-ethnicity, gender or mere propinquity) against 'otherness'. The symbolic benefit of the existence of alienation against (normalised) centredness, is that otherness can be definitively played out (Baudrillard, 1988). In the contemporary moment, the world in which we live is

> ... one which cannot be so neatly categorised and mapped, where the very distinction between mind and body, private and public space, and between who is inside or outside the boundaries of community, is obliterated and diffracted in a new and different cultural politics of real-and-imagined everyday life.

> (Soja, 1996: 116)

Soja's (1996, 2000) reconceptualisation of spatiality allows us to consider new cultural politics of belonging and difference, the powerful symbolic spaces and places of representation and the categories of inclusion and exclusion within the global ecumene. As Appadurai (1996) has famously narrated, the collapse of previously solid physical borders has been witnessed in the flow of peoples, technology, images, ideas and capital around the world that has resulted in the creation of dispersed communities, networks of trade and interdependence, media geographies and a reconfiguration of the human cartographic landscape and cultural politics. This interconnected spatial landscape is thus constituted by subjectivities that are hollow, decentred, fluid, infinitely adaptable and easily changed through the acquisition of new repertoires of products with the requisite marketing implanted images (Brown, 1995). Such a perspective contributes to the disassemblage of traditional, organically based national popular communities and identities, by generating globally oriented commercial initiatives designed to constitute transnational consumption communities. It is in this sense that we can see identities and subjectivity as hybrid, in the sense that members learn to inhabit multiple identities, speak multiple cultural languages and translate and negotiate between them (Featherstone, 1995).

Spectating spatialities: cosmologies of consumption

In today's media-saturated, virtual society, 'fans' do not necessarily inhabit a shared geophysical space (Ingham and McDonald, 2003). Rather, as Ingham and McDonald (2003) point out, fans can form symbolic communities in distantiated relational space. It is undeniable then that world football has undergone an extensive hypercommodified structural and spatial transformation in the last decade or so and that this has had a profound impact upon football's grassroots custodians – spectators (Giulianotti, 2002). To this end, noted football scholar Richard Guilanotti traces a taxonomy of contemporary spectator identities. He proposes four ideal-type categories: the supporter, follower, fan and flaneur. The supporter has a long-term, personal and emotional investment in the club, is likely to be from the surrounding community and have a topophilic relationship with the club's core space, namely the home ground. The follower, on the other hand, may display many of the above characteristics, but is more likely to identify with the club through vicarious forms of communication, most obviously via electronic media. The follower lacks the spatial embedding within the club and the surrounding community.

The fan experiences the club, its traditions, its star players and fellow supporters through a market-centred set of relationships such as consumption of related products. Of course, if the club fails to deliver on its market promises, then fans may drift into other markets (Giulianotti, 2002). The flaneur is, for Giulianotti (2002), the epitome of the intensification of the commodity-centred mediation of football qua entertainment. Drawing on Baudelaire's mid-nineteenth-century characterisation of the flaneur, and the subsequent remodelling by Simmell, Benjamin, and Foucault, the football flaneur adopts a detached relationship to football clubs, even favoured ones. The true flaneur belongs only to a virtual community of strollers who window-shop around clubs, whose shirts are adorned in tune with a couture aesthetic with the attachment to the commodity sign (as opposed to the signified), whose natural habitat is the virtual arena (non-places of the football ephemera) and who have little solidarity with other 'fans'. Given the reconsideration of spatiality in the contemporary moment, time is ripe for empirical investigation of transitions in football spectatorship – from the hot, grounded, traditional, place-bound fan to the flaneur, living in a cosmopolis of consumption and adorning club signifiers in a cool, transient, market-oriented style (Giulianotti, 2002). In doing so, it is important to stress the complex figures of difference and identity, past and present, inside and outside, inclusion and exclusion (Homi Bhabba, 1994) associated with a late capitalist mediated modern consumer culture. This complexity forms the basis for our initial investigation of the sporting empirical – the consumption of Global United within the rich cultural space of the United States.

Memphis United? Spaces of consumption

> Most of my recollections, all my memories, my entire narrative about this English football club were born and nourished without the benefit of having seen my team play (and trust me, this is a deeply proprietary relationship).
>
> (Farred, 2002: 8)

Grant Farred's (2002) deeply engaging 'long-distance love' narrative provides a personal account of his 'imaginary immersion' with Liverpool Football Club whilst residing in Cape Town. While harking to the romantic imagination of a 'boy's head', Farred's account is instructive, for it disclosed the arbitrariness of choice that was exercised in choosing Liverpool as a team to follow: his choice was based purely upon the availability (or lack thereof) of technology in the 1970s and his reading of the back pages of a Western Cape newspaper. Farred's fanship was thus based on the indexical forging of interpretation and affiliation within a culture formerly transposed through the 'Gutenberg Galaxy'. Farred (2002: 10) could easily have identified with

> ... the gritty Leeds United, Liverpool's great rivals in the early 1970s and firm favorites in the colored townships of my youth. Why not the flamboyant London side Tottenham Hotspur (Spurs) or their north London foes, the boring Arsenal ... why did I overlook the flashy West London side Chelsea?

The explanation offered for the relationship Farred developed with Liverpool is a 'click' between the word and his boyish psyche at that moment, a 'love' that grew in his imagination, as he was not able to 'see', given the predominance of the print media in the early 1970s.

Thirty years since the development of Farred's love, the acceleration of time–space compression, the development of communications technology and the realignment of spatialities mean that images of Liverpool, Manchester United or, for that matter, Bolton, Fulham or West Bromwich Albion are available in all corners of the world (or more precisely, those places that are connected to the informational society). The pervasiveness of this image was fundamental for the formation of the (male) soccer club 'Memphis United', who play in the Greater Memphis Soccer Association (GMSA) League Division One. Implicitly inhabiting the post-Gutenberg space, the team changed their name, formerly Shamrock Football Club (FC), after engagement with satellite television coverage of English Premier League games. Like Farred, for members of Memphis United, there was an arbitrariness of choice associated with 'becoming Manchester United'. The choice to 'follow' United was based around the dominant communications technology of the time and thus the availability of the image at a point distant from the source. As one interviewee in the study suggested:

> I'm 19, born and raised in the US ... my ancestors were mostly Welsh although I've got Dutch, Danish and English blood in me. Not bad regions, eh? ... I guess I identify with Giggs, Stam, Van Nistelroy and Smikes [Schmeichel]. But, to answer the question, it is because of matches on Fox Sports World, the coverage on Sky Sports news and Pay Per View (when I can) that I chose United.

While there was a certain degree of freedom of choice, like the previous respondent who perhaps captured the complexity of American cultural identity, the individuals within the study highlighted a number of other reasons for choosing United as the 'semiotic expression of social identity within the information age' (Castells, 1996). 'Soccer' in the United States has its very own peculiar gender politics and for male American fans and players of the game there was a need to associate with the success and status of the English game and distance themselves from playing a 'girl's sport'. One of the founding members of Memphis United explained:

> Well, you know, soccer over here is really for kids ... and girls at that ... for an adult to identify with it, well, there is a need to make clear that it's not like that, it's tough and physical.

This sentiment was furthered when considering the rationale behind choosing United. The decision to follow the team was built around the dominant players at the time and those in the history of United who had displayed so-called masculine characteristics and tendencies. In discussion of watching Mark Hughes playing in a Football Association Challenge Cup game, one respondent stated:

> Sparkie of course, he exemplified what soccer is all about, never give in, never die, not afraid to show who is boss ... that is what being United is for us. All I remember is the shirt, the white away one, with Sharp on it, actually no, the sponsor before Sharp, and Sparkie filling it out ... there has always been someone who plays that role, now it is Keane and Veron ... I mean Keane he is it at the moment and so are United, they are the epitome of success and that is what we need to associate with.

It is tempting to refer to the conditions of cultural production and propose that this identification is with exactly what is exemplified (violence, masculinity, overcoming pain, individualism, the star performer and so on) within the mediated version of sport (see Sabo and Curry Jansen, 1998; Whannel, 1998 for example). Indeed, Thompson (1996) has argued that such mediated symbolic ideologies tend to uproot traditions from particular locales and endow their symbolic content with some degree of temporal permanence and spatial mobility. Those within this study engage with United predominantly through electronic means, through what Baudrillard has called a satellisation of the real, in the form of televisual and the Internet representations that bring Old Trafford within easy and immediate reach (Brown, 1995). Further, we can suggest that the global footprints of United via electronic media are indeed recognizant of the new spatialities of our time discussed above and brings about new and complex accounts of difference and identity, inclusion and exclusion, and past and present. Whannel (1998), for example, has posited that Manchester United support has a nationwide character in which supporters are denounced by others as glory hunters and rival fans mock them by singing 'we support our local team'. Extending Whannel (1998), we can suggest that Manchester United has a truly global character that extends the tension between a situated local identity and a mediated symbolic identity that lacks any local embeddedness (Whannel, 1998). In this sense, and within the semiotic consumption of electronic media, what is being identified with is far from the rich, deep and historic traditions associated with the club; rather, there is an extremely superficial engagement with the recent success and commodity sign of the club. This is not to suggest that this attachment, like Farred's, is any less authentic, real or tangible than, say, Giulianoti's 'supporter' with a topophilic attachment to the club's core space. However, it does point to the palpable weakening of tradition inherent within the mediated consumption of United.

As the transmission of tradition becomes increasingly linked to com-munication media, tradition becomes increasingly miniaturised and detached from moorings in particular locales (Baudrillard, 1988; Thompson, 1996). Indeed, Baudrillard (1998: 124) extends this argument, by asserting that the signified has become abolished and *replaced* by the 'tautology of the signifier'. As a result, the increasing ideological and technical structure of the media serves to increasingly fluidise the 'social, historical ... [and] cultural specificity' of the original entity – Manchester United. Through the multimedia super corridor, the club's traditions become gradually and partially de-localised and increasingly dependent on mediated forms of communication for their maintenance and transmission from one generation to the next (Thompson, 1996). As the tradition and histories associated with Manchester United become detached from the local, they can become re-embedded in social life in new ways. This remooring of tradition through the global initiatives of the consumer-oriented global media therefore becomes a vital part of elucidating the contemporary lifeworlds of individuals, collectives and spatialities.

Through discursive consciousness (Maguire, 1999), the constituents of Memphis United immerse themselves in the mediated version of Global United, thereby engaging in cultural re-enactment in the new locale. Commodity signs, such as the club logo, are detached from their historical roots, decentralised, resisted in new locations and acquiring abstract qualities, remerging as elements within the reconstruction of spatiality. The Memphis United soccer team has re-articulated, and slightly altered, the club logo in a playful pastiche of the original sign. Now embedded with the words 'Memphis United' (as opposed to Manchester United), the refashioned logo designates simultaneously the historical roots and the local re-interpretation. In addition to the reworking of the club logo, a simulacrum of an early 1990s Manchester United uniform is worn by Memphis United players during their GMSA Division One matches. Tradition, then, survives in a generalised form, although superficially and designating multiple meanings within the neo-spatial soccer arena. In this way we can say that meanings have become more malleable, slipping across spaces and relating to more fluid boundaries. Further, and in addition to these depthless reconsiderations of tradition and meaning, we can point to the ways in which the global commodity sign signifies many differing degrees of belonging among different types of peoples.

Thus far, the discussion has been centred upon those people in the study who are of American 'origin'. Clearly, as a result of the intensification of the flow of peoples around the world, local soccer communities are ones which are far from spatially 'neat'; instead they are complex spaces where categories of inclusion and exclusion are obliterated and diffracted in a new and different cultural politics of real-and-imagined everyday life (Soja, 1996). Like many other soccer spaces throughout the globe, the Memphis community is made up of a complex amalgam of national subjectivities, many of whom use the sport as a cultural shorthand for their homeland.

Sporting diaspora: Manchester United's thirdspace

The advanced phase of globalisation has arguably enhanced the migration and flow of goods, services and people (Robins, 2000; Held and McGrew, 2001). In the latter regard, diasporic individuals, whilst often attempting to assimilate within a different place of citizenship, may find the ideologies and values of the culture different to that of their own. As people move from one region of the world to another, they often carry with them the sets of values and beliefs that form part of traditions. These mobile, nomadic traditions can be sustained partly through ritualised re-enactment and retelling of stories in contexts of face-to-face inter-action. Thompson (1996) sees this quest for roots as a way of recovering and inventing traditions which reconnect individuals to real or imaginary places of origin. Without such a quest, the individual can become decentred due to the apparent lack of grounding upon which to formulate beliefs, values and identity (Rojek, 1995; Thompson, 1996).

Increasingly however, there is the propensity for dispersed individuals to become closely interwoven with mediated symbolic materials, precisely because communication media provide uprooted traditions and thus endow local symbolic content with temporal permanence and spatial mobility (Thompson, 1996).

Communication media provide a way of sustaining cultural continuity despite spatial dislocation, a way of renewing tradition in new and diverse contexts through the appropriation of mediated symbolic forms. Hence, communication media and mediated quasi interaction (the resulting interaction that may occur) can play an important role in the maintenance and renewal of tradition among migrant or dislocated groups (Thompson, 1996: 103). The dispersion of traditions, transposed through the media and through the movements of migrant populations, has thus created a cultural landscape in the modern world of enormous complexity and diversity (Thompson, 1996: 103–4).

Capturing this level of complexity, Stuart Hall (1992) proposed a dialectic between tradition and translation. Tradition is seen as a powerful attempt to reconstruct purified, coherent identities whereas translation refers to those formations which cut across and intersect national frontiers and which are composed of people who have been dispersed from their homelands. These people construct hybrid identities and create new diasporas, where they learn to inhabit at least two identities, to speak two cultural languages and to translate and negotiate between them (Featherstone, 1995; Hall, 1992; Robins, 1991). Building upon the notion of translation, Edward Soja (1996) proposed that these dispersed individuals inhabit a 'thirdspace'; one that translates and negotiates structured binary oppositions, such as the native-other or local-global, and that tentatively disorders, dilutes and reconstitutes the polarities, providing space for consideration of an open logic of both. This liminal thirdspace is the site where counternarratives of belonging can be formulated and hybrid identities constructed, since the effacing of such polarities enables the continual expansion and expression of 'otherness' (Appadurai, 1990, 1996; Soja, 1996).

The pervasiveness of televised football, especially the ubiquity of the 'big red machine', can act as a source of identification for those dispersed from their homelands. In other words, transposed through the media, the Manchester United commodity sign provides (albeit perfunctory and depthless) cultural snippets of home. The global reach of United provides a source for dislocated individuals to reimmerse themselves in the consumption of the soccer team. Dislocated fans of Manchester United can watch the games, obtain up-to-date information and, importantly, generate an affiliation and identity upon a historic and familiar entity. Following Hall's (1992) notion of tradition, attempts were frequently made by those of English origin in this study to make consumption as similar as possible to 'home'. Examples abounded of the diaspora wearing Manchester United shirts, many well worn, outdated and considerably undersized (especially among the ageing male diaspora). Indeed, this was an important conduit to being 'connected' to other Manchester United fans within the locale. As one interviewee suggested:

> It's hard to feel physically connected in such a huge place unless one is fortunate to live in a district or city that has a good soccer heritage. The best way to find Man U fans is to do as I do – wear the kit out in public frequently and listen for comments in crowds and seek them out.

The pinning up of England or Manchester United paraphernalia, the construction of a mini-stadium in the basement, the drinking of 'real beer' (even at eight in the morning!) and the exclusion of wives were all attempts to reconnect to traditions, however superficial. There was also disappointment when there was not occasion to render the place of consumption familiar: 'There's no environment, there's no ... [struggles to find the word] ... there's nobody else out on the balcony going "we won!"' Indeed, there existed a clear expression of difference within the soccer space as individuals worked hard to reconstruct tradition through association with certain commodified symbols of Manchester United. One English female member of the soccer locale described how she associated with the former representative subjectivity of Manchester United – David Beckham. The respondent equated David Beckham as a quintessential marker of Englishness. By identifying herself as 'Becks' and sporting a former David Beckham hairstyle, she immersed herself in an English commodity sign, loaded with a plethora of English values and symbolism, whilst simultaneously remaining fairly unrealised and autonomous within US culture.

> I try to look like him ... you know ... I love the hair and whatever he's wearing in the latest magazine, I'll be wearing that kinda stuff, but ... people here might not know what the hell I'm doing ... which is better for me in some ways.

Of course, the subsequent sale of Beckham to Real Madrid may well disrupt such straightforward attachments, further complicating diasporic attachments to the increasingly fluid and mobile individuals who represent Manchester United. There was also evidence of contestation between those who were 'real' United (demarcated by extensive knowledge of and a 'hot' attachment to the club) and those who were tied to the club through the semiotic realm. When one 'true fan' discovered the result of a Manchester United fixture against another Premier Division club, she 'went crazy' after American friends asked if Manchester United's loss was 'that big of a deal?' The negation of a traditional or expected response resulted in a heterophobic and somewhat aggressively nationalistic response. 'From now on, I wouldn't sit an' watch it with Americans ... they don't hold the same feelings.' In this instance, tradition was arguably strengthened as a result of the communication with the individual's American counterparts. The negation of expected responses to Manchester United's loss exalted and destabilised 'sleeping memories', consequently serving to reinforce the I/we relations within the space (Maguire, 1999: 185).

In accordance with Featherstone (1995) and Werbner (1996), when the space of consumption failed to exalt cultural symbolism, the *place* of consumption became an important site for the rearticulation of symbolic content. Given this, the community gathered in particular places that have become demarcated within the locale as 'legitimate' sites in which to consume Manchester United and England games. Although faux exemplars of the postmodern simulated nostalgic 'sports' bar, the 'English' Fox and Hound and the 'Irish' Dan McGuinnes have become centres of consumption and platforms for cultural re-enactment in order to solidify identification within the diaspora. In this way, the availability of the communication media, along with the cultural re-enactment of tradition, has provided a way for these diasporic individuals to sustain cultural continuity despite spatial dislocation, a way of renewing tradition in new and diverse contexts through the appropriation of mediated symbolic forms. The s(t)imulated space of consumption (consumption practices are both a *simulated* version of the reality and a site for the *stimulation* of response from the consumer) became the site where collectives outside of the national sphere negotiated ideologies of locale that defined their subjectivity and identity. This may serve to recentre the individuals and allow for indulgence in a playful nostalgia, evoking pleasurable experiences (Featherstone, 1995) – the very dialectic that forms Stuart Hall's (1992) Tradition-Translation.

Among those within the Memphis soccer space there were those who we identified above as having gone through a process of becoming United (with the implicitly embedded mediated symbolic depthlessness in mind) and those who were in transit or were dislocated (at times temporarily) from their homeland. In addition to American 'nationals', the spatial landscape of Memphis soccer actually contained (although this is inherently fluid and far from exhaustive) English, French, German, Argentinean, Brazilian, Mexican, Uruguayan, Australian, Swiss, Russian, Dutch, South African, Cameroonian, Senegalese, Croatian, Ghanaian, Irish, Scottish, Welsh, Indian and Japanese. While soccer may have been the global vernacular, there existed a unity-in-football-difference. Football stood as cultural shorthand for nation, and Manchester United stood within this space for England as whole. Despite well-established historical and cultural difference within the English nation between supporters of different clubs, within the dislocated locale, these differences were obliterated, if not weakened. Coterminous with Thompson's (1996) quest for roots, Manchester United, or more precisely the sign associated with Manchester United, stood as a referent point for reconnection to the place of origin. In this regard, a telling example was conveyed in the recruitment of players to Memphis United. The current manager of Memphis United detailed a number of occasions in the last few years of attracting players from England to the club through their website. He recounted an example of a Liverpool fan that recently moved to Memphis and signed for Memphis United:

> When we asked him how he found out about the club and why he chose us he said it was cos of the website ... we keep it up to date and it has all the signage of Man U on it, all the updates on scores and players and stuff. When Dave [pseudonym] moved over, he didn't want to admit it at first, but after a while he said he chose the club as he thought it would be like home ... we had a lot of fun with him at first ... when he came to watch United games at the Fox and Hound he used to wear the Liverpool uniform, but he used to get such a hard time he soon stopped it.

The attempt to connect to a piece of home disrupted the traditional rivalry (however ephemerally) associated with Manchester United and Liverpool in an effort to belong within the soccer community. Equally as telling within the complexities of this globally diverse soccer space were the ways in which Manchester came to stand for the nation and the processes of cultural re-enactment that served to solidify identification within the diaspora. This unity-in-football-difference exemplifies the translation dimension of Hall's (1992) dialectic, where diaspora reorder the diverse identities associated with traditional rivalry, to produce a new platform upon which collective identification could formulate. In this sense we can suggest that tradition, order and control, as well as reflexivity, disorder, flux and uncertainty, existed simultaneously within the Memphis soccer space of consumption.

As the media increasingly exposes 'culturally recycled' symbolic materials loosely pertinent to any given nation or locale (Baudrillard, 1998), such as Manchester United, Manchester, or England, self-identity construction becomes far more open-ended and reflexive (Thompson, 1996). Exalting 'the immediate over the temporally distant', sporting consumption within a diasporic space renders spectators' observations relative to position (Gross, 1992: 59). From this perspective, the tradition–translation dialectic may be conflated into the more ethereal position of 'thirdspace' (Soja, 1996). The weakening or potential obliteration of the formerly structured demarcations within and between differential football clubs such as Manchester United and Liverpool conveys the fluidising of former polarities and a loose 'recycling' of cultural traditions within the dislocated space. From the position of 'thirdspace', therefore, the juxtaposition of tradition, order and control as well as reflexivity, disorder and flux may increasingly result in a combining effect, thereby generating a weaker, more opaque and plural platform upon which diasporic identity may be constructed. Further, Thompson (1996) posits that the media rearticulate symbolic content to such an extent that diasporic individuals no longer need to re-enact the traditional culturally symbolic materials. 'Being Manchester United' within the Memphis space of consumption entails a contradictory set of processes that simultaneously exalt, negate and recreate the traditions of Manchester United – a moment of transit in which complex figures of difference and identity, past and present, inside and outside, inclusion and exclusion (Bhabba, 1994) are continually produced and reproduced.

Coda: from Manchester to Memphis – the 'transparency' and 'obscenity' of consumption

Within the Memphis soccerscape there exists a hierarchy of cultural identities that surround the consumption, and use, of the Manchester United commodity sign. Although dispersed from their homeland and the topographic physicality of Manchester United, 'real/hot fans' (Giulianotti, 2002), heavily ensconced in the tradition–translation dialectic, saw themselves as superior followers of the team within the Memphis locality. In recreating an English 'reality' in a non-(English) place, these (even temporary) 'followers' (Giulianotti, 2002) consume a fragment of cultural continuity despite their spatial dislocation through a reordered mediated version of Manchester United. While the follower may lean heavily toward 'home', the weak 'cultural recycling' (Baudrillard, 1998) of the media product makes the fan float between binaries and thus marks the media as constituent, and constitutive, of 'thirdspace' (Soja, 1996).

The simultaneous existence of those who experienced Manchester United as part of the 'virtual community of strollers' (Giulianotti, 2002) further characterised the soccerscape within the Memphis locale. Following Giulianotti (2002) these flaneurs mark the epitome of the intensification of the commodity-centred mediation of football. These spectators consumed, and subsequently reordered, the signifiers of Manchester United and indeed reflected the disposable, fluid and transient nature of spectator identities within the ephemera of soccer space. The degree to which this investigation points to the detraditionalisation or loss of deep, rich, cultural content remains to be played out in the thirdspaces of soccer consumption. Yet, in viewing social relations, of which sport is clearly a central and prefigurative part (Lefevbre, 1991, in Soja, 2000: 199), we can go beyond a perspective that is abstract or ungrounded. Viewing spectatorship in spatial relations allows for negation of the rigidities of either/or binarisms and allows for a more creative, fluid and recombinatorial alternative of the both and also (rather than either/or) that opens new possibilities for a significantly different conceptualisation of the original opposition (Soja, 2000). In this sense, further empirical investigation of the multiple sites of the production and consumption of spectator identities will allow for a more complex account of belonging and exclusion, inside and outside within the contemporary moment – a consideration of the simultaneous existence of tradition and translation that can extend the preliminary account provided within this chapter. We suspect that when we place sport in material and symbolic spatial relations, we will be in a position to gain a more complex account of both the production and consumption of mediated transnational commodity signs such as Manchester United. Further, we propose that evidence will emerge that suggests that the transparency of the media – the 'more visible than visible' (Baudrillard, 1988: 22) – will negate the stage, the 'real' grounded Manchester United. The pervasiveness, reach and experience of the transnational commodity sign of Manchester United, then, is, as Baudrillard (1988: 22–3) has contended, just another reflection of the obscenity of the commodity: 'abstract, formal and light in comparison within the weight, opacity and substance of the object.'

Note

1 The research is based on a series of observations and interviews within soccer communities in the city of Memphis. Initially, we undertook ethnographic research with a team who play in the Greater Memphis Soccer Association (GMSA) League Division One. This team is called 'Memphis United' and play in old Manchester United uniforms. As a result of these observations, we identified a number of other Manchester United 'supporters' in Memphis and held additional in-depth, qualitative interviews. Again, as a result of these interviews, we were put in touch with members

of the Manchester United USA (MUUSA) supporters club and engaged in electronic interactions with members all over the United States via e-mail and discussion forums. While this type of snowball sampling technique enabled access to culturally and spatially diverse soccer enthusiasts, we recognise the limitations with this design and thus make no claims to be truly representative of Manchester United fans in the USA as a whole. Further research, especially that centred on those most likely to be targeted, and perhaps most vulnerable, by global capital, the youth market, is required to further tease out the complexities of soccer spatialities and subjectivities within the global marketplace.

References

Andrews, D. (1999) 'Contextualizing suburban soccer: consumer culture, lifestyle, differentiation, and suburban America', *Culture, Sport and Society*, 2: 31–53.

Andrews, D., Pitter, R., Zwick, D. and Ambrose, D. (2003) 'Soccer, race and suburban space', in R. Wilcox, D. Andrews, R. Pitter and R. Irwin (eds) (2003) *Sporting Dystopias: The Making and Meanings of Urban Sport Cultures*, New York: SUNY Press.

Appadurai, A. (1990) 'Disjuncture and difference in the global cultural economy', *Theory, Culture and Society*, 7: 295–310.

Appadurai, A. (1996) *Modernity at Large, Cultural Dimensions of Globalization*, London: University of Minnesota Press.

Barrett, S. (2002, 4 September) 'Fergie's digital army', *Revolution*, London: Haymarket Publishing Services.

Baudrillard, J. (1988) *The Ecstasy of Communication*, New York: Semiotext(e).

Baudrillard, J. (1998) *The Consumer Society: Myths and Structures*, London: Sage.

Bhabha, H. (1994) *The Location of Culture*, London and New York: Routledge.

Brown, S. (1995) *Postmodern Marketing*, London: International Thomson Business Press.

Business Wire (2002, 20 May) 'Manchester United', available online at http://www.lexisnexis.com.

Castells, M. (1996) *The Rise of the Network Society*, Oxford: Blackwell.

Dell'Apa, F. (2002, 23 July) 'Foreign Legions on way', *The Boston Globe*, Boston: Boston Globe Newspaper Company.

Farred, G. (2002) 'Long distance love: growing up a Liverpool Football Club fan', *Journal of Sport and Social Issues*, 26(1): 6–24.

Featherstone, M. (1995) *Undoing Culture: Globalization, Postmodernism and Identity*, London: Sage.

Fisher, E. (2002, 6 April) 'Soccer club's goal is to rule the world', *The Washington Times*, Washington: News World Communications, available online at http://www.findarticles.com/cf_dls/m1571/19_18/87024947/p1/article/jhtml (accessed 31 March 2004).

Giulianotti, R. (1999) *Football: A Sociology of the Global Game*, Cambridge: Polity Press.

Giulianotti, R. (2002) 'Supporters, followers, fans and flaneurs: a taxonomy of spectator identities in football', *Journal of Sport and Social Issues*, 26(1): 6–24.

Gross, D. (1992) *The Past in Ruins? Tradition and the Critique of Modernity*, Amherst: University of Massachusetts Press.

Hall, S. (1992) 'The question of cultural identity', in S. Hall, D. Held and T. McGrew (eds) *Modernity and its Futures*, Cambridge: Polity Press.

Harvey, D. (1989) *The Condition of Postmodernity*, Oxford: Blackwell.

Harvey, D. (2000) *Spaces of Hope*, Boulder: University of Colorado Press.

Harvey, D. (2001) *Spaces of Capital: Towards a Critical Geography*, London and New York: Routledge.

Held, D. and McGrew, A. (2001) 'The great globalization debate: an introduction', in D. Held and A. McGrew (eds) *The Global Transformations Reader*, Cambridge: Polity Press.

Ingham, A. and McDonald, M. (2003) 'Sport and community/communitas', in R. Wilcox, D. Andrews, R. Pitter and R. Irwin (eds) *Sporting Dystopias: The Making and Meanings of Urban Sport Cultures*, New York: SUNY Press.

Lefevbre, H. (1991) *The Production of Space*, Oxford: Blackwell.

Lefevbre, H. (1996) *Writings on Cities*, Oxford: Blackwell.

Luke, T. (1996) 'Identity, meaning and globalization: detraditionalization in postmodern space-tome compression', in P. Heelas, S. Lash and P. Morris (eds) *Detraditionalization*, Oxford: Blackwell.

Madan, M. (2000) 'It's just not cricket!': world series cricket: race, nation and diasporic Indian identity', *Journal of Sport and Social Issues*, 24(1): 224–35.

Maguire, J. (1999) *Global Sport: Identities, Societies, Civilizations*, Cambridge: Polity Press.

Morley, D. and Robins, K. (1995) *Spaces of Identity: Global Media, Electronic Landscapes and Cultural Boundaries*, London: Routledge.

Pieterse, N. (1995) 'Globalization as hybridization', in M. Featherstone, S. Lash and R. Robertson (eds) *Global Modernities*, London: Sage.

Robins, K. (1991) 'Tradition and translation: national culture in its global context', in J. Corner and S. Harvey (eds) *Enterprise and Heritage: Cross Currents of National Culture*, London: Routledge.

Robins, K. (2000) 'Encountering globalization', in: D. Held and A. McGrew (eds) *The Global Transformations Reader*, Cambridge: Polity Press.

Rojek, C. (1995) *Decentring Leisure: Rethinking Leisure Theory*, London: Sage.

Sabo, D. and Curry Jansen, S. (1998) 'Prometheus unbound: constructions of masculinity in the sports media', in L. Wenner (ed.) *Mediasport*, London and New York: Routledge.

Sassen, S. (1998) *Globalization and its Discontents: Essays on the Mobility of People and Money*, New York: The New Press.

Sassen, S. (2001) *The Global City: New York, London, Tokyo* (2nd edition), Princeton, NJ: Princeton University Press.

Soja, E. (1989) *Postmodern Geographies: The Reassertion of Space in Critical Social Theory*, London: Verso.

Soja, E. (1996) *Thirdspace: Journeys to Los Angeles and Other Real-and-Imagined Spaces*, Oxford: Blackwell.

Soja, E. (2000) *Postmetropolis: Critical Studies of Cities and Regions*. Oxford: Blackwell.

Sugden, J. and Tomlinson, A. (1998) 'Sport, politics and identities: football cultures in comparitive perspective', in M. Roche (ed.) *Sport, Popular Culture and Identity*, Aachen: Meyer & Meyer Verlag.

Thompson, J. (1996) 'Tradition and self in a mediated world', in P. Heelas, S. Lash and P. Morris (eds) *Detraditionalization*, Oxford: Blackwell Publishers.

US Census Bureau (2001) 'Mapping census 2000: the geography of US diversity'. Available online at http://www.census.gov/population/www/cen2000/atlas.html (accessed 1 April 2003).

Werbner, P. (1996) '"Our blood is green": cricket, identity and social empowerment among British Pakistanis', in J. MacClancy (ed.) *Sport, Identity and Ethnicity*, Oxford: Berg.

Whannel, G. (1998) 'Individual stars and collective identities in media sport', in M. Roche (ed.) *Sport, Popular Culture and Identity*, Aachen: Meyer & Meyer Verlag.

17 For the love of England

Scandinavian football supporters, Manchester United and British popular culture

Bo Reimer

The Scandinavian fascination for British football and for British football clubs is deep-rooted and intense.[1] Presently more than 50 British clubs have their own Scandinavian supporter clubs and in Norway alone the total number of members to such clubs exceeds 50 000 (Henriksen, 2003). The big supporter clubs are obviously devoted to Premier League clubs. But Scandinavian supporters have spread their interests all over the British map – and all over the league system.

Scandinavian fans watch British football games on television and they travel to Britain to watch their favourite teams play. This interest in anything British is unique; the major Spanish and Italian teams, despite their glamour and their more extravagant style of play, cannot compete. Why is that? What is it about British football in general – and Manchester United in particular – that is so fascinating for Scandinavians? And what does it mean for a person's identity to be a long-distance supporter of a football club such as Manchester United? These are the questions I will address in this chapter. I will argue that, in order to under-stand the Scandinavian fascination for British football, focusing on British football – or even on British football culture – will not suffice. This fascination has to be put within a broader context, and that is the context of British popular culture as a whole, and the Scandinavian fascination for that culture. In other words, I will argue for the need of historical specificity and contextualisation. However, by being historically specific, it may also be possible to say something meaningful more generally about both supporter cultures and identity formation. I will therefore move between more general discussions about identity and place and more specific discussions about Manchester United and their Scandinavian supporters. The article is based on historical research and on interviews with United supporters that produce Internet sites about the team. But my own experience of having worked for five years in the 1980s as a tour guide on football trips from Sweden to England with Scandinavian fans has also informed this article.

Football, identity and place

For many football supporters, the alignment to one particular team, to one's favourite team, is an important part of one's identity. This is of course not a novel statement. There is by now a rich literature on the subject, both of a more journalistic (Buford, 1991; Hornby, 1992) and of a more academic (Roche, 1998; Giulianotti, 2002) kind, supporting that statement. Supporters themselves would no doubt also agree.

An important aspect of a supporter's relationship to his or her favourite team has traditionally been its place boundedness. The supporter and the club share a physical space which makes it possible for the supporter to attend home games regularly and to become part of a 'real', live community. The ups and downs of the club are followed closely year after year and the allegiance to the club is handed down from parents to children.

A precondition for this kind of localised relationship between a supporter and a club is a fairly stable society, a society in which people lead their whole lives in the same city, keeping a close, physical contact with their favourite clubs.

That type of precondition does not hold in the same way today as it used to do, of course. People move from place to place, and from country to country, making the relationship for many supporters into a long-distance one – a relationship upheld with the help of the media.

The media have not only made it possible for old supporters to keep up their relationship with their favourite clubs, however. What is even more important is the addition of a new group of supporters, supporters that may never even have seen their favourite clubs live.

There is no questioning that today's most popular football clubs – Real Madrid, Manchester United, Arsenal, Glasgow Celtic, etc. – have their largest supporter base outside their home town, even outside their home country. As Michael Silk and Emma Chumley note in Chapter 16 in this book, Manchester United's fan community consists of 56 million people! And yet, as they also note, there is not a lot of research devoted to these fans.

The question of identity stands central for me in this context. If you live in the same city and support the same team your whole life, it is not unreasonable to believe that the team is important for your identity and your feeling of belonging to a local community. But what about a relationship that is only virtual? How significant could such a relationship be? Furthermore, what does it mean to have a strong relationship to two teams, one in one's home town and one somewhere else?

These questions are of general relevance in discussions of identity formation. They concern the notions of hybrid or fluid identities; identities that are fragmented, contradictory and constantly changing (Hall, 1996). Such notions – often but not always placed within a postmodern context (Gibbins and Reimer, 1999) – are contested. It may not be the case that there is a unified, 'essential' self. But how fluid can an identity be? This is of course a complex question of the kind that there never will be one answer to. Still, the point here is that studies of long-distance supporters may be useful within this context. What can such studies say about hybridity and fluidity?[2]

I will return to this question. But let us begin historically.

English football and Scandinavia

English football has traditionally had a high standing in Scandinavia. The game was of course introduced to Scandinavia from Britain and British teams started to visit Scandinavia already in the late 1890s.[3] A team like Arsenal, for instance, became very popular. But it was not only teams that visited Sweden, Denmark or Norway that became well known. In all three countries, games from the English first division were included on the state-run football pools when the national leagues took winter breaks.

However, British football was hardly crucial to Scandinavians. The knowledge of the actual football being played was not great; the interest was more of a curious kind, reading the strange names of the football clubs in the newspapers and on the pool coupons, and hearing them pronounced on TV or radio.[4] On the whole, British football was something exotic, something detached from everyday life.

Television changed this, even though it took a while. Television was introduced to the Scandinavian countries in the 1950s but even though sport became a 'natural' part of the television output in all three countries early on, it was not until the 1966 World Cup that England figured prominently on television. All three countries showed many World Cup games and players like Bobby Charlton and Bobby Moore became well known.[5]

Then in 1969 something exceptional happened:

> We sent our first commentator, Bosse Hansson, to England. It was the 29th of November, 1969. And it was the worst snowfall ever! I was home the night before and heard how one game after the other was cancelled. We called London. But we could not get hold of Hansson. The Norwegians called on Saturday and said that even more games were cancelled. It was something like 42 cancelled games if you counted all four English divisions. I was in the studio, feeling miserable. My hair was getting greyer. And then suddenly we get a picture from Wolverhampton! There is snow on the pitch, but there are also players. And finally we get to hear Mr Hansson! I relaxed, and announced that our first televised English league game ever, Wolverhampton–Sunderland, was about to start. Then it took 40 seconds and the screen turned black! I told the producer to return to the Stockholm Open Tournament in tennis. After 23 minutes we finally got the picture back. Ten seconds later Wolverhampton scored the only goal of the match![6]

In this dramatic manner, live English football was introduced to Danish, Norwegian and Swedish public service television. The idea came from the Swedish television commentator quoted above, Lars-Gunnar Björklund. He thought that there would be an interest among Scandinavian football fans for live games on television at the time of year when the national leagues were having their winter break – and at a time of year in Scandinavia when staying in front of the television screen seemed like a more attractive option than being outdoors. He also believed that the English style of playing football would suit Scandinavian football fans. In addition to this, British games were on the state-governed football pools.

He was right. The games were both an immediate and a long-lasting success. From 1969 to the late 1990s, Saturday after Saturday, Scandinavian football fans were able to follow English league games on public service television; each season between 10 and 20 games were shown within the framework of a sports programme that also included interviews, quizzes, horseracing and discussions of the results of the football pools.[7]

The sports programme had a direct impact on television viewing as such in the Scandinavian countries. Before this programme, television viewing had primarily been an evening practice. This now changed. The program succeeded in making television viewing on Saturday afternoons into a 'natural' practice for a large part of the male, Scandinavian population. It also made television viewing into a collective practice. Families had of course watched television programmes together ever since the start of television. But for the first time, friends met up at someone's home in order to watch a programme together. And they then often went out afterwards. A Saturday evening of drinking and clubbing suddenly had its own pre-game show – a football game. Mediated and interpersonal pleasure mixed.

The impact of the programme was not restricted to the transformation of Saturday afternoon practices, however. It also reshaped the interest in football among Scandinavian football fans. Suddenly millions of football fans became acquainted not only with Manchester United, Arsenal and Liverpool, but also with teams like Wolverhampton, Stoke and Derby. Scandinavian football fans acquired one more favourite team beside their local team favourite. People became serious Spurs supporters, Hammers supporters, etc. – often without ever having been to England.

It is almost impossible to overestimate this change in the interest in football in Scandinavia. The change concerned not only the focus on British football as such; it was also a move towards an interest in a British football culture as a whole.

Initially, watching the games on television was a specific, local activity, something friends did together. But soon this Saturday afternoon practice led to the creation of 'imagined communities' (Anderson, 1991) around the different teams. In 1974 a supporters' club was organised around Manchester City and in the following years clubs were organised around all major teams. In the 1980s and the 1990s the number of supporters' clubs exploded. Among the supporters' clubs you can now find Barnet Fan Club of Norway, Macclesfield Town Supporters' Club Scandinavian Branch, and Rushden and Diamonds Supporters' Club of Norway.[8]

In 1986, an organisation for the different supporters' clubs was started in Norway, 'Supporterunionen for brittisk fotboll'.[9] The Union organises 'The Groundhopping Club': every Scandinavian supporter who visits at least 25 British football grounds for organised matches can become member of this exclusive club. And since 1991, the Union organises a yearly football tournament between the members of the different supporters' clubs.[10]

In creating a football tournament, a step was taken from an imaginary to a physical community among Scandinavian fans. A person with an intense interest in a particular team that no one else in one's circle of friends cared about – say, Sunderland – was now able to meet other people with a similar interest.

For Scandinavian fans, living reasonably close to Britain, there was yet one step to take, however, and was that going from being a long-distance supporter to being a part of the crowd at the actual games. It was one thing to meet other Norwegians and Swedes who were supporters of Sunderland. It was quite another thing to actually be part of the experience at Roker Park. Thus, soon after the games had begun to be shown on Scandinavian television, special trips were started to Britain for fans wanting to watch British football 'really' live – not just live on television. You could travel by plane or by ferry over the weekend, watching games primarily in London, Manchester, Liverpool and Newcastle.[11] You could be one of 'the lads' (King, 1997).

Manchester United and Scandinavia

Manchester United were not among the teams that started to tour Scandinavia in the early days. They seldom left Britain altogether; before World War Two, the only countries United had travelled to were Austria/Hungary in 1908 and Switzerland in 1925. In the 1950s, however, United fairly regularly went to Denmark to play friendly games, the first game being against FC Copenhagen in May, 1951.[12]

The terrible plane accident in Munich in 1958 of course made headlines in Scandinavia and created sympathy for the team; and United's Northern Irish goalkeeper Harry Gregg, who survived the aircrash, was named best goalkeeper in the 1958 World Cup in Sweden. However, it was not until the 1960s that United found a solid supporter base in Scandinavia. The start was the 1966 World Cup Final at Wembley, a game in which United's Bobby Charlton and Nobby Stiles played significant roles in England's overtime victory over West Germany. Even more significant was the 1968 Final of the European Cup, also at Wembley, when United beat Benfica. In addition to Charlton and Stiles, Scandinavians now took players like George Best and Brian Kidd to their hearts.

The match against Benfica was exciting. But it was the end of the glamorous United era led by Bobby Charlton, George Best and Denis Law. Thus, when Scandinavian television started broadcasting English league football live in 1969, United were not the team they had once been. During the first decade of broadcasting English games, only once did Manchester United finish among the top three and one season United even played in the second division. However, together with Liverpool, United still became the team most often shown on Scandinavian television: between 1971 and 1995, Manchester United were on Scandinavian public service television almost 70 times.[13] There is no doubt that a large number of Scandinavians became Manchester United supporters during these years. And television played a major part in this.

The interest in Manchester United has continued to grow during the last decade. The reason behind this is of course United's tremendous successes and the star quality of players like Eric Cantona and David Beckham. It is also important that Scandinavian players have made the team. The Danish goalkeeper Peter Schmeichel was arguably United's best goalkeeper ever, and the Norwegian attacker Ole Gunnar Solskjær scored the decisive goal in overtime against Bayern Munich in the final of the 1998-9 Champions League. An indicator of the popularity of the club is that the Manchester United Supporters' Club Scandinavian Branch, founded in 1981, now is the largest supporter club for an English team in Scandinavia. The membership of the club presently stands at 23,000 and two people are employed full time. The club is acknowledged by Manchester United and Ryan Giggs is the current president.

Today, much communication around Manchester United is carried out on the Internet. Being a supporter does not only mean watching football games. Real fans want more. They want to read about their team. And they want to discuss the team with other supporters. The start of such specialised activities was the advent of physical fanzines: fanzines in which it was possible both to print more in-depth material than was possible in traditional newspapers and in which the writers could be more subjective. Such fanzines still exist, but today the Internet is more important. There are lots of sites devoted to English football teams. Scandinavian fans partake in the activities on the English sites. But there are also specific Scandinavian sites – both sites associated with supporters' clubs and sites that are just personal sites.

The main Scandinavian site devoted to Manchester United is the one associated with the official supporters' club. The supporters' club also publishes a physical fanzine, *United Supporteren*, eight times a year but the site – containing news articles, editorials and match reports – has more readers.[14]

The official supporters' club is formally oriented towards all Scandinavian countries. But the majority of members come from Norway. There are therefore sites oriented to supporters from the other Scandinavian countries as well. In Sweden, there are presently (at least) three sites, all started by fairly young fans who have interests both in United and in working with digital media.[15] All sites want to find their unique approaches to representing United on the Net. However, they do belong to the same genre, which means that they share notions of subjectivity and loyalty towards Manchester United. The idea is not to replicate traditional journalists' accounts of what happened in a particular game; much more important is to give a subjective view from the inside, a view based on the love for the team. But there are also similarities with journalism in the sense of trying to report on actions concerning Manchester United off the field, and criticism can be raised towards the team. When Manchester United were considering selling David Beckham to Real Madrid, critical editorials were published on the site for the Manchester United Supporters' Club Scandinavian Branch. When the deal was finalised, a number of fans left the supporters' club in anger (Myhre, 2003). However, the supporters' club accepted the decisions taken by the club. In an editorial, Christian Nilssen writes:

> I believe that people should be allowed to say what they want about Manchester United. But I also believe that it is important to show a common front. That is why United supporters in Norway and in the rest of the world have a mission to stand together and give the team and the manager all the

support we can. Let us show others that we are not a bunch of whiners. We are looking forward to new triumphs. And I can promise that if Keano gets to lift the Champions League trophy in Gelsenkirchen next May, then no one will think back upon the sad time when David Beckham was sold. Because then Manchester United will have taken the decisive step to become a better football team. Without David Beckham.[16]

Making sense of the Scandinavian fascination

English football has always had some kind of presence in Scandinavia. But it is quite clear that it is the start of the broadcasting of live first division games in 1969 that concretely 'created' the interest in English football.

Why did these broadcasts have such an impact?

First, it had to do with the regularity of the programmes. Watching English league football became a 'natural' part of everyday life. Scandinavian viewers could watch the ups and downs of their favourite teams and favourite players year after year. The Scandinavians who watched the games belonged to an imaginary community rather than to a physical one. But it was still a community – and the fans were knowledgeable. It was not a question of just knowing the main goal scorer of one's favourite team. A real Scandinavian fan knew very well also who played left full back.

Second, it had to do with the type of football played in England. Scandinavian supporters enjoyed the energy, pace and commitment of the English players. The football was exciting and it seemed honest. It also resembled the kind of play that Scandinavian fans thought themselves capable of – especially in the early years when the games more often than not were picked from the lower half of the first division. Games between Liverpool and Arsenal offered a kind of football that was far removed from the lower divisions of Scandinavian football. But Stoke-Wolverhampton? Bristol City-Birmingham? That seemed within reach even for mediocre Scandinavian amateur players.

Third, it had to do with the whole football culture. In relation to the games, the television broadcasts included interviews with supporters and pictures of the crowds singing and enjoying themselves. The broadcasts managed to transmit a feeling of excitement around what it meant to be a supporter; an excitement that did not exist at the time at Scandinavian games. It was not only that the attendance was low in Scandinavia; that was also the case in England in many places. But the supporters who were there enjoyed themselves anyhow.

The broadcasts started a process. First, Scandinavians took on the role as individual supporters, sitting at home. In the second step, an imaginary community started to take shape. And in the third step, people moved from being imagined to physical participants by travelling to England to watch games. In the terminology of Richard Giulianotti, some Scandinavians went from being Followers to Supporters.[17]

Travelling to England to be a part of the crowd could be done in two different ways. The most common one was going on an organised football trip. In a package, people paid for travel, a hotel, a ticket to a game and special coaches that brought you to the game. Not all Scandinavians wanted to go on such trips, however, since it meant sitting in a row with maybe 50 other Scandinavians. That was not the real experience. The Swedish Millwall supporter Magnus Hagström writes:

> I had been to London and seen football many times. Teams such as Tottenham, Arsenal, Chelsea and QPR [Queen's Park Rangers]. The big clubs, the ones that the Swedish travel agencies recommended and had tickets to. But me and my pals seldom went on the organised trips. We wanted something else from our football interest than sitting in safety with Swedish tourists. Something real, something that we could feel in our teenage bodies. That is why we always refused the travel agencies' pre-booked seats. We did not go with the coach to White Hart Lane. We took the tube together with *the real fans*.[18]

In an analysis of Norwegian supporters' relationship to English football, Hans Hognestad (2000: 115) argues that English clubs initially had an almost individualising effect on Norwegians. Instead of forming communities around a specific team, close friends tended to support different teams. In relation to identity formation, this seems to be a way of shaping one's identity by trying to be unique; to be different from everybody else. This is of course neither strange nor unusual. The quotation above indicates another tendency, however, and that is the need for belonging; the need for building one's identity by being part of a community.

It could be argued that English football culture plays a significant identity-forming role only for Supporters – not for Followers. However, it is probably more reasonable to distinguish between two types of relationships. The Supporter, who travels to England, partakes in the process of keeping the tradition of the club in question localised. But the Followers, who stay in Scandinavia, are not so much delocalising the club as re-localising them.[19] Manchester United gain new spaces in specific supporters' pubs. The fans look as much like fans there as they do in Manchester, dressed in United outfits.[20]

So what about the notion of hybrid or even contradictory identities? In an article about Israeli fans of British football, Amir Ben-Porat (2000) argues that the commitment to their British clubs is much stronger than the one towards their local Israeli clubs. This is of course a question that is not fit for one, general answer, but it would seem as if Scandinavian supporters at least do not feel that supporting two teams is problematic. Hans Hognestad writes that '… the attraction of English football provides a possible creative space for hybridisation based on parallel identities rather than conflict and rivalry as is often the case in football' (2000: 117). This is also my feeling after having taken care of thousands of Scandinavian (primarily Swedish) football supporters in England (primarily London). One reason for being able to support two teams is that they often belong to different universes; they seldom meet in games that count. And if they should do, the case is often that the two teams are of such different standards that the outcome is fairly certain from the start. That was definitely the situation when

I brought supporters for IFK Göteborg (Gothenburg) to Highbury for a Union of European Footballers Associations (UEFA) Cup game against Arsenal in 1980. To everyone's surprise, Göteborg scored the first goal, but in the end Arsenal won, 5-1. The Göteborg supporters who also supported Arsenal did not take this too seriously, however. It would have been worse for them had the loss been to Chelsea.[21]

All in all, it would seem that a relationship to two teams is often a fairly relaxed one. The addition of one more favourite team could maybe best be understood with the help of the word *extension*. One extends one's sense of belonging – and one's imagination. Grant Farred, growing up in South Africa, writes about how Liverpool fed his 'ever-hungry imagination' and how his emotional affiliation transcended geographical distances (2002: 9).

In Farred's case the distance to Liverpool was vast. For Scandinavians, England is close, and that creates another kind of relationship, one that is based on proximity. Aron Bergehall, editor of the Manchester supporter site www. mufcsverige.com, explains his interest in British football: 'I have always preferred British football. I have grown up with people who like it and I prefer the British way of playing – harder and with team spirit' (Interview, 3 October 2003). Bergehall's interest is based on tradition; older friends have supported British teams and he joins an already existing community. But it is also based on a fondness for the actual way the game is played in Britain. And this way of playing is not dissimilar to the Swedish way of playing; team spirit is a phrase often used in relation to Swedish football teams. Claes Höglund, editor of the site www.ManUtd.nu, makes clear a further connection between British and Swedish football by pointing to the relationship between one's way of playing football and the environment in which one plays: 'It is easier to picture yourself in England than in Italy, more go-ahead spirit, more rain' (Interview, 3 October 2003).[22]

Initially I stated that one cannot just focus on football and football culture in order to understand the Scandinavian fascination for Manchester United and other English teams. The quotations above indicate the importance of physical proximity and environmental similarities. Related to these are more general *cultural* similarities.

In the article 'A cartography of taste', Dick Hebdige (1988) describes how British youth from roughly World War Two became increasingly fascinated by American popular culture. In this form of culture, in American movies, in rock and roll, etc., British youth found something that seemed to speak to them in a way that the more formal and 'clean' British popular culture of the time did not seem to do.

I believe that the attraction British youth felt for American popular culture – the attraction for something different – is similar to the attraction and fascination Scandinavian people have felt for British popular culture.[23] During the whole of the twentieth century this culture has played a crucial role in Scandinavia; in the eyes of Scandinavians, there is a definite notion of 'quality' when it comes to British popular culture as compared to, say, American popular culture. The organisation of public service media in Scandinavia was based on the BBC model and British movies, British music and British television series have been extremely popular.

It is within this context that British football 'arrived' in Scandinavia; as yet one more part of an attractive whole. This is why football trips to England immediately became extremely popular. During a weekend in London, Liverpool, Manchester or Newcastle, Scandinavians could watch a football game, go on a pub crawl and watch a play or listen to a rock band. For most Scandinavians the language was comprehensible and, due to television and the movies, the English environments were immediately recognisable and familiar. The perfect weekend – for male Scandinavians, at least.

Processes of change

In this article I have traced the development of what could be regarded as a Scandinavian 'taste' for British football. However, things are presently changing. To start with, television has changed. In the late 1990s public service television lost the rights to the Premier League. These rights are now with cable stations demanding money for the pleasure of watching the games. This means that the possibilities for viewing top quality English football have diminished. In addition to this, today English football on television has to compete with Italian and Spanish league football as well as with the Champions League and the UEFA cup. In the 1970s, Scandinavian public service television tried to show German league football as an alternative to English football. It was not a success. The competition from the Italian and Spanish leagues is tougher, however. The flair and elegance that characterise these leagues today attract Scandinavians who have not been brought up on English football on television. Thus, due both to the coverage of football and to the playing as such, for the generations growing up in the 1990s it is not as 'natural' to support a British team as it was for previous generations.

This can be tied to a change altogether in Scandinavian taste when it comes to popular culture. The love for everything English – except for the food and the weather – is not as unconditional as it used to be. Today, for many Scandinavians weekend trips to Paris, Barcelona or Rome may be more exciting than a weekend in London. In relation specifically to football culture, it would seem as if the 'Lad Culture' that was so typical of British football fans, and which many male Scandinavians found so attractive, has lost some of its appeal.

However, this does not mean that the thrill of English football and of English football culture is gone. There is no doubt that the fascination is still strong in Scandinavia; it is enough to look at the membership of the Scandinavian supporters' clubs and their Internet sites.

Garry Whannel has argued that for teams like Manchester United and Liverpool there is a 'tension at work between a situated localised identity, and a mediated symbolic identity, which lacks any local embeddedness' (2000: 26). These are two separate identities, according to Whannel. But I would argue that this distinction is not as clear cut anymore. These two groups meet increasingly. Supporters who live in places other than Manchester and Liverpool – be it London, Oslo or Dublin – travel to games, trying to fuse a symbolic identity with a temporary localised one. Many visitors to a game at Old Trafford or Anfield do not live in Manchester or Liverpool.

This may of course create tensions of another kind than the one outlined by Whannel. Anthony King (1997: 335) writes that Manchester United, in distributing tickets to home games at Old Trafford, favour applications from fans living outside Manchester. Why? Because these fans are expected to spend more money on souvenirs.

The British football culture is changing. All-seater stadiums attract families and the affluent; and working-class youth, accustomed to the stands, become less visible. Where does this leave Scandinavian Manchester United fans? First of all, it seems hardly meaningful to speak of them as a homogenous group. There are Scandinavian fans who found the team when they were at the top and will forget about them when they become less successful. There are Scandinavian fans who travel in groups to Manchester in United colours and sit together, looking in amazement at the passion showed by the English crowd. There are Scandinavian fans who learn how to speak English with a Manchester accent and dress up in designer clothing for games, showing their belonging with United's 'true' fans.[24] Thus, Scandinavian fans of Manchester United do not constitute *one* subculture anymore – if they ever did. They mix and merge with other fans in intricate ways. Old communities disappear. New ones are created.

Notes

1 Scandinavia is the collective name used for Sweden, Norway and Denmark.
2 My interest is directed towards both a personal and a collective kind of identity. I will not get into the question of the relationship between sport and a national identity. For such questions, cf. Blain *et al.* (1993) and Bairner (2001).
3 The first game between an English and a Scandinavian (Danish) team was played in 1898. The English team consisted of amateurs (Andersson, 2002: 255). In 1904, the amateur team Corinthian became the first team to play in Sweden (Sund, 1997: 57). The first professional teams played Denmark in 1903, Sweden in 1910 and Norway in 1912 (Hognestad, 2000: 114).
4 The pronunciation of the names of English teams was not always easy for Scandinavians of the generations born before World War Two. The names Leicester and Norwich were especially difficult to pronounce.
5 Neither Sweden, Denmark nor Norway qualified for the 1966 World Cup. The interest therefore became larger for other countries' teams.
6 Interview with Lars-Gunnar Björklund, Swedish Broadcasting Company, 21 September 2000 (my translation). The interview was made in preparation for my book on the history of sports on Swedish television (Reimer, 2000).
7 The programme varied somewhat in content between the three countries but the matches were always the same.
8 Webpages: Barnet Fan Club of Norway (http://home.c2i.net/barnetfc), Macclesfield Town Supporters' Club Scandinavian Branch (http://www.silkmen.com/), Rushden and Diamonds Supporters' Club of Norway (http://www.rushden.tk/).

9   The Union for Supporters of British Football (http://www.supporterunionen.no).
10 The latest tournament was won by Manchester City. Manchester United have never won the tournament and is only placed 18th in the overall standings of the tournament (out of 51 clubs, over the years Exeter City has been the most successful team).
11 Due to the ferry links between Gothenburg/Århus and Harwich/Felixstowe, during the 1970s many Swedes and Danes went to Ipswich to watch football.
12 E-mail information from Mark Wylie, Curator, Museum of Manchester United.
13 The best goalscorers in these televised games were Mark Hughes (seven goals), and Steve Bruce, Ryan Giggs, Brian McClair and Sammy McIlroy (four goals each) (Bengtsson, 1995).
14 Available online at http://www.muscsb.no.
15 See online at http://www.mufcsverige.com, http://www.ManUtd-Swe.tk and http://www.ManUdt.nu.
16 Nilssen (2003), my translation.
17 Giulianotti's taxonomy of football spectators is based on two dimensions, one distinguishing traditional spectators from consumer spectators and one distinguishing hot spectators from cool spectators. The move referred to in the text, from being a Follower to being a Supporter, is based on moving from cool to hot. Both Followers and Supporters are traditional spectators (2002: 31).
18 Hagström (2001: 66), my translation.
19 Se also the article by Silk and Chumley about Memphis United.
20 Traditional-looking English pubs have become quite common in Scandinavia. You can also find American-type sports pubs showing football. Thus, television viewing has increasingly become a public sphere activity.
21 IFK Göteborg of course quickly became a much better football team, winning the UEFA cup in both 1982 and 1987, as well as knocking Manchester United out of the Champions League in 1994–5.
22 Mikael Dalkvist, Editor of http://www.ManUtd-Swe.tk: 'I prefer British football to Italian. It is too tactical and too many divings. I like the tempo of English fooball, besides the games are much closer' (Interview, 2 October 2000).
23 An important part of Hebdige's essay concerns the heated debates around taste that was the result of the process of Americanisation. That discussion is of lesser interest in this context, however.
24 'In response to the association of replica shirts and club clothing with inappropriate styles of support, the lads have self-consciously developed a style of dress by which they distinguish themselves from unacceptable support and sustain a distinct identity for themselves. Instead of replica kit, the lads have increasingly dressed in expensive designer clothing – such as Ralph Lauren and Henri-Lloyd – as a signal of distinction' (King, 1997: 339).

References

Anderson, B. (1991) *Imagined Communities. Reflections on the Origin and Spread of Nationalism* (revised edition), London: Verso.

Andersson, T. (2002) *Kung fotboll. Den svenska fotbollens kulturhistoria från 1800-talets slut till 1950* [King Football. The Cultural History of Swedish Football From the End of the 19th Century to 1950], Stockholm: Brutus Östlings bokförlag.

Bairner, A. (2001) *Sport, Nationalism, and Globalization*, New York: State University of New York Press.

Bengtsson, C.B. (1995) *Tipsextra 1969–1995* (A statistical summary of the Swedish television programme showing English league games), Stockholm: Tipstjänst.

Ben-Porat, A. (2000) 'Israeli fans of English football', *Journal of Sport and Social Issues*, 24(4): 344–50.

Blain, N., Boyle, R. and O'Donnell, H. (1993) *Sport and National Identity in the European Media*, Leicester: Leicester University Press.

Buford, B. (1991) *Among the Thugs*, London: Mandarin.

Farred, G. (2002) 'Long distance love. Growing up a Liverpool Football Club fan', *Journal of Sport and Social Issues*, 26(1): 6–24.

Gibbins, J.R. and Reimer, B. (1999) *The Politics of Postmodernity: An Introduction to Contemporary Politics and Culture*, London: Sage.

Giulianotti, R. (2002) 'Supporters, followers, fans, and flaneurs', *Journal of Sport and Social Issues*, 26(1): 25–46.

Hagström, M. (2001) 'Besatt av Millwall' [Obsessed by Millwall], *Offside*, 3(4): 65–100.

Hall, S. (1996) 'Introduction: who needs identity?', in S. Hall and P. DuGay (eds) *Questions of Cultural Identity*, London: Sage.

Hebdige, D. (1988) 'Towards a cartography of taste, 1935–1962', in D. Hebdige (ed.) *Hiding in the Light: On Images and Things*, London: Comedia.

Henriksen, A. (2003, 26 April) 'Fotballgal på heltid' [Full-time football crazy], *Aftenposten*.

Hognestad, H. (2000) 'Satellite transmitted passion? A study of Norwegians' relationship to English football', in *Idrett, samfunn og frivillig organisering*, Oslo: Norges Forskningsråd.

Hornby, N. (1992) *Fever Pitch: A Fan's Life*, London: Victor Gollancz.

King, A. (1997) 'The Lads: masculinity and the new consumption of football', *Sociology*, 31(2): 329–46.

Myhre, A. (2003, 18 April) 'Ut av supporterklubben i protest' [Leaving the supporters' club in protest], *Aftenposten*.

Nilssen, C. (2003, 21 June) 'Bedre uten Beckham' [Better without Beckham], *United.No*, available online at http://www.muscsb.no/.

Reimer, B. (2000) *Uppspel: Den svenska TV-sportens historia* [Re-Play: The History of Sports on Swedish Television], Stockholm: Prisma.

Roche, M. (ed.) (1998) *Sport, Popular Culture and Identity*, Oxford: Meyer and Meyer Sport.

Sund, B. (1997) *Fotbollens maktfält: Svensk fotbollshistoria i ett internationellt perspektiv* [The Force Field of Football: The History of Swedish Football in an International Perspective], Uppsala: Svenska Fotbollsförlaget.

Whannel, G. (2000) 'Individual stars and collective identities in media sport', in M. Roche (ed.) (1998) *Sport, Popular Culture and Identity*. Oxford: Meyer and Meyer Sport.

Interviews

Bergehall, Aron (2003, 2 October) Editor, www.mufcsverige.com. Telephone interview.

Björklund, Lars-Gunnar (2000, 21 September) Commentator, Swedish Broadcasting Company. Personal interview.

Dalkvist, Mikael (2003, 2 October) Editor, www.ManUtd-Swe.tk. E-mail interview.

Höglund, Claes (2003, 3 October) Editor, www.ManUdt.nu. Telephone interview.

Wylie, Mark S. (2003, 18 October) Curator, Museum of Manchester United. E-mail interview.

18 'Come on Red!'

An American tale

Jim Denison

> Until my twenty-second year I had never been further away from home than a five- or six-hour train journey, and it was because of this in the autumn of 1966, when I decided, for various reasons, to move to England. From the plane I gazed down lost in wonder at the network of lights that stretched from the southerly outskirts of London to the Midlands, their orange sodium glare the first sign that from now on I would be living in a different world.
>
> W.G. Sebald, *The Emigrants*

To begin, let me just say that my mother was never a soccer mom. Right place – Westchester County, New York ... the suburbs – just the wrong time. I was 14 years old in 1977, the year Pelé joined the Cosmos and under-13 soccer leagues sprouted up in every east coast suburban town. I learned to dribble an orange ball with my hands, not a white one with my feet. And nets belonged on rims not goals, I thought. Too bad really, because I probably would've made a half-decent soccer player. I had stamina, I had speed, and the few times I came across a game on television (usually a Spanish UHF channel) I'd pause before turning, something subliminal obviously catching my attention. Maybe it was the open style of play, or the announcer's sing-song Spanish, and, oh, my goodness, the ball handling and deftness of touch. But there was a strangeness to the proceedings as well. Like the exotic nature of Acapulco cliff diving, or ski jumping, two sports well-televised on ABC's 'Wide World of Sports' in the late 1970s. Perhaps it was the tempo – languid and drawn out – or how hard I found it to put a fix on the positions, and how that score just wouldn't budge. Those are common complaints from an American, I know. That's because soccer's just not our game. But last year I moved to England, and very quickly I discovered that if I was going to fit in, if I was going to participate in most men's conversations, I needed to get a handle on this game. And most importantly, I had to support a team. But which one, immediately became my next question.

England's not my first home away from home. I lived in New Zealand between 1994 and 2001. And like the narrator in Sebald's (1996) tale I quoted above – a man who left Munich for Manchester – various reasons also explain why I became a traveller. I never expected my university career to develop in New Zealand and then England. My aspirations towards travel, I can honestly say, were modest. After all, I didn't need to leave America for a more prosperous, more tolerant, more comfortable place. Unlike my ancestors who fled their homes on various British Isles because they needed to discover new ways to survive, New York and the rest of the United States was brimming with opportunity when I finished graduate school in 1993. But as Sebald conveys so elegantly through his sublime and beguiling novel of movement and wandering, to try and define the complexities of fate, relocation and ultimately identity is to begin a journey fraught with error. After all, memory never produces the truth, but rather a meditation on what would otherwise have remained in darkness or silence forever.

As anyone who has unearthed his or her past and crossed a border to live in another place will readily understand, such a journey always involves a form of shape-shifting or self-translation. This is even more so for those who have crossed a language barrier (as difficult as I find the English to understand at times, rest assured, I won't be claiming any linguistic liabilities). The English novelist Salman Rushdie, who was born into the Urdu language, has written of exactly this. 'A change of language changes us,' he said. 'All languages permit slightly varying forms of thought, imagination, and play' (2002: 32). So, too, would I add, do different sports create specific patterns of being and understanding. Canadian's hockey, Finland's cross-country skiing and the Japanese's sumo all show how sports' particulars influence national identity and individual character. Included in this, of course, must be the English and their football. And learning one's national game is a lot like learning one's language. To embody its subtleties and nuances it's best if you learn it young. Otherwise, you'll always play it, watch it and read it with an accent.

Displacement, travel and transplantation, of course, can also be something positive. For Rushdie, 'the crossing of borders, of language, geography and culture' (2002: 31) has given him his life's work. And of this he is clearly satisfied, not to mention wealthy. Similarly, I've not been unhappy in my nine years away from home. Moving to another place can inspire positive reflections on loneliness, frustration and discovery, and incite a revealing shift in perspective from parti-cipant to witness, or resident to alien. I enjoy experiencing differences: the sound of new expressions and modes of thought, food and landscapes. But foreign delights do fade. I first thought London's intricate network of roads, streets and alleyways mysterious and charming, whereas now I find them an utter nuisance. Some of my friends and family refer to me as a global citizen. But what does that mean beyond being able to enjoy the success of a number of countries at the Olympics? There is no global passport; elections are events for nationals only, and an accent remains what it is, an accent on difference. Moreover, I'm becoming increasingly aware that as my years abroad mount I might eventually have to face the fact that I've lived more of my life away than at home. What would that mean, then? And who would I really be? With movement away, I always believed, came the obvious corollary, going home. Growing up I saw that proven time and again. English, Dutch, French and German businessmen who moved with their families to my town for work in Manhattan always returned home. It was apparent through their manners, too – Englishness, Dutchness, etc. – that New York was only a stop-over on a round-trip journey.

I've recently come across a Welsh word that represents the idea of being away from home and feeling something akin to displacement: it's '*hiraeth*'. And for the Welsh, who tend to be quite emotional people anyway (compared to the English, that is), it means more than homesickness or heartache for a place and its specific varieties – a particular food, sound or scenic view. As I've had it explained to me, hiraeth 'is an evasive poetic regret that surfaces in the Welsh when they're away from Wales' (personal communication). Of course, homesickness, as the travel writer, Jan Morris (2002: 137), has written, 'is the most delicious form of nostalgia ... because, generally speaking, it really can be gratified'. We can never return to the past (the euphemistic Good Ol' Days) but we can, if the urge strikes us, return home.

Milan Kundera, who left Czechoslovakia for France in 1975, has recently written a novel on the very subject of returning home, titled *Ignorance* (2002). Kundera, who has carefully cultivated an image as the 'woe-is-me-exile', or the personification of *hiraeth*, has Irena, his main character and also a Czech emigrant in Paris, struggle with the idea of going back to Czechoslovakia following the downfall of Communism in 1989. She is shocked when a friend says, 'Shouldn't you now go home.' 'But Sylvie!' exclaims Irena. 'I've been living here for twenty years now. My life is here!' (Kundera, 2002: 70). Kundera, thus, problematises the identity markers of nationhood, residence and domicile. But these are high-stakes name tags that fortify the idea of belonging to something larger than one's self. Without them life can be confusing, and identity ambiguous.

In the foreign places I've landed I've always tried to be a good sport and accept their home field traditions and flavours. As one case in point, in New Zealand it was rugby (I even attended a game with my face painted in the colours of my local team, Waikato, when they went up against their arch-rival Auckland); now in England it has to be football. Sport has always provided me with a sense of geographical grounding. As John Bale (1994: 2) says, 'Sport landscapes – fields, stadiums, parks – do matter,' because they affect people's lives, their experiences and how they come to understand themselves. As a boy I believed my New York Yankees were precisely that – mine. I lived a better day following a Yankee win, and suffered terribly when they lost. Countless summer nights I fell asleep to the drone of announcers' voices on my bedside clock radio. There was comfort and security wrapped within their play-by-play banter and the players' names they pronounced – Chambliss, Munson, Nettles, Randolph, Guidry ... They also extended my world beyond the goings on of my house. They involved me in something bigger: culture, New York, America, not to mention manhood. But in an unfamiliar sporting landscape one loses that, and as regretful as that might be one must change if one wants to belong. So a native New York Yankee fan looking for comfort in English football would logically support who?

It's easy to understand why Manchester United are so hated in England (this became apparent to me almost immediately whenever I dropped their name into a conversation). It's jealousy, just like with the Yankees. They're too good, they're too rich. And just as any American baseball fan will tell you that he roots for two teams, his own and whoever's playing the Yankees, so will an English soccer fan, I've discovered, tell you that a loss for Manchester United is a win for everyone else. Ironically, Manchester United's success has made them more popular abroad than at home. Manchester United is for the shallow supporter I was told: the illiterate or displaced football fan who just wants to be part of the hype, like those screaming mad Asian girls who collect David Beckham paraphernalia.

But it was only Manchester United who emerged through the morass of football static I encountered in my first few months here. They were the only team whose games were shown on terrestrial television via ITV's coverage of the Champions League (since I didn't have evidence of six months' residency in the United Kingdom I couldn't get a subscription to Sky TV, thus gaining access to more games and more teams). Furthermore, David Beckham's face was truly everywhere – billboards and magazine stands. And his wife Posh seemed to be constantly singing, having babies, shopping on television, or talking about her life to some gossip columnist. Not to mention the Manchester United coach, Sir Alex Ferguson, who also seems to do nothing but talk, or more accurately spit and scream. He never has anything interesting to say, mind you, but there he is on television again ... talking, red-faced, shouting from the sideline. Old Trafford, too, quickly became the only ground I could associate with a specific team. Ewood Park, Maine Road, The Hawthorns, who plays there?

But more than all of that, becoming a Manchester United supporter, I found, brought with it a degree of safety and control, and a feeling of belongingness mixed with occasional instances of superiority. They win, after all, and as an immigrant you so often feel like you're losing and that you're lost – train routes and bus routes appear to be random and directionless, national insurance numbers and tax codes are baffling, certain towns are unpronounceable, and where do you go to buy anything? Nothing is familiar. No-one's face, no-one's name, no-one's house. At least with Manchester United I had one aspect of my new life sorted. Besides, did I really have a choice? Wouldn't it have been completely pretentious all of a sudden to start supporting Southampton, or Middlesbrough? There are people who know the entire history of those clubs. Their supporters have a grassroots trueness and authenticity rooted to those places that as a foreigner would feel too much like trespassing on the sacred. Siding with Manchester United avoids that. They're global, they're multinational, and like McDonald's and Coke, or the Yankees for that matter, they're a consumable brand present in all markets for everyone and anyone to enjoy (even in rugby-mad New Zealand the results of Manchester United's games were reported on the Sunday evening news).

In a lecture I recently gave to a third-year sport sociology class on the vagaries of identity and sport fandom, I read out loud from David Rowe's (2000: 96) fantastic story of Englishness and football fanaticism.

> ... when I start out in a new relationship I like to take it one game at a
> time, not thinking of the big prize at the end of the rainbow. But it was
> different with Charmain ... Things were never that great between the sheets,

I do concede, but I didn't think that was the be-all and end-all, and I thought it would get better with practice and a few more training sessions. Janice Nugent never minded my things with the scarf, socks, headband, and rosette – used to laugh like a drain sometimes, actually – but this one never seemed to go for it. I'd be really getting going and she'd say something that would put me off – like to turn my crowd chant tape down, or switch off the 100 watt lamps that I'd positioned above each corner of the bed for a bit of on-pitch atmosphere. I felt really humiliated, and I've got to admit I really lost it (and in more ways than one, if you take my meaning) when she said that she couldn't concentrate with my giant poster of Max Bootle on the ceiling.

Then I surveyed all 20 students, asking each one of them what football team they supported and why. The stories I heard were beautiful. Memories of grand-fathers and afternoons by the radio, childhood best friends and after-school kickabouts, trips to the home ground holding dad's hand, and souvenirs and replica shirts as Christmas presents. Naturally, I had no story of my own to share. And the students didn't seem bothered. 'He's not from here. He's an American, after all,' I'm sure they all thought.

References

Bale, J. (1994) *Landscapes of Modern Sport*, London: Leicester University Press.

Kundera, M. (2002) *Ignorance*, New York: HarperCollins.

Morris, J. (2002, November) 'Home thoughts from abroad', *The Atlantic Monthly*, 290: 136–8.

Rowe, D. (2000) '*Armour impropre*, or *Fever Pitch*, sans reflexivity', *The Sociology of Sport Journal*, 17: 95–7.

Rushdie, S. (2002) *Step Across This Line: Selected Non-Fiction 1992–2002*, London: Cape.

Sebald, W.G. (1996) *The Emigrants*, New York: New Directions.

Index